ALSO BY ROBERT KATZ

Death in Rome
Black Sabbath
The Fall of the House of Savoy
A Giant in the Earth
The Cassandra Crossing
Ziggurat
The Spoils of Ararat
Days of Wrath
Love Is Colder than Death

NAKED
BY THE WINDOW

NAKED
BY THE WINDOW

THE FATAL MARRIAGE

OF CARL ANDRE AND

ANA MENDIETA

ROBERT KATZ

THE ATLANTIC MONTHLY PRESS
NEW YORK

Published simultaneously in Canada

Printed in the United States of America

First Edition

Library of Congress Cataloging-in-Publication Data

Katz, Robert, 1933–

    Naked by the window: the fatal marriage of Carl Andre and Ana Mendieta / Robert Katz.—1st ed.

    1. Homicide—New York (N.Y.)—Case studies. 2. Andre, Carl, 1935–

    3. Mendieta, Ana, d. 1985. I. Title.

HV6534.N5K37 1990   364.1'523'09227471—dc20   89-77586

The Atlantic Monthly Press

19 Union Square West

New York, NY 10003

Design by Julie Duquet

To Susan Colgan and Peter Matson

As flies to wanton boys are we to the gods;
they kill us for their sport.

King Lear IV.i

CONTENTS

PERSONAE xi
AUTHOR'S NOTE xiii

MERCER STREET: | SUNDAY, SEPTEMBER 8, 1985 1
HAVANA: | 1948–1961 37
RIKERS ISLAND: | SEPTEMBER 9–10, 1985 48
QUINCY, MASSACHUSETTS: | 1935–1964 89
SPRING VALLEY, NEW YORK: | SEPTEMBER 11–14, 1985 106
IOWA: | 1961–1978 132
WEST BROADWAY: | SEPTEMBER 16–23, 1985 148
CENTRE STREET: | OCTOBER 1985–APRIL 1986 181
PARK AVENUE SOUTH: | 1965–1979 218
BERLIN: | 1986 239
HAVANA: | 1978–1982 261
BROADWAY AND HOUSTON STREET: | 1987 283
ROME: | 1983–1985 309
CENTRE STREET: | JANUARY 29–FEBRUARY 11, 1988 323
EPILOGUE: | BREAKING THE SEAL, 1988–1990 373

SOURCES AND NOTES 385
ACKNOWLEDGMENTS 419
INDEX 421

PERSONAE

ANA'S FAMILY
Ignacio Mendieta, *father*
Raquel Oti Mendieta, *mother*
Raquel Mendieta Harrington, *sister*
Ignacio Mendieta, *brother*
Tom Harrington, *brother-in-law*
Raquel "Kaki" Mendieta, *a cousin in Cuba*

ANA'S FRIENDS
Carlos Alfonzo
Dotty Attie
Hans Breder
Romolo Bulla
Alvin Curran
Natalia Delgado
Mary Beth Edelson
Wendy Evans
Leon Golub
Juan Gonzalez
Zarina Hashmi
Christian Haub
Annette Kuhn
Sol LeWitt

Carol LeWitt
Jim Melchert
Al Nodal
Ida Panicelli
Marsha Pels
John Perreault
Liliana Porter
Ruby Rich
Edith Schloss
Lowery Sims
Nancy Spero
Modesto Torre
Ted Victoria

CARL'S FRIENDS
Rudolf Baranik
David Bourdon
Rosemarie Castoro
Hollis Frampton
Jeremy Gilbert-Rolfe
Ronnie Ginnever
Nancy Haynes
Brandon Krall
Brenda Miller

Douglas Ohlson
Claes Oldenburg
Barbara Rose
Rita Sartorius
Frank Stella
May Stevens
Alice Weiner
Lawrence Weiner

ANA'S "OLDER AESTHETIC SISTERS"
Lucy Lippard, *feminist and art critic*
Mary Miss, *sculptor*
Carolee Schneemann, *artist and writer*

THE DEALERS

Paula Cooper, *Soho gallery owner*
Konrad Fischer, *Düsseldorf gallery owner*
Gian Enzo Sperone, *Rome gallery owner*
Angela Westwater, *Soho gallery owner, Sperone's partner*

THE NEIGHBORS

Alison Bierman, *the cleaning woman in 34E*
Mark Coler, *the neighbor in 34D*
Harry Leandrou, *night manager, Delion Delicatessen*
Edward Mojzis, *night doorman, 11 Waverly Place*
Spiros Pappas, *super, 300 Mercer Street*
Bobby Tong, *the neighbor in 34F*

THE LAW

Martha Bashford, *assistant district attorney*
Robert Baumert, *police officer*
Carol Berkman, *judge*
Louis Capolupo, *police officer*
Michael Connolly, *police officer*
Ronald Finelli, *detective, Sixth Precinct*
Elizabeth Lederer, *assistant district attorney*
Robert M. Morgenthau, *Manhattan district attorney*
Richard Nieves, *detective, Sixth Precinct*
Max Sayah, *judge*
Alvin Schlesinger, *judge*
Mark Sullivan, *assistant district attorney*

THE LAWYERS

Jack S. Hoffinger, *chief defense lawyer*
Gerry Ordover, *Soho art lawyer*
Gerry Rosen, *the "hippy lawyer"*
Mike Sherman, *defense assistant*
Gary Simon, *a Mendieta family lawyer*
Steve Weiner, *defense assistant*

AUTHOR'S NOTE

Experience suggests that the reader at some point, usually not at the beginning, may wish to know how this book got to be written. That can be found in the final chapter, an epilogue, perhaps best read at the end. For now, it may be enough to say that while all works of nonfiction are in some way bound to a structure imposed by the events recounted, I have, within those limits, sought to narrate these events as they were revealed to me, certainly not chronologically or in any other "logical" way. They came one calling for the other.

MERCER STREET

Sunday, September 8, 1985

—— 1 ——

Somehow, we possess a knowledge of the city. We may never have seen it with our own eyes, but we know the stillness of downtown streets an hour before the day breaks. We know how the breeze comes around a corner, and we can imagine the harsh, lonely light of an all-night store. These are among the things we can feel in our bones. We know the place the night sky starts to pale, the sound of traffic lights changing, how summer heat clings to our skin, and the simple truth that ghosts do not sleep.

It was into this darkness she fell.

MIKE CONNOLLY AND his partner John Rodelli had been working the Henry-Ida sector of Greenwich Village that hot and muggy, and unusually quiet, Saturday night, when at five-thirty Sunday morning, September 8, 1985, they got a call about "a jumper down at 300 Mercer Street."

Bobby Baumert and Lou Capolupo got the same call in Charley-David, which included the 300 block, but when they arrived a minute or so later, tearing up Mercer the wrong way, Connolly and Rodelli were already there. They were standing at the back door of the Delion Delicatessen, a twenty-four-hour grocery, talking to Harry Leandrou, night manager, salad man, and cook.

Leandrou, who spoke with a heavy Greek accent, was telling the cops that he'd heard something in the kitchen that sounded like a small explosion, a "small shake" on the roof just above his head. It was only a short while ago. His heart was still pounding. He and a couple of his workers had gone out the back door onto Waverly Place. There was a black guy across the street, he said, and a regular customer, the doorman from 11 Waverly, was coming down the block.

The black guy said something about a noise, and Leandrou went up to the doorman, who said he heard "some screaming, a scream . . . a voice from high up."

The cops looked up. The overcast sky was still dark, but the Mercer Street building could be seen towering over the roof of the one-story deli, itself an extension of the building. It was one of the tallest structures in the Village, thirty-five stories. Leandrou told them they had to go through the basement of 300 Mercer to get to the Delion roof. There was no time to lose; somebody might be dying. Baumert, at twenty-two the youngest of the four cops, was first over the six-foot fence that blocked the shortest route. Connolly, Rodelli, and Capolupo followed. Capolupo was the oldest; he was twenty-three.

They took a freight elevator and walked out on the tarred rooftop, making their way by the light of the street lamps on Waverly. Gravel crunched underfoot. About fifteen feet from the building line, a naked figure lay in the amber glow. A white female, thirty to thirty-five years old, was how she would later be described, but she was two months and ten days shy of her thirty-seventh birthday and Hispanic. She appeared lifeless, lying chest-down on her right side, one arm and one leg twisted unnaturally. She was small and unhumanly flat. Baumert approached her and kneeled. She wore blue bikini panties. He saw gaping wounds and recognized cerebral fluid; her damaged head faced one side, lying in a deep depression. The impact of the fall had dented the roof. He touched for a pulse in the neck and the wrist, feeling nothing but skin still warm.

Officer Connolly had the apartment number from which a call to 911 had been placed. While Baumert and Rodelli guarded the body and the site, Connolly and Capolupo decided to go there. They rode up to the thirty-fourth floor. Connolly wore thin-rimmed glasses. He had auburn hair. Capolupo had a thick droopy mustache. They rang the bell of apartment 34E. The door was answered by a short, stocky, barefooted man about fifty years old. He was dressed in blue overalls and nothing else. His balding dark brown hair was uncombed, and a full beard reached his chest. He had large dark eyes, ruddy skin, and, both officers noted, a wet, fresh-looking scratch on his nose. Sometimes a cop is called on to remember again and again, and this would be one of those times.

Sunday, September 8, 1985

Connolly asked if he was the person who had called 911. The man said he was. His name, he said, was Carl Andre. He seemed distraught. "My life is over," he said. "My wife is gone. I can't believe it happened. It's a tragedy. I don't know what I'm going to do."

Capolupo asked if they could be helpful in any way. Yes, the man said, he wanted to wash his hands. The young officers went with him to the bathroom, which was about ten feet into the apartment, to the right. They wanted to keep an eye on him for his own safety. On the way, Connolly saw a small room with the door open, and he looked inside. It was a mess of papers and files. Both officers watched the man wash his hands. He came out of the bathroom, shut the door to the disorderly storage room, and said, "I don't want you in there." He seemed to have regained his composure.

"Could you tell us what happened, Mr. Andre?" Connolly asked.

He and his wife were watching a movie on television, he said, sitting at a table in the main room, the living room, which was where the three men were now. The officers looked around. The lights of the city lay beyond a bank of tall, open windows. The room was sparsely furnished. The TV set sat on the radiator. There were two glasses and an empty bottle of champagne.

The movie had paralleled their lives, Mr. Andre continued, only the other way around. His wife wanted to go to bed with him and he said no. She got mad, going off without him.

Fifteen minutes after she went to the bedroom, said Mr. Andre, he looked in on her. She wasn't there. He went back again when the film ended, ten minutes later. Again, she wasn't there, and he called 911 to report that his wife had jumped.

"Maybe I was wrong," he said. "She wanted to go to bed. I wanted to watch TV. . . . I don't know, maybe I should have gone to bed with her if that's what she wanted. In that sense, maybe I did kill her."

Nobody had asked him if he had killed her.

Had he seen her jump? said Capolupo.

No.

Had he looked out the window?

No, he had not.

Had she written a note?

No.

"How do you know she jumped?" asked Capolupo.

"I just know," said Mr. Andre.

The officers went into the bedroom. It was in striking disarray, as though a summer twister had swirled through. A white folding chair was turned on its side, lying between a box spring and mattress and a bare wall. A clutter of wrinkled clothing and bedding was strewn about the room, scattered on the floor. Clothing shoved together, with neither rhyme nor reason, hung from the edges of open shelves. Two crumpled pillows on the bed lay corner-to-corner, forming the shape of a bow tie. One of them was sunk with as perfect an impression of a person's head as an ordinary pillow could retain. The couple's bed, its sheets bunched up, ribbed, and furrowed, faced two large sliding windows. The left one was wide open.

Connolly leaned out the window. The ledge crossed the center of his trouser pocket. He was six-foot-two. Below him, he saw the body and Baumert and Rodelli. Capolupo leaned out, too. He yelled to his partner.

"Bobby!"

Baumert looked up and waved.

On the way back through the apartment, Capolupo glanced in the kitchen. There were several empty wine and champagne bottles, some lying on the floor. Mr. Andre saw Capolupo looking. He said he collected the empty bottles for candleholders.

Capolupo called the precinct from the phone near the front door. Mr. Andre took down a book from a shelf and showed it to Connolly. He said he was an artist, in his prime, and this was a catalogue of his work. His wife was an artist, too, he said, but, "You see, I am a very successful artist and she wasn't. Maybe that got to her, and in that case, maybe I did kill her."

There was that funny phrase again.

Connolly looked at the catalogue. It showed photographs of a work called *Stone Field Sculpture*, a grouping of thirty-six glacial boulders emplaced at an outdoor site in Hartford, Connecticut. The young policeman was struck by this in a personal way; not too long ago he had considered going to college in Hartford but had become a cop instead. "I'll never forget it," he would later say. "Just a bunch of boulders."

ON THE OTHER side of Mercer Street, Ed Mojzis, the doorman at 11 Waverly Place, had finished drinking the coffee he'd picked up at the Delion grocery after he'd heard the scream and the "explosion." Something, perhaps the electronic howling outside, had drawn him from his desk in the lobby back to the street. He could see policemen standing on the roof of the deli, and there were men carrying a stretcher running through the courtyard of 300 Mercer. He still had two hours remaining before his midnight to eight shift ended, so he walked down Waverly once again to try to learn more about what had happened.

Mojzis was a Vietnam veteran, a portly man who had a cherubic smile but it wasn't entirely naive. He had started to work the double doors of 11 Waverly only two months earlier, leaving a job he'd had as a janitor at the Federation for the Handicapped. Once, in 1981, he had lived at 300 Mercer with his sister, but now he lived alone in Elmhurst, Queens. Today was his thirty-eighth birthday.

By now, higher-ranking police had arrived from the Sixth Precinct, including a lieutenant named James Brassel. They had been joined by medical technicians from Emergency Services, who had come for the body. Harry Leandrou, the Delion night manager, was back on the street again, telling his story once more; this time, Mojzis was also there to tell his. The cops took Mojzis into the lobby of the building, and he spoke to Lieutenant Brassel.

At about 5:30, said Mojzis, he went out for coffee. It was very quiet, like it had been all night, maybe because it was the weekend after Labor Day, and there was no traffic on Waverly. There was a "black fellow," a man in his twenties, across the street, and when Mojzis reached the fire hydrant between Mercer and Broadway, he heard a woman screaming "from my left."

He heard the woman "saying, 'No, no, no, no,' pleading don't," and the noes were "in a pleading sense, pleading with someone not to do something." It wasn't very loud from where he was, but there was something about the voice that stuck in his mind, something hard to put into words, he said, but it wasn't a scream of complete helplessness. There was some kind of self-confidence in the voice. A sharp "No!" then another and another and another. Then there was silence.

"I continued to walk toward Broadway," he went on, "and about four seconds later I heard what I thought was an explosion." It was a sound he'd never heard before, and he'd heard a lot of mortar in Vietnam. He remembered the man across the street looking up, or looking to his left, but he couldn't be sure if it was at the moment of the scream or the explosion. "Then Harry, the night manager, came out of the deli, and I said, 'What was that, an explosion?' And Harry said, 'No, I heard a thud, something landed over us.' 'Maybe somebody pushed somebody out of a window,' I said, 'because I just heard a woman screaming.'

"Then, I went into the deli and got the coffee I went for. There was a discussion of what I heard, and I went back to my post at 11 Waverly Place."

At the moment Mojzis told his story, neither he nor Leandrou had any way of knowing that the body on the roof was that of a woman. A police officer took down Mojzis's home address and his telephone number.

"WOULD YOU COME with us to do the paperwork, Mr. Andre?" asked Officer Capolupo. Lieutenant Brassel had told him to get Mr. Andre down to the station.

Mr. Andre agreed. He slipped into his shoes and a T-shirt with the sleeves cut off. He tucked the shirt into his overalls. He gathered up a bag of papers, and on the way out, he locked the door to his apartment.

Connolly and Rodelli accompanied Officer Patricia McGowan, who had arrived with the EMS. After the body had been zipped into a black plastic bag, they all went to the morgue. Baumert and Capolupo departed for the station house. Mr. Andre rode alone in the rear. Baumert noted the time. It was 6:25 A.M.

The Sixth Precinct was a modern, two-story building on West Tenth Street, between Bleecker and Hudson streets, no more than a couple of minutes away by police car. They arrived at a ramp that gave access to the 124 Room, a ground-floor eight by ten enclosure with a couple of desks where complaints were filed. Mr. Andre's complaint was, of course, that his wife had died. Capolupo filled in the form. He learned Mrs. Andre's name: Ana Mendieta. He spelled it incorrectly.

Mr. Andre sat alongside the desk. From time to time he held his head in his hands and murmured. After a little while he said, "Are you going to read me my rights?"

Baumert checked with Lieutenant Brassel, and when he came back, he turned to Mr. Andre and referred to a printed card he kept in his back-pocket memo pad. He asked Mr. Andre six questions, commonly called Miranda Rights. Did Mr. Andre understand that he had a right to remain silent; anything he said could be used against him; he had right to an attorney; if he could not afford an attorney one would be provided; and if an attorney were not available, he could remain silent?

At the end of each of those questions, Mr. Andre answered yes. Then Baumert asked him the final and, although he was speaking in the inscrutable monotone of complaint rooms, the most fateful one.

"Are you willing to answer questions?"

"Yes, I am," said Mr. Andre.

Again, Baumert made a record of the time. It was now 6:45.

2

When Ana Mendieta had arrived in New York from Rome ten days earlier, she went to the apartment on Mercer Street with some misgivings. For one thing, it was his place, not hers. It was an eyesore outside, and the inside made her uneasy. He'd lived there with a refrigerator full of champagne but in otherwise monkish simplicity ever since she'd known him, paying more rent than she could dream of. It had nothing to do with her, not in sentiment or taste, with those pale little Nancy Haynes paintings hanging frameless on the otherwise bare living-room walls and the curtainless windows standing naked and sooty atop Manhattan looking south. Many of her friends, and his, too, had gone wide-eyed with disbelief when they learned that Carl Andre, the sculptor who had given the world a new, unfettered way to see beauty and who, by the way, could have had his pick of half a dozen lofts in Soho, lived and labored in this protoyuppie high rise that darkened one of the nicest parts of town.

She had her own apartment. It was much more modest than his, but it was homely and earthy, which was her style in both her life and her art. It was on Sixth Avenue where it crosses Vandam, not Soho Soho, but you couldn't be nearer. It had a stoop with an iron railing that made it feel like a neighborhood, and her two little rooms were right over a funky antique shop, only one flight up. She had a crippling fear of heights.

But that apartment, though now unoccupied, was still in the hands of a troublesome subtenant she was trying to evict. Since she would only be in New York for thirteen days, she had decided to stay at Carl's. He was still in Europe, due to arrive in a couple of days, and it was the trouble with Carl, not his apartment, that vexed her most. She believed she had fallen out of love.

They had been married only seven months, though they'd been a couple off and on (rather more off than on) since they'd met in Soho in 1979. Only two weeks ago, dining with friends in the Piazza della Consolazione, they'd related the romantic story of their first encounter, but in a strangely skewed manner that revealed their malaise and upset rather than amused their company. They had been nasty to the waiters, nasty to each other, Carl was downright rude to one of their dinner companions, and when a cat swept by, Ana leaped to her feet in a histrionic fright. Still, he had tried to be nice to her. He told their friends how wonderful it was to put together a household with the person he loved, going around to the flea markets searching for this or that, and though he'd been married twice before, she was the first woman with whom he had begun to make a home. Afterward, he invited them to see the new apartment, which was just around the corner. They sat in the darkness of that midsummer night while Carl lit a candle and opened a bottle of champagne, and they went out on the terrace with its mighty view of the amber-lit ruins of Rome.

But that was all posturing to Ana, and nobody else was much entertained either. The next day he had gone off to Berlin; she no longer fretted about when she would hear from him again.

Sunday, September 8, 1985

"Dear Passion Flower," she had written not long before, "at every hour I am blue / for I don't hear from you. . . . Drop me a line / to say you're fine / For you I pine / to write a line / I'd feel much better / to get a letter."

What awful business had transpired to turn it all so sour so soon? Certainly those photographs she'd found of the bitch in Berlin were infuriating. The bitch called him Rainbow. And her stupid little postcards copying, as Ana herself had copied, Carl's penchant for sending postcards—he'd left them lying around practically out in the open: "It was so much beautiful, wonder - full . . . Thank you—I'm FULL!!"

But what really pissed her off was that she'd be in the bathroom, sometimes just after they'd made love—it happened in New York and Rome—and she could hear him calling the woman in Germany. That was back in May, barely a season after their honeymoon cruise on the Nile, and it was still going on.

And then there was the bitch in New York, whoever she was. You could take your choice of two, maybe both, the blonde she'd tracked to a certain restaurant in the Village, where she'd gotten the maître d' to admit he'd often seen them together, or the dirty-blonde whose little slate-gray paintings he'd bought and hung on the living-room wall. It used to be that she could, sometimes, with great effort, look the other way. They were often separated for long periods, and she would try to roll with the rumors, saying, "Well, Carl gets lonely. . . ." But that was before they were married, the first marriage of her life, to the only man but one who mattered.

The marriage mattered. Not the bourgeois legality but the commitment. It was his word, not hers. He'd told her he wanted to make a commitment. No other woman meant anything to him he told her. She was his "dear darling, sexy, beautiful Tropicanita," as he called her; his one and only, forever and forever, remembering their honeymoon and making love in Rome again and again. He'd said it in prose and he'd said it in verse.

R O M A N A M O R
my destiny . . .

"I want to marry your daughter because we are so much alike," he had told her mother when she'd put him on the phone the night before the wedding.

"Doesn't Carl look better?" she would say to friends who had seen them since their marriage. "Don't we look good together?" He was watching his diet, she said. She was changing his ways, she insisted, making him healthier. And she had said this as late as two weeks before coming back to New York, when he was with the bitch in Berlin, and she knew it couldn't possibly be true in the way that she wished or imagined it might be. Now the time had come to gather, or begin to gather, the many strands of her life that had grown awry.

3

By eight o'clock in the morning, when Detective Ronald Finelli arrived at the West Tenth Street station for a Sunday tour of duty, the sun had risen in a damp mantle of clouds. The temperature was already in the high seventies, heading like yesterday for ninety or more. A portent of dust-bearing rain was somewhere in the sky. Finelli had twenty-nine years on the force, five of them at the Greenwich Village precinct, and the things he'd seen over time had etched hard, straight lines on his face and a certain wise look around his eyes. He was not feeling well. He smoked too much, he had a gnawing discomfort in his chest that would not subside, and he became winded when he climbed the narrow flight of stairs that led to the detectives' squad room on the second floor. He had seen a doctor and was waiting for the results of the tests.

The squad room had a king-sized shield on the door, painted detective gold. The moment he went inside, he saw a civilian, just sitting, a heavyset bearded man in blue overalls and thick bare arms. He was alone on a bench by a wooden railing, reading a book. He did not look up, and Finelli walked by, heading for his small office off to the left.

"What do we got?" Finelli asked Mike Connolly. Connolly had come back from the morgue, and though he was already on overtime, he had been ordered to wait for and brief Finelli. What he had was called an investigate DOA.

Sunday, September 8, 1985

At the moment, Finelli was the only detective on duty, but Detective Richard Nieves soon arrived, getting the news of a female down at 300 Mercer Street. Both men had been assigned to the case. He went up to the squad room, made a mental note of the stranger in blue overalls reading a book, and reported to Finelli, the senior man. Nieves, a handsome cop with thick black hair rapidly turning gray, was in his early forties. He had made detective only two years back, sent it seemed from central casting, but in reality he'd spent fourteen years in uniform playing by even the stupidest rules.

The first thing Finelli did after listening to Connolly's report was raise 911. He wanted to hear a playback of the call made earlier that morning from apartment 34E to the police emergency number. All of these calls were routinely recorded and the time received was registered down to the second. The connection was made by telephone and from the commanding officer's office on the south end of the squad room, the two detectives listened to the tape. The recording had been made between 5:29:26 and 5:31:17 A.M. and was exceptionally clear.

> Operator: Police. Where's the emergency?
> Caller: Yes. My wife has committed suicide.
> Operator: Say again.
> Caller: My wife has committed suicide.
> Operator: Where are you calling me from, ma'am [sic]?
> Caller: I'm calling from 300 Mercer Street, apartment 34E.
> Operator: 34E?
> Caller: Yes.
> Operator: What floor are you on?
> Caller: Thirty-four.
> Operator: On the thirty-fourth floor?
> Caller: Yes.
> Operator: OK, and what's the telephone number you're calling from?
> Caller: 533-2609.
> Operator: OK. Uh, what happened exactly?
> Caller: What happened was we had—My wife is an artist and

I'm an artist, and we had a quarrel about the fact that I was more, uh, exposed to the public than she was and she went to the bedroom and I went after her and she went out of the window.

Operator: She jumped out of the window. How long ago did this happen?

Caller: Oh, I don't know, I don't know, I don't know. It was— I don't know.

Operator: What's your [sic] name?

Caller: Ana Mendieta.

Operator: Spell the last name.

Caller: M-E-N-D-I-E-T-A.

Operator: OK, you don't know. Did it happen recently? Did it happen just now?

Caller: Oh, it happened just now. I can't, I can't tell you.

Operator: All right, don't, don't hang up now. Don't hang up. Stay with me. So she, she jumped from the window, right?

Caller: Yes.

Operator: You near Waverly Place, are you?

Caller: Yes, it's a—oh.

Operator: Jumped thirty-fourth-floor window. Your window face the front or the back of the building?

Caller: It's the back. I don't know, I don't know, I don't know.

Operator: You face the back of the building?

Caller: Yeah. I don't know. It's, it's— I can't help you, I can't. Please.

Operator: OK, we'll be there as soon as possible. Don't—OK.

Caller: Please, please.

This was not the same story that Carl Andre had told Connolly and Capolupo, but was the caller Carl Andre? By now, the civilian outside had been sitting on the bench for over an hour, without complaining, and at last the detectives called him to the CO's office for questioning. Finelli introduced himself, and the conversation proceeded calmly.

He asked Carl for his "pedigree." He was five-foot-seven, weighed 175 pounds, and was one week away from being fifty years old. He had the same high voice heard on the 911 tape, and though quite collected now and unlike the distressed speaker in the recording, the detectives no longer doubted that he had placed the call. They asked him to tell them what had happened.

They had decided to spend a quiet evening at home, Carl said. Ana came home from jogging around Washington Square Park at 9:30 P.M. They ordered in Chinese food from a take-out place on Broadway. They watched the U.S. Tennis Open on television, the Yankee game, *Dracula,* and a Spencer Tracy–Katharine Hepburn movie called *Without Love.* Ana was drinking and at a certain point began to feel "tipsy," adding soda water to her wine. At about three o'clock in the morning, while they were watching *Without Love,* she said she liked the acting but thought the plot was "absurd," and she got up and went into the bedroom. At 3:30, the movie ended. He went into the bedroom and saw that Ana wasn't there. He waited twenty minutes, then called the police.

The detectives had both taken note that Carl's nose was inflamed and had an oozing scratch. Really oozing, Finelli thought, not deep, a piece of skin just pulled off the nose. By now they had also seen another apparently fresh scratch on his right forearm.

"Was she drunk, Carl?" Finelli asked.

"No."

"Did you think she might have left by the front door?" Nieves asked.

"No, I would have seen her. I was right near the door."

"What did you think happened to her?" Nieves asked.

"I don't know."

"Carl," said Finelli, "did you think she took a pill and disappeared?"

"I don't know. I don't know."

Finelli and Nieves couldn't put their finger on it, but both began to feel that Carl was in some way talking down to them, toying with them. They began to press.

Nieves asked, "Do you remember what you said to 911?"

"No."

"Do you remember that you said you had an argument with her?"

"I said what I said."

Finelli pointed out to him that his 911 call contradicted his story.

"Whatever I said, I said," he insisted.

Finelli asked Carl how he got the scratch on his nose. He had gotten it while he was out on his terrace at 300 Mercer, Carl said. A gust of wind had blown the door in his face. It happened the Thursday before last, he said. That was ten days ago.

Finelli smirked. Listen, pal, the detective felt like saying, don't insult my intelligence. Instead he asked if Carl would allow them to go to the apartment, to view it and photograph it? He didn't say so to Carl, but he wanted to get a better "feel for the case." Carl refused.

"Why don't you want to let us go to the apartment?" Nieves asked. "You got anything to hide?"

"No."

This turned into a discussion of its own and finally Carl agreed in writing to permit them to photograph his apartment, but with a stipulation that no pictures be taken either of himself or his "attic room." That was fine with them, though they had no inkling of what he meant by an attic room.

4

Carl had arrived from Belgium eight days ago, so for the first two days of her stay, Ana had the apartment all to herself. As usual—this was her third trip back this year—from the moment she walked in the door she was on the old rotary telephone in the entrance foyer for hours at a time. She had an astonishingly large number of friends and acquaintances with whom she kept in touch, but the people uppermost in her mind on the eve of that Labor Day weekend had something to do with resolving the problems with Carl, the subtenant on Sixth Avenue, and her career. Among the first friends she called were the only two in whom she confided her most intimate thoughts. Both lived outside New York. One was her sister, Raquel, who was vacationing upstate with her children and couldn't be reached; the other, Natalia Delgado, in Chicago, said she would have to call her back so that they could speak at length, though Ana managed to bring her up-to-date on where she thought she stood with Carl. The conversations she had with others that first Friday portray other dimensions of her mood and its contradictions. She was very optimistic about a talk she'd had with a Soho gallery and filled with enthusiasm for a major piece of sculpture she had been commissioned to install in Los Angeles. She spoke of being very happy in Rome, and was looking forward to celebrating Carl's fiftieth birthday in a special way (though she'd told Natalia she was going to see a divorce attorney before going back to Rome). The lawyer who was working on getting back her apartment reported that he'd succeeded, and she planned to spend Saturday morning cleaning up the mess she was sure she'd find. One friend was interested in renting it while Ana continued to live in Rome, another knew someone trustworthy who had the same idea, and both of them offered to help her get the place ready to live in.

She had begun doing what she'd come to New York to do.

WHEN SHE USED to spend the summers in Mexico with Hans, every morning the maids would braid her long black hair Zapotec style, parting it in the middle, pulling it tight behind her ears, and twining a bright ribbon with her tresses to thicken and add color to every lock of the braid. They called her Ana Maria because that's what she called herself before she went to live in New York, and they treated her with fondness because she spoke their language and she came back to them and respected the Oaxacan tradition of celebrating death and the Day of the Dead.

One of those mornings, when she was twenty-four, she awoke beside Hans, moved by the light of Oaxaca at dawn. She slipped out of bed and left the hotel. She went to a butcher and bought a cow's heart and a bucket of blood. It was still very early when she returned, but Oaxaca had begun to stir. They would have to work fast, she said to Hans, dragging the sheet from the bed, laughing. As they climbed the stairs, she told him what she wanted to do. They went to the roof of the hotel, carrying the sheet, the bucket of blood, and the cow's heart wrapped in a newspaper. It was a flat roof of large red bricks, perfect, she thought, and she threw off her clothes and lay on the roof, looking up at the deep blue of the Mexican sky. Hans, following her instructions, covered her body with the bedsheet, and she helped him tuck it under, head to toe, all around. It was hot. Pour, she said in a muffled voice, and he poured the blood on her covered face, between her breasts, and on her stomach, until it overflowed the basin of her pelvis, forming a puddle between her legs as she held her knees together tightly. Put the heart on my heart, she said from beneath the blood-drenched sheet soaking through and through, making her sticky wet and staining her body slaughterhouse red. He placed the heart, twice as big as her own, on her chest, drained the last of the blood, and shot a roll of 35 mm color film. Then they cleaned up the mess and when the maids came, they did her hair, laughing into the mirror, telling her how beautiful she was, saying nothing, to be sure, of the soiled bedsheet.

Days later, when the thought of the bloodied body supine and inert on a rooftop had been paled by fresh adventure (because when she did these things, making art with her body, she got up and forgot it, going on to the next thing), they examined the slides, and she said, "Oh, that's a good one. What do you think?" And Hans said, "OK, I think you should keep that." But Hans, who was her teacher, thought it naive, less interesting than some of the other new work, and he might have told her one day soon, but they never looked at the slide or spoke of it again.

THE FIRE AND ice that lit her large brown eyes and ignited her eminent smile were squeezed inside a tiny body. "What can I take so I can grow taller?" she would ask her sister when they were teens in the children's home in Iowa and she'd set her heart on becoming a stewardess so she could travel all over the world, but first she had to be five-feet-five; Raquel, who was older and taller, would reply, "Ani, I don't think you're going to get that much taller." Whenever she was asked, Ana would always say she was five feet tall, and she had her passport and driver's license to prove it. At half-past ten that morning, when they laid out the broken body on stainless steel, it was shorter, but of course every vanity had departed with the spirit.

The autopsy was done at the Manhattan Mortuary on First Avenue and Twenty-Ninth Street by Joacquin Gutierrez, a pathologist, whose title in the city bureaucracy was junior medical examiner. He had come from the Philippines to study and specialize in unnatural death. His performance this morning was overseen by two other physicians. As he observed, palpated, and in the end disassembled the dead woman,

Sunday, September 8, 1985

Gutierrez dictated his remarks to a stenographer named Dorothy Stevens. "The body," he began, "is that of a thirty-six-year-old white female fairly developed and fairly nourished measuring four feet, ten inches and weighing ninety-three pounds. . . ."

Proceeding according to custom, his external examination began from the head down:

"Head hair is black and slightly curly," he said to Stevens. Touching the head, he felt multiple fractures of the skull. As was the practice in examining unnatural death, he searched for evidence of foul play—wounds, for example, that might have been inflicted prior to the fall. He made note of a bruise on her right eyelid. The eyes were free of hemorrhage, the irises brown. The nasal bones were intact, and when he opened the mouth, he remarked that the teeth were natural and in moderate repair. The jaw was broken. The collarbone was sticking out of the right shoulder, and the skin of the right upper arm was detached down to below the elbow, the muscles and tendons visible. Both arms displayed multiple abrasions. He lifted them and examined them closely for talebearing needle tracks and wrist scars. There were none. The right middle finger was cut. The fingernails were long and dirty, wads of roofing tar wedged underneath. The flesh was torn on the stomach, the right thigh, and both legs, but he saw no indication of trauma in the genital area, which appeared to be "that of a normal adult female." Then, after he had raised the body to observe the extensive abrasions on the back and set it down again, he paused and opened the chest.

Later, a physicist would calculate that Ana had fallen 269 feet in 4.21 seconds; at the moment of impact, her velocity was 120 miles per hour. As a result, almost all her bones were shattered and all her major organs lacerated, including her brain and her heart. A year or so earlier, she had complained of an irregular heartbeat to a friend in Rome, who recommended a cardiologist. After a series of tests, she was told there was nothing wrong, and now Gutierrez's examination confirmed that her heart was structurally normal, the coronary arteries clear. Her heart weighed 250 grams. There was little else worthy of note; "unremarkable" was the neutral medical word used repeatedly by Gutierrez when not describing the injuries. Some of the Chinese food she'd eaten with

Carl the night before was still in her stomach, green vegetable matter
undigested. This, along with nail clippings, some scalp and pubic hair,
swabs of every orifice, and samples of other body fluids, was submitted
for laboratory study to aid further inquiry. Finally, Gutierrez dictated
his conclusion as to the cause of death:

> Multiple skeletal fractures and internal injuries. Fell from building
> at 300 Mercer Street on 9/8/85. Circumstances undetermined
> pending police investigation.

Ana's remains were returned to the morgue; she had yet to be viewed
by someone who knew her, who could claim her within the terms of
the law and put her to rest.

5

"Carl, now we're going to go over to your apartment," Detective Finelli
announced after he had called the Crime Scene Squad to meet them
at 300 Mercer. It was about eleven in the morning now. Connolly, who
like Carl had been up all night, drove. Carl sat in the rear of the
unmarked car. "It was low-key, nobody was excited," Nieves would
later recall.

When they arrived, and Carl had let them into the apartment, there
was little to do but wait for the Crime Scene photographers. Connolly
showed the detectives around. They were struck by the mayhem in the
bedroom. Finelli looked out the fatal window. It seemed as though it
was going to rain. He leaned out. Oh, my God, he thought, living a
moment of terror at the sight of the sheer drop.

In the living room, Finelli asked Carl if he had any of his sculptures
around. Carl said, "You want to see some of my artwork?" He showed
Finelli one of his catalogues. Finelli's eye was caught by a photograph
of another Andre outdoor piece called *Joint;* lying in a field, it was a
hundred yards long and consisted of 183 bales of hay placed end to end.
Connolly already had had enough of that sort of art; he stood by doing
nothing.

"Would you mind if I make a few phone calls?" Carl asked.

Sunday, September 8, 1985

"Listen," said Finelli, "you can do what you want."

Carl flipped through the pages of his personal telephone book, scanning the tidy block-lettered entries. He began to dial from the black phone on the table in the entrance way. The cops pretended otherwise, but they all eavesdropped.

The first call was to someone who apparently wasn't in, because Carl spoke as if he was leaving a message on an answering machine. His voice was unsteady. He said, "Hello, this is Carl. Ana is dead. We'll have to cancel our dinner engagement. Sorry."

Connolly had the impression that in the second call Carl was speaking to a man. Connolly heard him say, "Hello, this is Carl. A tragedy has happened in our lives. I'm sorry, I can't talk now." Finelli heard him use the phrase, "something happened that is unmendable."

Carl continued to make these laconic calls, four or five of them, all to cancel the same dinner party. Detectives Ward and Mahoney arrived from Crime Scene at 11:40 and began to set up their equipment. Finelli sent Nieves to canvass Carl's neighbors for anything pertinent they might have seen or heard late the night before. Ward and Mahoney took seven photographs of the bedroom and living room; as bargained for, the "attic room"—the disorderly storage space—remained inviolate.

Connolly then brought them to the Delion rooftop. It was standard police procedure to photograph the body before removal, but this had been overlooked. Now, they photographed the indentation made at the point of impact and took measurements of its position relative to the building, which showed that the victim hadn't landed directly above the deli but on the adjoining space, a restaurant on Broadway called Montien Thai.

In the meantime, when Carl was alone with Finelli, the ring of the telephone shattered a quiet moment. Carl answered.

"Hello?"

"Hello, Carl, this is Natalia. . . ."

It was a wake-up call for Ana, placed from Chicago by her friend and confidante Natalia Delgado. Carl had had precisely this exchange with her when he had answered her call less than twelve hours earlier; after a polite word or two, he had passed the phone to Ana. Ana had remained on the line for about half an hour, and the conversation would have gone on longer if Natalia weren't being badgered by her husband to hang up. She had told Ana that she would call her first thing the next morning to pick up where they had left off, and Ana had asked her to wake her, saying that she shouldn't call early in the morning because she wanted to sleep late.

"May I speak with Ana?" Natalia said now.

"No," Carl replied in a vacant voice, "you may not."

"Well, isn't she there?"

"She's not here right now."

"Would you ask her to call me when she gets in, would you give her that message?"

"Yes, I'll give her the message."

Nieves returned to the apartment from his survey of tenants on the thirty-fourth floor. The neighbors adjoining both sides of 34E reported hearing a violent argument erupt at the Andres' three nights back, the second that week, said Mark Coler of 34D, but only Bobby Tong, in 34F, heard something last night: a noise in the Andre bedroom, then a crash outside.

After Crime Scene left, they all went back to the West Tenth Street station, Carl dutifully obliging a request that he come along with them once more. It was one o'clock that afternoon when they reentered the squad room. Finelli and Nieves learned that they had gotten another assignment, and they told Carl they had to go out but wouldn't be very long. By now both detectives, and Connolly, too, suspected Carl of having murdered his wife. Finelli had sensed it "right from the word get-go"; Carl's story was cockamamie baloney, he felt, like scrambled eggs.

Both cops continued to pursue a carrot-and-stick strategy that they hoped would lead to a confession. Finelli called Connolly aside and said that if Carl wanted to leave, he should try to talk him out of it, but if he insisted, he should let him go. Alone with the suspect, Connolly asked Carl if he could get him anything. Carl said no but complained of being very tired. There was a cot in the CO's office where he could lie down for a while, said Connolly. Carl went inside and fell asleep.

Sunday, September 8, 1985

I T   W A S   T O have been a dinner for twelve that evening, planned by Ana as an early birthday party for Carl before going back to Rome. Some of the guests had been invited for drinks at the apartment at six, and the whole party was due to convene later on at Sabor, on Cornelia Street, in the heart of the Village. It was a long and narrow intimate spot, almost posh, serving refined Cuban dishes, but more Carl's place than Ana's. He'd been going there for years and had turned it into an art-world power lair of low visibility, a quiet little elegance in a neighborhood of phony eateries, a place where he'd bring his important Soho and uptown or European curator friends and where he was famous for erudite discourse and picking up the tab. On the day after Labor Day, Ana had been by with her friend Mary Miss to make the reservations. They'd sat around drinking wine and talking with the chef, Ronnie Ginnever, an ex-wife of artist Charles Ginnever, both pals of Carl's since the sixties. Ana, slowly getting drunk, Ronnie thought, seemed happy to be back, "quite feisty." The following evening, Ana planned the Sunday party over dinner with another friend, one she'd made in Rome, a young architect named Wendy Evans. It was a foursome, but the women didn't pay much mind to the men, Wendy's date and Carl. Ana wanted to do the birthday dinner Roman style, meaning getting lots of friends together from different circles. It was a low-alcohol evening, "delightful," as Wendy remembers it, and Ana's spirits soared. "We were both on a we're-gonna-be-famous high. I'd just received a major promotion, running a billion-dollar project, and Ana felt great about her new work on the tree trunks, which I thought was her best so far." That same night, though, the neighbor in 34D heard the Andres shouting next door.

T O   T H E   P E O P L E he had actually reached on the telephone, Carl didn't say why the dinner was canceled. To Wendy, for one, he had simply said that it had been called off, and he asked her to phone the others and tell them not to come. "Is it Ana?" Wendy asked, but only because it had been Carl and not Ana who had called, and though Carl replied yes, he revealed no more. Wendy thought nothing of it, "just another weirdness," and she told him to tell Ana that if she needed anything at all she should let her know. So it was not until Carl's more explicit messages were replayed that Ana's world began to learn that she was dead.

Doug Ohlson, a bearded man in his late forties who taught art at Hunter College and made color-saturated, figureless paintings in his loft on Bond Street, was on the guest list, and he had one of those terrible messages on his machine. He'd heard it at about noon.

"Ana is dead," it said. "There'll be no dinner tonight. The police are here."

He played it again, utterly chilled. He hadn't known Ana very well, maybe two dinners together with others around, but he had known Carl since the raucous Max's Kansas City days when they were the boys of the new art and Carl would come to dinner with his French-horn case, its velvet-lined interior filled with bottles of champagne. Ohlson didn't know what else to do, so he walked the seven blocks to Carl's place, only to learn that Carl was gone and the doorman who might know something was out to lunch. He waited in the Chinese take-out place around the corner, and when he returned, the doorman still wasn't there, but two detectives in the lobby asked him what his business was with the Andres. They told him to go to West Tenth Street to see Finelli, if he cared to.

Ohlson arrived at the Sixth Precinct sometime after two. Finelli was back, but Carl, he said, was still asleep on the boss's cot. After Ohlson told him about the terse phone message Carl had left, Finelli questioned him briefly. He asked what the nature of the dinner date was and who else was going to be there. Ohlson, who wasn't sure about the first and knew less about the second, asked if he could see his friend. Not now, said Finelli, but he added, "We'll let him go later this afternoon." Ohlson felt a sense of relief, which lasted walking all the way back home. But when he got there, another taped message from Carl was waiting. It was almost identical to the first, but somehow it sounded even more plaintive, for as his voice trailed off at the end, Carl was heard to say faintly, "So, if you know a good lawyer . . ."

FINELLI AWAKENED CARL at 3 P.M. and asked if he cared to eat something. Carl said no. He wanted to make some more phone calls;

while he did so, Finelli went off to brief his superior, Joe Ayers, chief of detectives.

Sometime between 3:30 and 4:00, one of the people Carl had telephoned arrived at the precinct and managed to have a few private words with him. Who this person was and the purpose of the visit was known to no one but themselves at the time, but both Detectives Finelli and Nieves observed Carl passing his visitor the keys to the 300 Mercer Street apartment.

Finelli and Nieves again sat down with Carl—for a final round of questioning, Finelli told him—still believing he was leading his man down a path to confession.

"Did you have an argument last night?" Finelli asked.

"None," said Carl. Nor could he recall the vociferous fighting heard by his neighbors two nights earlier. He began instead to paint a picture of what a happy couple they were. They lived in Rome and they had lots of money and he'd just bought her a new car.

"Why would she do it?" asked Finelli.

Carl didn't know why she would do it.

Finelli wanted to run through the Saturday-night story again. Carl, seeming calmer than ever now that he had caught some sleep, sailed into it once more. Ana came back from jogging. They ordered in Chinese food. Finelli was taking it down on paper, this time as a formal statement, but he had an old cop trick up his sleeve, and he suddenly turned to Carl and said, "Listen, Carl, you can write and read English better than me; why don't you write it?" It was a lot more kosher to have the suspect's statement in his own hand.

Carl, as he had more or less all day, obeyed. He set one small block letter beside another, composing the version, or a version of the versions he'd been recounting since the police had arrived at his door. Like all the others, it remained hopelessly at odds with his 911 call. On paper, however, the story grew somewhat vaguer. Instead of saying he called the police twenty minutes after discovering that his wife was not in the bedroom, he wrote that he did so "later," when "I had the horrible belief that Ana had fallen from the window." What had been termed a suicide when he had cast himself as an eyewitness to 911 had passed through a stage in which the operative verb "jumped" had now evolved into "fallen." It was an evolution that suddenly opened a whole new possibility: that Ana Mendieta had met her death accidentally. Once again, Finelli and Nieves had the sensation that Carl was trying to outfox them.

They left him alone and went to see Joe Ayers. Ayers, a beefy old-timer with sixteen years supervising detectives, went over all the paperwork and Carl's written statement. What else did they have? Other detectives were out canvassing the neighborhood. They called Ed Mojzis, at home in Elmhurst on this unforgettable birthday, and had him repeat his story of the woman screaming no, pleading. It was half-past four. Ayers told his men to up the pressure on the suspect. Experience taught cops that the game players sooner or later tired of playing; they often said oh the hell with it and then confessed. Keep him talking. Lean a little harder. Bring in the D.A.

6

Apart from the Sunday dinner date, scheduled to begin with six o'clock cocktails at Carl's, Ana had made appointments for earlier that day, and by now the telephone was ringing in vain in 34E. Out walking on Saturday, she had caught sight of two of her Sixth Avenue neighbors, poet Jayne Cortez and sculptor Mel Edwards, and she'd dashed across the street to hug and kiss them and remark how long it had been. They'd planned a catch-up brunch for today at 12:30, so for several hours now her whereabouts were being questioned and the puzzlement, if not yet concern, was mounting.

Since 3:45 P.M.—it was now almost five—Ana's sister, Raquel, had been sitting on a public bench near the stoop on Sixth Avenue with her husband, Tom, and the children. They had driven down from their home in Spring Valley upstate to spend the afternoon with Ani. The traffic had been heavier than they expected and they were a little late; they thought they had somehow missed her. Or, less likely because it was unusual for Ana to be late, she had gotten held up with one thing or another and she would surely show before much longer.

The murky sky had yet to shed its rain, which would have made the waiting harder, but both the temperature and humidity hovered in the low nineties. Raquel, six months pregnant with her fifth child, had felt a strange unease all day. Unable to sleep the night before, she too had watched part of the Tracy-Hepburn film *Without Love*. It had seemed like a tale of a hollow marriage and unrequited love and it had echoed her sister's displeasure with Carl. She had switched off the set before the turn for the better and the inevitable Tracy-Hepburn happy ending, being left with only the worst of it all.

She had hoped to see Ana that Saturday afternoon, but when she got her on the phone, Ana poured out her anger at Carl in a way she had never heard before, after which Raquel said she'd prefer to see her when Carl wasn't around. How could she act civilly toward him knowing what she knew now? They had made the appointment for today at the place on Sixth, which Ana had been tidying up off and on all week and where, because Carl had never seemed like family, Raquel and Tom and the kids felt more at home.

That was why Raquel, in spite of the endless waiting, shrank from calling 34E, fearing she'd get Carl on the phone. She'd gotten him yesterday when Ana was out, before she had spoken to her, and though she knew from the last trip to New York that the marriage was faltering, maybe they had set it right, and she chatted with Carl the way sisters-in-law were meant to.

"What are you guys doing tonight?"

"We're just going to stay home," Carl said, politely, but not the way you speak in a family. "We're going to eat in and watch the Dracula movie on Channel 13."

"Well, maybe we'll come over tonight and we can visit and stuff. So why don't you have Ana call me as soon as she gets back, because I have to take the kids to the dentist at three o'clock."

Within ten or fifteen minutes, Ana called. Speaking in Spanish as always, they talked about when they were going to meet, and then she started telling her "all this stuff" about Carl. That was when they changed the time and place, which was why she'd sat for an hour and a half on the wooden bench, aching, watching the uptown Sunday traffic grow, until Tom, thinking of the long ride back, saw one of Ana's neighbors open the locked entrance to the building, and Raquel slipped inside. She banged on Ana's door for no good reason, saw a piece of cardboard lying on the floor, and scribbled a note saying they'd been there and she hoped they'd see her soon, sending love and kisses from them all. She balanced the piece of cardboard on the doorknob and left.

A FEW BLOCKS away, in Bond Street, a grizzly faced man in running gear rode in the elevator of the loft building where Doug Ohlson had his studio. There had been a ten-kilometer race in Central Park during the hottest part of that afternoon, and he had been in it as a walker, which was punishing enough for anyone around as long as him. His name was Gerry Rosen. One of his calling cards, so to speak, was that he had been a classmate of Supreme Court justices William Rehnquist and Sandra Day O'Connor. When O'Connor was appointed, *Newsweek* singled out Rosen as someone else of note in her class. The magazine called him the "hippy lawyer" because he used to wear boots, leather clothes, and earrings to court, and Charlie Manson had sought him out to defend him, only to be rebuffed. But that was southern California in the sixties, and it was something Rosen had outgrown when he'd come east to practice law in New York. But the essence had never quite left him. He'd married an artist and represented artists, campaigning for their creative rights, lecturing at the downtown art spaces—the Kitchen, the Franklin Furnace—moving and doing a little business in the Warhol-pop-art-happening world of the seventies, and when performance artist Chris Burden had himself nailed to a Volkswagen, the man with the hammer was Rosen.

Lately, though, he'd been wearying of it all. He was pushing sixty and sixty was pushing back. Red eyes and too many wrinkles made him look older. He rarely shaved. If you came across him in the VG Café on Broadway eating his breakfast of coffee and roast potatoes before getting into his reasonably well-tailored courthouse suit, you'd be sure he was homeless. He worked out of his loft on Bond Street, his wife, Jane Logemann, painting in the same space, but he was trying to get back to where he'd begun, with Rehnquist and O'Connor, in criminal law.

———

Sunday, September 8, 1985

DOUG OHLSON HAD the loft directly below the Rosens, and when he heard the noisy old elevator climbing, he thought it might be his neighbor. Since the second message from Carl, he'd been on the phone, calling friends who might know a suitable lawyer, and one of the first persons he tried to contact was Gerry Rosen. His wife said he was out but ought to be back soon. Rosen had successfully represented their mutual friend art dealer Susan Caldwell in a civil case, and Ohlson had seen and been impressed by Rosen's courtroom manner, so he wasn't simply the attorney next door. In the interim, he had also called Caldwell, and she had joined him in the formidable task of coming up with any kind of lawyer on a hot New York Sunday afternoon. Now, Ohlson ran into the hallway, and having guessed right about the elevator passenger, flagged him down as he began to pass.

"I've got to talk to you," he said with an urgency Rosen understood. He stopped the elevator and followed Ohlson into his studio. "Something terrible has happened. Ana Mendieta is dead. And Carl is at the police station and I don't know what this is all about but he's called me twice and the last time he said he thinks he needs a lawyer."

Rosen barely knew Carl, Ana even less. Over the years, he'd run into Carl often enough at one art event or another, their acquaintanceship never progressing beyond him wiggling the sculptor's reluctant hand. But he was as keenly aware of Carl's priestly eminence as anyone else in the art world. He wanted this job. His nose smelled the Big Case, and thirty years of lawyering told him to get his nose in the tent. He picked up Ohlson's phone and called the Sixth Precinct, asking for Finelli, the only name his neighbor recalled. Rosen had a practiced voice that rang tough, but he didn't reach Finelli. The cop at the switchboard claimed that the detective was away from his desk; when Rosen asked to speak to Finelli's partner, he was told that he was also unavailable at the moment. Rosen suspected the worst, that the police were stalling, probably hounding their quarry right now.

He explained this to Ohlson, saying that they ought to go there in person without further delay. He went upstairs to shower and change, but the heat suddenly hit him, and he had to nap for an hour before he had the energy to get out of his running clothes. When he returned, dressed now in khaki pants and sneakers, he found Ohlson on the phone. After listening for a few moments, he sensed that other lawyers had somehow begun to descend while he'd been upstairs. The calls Ohlson had made earlier seeking above all to come to his friend's rescue were now being returned. A Gerry Rosen was an unknown quantity, dubious at best, while the people calling back were talking about solid connections with the best litigators in town. There was tension in the air and Ohlson seemed in a quandary.

"Look," said Rosen when there was a break in the calls, "Carl really needs help right now. You can change lawyers later, but he needs a lawyer now and we should get our ass over there quick!"

ASSISTANT DISTRICT ATTORNEY Martha Bashford, Yale Law, five and a half years in the D.A.'s office, thirty-one and overworked, was at home on homicide call when Finelli phoned at about a quarter to five that afternoon. Her shift was almost over, and she had made plans to have dinner and go to the movies with her friend Jane Feldman, another assistant D.A.

Finelli told her what he had: a suspect telling conflicting stories about how his wife went out a thirty-fourth-story window, trying to make them believe that she jumped because he wouldn't go to bed with her—"some hotshot artist named Carl Andre, who has these books about his work." The detective said he was ready to make an arrest, particularly since he'd learned that the man had plans to leave the country in a couple of days, but Bashford was not entirely convinced by what he told her on the phone. She asked him to send for the video unit, and she said she would question the suspect herself.

Bashford, an attractive woman with a broad, fair-skinned face, eyes set wide apart, and a girlish smile, had never heard of Carl or Ana. She happened to live in the Village, too, in a small apartment on West Fourth Street not far from Mercer. It was also close enough to the precinct house to go over on foot, in spite of a physical disability that made walking difficult. She called her friend to cancel their date, but Feldman asked to come along just to watch her at work.

The two women arrived in the squad room some time before six. The video unit was already there, and while Finelli plied her with more details, the gear was being readied in a room nearby. Bashford asked where the suspect was. He was probably making phone calls, said Finelli. He told her that Carl was putting on some kind of act. When he wasn't on the phone, he was reading or figuring out his taxes, or something like that. What impressed Bashford, apart from Finelli's report about the suspect's odd behavior, was a look at his passport. Carl's claim that he had scraped his nose on the terrace of the Mercer Street apartment a week ago Thursday was contradicted by the most recent customs and immigration stamp in his passport. It showed he had not arrived in the United States until Saturday, two days after the alleged accident. The camera was ready now, and so was she.

When they came out of Finelli's office, Carl was sitting on the bench. Another friend he'd called had come by an hour or so ago offering a bag of take-out food and sympathy, and by now he'd finally had some nourishment. Finelli approached him with the young assistant D.A. and introduced her. She looked for and saw the scratches, making mental notes for later recall. The face scratch was red and "open on his nose"; the arm scratch was "long, very thin, it was red . . . it looked like a cat scratch; it was several inches long, three or four inches, above the elbow, on the fleshy part of the upper left arm." She wanted photographs, though she said nothing for the moment. Carl had already told Finelli that he wouldn't allow any pictures taken of himself, but now they'd get him on video.

Bashford had not had much experience with this kind of questioning. It was a relatively rare event that happened once or twice a year. But she knew precisely how she would proceed, or at least begin. She would say very little to him until she had him in front of the camera. She wanted everything on tape. She would start by establishing his awareness of his rights, then go on to point out the discrepancies in his story and see how it developed from there. First, she explained to Carl that she would like to ask him a few questions, just the two of them in a room, with Finelli present. The video equipment, she said, was in an adjoining room behind a glass panel. They walked toward it. Carl, as he had done all day, dogged along. Suddenly, however, someone hit the power switch, and the place lit up in white-hot light. Carl stiffened.

"Shit," he said, "this looks serious. I want to talk to a lawyer."

The game, if it had been a game, was over. There was disappoint-
ment, but no one argued. Unimpeded access to an attorney was Carl's
right. Finelli led him to a phone and left him alone. Carl closed the
door.

Almost at the same moment, a taxi drew up outside carrying Ohlson
and Rosen. Rosen lit into the desk sergeant, bluffing he'd been retained
by Carl Andre and wanted to confer at once with his client. He was
escorted upstairs to Finelli, who made a crack about the stubble on
Rosen's face and introduced him to Bashford. Bashford was put off by
what she took to be gym clothes, thinking he didn't look much like a
lawyer. She was on the verge of asking for some sort of identification,
but Finelli's friendly manner moved things seamlessly along. Carl, who
hadn't got very far on his own, was back on the bench, and Ohlson
went to his side, bearing the news that he'd brought him Gerry Rosen,
counselor-at-law.

Rosen, hearing about the video unit, took Bashford by surprise,
saying there would be "no problem" going ahead with that, but of
course he'd have to speak privately with Carl first. They were shown
into a room and left to themselves.

"Can you believe this?" Bashford said to Feldman while they waited.
It was a rare lawyer who allowed his client to do anything more than
remain silent.

Alone with his attorney, Carl gave him a short summary of the story
he'd set out in his written statement. Rosen didn't want to know more,
and though he couldn't help but notice that the scratch on Carl's face
looked "very, very fresh"—it had no scab and he saw blood—it appeared to be a trivial wound. This was not the time for a lawyer to
anguish over truth. The issue was plain and simple. Should Carl submit
to the videotaping, and what were the consequences of a yes or a no?
Bashford, he told Carl, was saying, or at least implying, that "if you will
accede to our request and we're satisfied that you've cleared yourself,
you can walk out of here tonight. On the other hand, if you refuse, the
risk of your being held and charged with homicide is greater."

Rosen's advice to Carl, from what he'd heard so far, was to take the
higher risk. He had in mind a recent case in Brooklyn that had caused

a stir among his colleagues. The defense counsel had told his client to talk to the police, and this move was being highly criticized.

"You aren't going to help yourself," he told Carl, "and you could do something harmful."

Carl agreed, and after fifteen or twenty minutes they came out of the room.

"No video," Rosen told Finelli and Bashford.

"Fine," said Bashford. Would Carl allow them to photograph him?

The two sides withdrew for further consultation. Carl refused. Finelli carried the news to Bashford.

"The man won't let me photograph him," he said.

"Now, fuck him," said Bashford. "He's under arrest."

It was seven P.M.

Finelli shuttled back to Rosen. Carl was standing nearby with Ohlson.

"Gerry," said Finelli, "we have to arrest Carl."

Carl didn't react.

Rosen nodded. "Do me a favor," he said. "Don't cuff him behind."

Being handcuffed with your hands behind your back made it hard to keep your balance going down a flight of stairs or getting in and out of a van or a car. Both men knew that's where Carl was headed next, on his way to Central Booking, Police Plaza, downtown.

Ohlson, like Carl, had no notion what would happen now. He asked his friend if he could get him anything. Carl said he'd like a container of milk. There was nothing further Rosen could do until Carl's arraignment, which would take place the following morning, he had been told. He left with Ohlson, who headed for a deli and returned once more to the precinct to drop off a quart of milk.

In the meantime, Bashford had also gone, ordering that Carl be photographed before anything else. She wanted the earliest possible record of the scratches and, of course, the more time passed, the more they would knit. Lately, she had been having poor results with police photographers, and on one recent occasion she'd gotten an infuriating complaint that they couldn't do a job because they had no film. This time, before leaving, she expressed her concern. When Finelli said he had a Polaroid camera handy, she asked him to take the pictures himself.

HE HATED TO be photographed, the unconcealable hate of it staring out of each rare frame into which his image had been trapped. Where were the pictures of Carl Andre, subject, author, title of hundreds of articles, interviews, catalogues, and books since he first appeared in public in 1959? One might search through the years and find no more than a dozen in all and much fewer of the sculptor matured and in the days of his glory. Photograph the work but not the artist he would tell the writers who came calling, drawn by the diaphanous landscapes of his sculpture. His loathing of surrendering his likeness seemed an artist's quaint, even charming, idiosyncrasy to some, but there were women, lovers taken by the charm, who perceived him at odds with his fleshy body when shed of the cumbersome, cover-everything overalls he always wore. Once, two or three years back, Ana had coaxed him into an arcade photo booth. Squeezed behind the plastic curtain, she climbed on this side of him and that, pointing him at the camera, stealing a kiss as the lights flashed. If she had gotten him to smile in only one photo, which she almost did, there would have been a record that had never existed before or since.

Now he would have to face a camera again, Finelli's cheap, fast-photo Polaroid, pose for him alone in the squad room with all the fluorescent lighting turned on because the days were getting shorter and it was eight o'clock and fully dark. Finelli flashed at the scratch on his nose; when the first picture came up, he took a second then a third while the others dried. Then, to get a clear shot of the arm scratch, he asked the prisoner to remove his T-shirt. Carl did not resist. He undid the straps of his overalls, getting naked to the waist.

No one could remember when he began to dress that way, in workmen's blue denim overalls, day after day, year in and year out, hand tailored in Germany for his wedding day. Maybe it started in the sixties, but one simply wouldn't bring oneself to ask him, and he would be the last to say. Ana would make sport of his methodical ways and how he kept the monotonous wardrobe stacked so neatly on open shelves in the bedroom. She thought it was so American. Sometimes she would tease him about it in company, and when she'd had too much to drink there'd be a hint of malice somewhere way down, but he would only laugh, not even laugh, just smile, his shiny red cheeks getting round and looking a bit like polished apples.

The detective pointed, squinted, and he snapped. Suddenly, his eye was caught by something that had remained unseen until now, and he had the prisoner hold still for just one more. There was a third scratch. Like the others it was still red. It was on Carl's back, just below his neck. Finelli imagined Ana's arms around him, struggling.

—— 7 ——

Mary Perot Nichols and Annette Kuhn, writers for *The Village Voice*, had been Ana's poker pals in Rome, and they were both back in New York, invited to the eight-thirty dinner at Sabor. They had gone to 300 Mercer Street for the six o'clock drinks, and when they asked the doorman to ring Carl Andre's bell, he said, well, there's been accident; Mr. Andre's wife fell out of the window. The two women wandered into the clammy night, finding Sabor, where they spoke to Ronnie Ginnever, who said that Carl, sounding awful, had left a message on her machine saying that something "unmendable" had happened. That was all she knew, but it seemed to confirm the Mercer Street doorman's story. Ginnever burst into tears, and the other two women, not yet ready to cry, fled. They went to the Lion's Head on Christopher Street—a writers', not an artists', place—and then got drunk.

Wendy Evans, to whom Carl, without saying why, had given the task of calling "the others," had only reached two or three of them. One was Mary Miss, the woman who had been to Sabor with Ana to make the reservations. She had been calling Carl's number all afternoon, and between the no answers she had spoken to another friend of Ana's, Liliana Porter, expressing her feeling that something was terribly wrong. That evening, after eight-thirty, Mary Miss received a call from a guest unaware of the cancellation who had showed up at Sabor to be told by Ronnie Ginnever that Ana was surely dead. Again she called Liliana, who said she didn't believe it; Mary Miss had probably gotten it all wrong. "What you heard," said Liliana, "was that Ana was dead *drunk* and couldn't get to the dinner." But the calls kept coming because Mary Miss knew Carl long before Ana, and his friends who had been at the precinct were airing the bad tidings. It was true, they were saying, somehow echoing Carl's latest, more ambiguous account, Ana had fallen.

IT WAS NOT until one o'clock Monday morning when a telephone rang beside a couple fast asleep in Spring Valley, New York, that the sorrowful news of what had happened that Sunday reached Ana's next of kin.

"Is this Raquel Harrington?" said an unfamiliar voice at the other end of the line.

"Yes." Raquel had not been herself all day, and now, roused from unconsciousness, she was less so.

"You're Ana Mendieta's sister?"

"Yes." It is a man, she thought, and he is hesitating, having difficulty forming sentences.

Tom had been awakened, too. He listened in silence, waiting for the clues that would tell him what it was all about.

"This is Detective Finelli of the Sixth Precinct."

He had been trying for hours to reach her. Sometime in the afternoon, he had asked Carl about Ana's family, learning that she had a sister in Rockland County. Finelli had gotten her number from information, and when he wasn't busy with Carl, had tried it from time to time. But Raquel and Tom and the children, after they had given up waiting for Ana, had gone to a meditation program in Manhattan and then to dinner; they had not gotten back to Spring Valley until nearly midnight.

"Your sister and her husband were arguing in their apartment," said Finelli, "and the window was open and she—she went out the window."

He is having a very horrible time, Raquel thought, because he's trying to tell me something about a window and he's struggling for words. She saw a window, the window of Ana's apartment as she had seen it only hours ago, above the antique shop looking out on Sixth Avenue from one flight up.

Sunday, September 8, 1985

"Where is she?" asked Raquel. "Is she in the hospital?"

Finelli said, "She expired from her wounds."

She expired from her wounds? Raquel thought, and she said, "What?"

Carl had been arrested, Finelli said, charged with homicide. He'd been telling conflicting stories. There were scratches on his body. The bedroom was the scene of a struggle. A doorman had heard a cry of terror. He had pushed her out the window. Could Raquel come downtown later today?

Finelli heard the weeping.

"Is your husband there, ma'am?"

She passed the telephone to Tom. He wept, too.

RAQUEL HAD A younger brother. His name was Ignacio. He was on the night maintenance crew at the University of Iowa, which was where she called him at one-thirty in the morning, to tell him that their sister was dead.

"Carl killed her," Raqui said, because she had no doubt in her mind that it was true.

Ignacio went home to his wife, Laurie, and the baby. He found a notepad and called back, taking notes of everything Raqui said the police had told her. The last time he saw Ani was the only time she ever saw the baby. It was in January, just after her wedding in Rome and before the cruise with Carl on the Nile. She had come back to Cedar Rapids, where Ignacio, the boy, had watched her grow to womanhood. She looked so different married. She was always beautiful, a natural beauty who wouldn't waste time on how she looked, but now she was really fixing herself up nice, elegant. On one of those days, they went out to lunch, with her looking so attractive, and she said that Carl would have liked the restaurant he picked. He'd never met the man, but he'd been in his apartment. That was in 1982, long before the baby, when Laurie and he spent two days and one night in New York. They had gotten on the subway to Greenwich Village, and Ani had met them at the closest stop, walked them over to Mercer, and taken them to 34E to show them how she lived. He was not all that crazy about heights either—perhaps it ran in the family—but he was taken with the Manhattan sky and he went out on the balcony, crying, "Hey, Laurie, come here!" while Ani waited inside. The bedroom was real simple, he recalled, neat like the rest of the apartment; just a box spring and mattress on the floor, a wall on your right as you came in, the other wall, open shelves to stack your clothes, and the window, that window. In his wet, mourning eye, he saw the sill of that window as high as his chest, and his sister, when she was alive, had only come up to his shoulder.

He spoke to Raqui until the day broke, and then he got into his car, heading for a tract house in Danbern Lane. It was almost seven when he got there. The leafy street was empty, the sidewalks blinding white. He let himself in by the side door. She was already up, getting ready for work, and she wasn't surprised to see him because he was on the night shift and would often come by at strange hours.

"Mother," he said, "come here."

He embraced her, holding her tight, and she could feel his body trembling.

"I have something very bad to tell you," he said, and he told her everything he knew, which was so very bad just telling it, he wouldn't wish it on anybody.

Ani's husband killed her, that's what Ignacio said, and his mother believed it because she had spoken to Ani on Friday and she had said, "Mother, don't call me this weekend. I'm going to be very busy. I will call you on Monday." So she could only be dead if she had been killed, and besides, she thought, well, maybe her husband didn't call us to tell us she was dead because he feels guilty.

——— 8 ———

Until she was twelve years old, Ana grew up like a little princess in a fairy tale. The family, the two sisters and their mother and father, lived in Cuba in a very big house with a lot of servants. After lunch, the adults would take a nap, and because the girls—Ana Maria and Raquelin they were called then—were "too noisy" they had to go "somewhere else," and Ana would whisper to her sister, "Let's go to the kitchen," or simply, "Let's go listen." She loved to listen to the maids talking. They would gossip about this boyfriend and that boyfriend and about everything that was going on, and Ana, especially, would sit there enthralled.

The kitchen maids were very devoted to Santería, an Afro–Latin American religion of black gods and goddesses and white Catholic saints who sometimes endowed their worshippers with the power to ward off evil and foresee and shape the future. Many Cubans, even in the upper classes, were *santeros*, followers of Santería, but the Mendietas were orthodox Roman Catholics and always discouraged anything that had to do with the cult because they felt it was pure superstition. So the kitchen was a place of forbidden mysteries unfolding, where Ana grew interested in magic, in the secrets of nature and how to divine them.

The house was in Havana. Ana's maternal grandparents, to whom both girls were very attached, lived in Cárdenas, in the province of Matanzas, and they had two beautiful, family estates, one in Cárdenas and one in Varadero Beach, with its gleaming sea and sparkling sand shaded by pines. The girls would spend the school year in Havana and their summer vacations, Christmas, Easter, and most weekends at either Varadero or Cárdenas. Sometimes fifty people, dressed in all their finery, would come to dinner. The living room had a staircase with seventy-five steps and beautiful glass cabinets filled with fascinating objects. The house on the beach, where Ana's mother was born, had a tower and twelve bedrooms. It was called the old house, and with time it had grown so revered that it had its own birthday parties, family members bringing gifts to adorn it.

Ana's grandparents were very well known in Matanzas. Her grandfather was a physician, and he had a private clinic there. Her grandmother was the president of the Descendants of the Veterans of the 1895 War of Independence, and on patriotic holidays Ana always marched in the parade to Puerto Rojas, a fort named after her great-grandfather, Carlos Maria de Rojas, who was a general in that war. General Rojas was revered in all of Cuba because when he was ordered to burn the sugar mills controlled by the Spanish troops, he burned his own mill, too, destroying all his wealth to save his country. There were many heroes in Ana's family, and great-grandfather Carlos was a disciple of Longfellow who had studied at Harvard, helping the bard practice his Spanish at teatime. These were the stories the children heard.

Ana's father, Ignacio Alberto, was born in Havana. He was an attorney and even as a boy very much engaged in politics. His father had been a consul to Spain, a colonel in the War of Independence, and later a general in the army. Ana's great-uncle, Carlos Mendieta, was the president of Cuba in the thirties.

Her father met her mother because he used to be an oarsman. The country club in Matanzas was rowing against Havana, and Ana's father was there for the race. Her mother had just been voted by the men of the club as Miss Varadero, the queen of "sympathy and friendship." She was seventeen and he was twenty and the year was 1938. She studied chemistry and physics at the University of Havana, and along with Ignacio joined the University Students' Federation, which was full of rebels (one named Fidel Castro); when her mother found out, she made her quit. Not until she finished her thesis did her father give her permission to marry.

Ana was born before dawn on November 18, 1948, two years after Raquel. Her mother began to keep a baby book: Ana Maria Mendieta y Oti arrived weighing six pounds, six ounces, with chestnut hair, dark brown eyes, and she was *delgado,* slender. She took her *primeros pasos,* her first steps, at nine months old. She was a very sickly baby. In the first year of her life, she needed three transfusions of her father's blood, and her mother thought this child was going to die. She recovered very slowly and grew up tiny, all her wishes indulged—everyone, a little fooled because she always looked younger than her age, remarking how precocious she was.

She was a show-off, and whatever she did, no matter how silly, everybody laughed. She had a birthmark on her shoulder, and when there were people around she would show it and say, "When I was born, God was going to make me black, and he started working on my shoulder, but then he changed his mind, but it was too late because my shoulder was already black." She had been dramatic that way since she was a baby, the frail child everyone felt for and pampered.

There was nothing but love in the Mendieta home, but one day, when Ana was eight years old, she heard that the father of a schoolmate was leaving his wife, and Ana began to wonder if such a terrible fate could happen to her. So on Valentine's Day, called Lovers' Day in Cuba, Ana wrote a very special Valentine to her own mother: "This day, Mommy, is the happiest day in my life because I think you are in love with my Poppy."

She had a bad temper, too, even when she was little, and Raquel loved to get her mad just to see someone so little so mad. She used to tease her, making funny faces, and Ana, getting really mad, would back her into a corner. Raquel would be laughing, and the madder she got the more Raquel laughed, until she'd be defenseless; as little as Ana was, she could beat her sister up because Raquel couldn't stop laughing even when it hurt, which made Ana madder than ever.

The best fun was at the old house. Ana and Raquel and their younger cousins would play games on the beach, and Ana was always the leader. They would build castles, bury themselves in the sand, and Ana would decorate the bodies with plump hips and huge breasts, and everyone would laugh. Then, following Ana, they would float on the still Caribbean water, mouths open wide to let the tropical sunshine in their throats, because it kept them from getting a cold, and when Grandmother rang the big bell on the porch, all the kids had to come out of the water.

She was very good in school. She went to a Catholic school, El

Apostolado del Sagrado Corazón. Like all the other girls, she wore a
blue skirt with pleats and two straps and a white linen long-sleeved
blouse every day. She behaved badly in class, clowning, and sometimes
she had to stay after school until six o'clock to do her homework, and
her mother would come to pick her up, seeing her sitting there all alone,
looking so tiny. She did not have to study very much to get good grades,
and she hardly ever did her homework. Every now and then her mother
would say, "Are you sure you don't have any homework?" And she'd
say, "Well, I have homework but that page is missing out of my book,
so I can't do it." Then one day when her mother was changing the
sheets in Ana's room, she picked up the mattress and pages and pages
of her school book were underneath.

Only Ana could get away with these things. Everybody would laugh
and say, "How funny!" If Raquel had ripped a page out of her book,
that would have been the end of her. Raquel had to go to the music
conservatory on Saturdays, take piano lessons every day, and perform
her chores and errands, while Ana, being younger and bolder, was free
to gather crooked sticks and snails and horsehair and all the other little
things that pleased Changó, the great Babalú-Ayé, Yemayá Star of the
Sea, and the rest of the sainted pantheon of Santería.

THOUGH HARDLY NOTICEABLE in the never-ending lives of little
girls, everything began to change in 1958. They were returning to
Havana from an autumn holiday in Cárdenas, the girls with two cousins
in the back seat of their parents' car, as always joking and laughing and
singing happy songs, when Ana's father, at the wheel, snapped around
and yelled. "You children should be quiet!" he cried. "Don't you know
that people in Cuba are dying! You should have some respect!"

People in Cuba were dying. They knew that now. Fidel and Che had
beached in Oriente in a boat called *Granma*. They knew that because
Fidel, before he fled to Mexico, had been in their house talking all night
long, and when he landed back in Cuba their father and mother had
been so happy on hearing the news. Fidel and his army of *campesinos*
were battling in the Sierra Maestra, fighting to overthrow the wicked
dictator Batista, fighting, as their great-grandfather had fought with

José Martí against the brutal Spaniards, for the freedom of their country, and Cubans were dying.

Whole weeks went by, strange people came and went from the house in Havana, and the girls were not allowed to be around them. Suddenly it was joyous Christmas and time to go to Grandmother and Grandfather once more, which they did, but this time without their mother and their father. And why were they going to Cárdenas and not the house on the beach as they always did for Christmas and New Year's?

One night after Christmas and before New Year's, the whole town was in the streets of Cárdenas, singing and dancing and throwing confetti at Fidel's army marching on Havana. Ana and Raquel, watching in awe from the balcony, had never seen grown-ups so happy. The next day they had to leave, and they weren't told why they were going back to Havana before New Year's Eve in a stranger's car and why their father hadn't come to pick them up. They arrived at the house in Havana, hearing funny sounds in the living room, and when they went there, they couldn't believe their eyes. Their father was destroying the living-room furniture, taking apart the big square sofa and the massive armchairs, the insides yielding an arsenal of submachine guns and ammunition, and all these years the girls had been bouncing and wrestling on that couch. "Remember when we jumped on that?" the sisters, feeling scared, were saying to each other. "Look at all the bullets in there."

On New Year's Eve, the wicked dictator fled in the middle of the night, and on New Year's Day, 1959, the *campesino* army marched into the capital, Fidel and Che leading the way and the whole world cheered, so there was nothing to be scared of anymore. Instead they felt proud of Fidel and their country, proud of their father being part of a glorious revolution.

A heroic picture of Fidel went up on the living-room wall, and little by little the girls learned that their father had been a hero, too. Right from the beginning he had fought Batista, refused to practice the dictator's law, been briefly jailed, then gone underground. He had moved Fidel, a younger man, into the revolutionary party, had secretly joined Fidel's 26th of July Movement after the raid on Moncada, and of course had hidden guns and ammunition in the furniture. The dictator, rounding up his enemies, had sent someone to kill their father in those final days, and Ana and Raquel had gone to Cárdenas alone that Christmas because he was in hiding. Fidel, rewarding him, had given him an important job in the foreign ministry, sending him on a mission to bring back one of Batista's fugitive henchmen, and when he returned to Cuba, pictures of Ignacio getting his man were in all the newspapers.

The new Cuba had new enemies, at home and abroad, and Ana and Raquel began to grow up faster. How could you think of Varadero Beach when people you knew were suddenly besieging Fidel? They were slandering him, calling him a communist, an atheist, an anti-Christ, and the girls would fight back, joining their mother and father, saying he was none of those things and that was just loose talk against the revolution. But one day, in 1960, their father fell silent.

A security check had revealed that during World War II, he had been a counterintelligence agent, trained by and an informant of the FBI. Afterward, he had become a major in the National Police, tracking down clandestine Cuban communists. He could clear all suspicion, he was told, if he would join the Communist party. So the loose talk was true, and before long Fidel said so, calling himself a Marxist-Leninist, and their father, who never went to church on Sundays, refused to join him, saying, "I believe in God. I'm a Catholic. The communists have an atheistic belief and that goes against my belief." He broke with Fidel, going underground once more in search of a new deliverance, seeking the new Martí but finding only the CIA.

ANA, SECRETLY TO be sure, began to smoke. It was 1961. She was twelve years old. She had a boyfriend. She taught her older sister how to smoke, to inhale, because she didn't like Raquel's "dummy" ways. Fresh faces were seen around the house in Havana, good-looking young men coming to see her father, to discuss things that were kept from the girls, but Ana had begun to disobey her father, and whenever the girls could, they watched the young men and smiled.

That year was the Year of Education. Private schools were to be abolished; in February, the revolutionary government turned to the

Catholic schools. All teachers, nuns, and priests who were not Cuban born, which was most of them, were deported to their homeland, usually Spain. The schools and their chapels were closed, the statues and relics often stolen. Ana and Raquel were saddened by the thought that they would never see their teachers again, but there was ample compensation. These were exciting times, school-free days of hanging out with friends, meeting boys, smoking, and wondering what was going to happen next.

"Education *is* the revolution," Fidel said, and he issued an order: all school children fourteen or older would be sent into the hinterland to teach the *campesinos* how to read and write. Camps would be established in the countryside where the teenagers would live away from home for a period of several months, bringing literacy to the peasants, whose revolution this was. Raquel had turned fourteen months ago, and in the Mendieta household, as in those of many of the old Catholic families of Cuba, this decree, above all the godless others, was greeted with outrage and fear.

Girls, good girls, though they nurtured private "imperfections" suspected by their parents and known only to their confessors, were still chaperoned when they went to a dance or a movie with a boy, and now they would be wrested from the family by the same men who had robbed saints from the altars, assembled, dark-skinned and white-skinned together, to live in promiscuity with other children of unknown provenance, thrown at the mercy of toothless sugar-cane workers with rifles and machetes at hand. Worse, these communist camps of captive children were ideal brainwashing centers; if Marxist-Leninist Castro hadn't thought of that, his Soviet masters surely would. This was what was happening to Cuba. The end of venerated Spanish tradition, the end of God-given parental authority, the end of the sacred family, was surely near.

Then, in April, came Playa Girón, the Bay of Pigs invasion. Fifteen hundred anti-Castro Cuban exiles financed, trained, and directed by the CIA were stopped ignominiously in their tracks, more than eleven hundred taken prisoner by the Fidelistas. Ana's father, by now deeply enmeshed in other matters with the CIA, was taken by surprise by the news of the landing and infuriated that his network had been excluded.

His nephew had been one of the captured, and his self-exiled sister, Concha Mendieta, the young man's mother, was suddenly in the center of the humiliating aftermath. Nicknamed La Madrina, the God-mother, she had flown in from Miami to negotiate the high price for the release of the eleven hundred prisoners with an unforgiving Castro.

Ana's mother became truly frightened now. The Bay of Pigs debacle was followed by a wave of indiscriminate arrests and summary trials bringing either swift execution or interminable imprisonment. There was a baby in the family now, a boy named after his father, and she felt certain her husband could not avoid capture for very long. The revolution had divided the loyalties of the larger Mendieta family, as it had her own. Her brother, for example, had already been arrested by the regime, even though her sister was married to Fidel's personal physician. Many of the old families were torn by the same dilemma, blood turned against blood. Some, including several of the parents of Ana's and Raquel's friends, had begun to send their teenage children out of the country for the time being. Old families, more than any other thing of nature, abhor the vacuum of rootlessness, and thus the belief was strong among these families that in spite of, or even because of, the Bay of Pigs, which had so embarrassed the new American president, John Kennedy, Fidel would be driven from power at most within a year or two.

As a boy, Ana's father had himself been sent to high school in Miami under the dictator Machado's reign of terror, so it was anything but outlandish for Ana's mother to suggest that the time had come for the girls to go too. A Catholic organization was already in place, and the dowager niece of pre-Batista president Ramón Grau, Paulita Grau, was acting as a go-between, circulating among the families. Ana, who had grown "mouthy" and was not getting along with her father, was thrilled with the notion of going to America, but Raquel was set against it. More important, their father said no. Cuba was his country, he said, and this was where they all belonged, fighting for freedom, keeping the family together.

ANA'S BOYFRIEND'S BROTHER was a young man of twenty-two, and one day that year he asked the two sisters and another girl to distribute some leaflets to the shoppers going in and out of a Woolworth's store in downtown Havana. The leaflets railed against the revolution that had closed down their schools, and the girls had lots of free time and they were getting bored, so they all said yes. They did it, then did it again and again. Once they were chased by militiamen. They ran for their lives and lay low for a while, but this scary episode was only one part of the adventure, and they began to make phone calls, too, which really got their hearts drumming in their chests. They would meet with Ana's boyfriend's brother, and he would give them a list of messages and places to call. Ana and the others would dial the numbers and say that a bomb was going to explode in this or that building in five minutes. There were never any bombs, but there were many evacuations accompanied by sickening fear.

Soon they learned they were part of a larger enterprise. An older girl, a seventeen-year-old whom they knew from school, got caught with her boyfriend and a car full of leaflets and who knew what else; she went to trial and got thirty years in jail. They heard of someone above Ana's boyfriend's brother and someone above him, too, and that they were all bound together like cells, and you never knew who was above, adjacent, or below, but somehow the man at or near the top found out about Ana and Raquel and they found out he was their father. That was when Ignacio Mendieta, without saying why, agreed with his wife to send the girls to America.

THE ORGANIZATION GETTING children out of Cuba had grown quickly. It was backed by Protestant, Catholic, and Jewish welfare groups in the United States and given Washington's blessing and funding, along with cooperation and guidance from the Department of State and the CIA. Calling it Operation Peter Pan was one piece of guidance, and giving it a political spin to help discredit the revolution was another. In Cuba, the enhanced operation was known as Patria Potestad, a slogan meaning "parental authority" as opposed to Castro's authority and his plan to draft teenagers in the war against illiteracy. Literacy was fine, but the revolution was violating parents' rights, breaking apart the family and undermining its values. Who knew what other evil lay ahead? A fear campaign sought to depict the countryside

teaching camps as the staging grounds where sooner or later the children would be spirited off to atheist Russia for indoctrination. A full-
blown cold war airlift began. It was less reminiscent of Barrie's Peter
Pan than the Pied Piper of Hamelin.

Ana, full of joy, packed her own suitcase, deciding on her own what
she would bring to America. They were only going for a while, to wait
out Fidel's impending demise. The Catholic organization had promised their mother that the girls would not be separated; staying together
was after all what it was all about. Raquel, however, refused to go and
wouldn't pack her suitcase, crying to her mother, "I'm not going and
you're going to have to tie me up and throw me into the plane if you
want me to go!" Even Ana would cry at the airport.

It was September 11, 1961, a steaming Monday. The girls were
accompanied to José Martí International Airport by their parents and
their grandmother, up from Matanzas. The departure terminal was
packed with families that had chosen to disband rather than suffer the
fear of being disbanded. More than two hundred passengers had been
booked on the regularly scheduled KLM flight to Miami, but the only
people being given exit visas these days were children, and the plane
would be filled with children only, all between ages ten and eighteen.
The revolution was keeping these parents hostage. The children, with
hardly time for one kiss good-bye, were whisked off to customs, where
they stood for hours undergoing a thorough search. The parents
watched from behind a plate-glass partition. Everyone was crying.
Some children were taken off the lines for internal body searches, but
most were simply frisked for concealed hard currency and jewelry. Ana
and Raquel were wearing gold earrings. Ana's were confiscated, but
Raquel had trouble removing one earring, and the customs woman
couldn't bring herself to send her to America wearing only one, so she
gave her back the other, a gesture that would travel with Raquel for
a lifetime. All of the children carried the allotment of rum and cigars
allowed by customs; for some like Ana and Raquel, when traded in
Miami, these goods would bring the only dollars they would have.

After clearing customs, the children and their parents pressed themselves against the plate glass on either side and mouthed their last
good-byes, planting and throwing kisses, tears running from their eyes,

leaving only handprint smudges behind them. At last the flight departed, lifting for a thirty-five-minute hop across the Straits of Florida. The children's tears were drying on flushed cheeks, a quiet sadness setting in, when suddenly the flight attendants brought out trays piled with Hershey chocolate bars, which had long been gone from the shops in Havana, and everyone brightened. Soon they were all singing at the top of their lungs, expelling every trace of gloom, and when they crossed into American waters, an announcement was made by the captain, everybody cheering and shouting, *"Somos libres! Somos libres!"* Ana may have been the gladdest, certainly the most demonstrative because when they landed in Miami and the children scrambled down the flight stairs, she alone, in a burst of exuberance, fell to her knees and kissed the blistering tarmac, making her sister blush.

"What are you doing?" Raquel whispered harshly. "Get up from there!"

And Ana turned to her and cried, "I'm free!"

—— 9 ——

Carl spent a restive night in a cell in Central Booking, a massive Rubik's Cube-like building of dark red bricks and tall, narrow windows. He was fingerprinted and photographed again at 7:30 in the morning, full-body mug shots. At eight o'clock he was taken under guard a few blocks north to the Criminal Courts Building at 100 Centre Street, the Tombs, and led past the inscriptions in the granite facade meant to chill the stoutest heart. He went in a back way, through a cagelike maze, and was shown into a ground-floor courtroom. He was in AR1, arraignments, the transmission belt where the clanging, cantankerous system of justice begins.

Gerry Rosen wore the only smile he saw. Accused felons lumbered in and lumbered out. Guards, arms bulging in their short-sleeved white shirts, stood by, waiting with crossed arms for disorder. There was, in AR1, an unrelieved assumption of latent violence. When his turn came, Carl was brought to a table in front of the judge's bench. The thigh-high table had a large arrow painted on it, and the court clerk barked at him to stand at the point of the arrow, so as to face the judge. The lobster-shift assistant district attorney was there for the people of the State of New York. State supreme court justice Alfred Kleiman was on the bench, handling one of the last cases of the weekend night-court session. Copies of the felony complaint, sworn to by Detective Finelli, were handed out. When the case was called, Rosen waived the ritual reading rather than risk irritating a judge who, experience guided, was apt to be eager to get home and crawl into bed. Besides, he had already gone through Finelli's deposition with his client. It accused Carl of homicide; he had intended to kill his wife, had pushed her out of his thirty-fourth-floor window, and had succeeded in killing her. When he read the document, Carl had betrayed no emotion, but when he got to the part in which Finelli declared that the defendant called the police twenty minutes after he had noticed his wife was missing, at 3:50 A.M., Carl turned to Rosen and whispered, "I didn't. That's not true"; he hadn't said he'd called the police at 3:50. Rosen himself noticed something in the complaint that seemed to favor Carl. The informant who had heard the woman screaming (Mojzis's identity was being kept secret until he could testify before a grand jury) was said to have told Finelli that she was crying, "No, no, please don't," but the words "please don't" had now been crossed out, widening the gap in any leap of logic that might have to be made.

The assistant D.A. told the court he'd received word that the defendant had a plane ticket to return to his home in Italy on Wednesday, and he asked that he be kept in custody. The judge so ordered. Rosen tried to make a pitch for bail. The judge told him to pitch elsewhere, presumably anticipating the end of his day. The accused was taken back to his holding cell.

CARL HAD NOT yet actually retained Rosen, but he was his only line to the outside world and he wasn't letting go. Before parting that morning, the two men had a few moments to confer. Rosen said he would do all that he could to get him a bail hearing as soon as possible. He also gave a high priority to photographing Carl's apartment; the police were claiming that the bedroom was the scene of a struggle, and any evidence to the contrary had to be preserved. Carl had no objection. He wrote a note to the doorman of 300 Mercer telling him to admit Rosen "until further notice." He instructed the attorney to pick up the keys to his apartment at the home of Nancy Haynes. These were the same keys he had given to the unidentified person who had visited him yesterday at the precinct. Haynes had been one of the first persons Carl had telephoned after Ana's death. A tall, slim woman of thirty-eight, she was the artist whose grayishly meditative paintings, to Ana's chagrin, hung on the Andres' living room wall. She had most decidedly not been invited to Ana's dinner party for Carl, so he had called her for something other than to cancel. She had either been the person to whom he gave the keys directly or she had gotten them shortly afterward.

Haynes, Carl said to his lawyer, would also give him a leather shoulder bag containing his personal papers. He then directed Rosen to a bookshelf in the apartment where he said he would find something he called a portfolio, a folder containing financial documents. Carl wanted Rosen to retrieve the bag and the portfolio. He had checkbooks in both places giving him access to about $125,000 in various accounts, and he wanted to expedite whatever transactions might be required in the event he would be allowed to post bail. All along, Rosen had been reassuring him that bail would be "no problem," and before they separated, Carl took the extra precaution of telling Rosen to cancel his now suggestive flight plans to Rome.

Scurrying about the courthouse, Rosen managed to get a bail hearing on the docket for two o'clock that afternoon. It was still early morning. He retrieved Carl's keys and musette-style leather bag at Nancy Haynes's loft, stopped off at Turon Travel in Soho to cancel the plane reservations, headed over to his own loft on Bond Street to fetch his 35 mm camera, and then went to 300 Mercer, where with the blessings of a solicitous doorman he let himself into 34E.

He scouted. Although he had trouble locating Carl's portfolio amid the clutter, the apartment seemed ordinary enough to him. But when he saw the bedroom, he understood why the police might take it for an arena where violence had occurred. Still, it was a matter of interpretation. A case could be made that cops were accustomed to conventional apartment settings, with things in drawers and the bed made military style each day, and that they were unprepared for an artist couple's bohemian, loosely lived-in space. He began to photograph the apartment with that in mind, though in his own experience he had generally found artists to be as fastidious about their surroundings as anyone else.

The telephone rang. He wondered whether to respond. Why the hell should he answer the phone? he thought. On the other hand, maybe he could get some new information. The ringing persisted. On impulse, he swept up the receiver and said hello.

"Is Ana there?"

It was a woman's voice. She gave her name, but it passed him by. She was Ana's friend, she said.

September 9–10, 1985

He wondered what to do next, already regretting having gotten into this predicament. "You can't speak to her," he said.

"Well, may I speak to Carl?"

"Carl isn't in." Why wasn't there a handbook for this sort of thing?

"Well, when is Ana going to be back?"

"Ana is dead." He had decided to be straightforward, but when the terrible words fell he stopped cold, unable to fill the hissing silence with any other sound. Finally, he muttered something incomplete about Carl, then, "She went out the window."

The woman was stricken by the immeasurable horror. "And Carl?" she sobbed. "Where's Carl?"

"He's, he's in custody."

"Well, what are you doing in the apartment?"

"I'm his lawyer. I'm here just looking for some things. I'm really sorry, I can't talk to you anymore. I'm sorry about this. I'm very sorry to have to tell you like this, but I gotta go." He hung up. He was really sorry.

IN THE COURSE of this conversation, Rosen had chosen frankness rather than anything less because he judged it to be, apart from human considerations, the legally correct position. If his presence in the apartment were somehow to be called into question, he could not, he believed, be accused of having dissembled. What he did not know was that the woman to whom he had spoken was also a lawyer; as soon as she composed herself, she began to suspect him—particularly because he had said he was "looking for some things" and then had seemed in a hurry to hang up—of the crime of complicity after the fact. Moreover, she thought she knew precisely what he might be looking for.

The call had been placed from Chicago and the caller was Natalia Delgado, who had called twice yesterday, had spoken to Ana hours before her death and to Carl hours after to tell him to wake her. She considered herself Ana's closest friend, and certainly she knew more of her most private affairs than any other friend.

A handsome woman with candid eyes and a strand or two of gray in her hair, Natalia was four years younger than Ana, like her a childhood émigré from Cuba. Long before she met her, from the time Natalia was a little girl to much later in America, Ana had woven through her life. She had no remaining memory of the summer excursions with her mother and father to the old house in Varadero Beach to visit Ana's family, but Ana's cousin had married Natalia's uncle, so there were always Mendieta stories in her house. In the early seventies, as an art student at Oberlin, Natalia had a teacher who had somehow come across and been taken by the work of a then entirely unknown artist and that was Ana. Years later, in 1981, when Natalia had given up the notion of being an artist herself and was living in Brooklyn studying for the bar, she met Ana and Carl one evening at a party. He looked like Karl Marx and he smiled at her and was very quiet, while Ana and she, becoming friends, spent the evening going over their pasts, discovering all the distant people they knew in common. There were other parties together, but Carl was rarely there. Natalia would never forget one in particular—a reception for visiting Cuban writers—when Ana arrived glowing, eager to tell a Carl story. They had been on their way uptown in a cab, said Ana, when Carl, watching the street numbers get higher, discovered they were going to East Harlem and he wouldn't go past Ninety-sixth Street, which was where he stopped the driver, leaving her alone laughing at him for being so American. "Ah, these gringos," she said to her friends that evening, "they are really very different. . . ." She always had a Carl story ready for Natalia. One night, when Ana was alone, she called and they went to a Frida Kahlo opening. One of the paintings was Kahlo's incandescent portrait of herself standing with her legendary husband, Diego Rivera. "You know," said Ana, seeming as always thoroughly amused, "Carl thinks that our relationship is like Diego and Frida. Can you imagine the ego?" And that night, wrenched perhaps by Frida, she spoke of Carl in a way she rarely spoke of him to anyone, and it wasn't all in amusement. The women grew closer, becoming kindred, and Natalia, following Ana as one follows a shooting star, became the repository for all the fading lights in Ana's love for Carl.

Within a couple of hours after receiving the calamitous news of Ana's death, Natalia was seated in a downtown office with two detectives of the Chicago police. She realized that she was probably the last person besides Carl to have spoken with Ana, and the substance of that half-hour conversation might have turned fatal. Now, she told the detectives, supportive evidence, which might provide a motive for the alleged murder, appeared to be in jeopardy. They made some notes and some phone calls. They advised her to get in touch with New York, Detective Finelli, Sixth Precinct.

LOWERY SIMS, A curator at the Metropolitan Museum of Art, arrived at Penn Station somewhat frantic about her lunch date. The first thing she did was call her office on Eighty-second Street to leave word that she was on her way. Ana had called her last Friday to say she was back in New York and Lowery had said, "Well, you want to get together this weekend? I'm going out of town and I can be back for dinner Sunday night." And Ana said, "No, no, let's just do lunch on Monday." And on Sunday, Lowery was flying back from North Carolina when the plane ran into thunderstorms. It was forced to land in Washington, where she spent the night and took the train the next morning.

They had met in the late seventies when Ana had just gotten to New York. Lowery, black and feeling beautiful about it, was working with a new feminist magazine called *Heresies,* preparing a special issue on Third World women, and Ana was contributing, too. They became friends, getting closer, oddly, after Ana left for Rome. Lowery, like many others, would receive one of Ana's newsy but custom-fit postcards now and then, and when Ana came to town, it was, like this trip, catching-up time. Lowery had risen to a powerful position in the art world—helping to decide the purchase of contemporary art for one of the world's greatest museums—and she grew sensitive to the way Ana managed her ambitions. Lowery had become used to being "handled" by artists hoping to sell their work, but with Ana she never felt she might be giving more than she received. That was when she recommended a few of Ana's drawings, abstract but unmistakable female forms, to her boss, and the Met bought them. Ana had been ecstatic, and Lowery shared her joy. As an artist and a curator, Lowery felt they had joined forces in a kind of movement she thought of as mainstreaming minority artists.

Now this big rush to get to the office, and then, no Ana. Getting busy with her work, she quickly forgot about the missed appointment, but before long she got a call from a friend who asked if she had heard anything about Ana. Lowery said she'd been stood up for lunch, and the friend said he'd heard Ana was dead, and Lowery said that was ridiculous. Before long they spoke again; there was more news, and she knew it was true. "You go through your life," she would say later, "and sometimes people don't show up and there's always some anxiety about what happened; but this was the first time in my life that something really happened."

AFTER HE HAD completed photographing Carl's apartment, Rosen raced downtown to criminal court at 100 Centre Street to argue for his client's freedom. There had been no press reports of Carl's arrest as yet, but the circle of his friends who knew continued to widen by old-fashioned smoke signals of one sort or another, making its presence felt in more and more tangible ways. Both telephone lines in Rosen's loft had been ringing all morning, messages of support for his client piling up on his answering machine.

Nancy Haynes and Doug Ohlson were comforting Carl in body as well as spirit when Rosen at two P.M. went before Judge Max Sayah to plead for his release. Also present in the courtroom, besides assistant D.A. Martha Bashford for the People, were staff reporters from the *New York Post* and the *Daily News,* so the story would break very soon. Apart from his celebrated client's interests, Rosen had a sense of something of himself at stake, too. His itching hand was on the throttle of the Big Case but as yet restrained by an absence of a clear signal to go. Carl simply hadn't retained him yet, and Rosen, bending the first rule of practice—up-front, cold-cash commitment—was working good-Samaritan style. He had thought winning bail would be easy but his failure to budge Judge Kleiman at the arraignment had preyed on him all morning and by now he quietly despaired, and Haynes and Ohlson looking over his shoulder was hardly cheering.

He got off to a bad start. Judge Sayah couldn't figure out what Rosen was doing in his court. Bail, the judge pointed out, had already been denied in night court, but Sayah did hear the lawyer out. He listened patiently while Rosen portrayed Carl as an upright citizen by virtue of his renown, absence of past offenses, the "thinness" of the case, and his bondable assets. "I'm talking about bail of one hundred, two hundred, three hundred thousand dollars," he said, prepared to buy at any price and worry later.

Bashford for her part rehearsed the evidence in Finelli's complaint and cautioned that the defendant, because of his assets, particularly those abroad, might abscond. Although she did not say so, she felt that while Carl might be too well known to simply disappear, she might lose him to the complex machinery of extradition. The working premise in the D.A.'s office was, "Before you know it, they're in the Dominican Republic," with which the United States has no extradition treaty.

Rosen parried with the prudently cancelled tickets to Rome, and he added his willingness to surrender Carl's passport. He would personally keep Carl on a leash, he added, remain in daily contact with him, and, as an officer of the court, report any infraction.

"My real problem is," the judge told Rosen, "that you went before a supreme court judge in arraignments and nothing has changed since last night."

"He didn't hear me," Rosen replied with passion. "He wouldn't even hear me."

"I don't understand that. That, to me, doesn't make sense. You're asking me to overrule one of my colleagues."

Rosen, sensing all else was failing, reverted to his hippy lawyer days. He went into what his California trainers called the "poor Joe" routine, in which feigned ignorance and deference were used to work oneself out of a morass. "Your Honor," he said, addressing Sayah's dilemma, "he did not entertain it. You're not overruling it. He said he was in no position. Maybe I'm a little short on my knowledge of the procedure, but I took him at his word. He said he cannot make a bail determination here."

"It was his duty."

"Well, he didn't do it, or maybe he did it negatively. We didn't get a hearing. . . . I don't think he would feel that you have—"

Sayah began to succumb. "Are you prepared to put up $250,000?"

Rosen pumped his head. "Yes. In cash and collateral. Like $75,000 in cash and the balance in collateral of artwork."

Sayah winced at the idea of the defendant pawning sculpture in his courtroom, and Bashford, who'd been told by Finelli about the picture he'd seen in Carl's catalogue, had a fanciful vision of 183 bales of hay being stored for safekeeping in her cramped little office. When Sayah asked who would determine the value of Carl's work and Rosen began to speak of bringing in experts, the judge retreated to his original claim that the defense should have acted in night court.

"Wait a minute," said Rosen, poor-Joeing anew, "I was at the station house with [Carl] from 5:00 to 8:00. . . . And the only dereliction that I may have committed since then is that I didn't go sit in the court-house all night. I determined that it was pointless to come and sit in the courthouse all night, and I got here by eight o'clock this morning, and I've been aggressively pursuing this. I asked for a station-house release and they laughed at me. They said, 'That's the old way; you must have been around a long time.' But, basically, I have been pursuing and urging that he be granted bail or some kind of release for almost four hours at every juncture, and I'm doing it here."

This poor Joe had been laughed at and sent packing, but he hadn't surrendered. "Well," said the judge, "I would entertain $250,000 cash. I'm concerned with the artwork. I don't believe the People [sh]ould have to have an obligation to convert artwork."

"All right, $250,000 cash. That's your ruling then?"

So it was ruled. Neither works of art nor promissory bonds. Cash. Carl would also have to surrender his passport to the D.A. He did so on the spot, pending grand jury action, which was scheduled for the end of that week, Friday. The court adjourned. The problem now would be to raise the money. In the meantime, of course, Carl would continue to remain in custody. But that took away nothing from the tonic of winning. Indeed, before being hauled away once more, Carl came up to Rosen bearing a smile. "I want to retain you as my lawyer," he said.

Carl was trundled off to the cloisters of Rikers Island. Rosen gave interviews to the press. He defended his brand-new client, saying that he believed Mrs. Andre might have stumbled out the window as a result of jet lag. The lawyer also urged the reporters to mention his artist-wife, Jane, in their stories.

September 9–10, 1985

———— 10 ————

Martha Bashford, poised and looking sure of herself in the courtroom, was less so riding uptown to West Tenth Street to meet with Ana's sister, Raquel. She had already suffered her first setback in Judge Sayah's court, and while that had not been unexpected, the hearing foreshadowed the inhospitable terrain that lay ahead for the prosecution.

The judge may not have displayed much regard for the real worth of the defendant's art, but he had also raised a juridical eyebrow at the district attorney's charge that the artist was a murderer. After listening to the facts adduced by Bashford, he expressed a doubt that she would win an indictment. "The grand jury is not a rubber stamp," he warned when Bashford affirmed that the murder charge would stick. Rosen had raised the most clear-cut alternatives to homicide—accident or suicide—arguing that both were a long way from being excluded. Bashford, who had spent the morning on the telephone interviewing many of Ana's friends, could do little more than air their opinions that the deceased had been in a forward-looking, optimistic mood and that there was no reason to entertain any thought of her taking her own life. In a frail attempt to refute the notion of an accident (she had not yet learned of Ana's fear of heights), Bashford cited, rather selectively, Carl's early claim that his wife had jumped, adding that the height of the window ledge in relation to Ana's diminutive stature rendered an unintentional fall highly unlikely. It was of course premature to judge the substance of a case still under investigation, but as yet Bashford had no more answers than anyone else to the hard questions that were bound to rise like a whipped tide.

As head of the domestic violence unit, the young prosecutor had been in the war room of the D.A.'s office long enough to recognize the rare and catalytic nature of her assignment. Thirst for it or not, this had every potential for a front-page, career-making case—an event for most assistant D.A.'s that comes to them only in the ether of their dreams. The travelers on the highway of justice in the Manhattan judicial district were almost always wretched men of color on their way to prison. Light years away was Carl Andre. Although not a very visible star in the universe, he shone among the brightest in the art world, and the city of New York was the undisputed capital of that world. The murder trial of an acknowledged founding father of an entire school of modern art could be counted on to turn public attention to a stage where new stars were born. In her impassioned plea that Carl be held in custody, Bashford had bowed nonetheless to his elevated status. The people had no objection, she said, to the defendant being held in administrative segregation—a bureaucratic phrase for celebrity row, the closest thing to the presidential suite for a prisoner at New York's Rikers Island. At the moment, however, Judge Sayah's admonition that, on the evidence he had heard—which lacked even a hint of why the alleged crime had been committed—the case might not get past a grand jury, seemed to counsel caution.

DETECTIVES FINELLI AND Nieves were proceeding with firmer, if less elaborate, persuasion than Bashford's. They were in Finelli's smoky squad room office with Raquel and Tom Harrington, questioning Ana's sister while they waited for the assistant D.A. Finelli hadn't had much sleep in the past thirty-six hours, and he looked it. Worse, he felt it.

"No woman commits suicide in her underwear," Finelli had told the grieving couple not long after they arrived at one-thirty that afternoon.

The dead woman's husband, he was thus admitting, had been a suspect in his mind from the first fact of the case—the body lying all but naked on the Waverly Place roof. Old cops with chest pains do not gather facts and figures, but they know about such things. From that moment on, Carl had set off Finelli's every alarm with the ring of guilt.

"He thought he knew more than anybody else," Finelli said, "so we were thinking that was the thing that was going to do him in. Right from the beginning we felt he was going to slip up because he thought he was so smart. And we almost got him. He kept saying things like, 'I don't know,' or he didn't recall, or something like that. But a couple of times it looked like he was going to answer something, and then he would stop himself from saying too much."

Listening, Raquel remained in the thrall of an unearthly feeling that

September 9–10, 1985

Ana was not really dead but only in hiding from a vengeful husband, believing at the same time that by this fiction she was shielding her unborn child from irreparable trauma. Somehow, though, she took an instant liking to Finelli, who seemed so worn by time yet so vigorous in what he was saying.

His greatest regret, Finelli went on, was that he had not gotten his dry-eyed man under the vaporizing light of the video equipment.

"I didn't talk to him the way I'm talking to you," the detective said, conveying a sense of the pressure he had been applying. "He was on the verge of confessing. If it had just gone a few minutes longer, but then he saw the video and he just snapped out of it."

As the matter stood now, he went on, the case against him wasn't strong enough to get past first base, and if it hadn't been for the doorman who heard Ana's screams, there might not even have been probable cause to justify an arrest.

Both Raquel and Tom were taken by surprise hearing Finelli's assessment of the outlook for the case. They had assumed Carl had in fact confessed. His failure to mourn with them, to have made no attempt to even call them, was all the confession they needed.

What had stumped him, Finelli admitted, was the motive. "He was going on and on about what a loving relationship they had and how they were practically newlyweds, and he bought her a car and gave her an apartment in Rome, so if she was so happily married, why would she kill herself?"

"That's not true!" Raquel shot back, suddenly coming alive. "It wasn't anything like that." She felt a rush of anger, and the thought of Carl going free brought out all that she knew.

It was at the end of May, on her last trip to the States, that Ana went to see Alton Abramowitz, a divorce attorney whose name she got out of a New York Bar Association listing, and it was either on the first or the second of June that Ana finally came clean with Raquel, telling her what it was all about, speaking for hours about Carl bringing his girlfriends to the apartment and being so unsubtle about leaving things around. She called Raquel three days in a row, venting her anger on the phone from Mercer Street while drinking Carl's champagne out of spite or, on the day she left to fly back to Rome, pouring it down the toilet because she didn't want to mix it with the sleeping pill she'd taken to overcome her fear of flying.

When Raquel had talked to her two days ago, all the things Ana said this time—about the photos and the postcards and letters—made her so upset by Carl's callous ways that she didn't want to go to their apartment that night. It sounded like he was getting worse by the minute instead of better. Ana was feeling very spiteful. It wasn't like she was just saying, "I'm so angry, I'm so angry." It was like, "That son of a bitch, I'm gonna do this to him and I'm gonna do that to him." That was her tone.

Ana said, "Everybody thinks Carl is such a generous and nice person; well, they don't know the real Carl Andre, and I do, and I'm going to expose him to the world!" And she said, "When I'm finished with him, nobody's going to want to talk to him! Nobody's going to want to have anything to do with him!" Raquel couldn't imagine that her sister would be so naive to think that no one was going to want to talk to him merely because he had a couple of women on the side, though she also could not imagine what Ana meant by saying she would "expose" him. Now that Raquel knew that Ana and Carl had argued after watching *Without Love* and that Ana had in some way been touched off by the movie, Raquel could understand how Ana might have cut him in half with a word like "expose" because that was her fighting style. And hadn't he used the word, too, speaking to 911? But she just hadn't gone into it that afternoon, hadn't said, "What do you mean by that?" because Carl was there in the same apartment when Ana was talking to her, and Raquel had figured, well, we're going to talk the next day and Ana would tell her whatever it was. But Raquel had a feeling Ana wasn't just making empty threats, and she did ask why Ana didn't confront Carl, who knew nothing of all this. Not yet, Ana replied. She had to wait a few months. The way she put it was that something big was happening, something to do with one of those northern countries in Europe where Carl was always going, and the people interested in her work were connections of Carl's. She was clear about that—Carl's friends, his connections—and that through these people she could get a show at the end of 1985. She said it would mean a real breakthrough in her career. She didn't want to ruin that. She felt that once she started the divorce then Carl would get mad and kill her chances for the show.

By the time Raquel had told her story, Bashford had arrived, and they went over it again. In terms of courtroom evidence, it added almost nothing. It was textbook hearsay. Suggesting any scenario in which the substance of that phone conversation between sisters had somehow become known to Carl and had resulted in his reacting with homicidal violence would be dismissed as speculation supported only by the word of one egregiously injured party. There were exceptions to the rules of hearsay, but this was not one of them. Nevertheless, it helped Bashford make sense of it all, and it would make others understand what might have happened that night. Such testimony could be introduced, at least to a grand jury, to show Ana's nonsuicidal state of mind at the time of her death, that far from being depressed, she was actively planning, scheming for rewards in the future. The way to present the case to a grand jury appeared clearer than ever now. Grinding away the possibilities of suicide and accident—Raquel's information about Ana's fear of high places further undermined the latter—left evidence supporting homicide only. Bashford was as convinced as the detectives that Carl was guilty. She was less pessimistic about bringing him to justice, but she wanted Raquel to be prepared for "the worst."

In the meantime, however, Finelli, who had been called to the phone, bore news of a fresh development in the case. He was on a long distance line to Chicago with Natalia Delgado. Keeping Natalia on hold, Finelli reported to Bashford that the caller had reason to suspect that Carl's lawyer had searched the Mercer Street apartment that morning, looking for and possibly removing incriminating evidence.

Natalia asked to speak first with Raquel, and when they had done what could be done to soothe each other's sorrow, she got on the phone with Bashford. She repeated the details of her conversation with Gerry Rosen and revealed that Ana, since her return to New York, had discovered and photocopied an array of documentation she had intended to use in a divorce suit based on charges of adultery. This evidence was in addition to records she had already compiled and kept hidden in her apartment in Rome. She wasn't interested in a peaceful, no-fault settlement. She wanted to hire a detective and get pictures and tapes and haul him into court because she didn't want peace, she wanted war. Besides, Abramowitz had told her that she'd been married for so short a time that she couldn't get her hands on most of his assets. The only thing left was satisfaction and maybe the lease on the apartment in Rome with the twelve months' rent that had been paid in advance by Carl.

For more than a year now, Natalia had held power of attorney to manage many of Ana's legal affairs when she was out of the country. Thus she knew a good deal more than Raquel did about the details of Ana's divorce plans and the underlying nature of her case against Carl. Much of it, she said, perhaps too much, had been discussed on the phone in their final, late-night conversation. Natalia didn't know where in either the Mercer Street or Rome apartments Ana had concealed the material she had been secretly duplicating and collecting, but, she said, Ana had told her that on this trip to New York she had been "photocopying like crazy," and that by way of wry satisfaction what she had found had made her very happy. Furthermore, when they had spoken on the night of her death, all of these papers were firmly in place somewhere in both apartments.

When the person who claimed he was Carl's lawyer said he was looking for "things," Natalia's first thought was that he was after Ana's photocopies, which in the last moments of her life, Natalia imagined, had in some horrifying way come to light. Her concern now was to safeguard whatever she could, and since she also knew that the Rome lease was in both Carl's and Ana's names, she wanted to alert the district attorney that Carl had legal access there, too.

Bashford assured her that she would see to getting the Italian police to seal that apartment. More pressing was the need to go before a judge in New York to obtain a warrant to search for Ana's papers in 34E. Natalia's story had reinforced Raquel's. As the last person other than the accused to speak to Ana alive, Natalia had suddenly emerged as a potential star witness. She had to be questioned as quickly as possible. Some word that Ana had uttered to Natalia that night might, if recaptured, contain the key to understanding her demise. Bashford asked if Natalia would come to New York to testify before the grand jury. There was no length Natalia would not travel now.

——— 11 ———

Wendy Evans was in her office on the Upper East Side trying to call everyone she knew among Ana's friends. She hoped to spare them the shock of reading about Ana's death in the morning papers. Not many years ago, a friend of Wendy's, a fellow student at Harvard, was found murdered just after graduation, and the story was plastered in lurid detail all over the *New York Post.* That was what she expected now.

A slim, stylish woman with luminous brown eyes and a ready smile, Wendy thought of herself, an architect in the well-known firm of I. M. Pei, as a corporate person, the only take-charge sort among her artist friends. Somehow she felt it her duty to manage this crisis. She had always been surprised that Ana would want to be her friend. She admired Ana for having been constantly true to her art; because of that, Wendy believed, Ana would surely regard her as someone who had sold out, of having become the yuppie-like "Wendy doll" she called herself for fun. But the two women had become close chums that first year in Rome.

Of the forty or so fellows at the Academy, only Ana and Wendy had dared to venture boldly from that American sanctuary on a hill overlooking Rome but really a planet away. From the start they both took on a new look—dropping their Americanness and going Italian. Wendy changed her makeup, her hairstyle, put on high heels, and never wore jeans again, while Ana, though less capricious when it came to fashion, set the pace. They both bought old cars, and they both learned Italian, learned to shout it for the life of them as they whipped through the traffic of Rome, making the rounds of the galleries near the Spanish Steps and hanging around the Pasta Factory, an old commercial building in a decrepit part of town, converted Soho style into artists' studios. Wendy got herself an Italian boyfriend, and when Carl would show up from time to time they'd double-date, starting the evening with champagne. Carl always treated Wendy very cordially, always picked up the bill, and always had something smart to say. He liked to go Il Galleone, a touristy fish restaurant decorated like a ship, a place he wouldn't be seen dead in back in New York. He liked it because it had a large menu in English, and he tried his best to make a virtue of being "monolingual by choice," he would say. Those Roman days. Running around with Ana from one bureau to another, piling up the stack of incomprehensible certificates you needed to get married in Rome, Ana loving marriage, yearning for the breakthrough in her art, craving fame and rank, and growing gracefully old. They were good times always, except, sometimes, the "getting home scared," blacking out after champagne evenings with Ana and Carl. Now it was all going to be in the *New York Post.*

ONE OF ANA's friends, whom Wendy could not call, was sitting on the stoop of Ana's apartment building at 188 Sixth Avenue. Her truck was parked at the curb. It was late afternoon. Her name was Marsha Pels. She was a thirty-four-year-old sculptor who had won the Prix de Rome during Ana's second and final year in Italy and who in a way had taken Wendy's place as a sidekick after Wendy had gone home. Only a few weeks ago, when they were both still in Rome, Ana had given Marsha Wendy's telephone number as someone to look up when she got back to New York. But Marsha hadn't gotten to that yet, the days since her return having been filled with setting herself up again after more than a year abroad. Marsha made large, sinuous bronzes, and like many foundry sculptors she traveled heavily and sluggishly. She hadn't even seen Ana yet, though they had talked by phone twice last week.

She had been waiting for nearly two hours now and was at the limit of her patience. She had called the Mercer Street number a couple of times without an answer. They had made an appointment to meet here to move Ana's belongings. With Marsha was a stocky young man named Marc Mancini, whom she had hired for Ana to help with the moving. He was also hoping to become Ana's assistant. Ana had asked Marsha to help her find someone to work with her on her project in Los Angeles, the permanent outdoor sculpture to be installed in MacArthur Park. The original plan had been to move Ana's things from Sixth Avenue to Carl's place and go out for a drink. Marsha was also eager to sublet Ana's apartment, and Ana had agreed, but the last time they spoke there had been changes, and from what Ana said, Marsha suspected that something was very wrong.

September 9–10, 1985

The first call had come last Wednesday. Marsha had gotten back ten days before her. Ana seemed high-spirited, but she was concerned about her friend. In Italy, Marsha had expressed apprehension about returning to the doldrums of her real world after an exhilarating and productive stay in Italy. Marsha admitted to being somewhat of a mess under the impact of culture shock, but she was glad that Ana was going to help her out by letting her rent the Sixth Avenue apartment.

On Friday morning, however, Ana called again. She sounded upset.

"I can't talk to you now," she said. "The plans have changed, but I still need your help. I'm going to be moving things the other way, from Carl's apartment to my apartment. So can you help me anyway?"

"Sure, it's all arranged. We'll just show up the regular time."

It had to be something with Carl, Marsha thought, though Ana had never spoken badly about her relationship with her husband. Marsha disliked Carl. She knew him well before she'd come to Rome and met Ana. She considered herself one of the few women who was not under his spell and the only woman among her artist friends who had not become his mistress. Unlike the way he treated Wendy, he hadn't always been cordial to Marsha. She had met him in the early eighties, watched him court her friends, watched him hold court night after night at Chinese Chance, Mickey Ruskin's place in the Village and the successor to Max's, but it was not until Rome, when Carl discovered that Marsha had become Ana's close friend, that he began to break out the champagne around her. She had been as surprised as he was learning they shared a bond with Ana. One day, Ana announced that she was going to the Rome airport to pick up Carl Andre, which was startling enough, but not long afterward, she came into Marsha's studio at the Academy and said, "Carl and I are having a small reception out in the back, and I want you to come if you can." And Marsha said, "Oh, that's nice, what for?" And Ana said, "We're getting married." And she seemed so very happy.

Marsha called Carl's number again. Again, no answer. She scribbled an angry note: "Where the hell are you? I've been waiting two hours. And I had to pay the guy."

She got into her truck, paid the guy, and drove him home.

———

BY THE TIME Gerry Rosen arrived at his loft to return his phone calls, his answering machine had been filled with new and renewed messages from the art world and the media. He was impressed by the way the New York "art infrastructure" was so swiftly closing ranks around his client. He labeled this coven of reigning dealers, curators, collectors, critics, and artists the art infrastructure because, like many who spoke the argot of Soho, he liked to mix street talk with uptown phrases. But this was not the infrastructure he knew.

Once, in the California days, he believed in the culture of art as a cathedral in which one might find communion with the essence of one's times. But the artists he'd met and known since then inhabited another, savage temple, holding drawn knives, letting the blood of their rivals to move from one exposure of their work to the next. He saw money-grubbing, covetous, piglike New York as the cruelest temple of them all. Now, however, he perceived a vector gathering in that culture, and speaking in artspeak, it was saying, "We've got a major, seminal figure sitting in the destructive, discreative environment of Rikers Island and what can we do to help?"

It had been a rare, winning day. This was hardly the time to celebrate, but, alone in his office, a walled-off corner of the loft among the cartons of his past, with an old two-bladed ceiling fan cooling him down, an old-fashioned pat on the back was OK. Today's victory in court was an inrush of steroids melting the flab on his self-esteem. Where in all New York, he wondered, was there another practicing criminal lawyer who could have gone before a middle-brow public disciplinarian and matched his stand-up, impromptu portrayal of Carl Andre as the great and wealthy museum-class artist—this guy in blue coveralls charged with murdering his wife who sells boulders to Hartford for a living. How, without a unique combination of skills, do you make sense of *that* to an unenlightened judge? Sure, the inspiration was out there: Very Important Artist, Hundred-Grand Case, and those were the incentives by which he had advanced a pretty strong argument, very forceful and dramatic, in the way he'd come right out front, California style, "confessing" ignorance of the niceties of New York law only to dress up his appeal: "Hey, listen, you're smarter than I'll ever be, but I've got rational arguments that should convince you to let him out." The judge had bought it. The press had bought it, too, or something like it, and he'd just picked up on it, like the story about Carl's wife having jet lag popping into his head when he'd needed it.

But there were problems, and they waxed as the evening wore on. Calling back, fielding new calls, and coming down slowly from the intoxication of it all made it clear to him that it would not be a simple matter to put together $250,000 in cash without trying the patience of a man unaccustomed to having his freedom curtailed. What had struck him, even disturbed him, about Carl was his cool-headedness, the white-knuckle grip on himself and his predicament, unruffled, at least to the observer, by either the gross ambitions of the law or the wounds of loss. Jail, even in a gilded cage, was as suddenly disabling as a burst appendix, and though Carl had been pleased with Rosen in the afternoon, the span of his pleasure was bound to collapse by morning.

Rosen's feelers were already receiving signals. The drift of some of his phone conversations with Carl's friends seemed to be that the bogey contesting his worthiness to defend Carl Andre had not been laid to rest by today's performance. Nancy Haynes, for one, having observed him in Judge Sayah's courtroom, was somewhere out there brooding quietly but not silently about his courtroom manner. She had apparently taken his poor Joe ploy in earnest, and she worried about how well Carl's interests were being served.

He would take this up with his client tomorrow morning when they met on Rikers Island, but the news he would carry to prison was still unclear. The woman who represented his artwork in New York, Paula Cooper, a prominent Soho dealer who had known and adored Carl for twenty years, was the person in the best position to convert his assets into cash. But she was in Washington on business, and though she had cut it short, she was not due back until sometime tomorrow. Even so, Rosen saw middlemen and haggling in his future. Some of the callers had expressed a willingness to contribute to a bail fund, but that was probably the longest way home. Carl, no matter what, was facing many days in jail, five at least, Rosen figured. His first duty, he felt, was to his client's defense and the stewardship of his rights. So what if he spent a couple of days more locked up? But he knew the pressure to post bail would be fierce.

The hardest truth was that he felt himself launched into a big league in which he was not yet ready to play. For one thing, the gaps and the nagging contradictions in Carl's story made him doubtful about how to proceed. For the first time in his life, he understood that a criminal lawyer in a circumstantial case such as this one had no business wringing his hands over whether his client did or did not commit the offense he is charged with. The attorney really has a much more objective situation to evaluate: the evidence the prosecution might produce and its probable weight in a court of law. The defending attorney, Rosen saw now, need not ever face the ultimate question simply because no one but the accused can ever know with absolute certainty to what extent, if any, the charges are true. People, he thought, are convicted and executed and you don't know the absolute truth. Yet wring his hands he did.

There was the business of the two portfolios, the bag he had retrieved from Haynes and the folder he'd taken from Carl's bookcase. They were at his side now, but he was loath to look through them, uneasy about what he might find. At a glance, the one that Haynes had given him appeared to contain Carl's "guts stuff," his most personal papers. The other, the financial file, seemed innocuous enough, but who knew? Carl was eager to have both portfolios, but surely it would be imprudent to bring them with him to Rikers, where they might be searched, if only for drugs. By the number of empty champagne bottles lying around in 34E, who could say what other substances the Andres indulged in? The questions mounted.

In Judge Sayah's court, he had, for tactical reasons, declared that his client was considering going before the grand jury to testify in his own behalf. This in fact did appear to have an effect on the judge's decision about bail, and he had even chided Bashford that she might fail to get an indictment. Taking the stand in a grand jury proceeding, the all but unfettered domain of the prosecution, is a powerful demonstration of one's belief in one's own innocence, but Rosen was unsure about advising Carl to do so. If he were guilty, or in some way responsible for his wife's death, his testimony could be disastrous. Perhaps he should consider pleading temporary insanity. Or was plea bargaining the best course to follow? Review the facts, he thought; these questions could be answered tomorrow at Rikers.

Earlier in the day, he had spoken with an old lawyer friend, William Kunstler, one of the most famous litigators in the country. Rosen wanted to explore the idea of teaming up with a man of greater experience than he had, a major leaguer. Kunstler seemed interested. That, too, he would take up with Carl in the morning. Tonight, however, he remained at a loss. He began to make a checklist. He headed it "Things to do."

RON FINELLI AND Chief of Detectives Joe Ayers arrived at 300 Mercer Street at 10:30 P.M. to execute a warrant to search for evidence of a murder committed in apartment 34E. The warrant had been drawn up by Martha Bashford, and Finelli, going before a judge, had obtained court authorization two hours earlier. Under laws that had evolved over hundreds of years to protect civil rights, search warrants had to be written in language so unequivocal that the searching parties were left with no discretion as to what they might seize. Thanks to Natalia Delgado's call from Chicago, Finelli and Ayers would not have to bend any rules. They knew exactly what they were looking for—the photocopies Ana had been secretly compiling to use against Carl in her suit for divorce.

The two detectives waited in the lobby for the Crime Scene Unit and Emergency Services. Finelli, killing time with his smokes, was in a good mood. Bashford had been in touch with Interpol about sealing the apartment in Rome, and she had asked him if he would mind going to Italy to work with the Rome police. He had leapt at the chance. He was of Italian descent and was that much more excited about going, but a lot would depend on what the doctor would say when he got the results of his tests.

Crime Scene and Emergency Services showed up at about eleven o'clock. The latter unit had been summoned when it was discovered that nobody had Carl's keys, and Crime Scene was there to officially "process" the apartment in search of clues.

Once they had broken in, the first thing Finelli did was open the door to Carl's mysterious inner sanctum so sternly forbidden to him and his men until now—the "attic room." Nothing could be touched until Crime Scene had done its work under so-called sterile conditions, but Finelli's curiosity held sway, at least for a look. It was a chaotic lair, worse than the bedroom. File cabinets, papers, a chair, all overturned and on the floor.

Crime Scene detective Anthony Amplo, working the sixteen-hour turnaround shift, began with the photography. He was assisted by his partner, making it a foursome in the apartment now. All of the detectives spoke with a New York accent, but Amplo, who looked like a comic-strip sleuth, talked a particularly pronounced New Yorkese. He and his partner photographed the "attic room," the entrance to the bedroom, the inside of the bedroom looking toward the window, and the bedroom window facing the street. With his partner holding him by the back of his belt, Amplo shot the view leaning out of window. He also took two close-ups of the radiator in front of the window.

The reason for the close shots was that Amplo, who had twenty-two years on the force, considered the configuration of the radiator relevant to the case. The heating element was encased, and he wanted to show that apart from the narrow grillwork there was a wider, smooth surface on which prints may have been left.

He then applied a powder to the window area, including the walls, dusting for fingerprints, footprints, and palm prints. Four partial fingerprints came up, three on the windowsill and one on the wall. They were lifted with a kind of cellophane tape with an opaque backing.

The detective made measurements in the bedroom next. The height of the windowsill from the floor was two feet, eleven and one-quarter inches. The sill extended five inches into the room. The baffled radiator abutting the window was narrower than the sill by ten inches on each side and not as high. It was two feet, ten inches from the floor and jutted another nine and one-half inches into the room. The two-panel sliding window was five feet, one inch in height, and the left panel, which was the side that was open—the side from which Ana had plunged—was two feet, eleven inches wide. The right panel was two inches wider.

September 9–10, 1985

Crime Scene packed up and left at 1:45 A.M., and Finelli and Ayers proceeded with the search.

By now, they had seen a purse lying on the bedroom floor. It was a beige leather handbag with a shoulder strap and a leather handle. It had been bought by Ana in Italy, and though the cops had no way of knowing that, they assumed correctly that it was hers. It contained eyeglasses, a cosmetic pouch, a Blue Cross card, Ana's driver's license, her passport, her business cards tucked inside a mirrored case, another packet of business cards (her own, one of Wendy Evans's, and one of another friend's whose name was Eduardo Costa), her wallet, a flashlight, and some subway and tunnel tokens.

The "attic room" yielded most of what would come to be called the infidelity records: a letter to Carl from a woman in Berlin, which ended with "hugs and kisses"; four postcards from other women; credit card receipts, a hotel bill, and a phone bill from Munich; and other papers that would be catalogued as miscellaneous. Another source of these documents was a scatter of magazines and papers on a table near the front door and a bookcase in the living room. This produced a collection of Carl's telephone bills, credit card receipts, and a spiral notebook.

Finelli also gathered up some of Ana's papers, such as her bank statements and checkbooks, as well as some photographs that were lying around. One of them was a picture of Ana, another woman, and Fidel Castro.

That was the long and short of it. At about two-thirty in the morning, Finelli and his chief agreed they had gone through everything that might yield what they had been authorized to seize. Finelli put everything collected, the "whole schmeer," he said later, into Ana's purse. Back at the West Tenth Street station, he stashed it in his locker.

Only later would it become apparent that the most significant result of the search was what it did *not* produce: there were no footprints on the windowsill. Moreover, not until more than two years later would anyone realize that not one of the infidelity records was a photocopy. The material described by Natalia Delgado as having been in the apartment when she spoke to Ana very early Sunday was nowhere to be found late at night on Monday.

—— 12 ——

SCULPTOR HELD IN DEATH
PLUNGE OF ARTIST WIFE

This four-column headline in the *New York Post* hit the stands on
Tuesday morning. Carrying the usual number of errors, the story read,
in part, like this:

> One of the world's most controversial sculptors, Carl Andre,
> is under arrest—accused of murdering his artist wife by throw-
> ing her out of the window of their Greenwhich [*sic*] Village
> apartment. . . .
> Andre, a minimalist artist, was held without bail at his arraign-
> ment Sunday night [*sic*].
> But in a fervent argument for bail, his lawyer, Gerry Rosen,
> moved in Criminal Court yesterday to have the bond fixed at
> $500,000 [*sic*] "in collateral artworks." . . .
> Later, lawyer Rosen—who is the husband of artist Jane Loge-
> mann—said . . . he believed that Miss Mendieta had stumbled
> through the open window, and pointed out that the couple might
> still have been suffering from jet lag. . . .

The only explanation of why Carl ranked among the "world's most
controversial sculptors" was that some years back an Andre piece
bought by London's Tate Gallery, which consisted of a rectangle of 120
bricks, "touched off an international furur [*sic*]."

The *New York Daily News*, with a similar headline, got the story
slightly straighter, beginning with the following lead:

> An internationally known sculptor was jailed on Rikers Island
> yesterday following his arraignment on charges of pushing his
> artist wife to her death from the couple's Greenwich Village
> apartment. He was jailed when unable to post $250,000 cash bail.

September 9–10, 1985

The *Daily News* made a point of the judge refusing Carl's art as bail, and while it quoted Rosen, it used the space the *Post* dedicated to Rosen's wife to say something about Ana being "herself a distinguished sculptor." Neither did it rely on Rosen alone, presumably because it had two reporters on the job. They managed to get Manhattan district attorney Robert Morgenthau to say that Carl's denial of wrongdoing "was nonsensical and does not agree with the facts." They also got an interview with one of the employees at 300 Mercer Street. "They always looked happy," the employee said of Carl and Ana.

The *New York Times,* in its own low-temperature style, gave prominence to the story, too. Scoring highest on getting the bare facts right, it cited Morgenthau at greater length, going for the police account of the incident without a single "balancing" word from Gerry Rosen. The only interview in the *Times* piece was, in a sense, with itself. It quoted its chief art critic, John Russell (a longtime enthusiast of Carl's work), as saying that Carl had been "internationally known as a gifted and serious artist since the late 1950's." Russell, or as the case may be, the *Times,* knew much less about Ana; apart from mentioning her having won a Guggenheim Fellowship in 1980, the article listed only a couple of her minor achievements.

The electronic media simply recycled the morning papers, extracting little sound bites for airing throughout the day, mostly on radio. The only article of merit in terms of daily journalism was still being written by a New York correspondent named Paula Span. She would report at length on the utter shock the news was causing in the art world. It would appear in tomorrow's *Washington Post,* but by tomorrow the story would be gone from the New York papers, replaced by a disquieting silence that would endure for a long time.

PEOPLE IN ANA'S world would remember what they were doing when they heard the news much in the way whole generations remember where they were the day Kennedy was shot.

One such person was Carolee Schneemann, a performance artist of high acclaim, whom Ana had thought of as her older "aesthetic sister," the feeling being mutual. Carolee was asleep in a corner of her loft when a friend who had a key let himself in. He was helping her refurbish and his arms were laden with tools and plasterboard, which he dumped on the floor. He threw his morning newspaper at Carolee to wake her and get her on the job. "Wait'll you see this," he said. "Carl Andre's wife is dead." Carl Andre's wife, she thought, trying to place whom that wife might be. His wife? She gasped. Ana? And there was a *Daily News* beside her.

Lucy Lippard, an art critic, feminist writer, and another older "sister" heard it on the radio. "God, I heard it," she still remembers. "I'd spent the night with my mother in Connecticut and I heard it driving down to New York. It said, 'sculptor something,' and I thought, oh, they're always calling people artists, and it's probably nobody I know, and all the way down I heard it, and it was Ana. First they mispronounced her name, then in the next twenty-minute interval somebody told them how to say it, and it just kept going on, over and over and over, and I don't know why I kept listening." She was always about to write an article praising Ana's work, and Ana had known it. Every now and then, because Lucy's name went far in the art world, Ana would call her or write and say, "This would be a good time." And Lucy would say, "Right now I'm doing something else, Ana," and she'd think, Ana's work is getting better and better, no hurry.

IT WAS NOT an easy trip to Rikers Island, even when you went voluntarily. The New York City jailhouse sat in a limbo, between the Bronx and Queens, straddling an imaginary line between the East River and Flushing Bay. It was far from the last stop on any subway line, and neither private car nor taxi was allowed to cross over. You somehow got to the foot of a narrow bridge to the island and took prison transportation to a window with a number to state the reason for your call. Manhattan lawyers, whose fees began at a hundred dollars an hour, did not regularly go there to see their clients. It meant hours of hassle for minutes of consulting time. They preferred to meet them when, invariably, they were trucked into the city for one or another appearance before a judge, of which in even the most humdrum criminal case, there were more than enough.

Gerry Rosen's hourly consultation rate was $110, but he was not that kind of lawyer. A client in jail was infirm, he believed, and his lawyer had to become his surrogate, performing beyond the line of duty and being prepared to serve as both moral support and messenger boy.

As was his custom, he was up and out early, and, after he read the newspapers, off to see Carl. Today would be particularly strenuous, and faced with so many hours away from his answering machine, he succeeded in pressing his wife into secretarial service, going "live" on both his phones. Persuading her had not been an easy way to start his day. Jane had not been flattered, given the subject matter, by seeing her name flung out of left field and into the *New York Post*.

Rosen's list of things to do contained eighteen separate entries by now. The parts about getting Nancy Haynes off his back, teaming up, maybe, with Kunstler, working out the best defense strategy for confronting the imminent grand jury action, and, of course, raising the bail money had all been put to paper. But chief among Rosen's concerns were the items that had to do with clarifying Carl's version of the primary events. Earlier, when they had learned that a witness had heard a woman screaming, Carl had told Rosen that he was "dozing" in the living room at the time of his wife's fall and that he had not heard any scream. Rosen hoped Carl could help him reconcile this with his claims, particularly to the 911 operator, that she had jumped. Highlighting this item with a little arrow, he wanted to ask Carl if he hadn't heard a scream, what, then, drew his attention to the bedroom two hours after the Tracy-Hepburn film ended? If he had been dozing, how could he be sure that she had not slipped out of the apartment? In spite of denying it to the police, had he looked out the window?

This was the agenda he had come to Rikers to discuss, but the prisoner, when he was brought in at about nine-thirty that morning, had his own agenda in mind.

"You've got to get me out of here," Carl said, a pitch of despair in his voice. He looked far from his ruddy self.

He had passed another bad night, confined to a temporary pen, wakened at five A.M. He had not been assigned to the relative luxury of the thirteen-cell dignitary ward. That was not to be until tomorrow so tonight would be more of the same.

He had to make bail. There was a museum show coming up in Krefeld, West Germany, and a one-man gallery show in Rome. The

Krefeld exhibition was being handled by his German dealer, Konrad Fischer of Düsseldorf. Fischer was a good friend of many years, and Carl had money and sculpture there, and goodwill as well. Fischer, he told Rosen, had to be contacted at once, not only about wiring bail money, but, since Carl's European travel plans had been canceled, Fischer had to be instructed how to install his work in the museum. The same was true for his Rome dealer, Gian Enzo Sperone, who had been expecting Carl not only for the installation but for the September 17 opening, too.

Carl asked Rosen for his two portfolios. Money had to be moved from various accounts. It had to be done today.

Rosen said he had them but hadn't brought them with him.

Carl erupted in anger. He yelled at his lawyer. Stupid was what he called him.

Rosen, the person who drove the nails through Chris Burden's hands when no one else would, was not the sort of man who allowed insult to go by unchallenged. But these were unusual circumstances. He tried to assuage Carl's ire.

"Look," he said, "no problem. I'll go get them. I'll be back in a couple of hours."

Why hadn't he brought them in the first place? Carl insisted.

He didn't know why, he said. His perfectly sensible reasoning, that they might be searched and contain something illicit, escaped him for the moment.

Rosen gathered up his list of things to do and prepared to leave. Carl dashed off a note in his block-lettered, upper-case style and told him to get it to Paula Cooper. The terse message asked Paula to get in touch with Carl's European dealers Fischer and Sperone. They were to be informed that Ana had died and he would not be able to go to Europe as planned. He then gave precise instructions, measurements included, of how the Krefeld and Rome shows were to be installed.

It ended with Carl wishing Paula well and his informal signature, a small flourish of his initials that looked like an @ sign. Rosen, as he read it, marveled at his client's equanimity.

———

September 9–10, 1985

MAKING HIS LOOP to the city, Rosen was unaware that another downtown lawyer named Gerry had entered the territory he was trying so earnestly to consolidate as his own. The new man had appointed himself to an emerging council of war eager to do all they thought best for Carl.

His name was Gerry Ordover, a buoyant Soho figure well known to famous artists. Operating in shirtsleeves out of an old row house on Sullivan and Prince streets, he went back to the earliest Max's Kansas City days, servicing the eccentric legal demands of the art community with lively chatter and a smile. His chief client since the sixties was Leo Castelli, the doyen of dealers, and he had represented Frank Stella during the minimalist painter's rise to first-magnitude stardom.

Art law was Ordover's specialty, but he had been on the scene when Soho was coalescing out of the ratty dungeons of rag balers and doll makers, and he had negotiated many of the sweetheart leases and sales of what would become some of the world's handsomest spaces where art is created, shown, and sold. Unlike Rosen, however, he had almost no criminal law experience. His only three penal cases involved sculptor John Chamberlain, busted in the Village for drunk and disorderly conduct; Stella and his wife at the time, Barbara Rose, both busted in Central Park because Barbara, so went the complaint, wouldn't take her foot off a bench when a cop told her she had to and Frank bit the cop's arresting hand; those cases dated back to the sixties, and in the early seventies, he had defended dealer Tony Shafrazi, busted at the Museum of Modern Art for spraying paint on the *Guernica*. Not that Ordover had any ambition to topple and replace Rosen—a friend as well as a colleague—but the common denominator of his criminal law experience was that in all three cases he had posted the bail and brought his clients home and now he saw a way he might also rescue his old acquaintance Carl Andre.

Carl had never been Ordover's favorite person. At Max's and later at Chinese Chance, he would run into Carl, say hello, and as often as not get barked at. "Send the lawyers to Tahiti!" was Carl's favorite bark, or so it seemed. Ordover, however, practicing one of his other sidelines, had handled Carl's divorce, long before he met Ana. Carl, in the sixties, was married to another artist, Rosemarie Castoro, the second of his three wives. It was Stella who sent Carl to Ordover when the couple decided to split. They parted friends, and the way Ordover remembered it now, Rosemarie told him that she and Carl had always been perfectly compatible living together in their studio; Carl, the sculptor, had the floors, and she, the painter, had the walls. But, alas, she too had taken up sculpture, so Carl, with Rosemarie's blessing and Ordover's instructions, had gone off to Mexico, in those days the favored halfway house to the quickest and most civilized divorce.

Carl had come in and out of Ordover's life often since then, though not as a client. He had known Rosemarie quite well, and she continued to see Carl, at least for a weekly game of chess when he wasn't traveling. The rumor even now was that the weekly game, a routine that endured, irking Ana, had been stipulated by Carl as a condition of the divorce, but Ordover knew better. After Rosemarie, Carl paired up with Angela Westwater. She had come to New York as a twenty-nine-year-old managing editor of *Artforum*, moving to the gallery side of the business as Carl's dealer and living with him through much of the seventies. Ordover had known her well, too, but he hadn't had much contact with Carl lately, and he had never met Ana.

Hearing the news yesterday evening through someone who had a friend living in 300 Mercer, Ordover had no doubt that the woman's death was a case of "sudden suicide" and that Carl was being held unjustly. He had tried to track down more details, but it was not until this morning that he had spoken with an artist friend of Carl's, Larry Weiner, who knew more than what was in the papers. Weiner, in fact, had been one of the friends who had come to the Sixth Precinct on Sunday to support Carl in his ordeal. The main concern now was getting him out. Konrad Fischer had already been contacted in Germany and was sending $150,000, but even by telex that meant days of delay that would stretch into the hiatus of the weekend. Everyone was waiting for Paula Cooper's return, said Weiner. The thinking was that she could arrange a quick bank loan. Ordover checked this out with Douglas Baxter, who worked for Paula. He was unaware of any talk of a bank loan.

Sometime around noon, Ordover got Paula herself on the phone.

September 9–10, 1985

She had just arrived at her gallery a few blocks east on Wooster. The only thing certain so far, she told him, was the money coming from Fischer, and even when it arrived and was added to Carl's money, they would fall substantially short of the mark. She had already heard from the other Gerry, she said. He had been out to Rikers but hadn't brought Carl's checkbooks, and Carl was annoyed. Rosen was going back with the stuff, but by the time he'd return to the city, the banks would surely be closed, losing another day.

That was about the moment that Ordover, saying nothing to Paula, realized that he knew someone he might tap for ready cash. He telephoned his former client Frank Stella.

TOM HARRINGTON HAD driven down to the city to spare his wife yet another ordeal. He told the clerk who he was and showed his Social Security card.

They wheeled out the body at one P.M. It was, of course, covered with a sheet. He waited for a doctor to peel it away. He had been there the first time Ani spoke to her sister about this guy she had met who was interested in her. She had just gotten out of the long relationship with Hans, and along he came. He remembered Ani saying she had never been with anyone who treated her as nicely as he did and that she wasn't quite sure how to respond. He remembered her talking about how he was so very sweet to her and how he was always bringing her gifts and flowers and poetry and how he really seemed to love her. She hadn't wanted to get involved with him at all. He remembered her saying that, too. But he kept wooing her all the same. And the way she described him, not physically, just the way she felt about him, was so romantic, Tom thought he was some handsome young artist and was surprised when he learned he was Carl Andre, a man much older than she.

The doctor came by and turned back a corner of the sheet. Only the face was exposed. He identified her.

SOMETIME DURING THE prison day, Carl spoke to a psychological counselor. He said he wanted to see his wife's body. The counselor, who like everyone else who had contact with him, had been perplexed by

Carl's stony demeanor, approved his request and said he would pass it on to the authorities. Carl seemed less distressed when Rosen returned to Rikers with his papers. He began to go through them, and Rosen took up the matters on his list.

"Don't cop out on me," Rosen said, hoping to make it clear that he was not aiming for an admission of guilt, but simply wanted to go over the facts. Carl denied or admitted nothing. His written statement to the police was as far as he would go. As for his "dozing" prior to discovering that his wife was no longer in the apartment: when Rosen tried to pin this down and asked him how he knew that she hadn't gone out the front door, Carl, as he had told the police, replied that he just knew.

This was not the sort of answer that would endear any jury Rosen had ever faced. It also seemed to be the best Carl would ever do. "You ought to consider the idea of a temporary insanity plea," Rosen suggested at this point. Carl listened attentively.

The conversation bogged down in the details of finances and the possibility of Rosen getting to his client's bank before closing. The attorney had trouble understanding the reason for Carl's complicated checking maneuvers, and he asked him why he didn't, for convenience's sake, write just one check in Rosen's name and let the attorney disburse the funds as needed. Carl looked up from his checkbook, stared at him, and smiled. He would keep his own books.

ROSEN GOT BACK to town in time to make the bank. He was unaware of the efforts at raising bail being made by others, but when he returned to his Bond Street loft, he saw that the tidy list of phone messages kept by his wife was filled with offers of money to help get Carl out of jail. The most specific one had come from a man who had only recently posted $100,000 bail to free himself. He was a powerful and lately notorious art dealer named Andrew Crispo, who had been arrested the previous May, charged with a sexual assault felony. "If you need money," Crispo told Rosen when he returned the call, "I know where you can get money on his art." There were art financiers in New York, he said, who could provide unlimited funding. One of them, a firm called Rosenthal and Rosenthal, was "wonderful—but a little expen-

sive." Rosen, however, felt confident that the outpouring of support
would now gather quickly. Gerry Ordover had called twice to say that
he might be able to help in raising the bail, and Rosen, though he
couldn't get Ordover on the phone just now, considered him a powerful
ally to have in the art world.

Apart from the cash offers, there was a fresh ground swell of art
establishment solidarity with Carl. Both Angela Westwater and ex-wife
Rosemarie Castoro stood ready to help with whatever might be needed.
Artist Rudolf Baranik, speaking for both himself and his wife, May
Stevens, also an artist, revealed that they had been to dinner with Carl
and Ana the Friday evening before her death, and they wished to do
whatever they possibly could to stand by her husband in his misfortune.

Uplifted from the low points of his day, Rosen turned again to
thoughts of Carl's legal defense. He hadn't gotten passed the "dozing"
and insanity-plea entries on his checklist, which left everything unan-
swered, and new ideas had occurred to him since. He began making
inquiries about hiring a private investigator to track down any potential
witnesses and evidence in Carl's favor. Curious about the Friday-eve-
ning dinner mentioned by Baranik, he called him back. It had been a
foursome at Pirandello's, an Italian restaurant around the corner from
Carl's place, pleasant enough, said Baranik. Did Carl have any
scratches on his face? Rosen asked. Without saying so, Rosen was
attempting to corroborate Carl's claim that the nose scratch was several
days old, though it had appeared fresh to him when he first saw it on
Sunday. Baranik said that Carl's face was not scratched. Shortly afterward, however, Baranik called again to add that he could not be sure.
The reason was, he said, "I always look at a person's eyes."

Sometime before five-thirty P.M., Paula Cooper, who had been trying
to reach Rosen for the past two hours, got through. She was a soft-
spoken woman whose voice sometimes fluttered so low that it was
difficult to hear, but Rosen was hearing her fine as she thanked him
for all he had done for Carl. His services were greatly appreciated,
she said. They were, however, no longer needed. "We've hired
another lawyer," said Paula. She was so gentle with him, he thought,
so civilized.

"Good luck!" he said. He hung up. His nose was out of the tent, his hundred-grand case out the window; so, he wasn't in Kunstler's league, but he was immensely relieved.

——— 13 ———

Paula Cooper, a comely woman with large brown eyes, was making her telephone calls from her office at the back of her gallery at 155 Wooster. She had spent part of the afternoon hearing Carl's friends argue the case for dumping Gerry Rosen and interviewing the lawyers they recommended. By three o'clock, she had made her decision.

Her expression of gratitude to Rosen had certainly been sincere, and his comportment had been aboveboard and effective. He had in fact won the first round in the courtroom, and if he had irritated Carl this morning, he had gone to great lengths to make amends. What would bother Carl most, Paula knew, was something Carl was probably still unaware of: the story in the *New York Post*, most of which originated from Rosen himself and had the appearance of self-promotion. Who could tell what that might augur? The man she had taken upon herself to replace Rosen, an advocate of a low-profile, as-little-press-as-possible strategy, seemed more compatible with the Carl she knew, and she had known Carl well for a very long time.

As a woman of thirty, Paula Cooper had made art-world history by planting a flag of discovery in Soho. She established the very first gallery there, drastically shortening the supply lines between where artists had begun to live and work and the art marketplace uptown. That was in 1968, a boom year for art sales, and by the next boom year, 1973, scores of galleries had followed her lead, shifting the center of gravity of the entire art world.

That first space was a five-thousand-square-foot loft on Prince Street, two flights up, the grand opening a grand happening, sixties style—a benefit show for the Veteran's Against the War in Vietnam. It was organized by Lucy Lippard, and Carl was in it, too. Fantastic was the way it would be remembered by Paula. Those were active, political days, when the Art Workers Coalition, a band of radical artists, would meet after hours at Paula's, and Carl, one of the founders, would plot with others to overthrow the old art world. Being an artist, Paula thought, was different then. You were an artist, you were doing your work. You went across town to Max's Kansas City, went there all the time. You hung out. You talked, you argued, you drank. You paid your tab with your artwork and you never thought of money. Now all those same downtown people were very middle class and rich, doing all the same things their uptown collectors do, dressing the same way, eating the same foods, going to all the same places around the world. The magnificent separation, the once fiercely independent nation outsiders called bohemia, just wasn't anymore. Carl was perhaps the last of a vanishing tribe.

She had met him earlier in the sixties, when he was slim and under thirty, a clean-shaven poet-sculptor with closely cropped hair and mysterious eyes. She worshipped his art. She had been learning the dealer's business in a gallery that represented his wife Rosemarie, and Rosemarie brought Carl, whose minimal sculptural cut was beginning to interest dealers, and he was invited to exhibit his work. In those days, before an aesthetic revelation that was still only gathering in his eye, he was doing massive Styrofoam pieces, jamming and enclosing "negative" space with nine-foot slabs of the white plastic latticed this way and that. Paula loved it all for its fragile, weightless simplicity in spite of its size. She would never forget how Carl had shocked her at the end of the show when she asked him where she should send the sculpture and he said, "Ah, give them away," and she thought, "Oh, my God." Soho oral history had it that Carl had suffered an uncommon romantic frustration, failing to win every corner of Paula's heart, but that being neither here nor there, the truth was that she, even in the brawling, most macho days of Max's, never thought of him as anything but kind and gentle and fair-minded, a man of rare brilliance and artistic valor.

True, he could get irascible, "verbally very acerbic," Paula would say. More often, he was exceedingly contained and formal in his everyday behavior, but when you were as sensitive to him as she, you could weigh nuance in this apparent aloofness and perceive his inner mood.

Only a week ago, on his return from Europe, he had behaved in all of these ways with Paula. The neoexpressionist eighties were displacing the minimal masters without pity, and Paula's sales of Carl's work were plummeting. The one-man show she had given him last winter hadn't reversed the trend. His close friends noticed that Carl seemed to be growing crabby, and even the *New York Times*, reviewing the January exhibition, complained of it being "emblematic of his cantankerous attitude toward the art establishment and possibly the audience for art as a whole." Paula hadn't seen much of Carl lately. The gallery had been undergoing renovation all summer and was closed to the public, and she was often away. Carl had been in with Ana one day that week, and finding Paula gone, had given her a difficult time on the phone. Then he had been back again on Friday, knowing she was still away, but this time bearing a note of apology, which he left with the book-keeper for Paula's return. She had gotten it only today, its import eclipsed by the terrible events in the meantime and his jailhouse plea for her help.

At about 5:45 that evening, a gray Olds Omega pulled up outside the gallery. She was expecting the car. Gerry Ordover was at the wheel. Paula got in and they headed over to the Bowery, picking up Larry Weiner at his studio on Bleecker before pointing for the Triborough Bridge. It was grim company, and night was coming on, but Ordover felt good. He had a certified Citibank check in his pocket made out to the Department of Correction in the amount of $250,000. They were going over the river to bring Carl home.

FRANK STELLA, a forty-nine-year-old painter considered among the world's most important living artists, had agreed without hesitation to contribute substantially to a bail fund. One of his earliest paintings had recently sold for more than a million dollars, and though he was not a beneficiary of that sale (he had been happy to let it go for $1,200 years back), his success had made him an extremely wealthy man. He and Carl had known each other since boyhood. They had been classmates at a New England prep school, Phillips Academy, at Andover, and while they hadn't run into each other much there, they became close friends when they got to New York in the late fifties, sharing the same spaces, the same dreams, and, at different times, a love for the same woman.

Carl, however, would come to look upon Stella, who so clearly em-bodied the element of genius in creative work, as his mentor. Carl had given Stella the intriguing titles of some of his early paintings—*The Marriage of Reason and Squalor* was one—but Stella, with customary throwaway acumen, had given Carl perhaps the greatest gift of his career. In their green days, Carl made his sculpture in Stella's West Broadway studio, and one day Stella, as he often did, took a moment from his painting to see what his friend was up to. Carl, trying to emulate Brancusi, was hacking away at a six-foot length of timber standing upright, carving one of its sides. Stella stared at the carving. He was a man of daunting silences. He walked around it. He ran his hand along a smooth side that hadn't been touched at all, and finally he said, "You know, Carl, that's sculpture, too." At the time, Carl was offended, but he would learn to cherish every word. Stella's "prophetic remark" was what he would call it when materials untouched by the sculptor's hand would become the essence of his art. It was, Carl decided, the cut matter made into space—not the space cut into matter—that was his sculpture. Turning the tables on venerated tradition, Carl had in one sentence created a theory of a new, minimal art form, and though there were many who disdained Carl's work, no one, once it had been so cogently explained, could say he or she didn't understand it.

This genesis story was deeply inscribed in art annals by now, Carl never needing much coaxing to tell it. Lately he had told it to writer Calvin Tomkins, and Stella, if he had not known it earlier, had seen it incorporated in his 1984 *New Yorker* profile, written by Tomkins and called "The Space Around Real Things."

Over the years, the two artists, both upholding reputations as very private men, had drifted apart, seeing far less of each other than in the past. Now, however, it was Stella's turn to give again. After Ordover's call, Stella had spoken with his present wife, Harriet McGurk, and they had decided they wanted Carl freed without further delay. Ordover was called back and told that the entire quarter of a million in cash could be picked up at once at Stella's bank.

Ordover had been in touch with Carl's new lawyer, who had given him instructions on how to make out the check and where to bring it, but they ran into trouble when the Department of Correction's computer went down, so the check had to be brought out to Rikers and hand-delivered to the officer in charge. But no one was complaining now.

The party arrived at the Rikers bridge at about half-past six. They bused over to the other side, ending up in a dismal waiting room while Ordover tried to pull strings to get around a minor error in the way the check was written. That obstacle was hurdled when the guard who had questioned the check was overruled by his superior, but only Ordover was given a pass to go to the section of the prison where Carl was being held. Paula and Larry remained behind with a candy vending machine.

Ordover got to the next waiting room a little before seven. He was alone with four drab walls, a hard place to sit, and a single magazine he found in his briefcase. Thank God I'm not a prisoner here, he thought. Soon he wished he'd brought a book. Cops came and cops went, but no Carl. There were posters on the walls, and Ordover, who knew of well-meaning people who sent posters to brighten city hospitals and jails, was anything but cheered; they had been hung so unfeelingly that their only possible function was to gather grime.

Paula and Larry, eating candy bars for dinner, paced the floor. Larry had a long gray beard and was dressed in gray, a loose-fitting Brooks Brothers suit. It had become his signature costume almost in the way blue overalls had become Carl's. A man with a booming voice, he was quite articulate, perhaps as a result of his use of language in his art. Early flight from the South Bronx to Kerouac's San Francisco might have also helped. He was five years Carl's junior. The two men had met in the Max's sixties days, when people believed in nightly barroom argument as essential to making art. Like Paula, he regarded Carl as a gentle, charming person of great talent, reserved and sometimes "bitchy." He had also gotten to know Ana over the last few years, going drinking with her and Carl. She brought him Cuban cigars from her travels, brought his daughter coral from the Caribbean, and he, as a traveler himself, was touched that somebody remembered to throw a couple of packs of Cuban cigars in a sack for somebody else. He admired her courage, the risks she took in her work, and he thought of her as being very Latin, a fiery, feisty person with the same temperament as Ricky Ricardo in *I Love Lucy,* and, because he believed that opposites attract, Ana and Carl's being together was classic and very romantic. He'd seen her yell and swear, then suddenly realize she might be hurting someone's feelings. She'd stop and say, "Oh, I didn't mean that." She was a good-natured soul.

When two hours had passed, a guard appeared at Ordover's side to explain the delay. Some prisoners had created a disturbance, he was told, and the captain had been too busy to check Carl out. But he was coming soon, being brought out a back way. Ordover would have to take another bus and wait in the darkness outside at a door whose location he could not clearly understand.

"Isn't it possible to bring him down this way?" he pleaded, fearing he would never find Carl. "I really don't know the ropes around here, but I brought the bail out for the guy and, you know, it's late, and I'm afraid I'll lose him. I gotta get him back to the city."

Another hour and a half went by while the guard was seeing what he could do. At 10:30, Carl appeared. He looked somber, haggard, his blue clothing rumpled; he was mute at first, but he came forward bearing thanks and looking the happiest he had ever been to see Gerry Ordover.

They took the circulating bus back to the entrance building, joining Larry and Paula and driving back to the city in silence. "It was a sense of total tragedy," Larry would remember. "It was one of the saddest rides I've had in my life. That's not the kind of thing you intrude on. You ask, 'Do you know what happened?' And he says no. And then he says there is a deep sense of loss and he is totally broken up about it. And that's the end of it." Once, in San Francisco, Larry had almost been killed in a car crash and had lost chunks of three days of memory, so, he thought, what else was there to say?

They stopped first at Paula's to pick up Carl's keys, but Carl did not want to go home because, he said, there might be reporters in the lobby and the telephone in the apartment would be ringing. They searched for a hotel, finding one after another booked full with buyers in town for a dress manufacturers' convention. Ordover remembered a place on East Twenty-eighth, off Madison, the Deauville. They stopped there. The lawyer went inside to make sure it hadn't become a hooker's hotel. It was OK, and there was a room for Carl.

After he had dropped everyone off, Ordover stopped to get some milk on the way home, and he ran into a bunch of Carl's friends. They were coming out of a bar on Prince Street, an old-timers' place whose name nobody could ever remember, but it was called the Pool Room because of the pool table inside.

"Hi," he said, "I guess you'll all be pleased to know. Carl's out." He gave them a rundown of what had happened, and that, he thought, made them feel pretty good. He himself hadn't felt better in a long time. He had called Stella to let him know that the operation was a complete success, and Stella also felt good.

Paula called Stella, too, to thank him for coming to the rescue. That was a hell of a lot of money to put up, she thought. "Well," said Stella, "Harriet and I certainly didn't want him in jail." Then, wondering aloud who might be as supportive of him, he added, "Well, Carl's lucky."

—— 14 ——

If Ana's early life recalled the wonder of a fairy tale, Carl's, in the telling, had all the heft of legend. In 1984, by which time he had exquisitely honed his interview persona, an unsuspecting questioner made a reference to what other writers claimed to be the early influences in his life and Carl, cutting through, responded, saying that whatever had been written had been written "because I have told them so." He had always been the master sculptor of his distant past, arranging and sometimes rearranging the modules of his memories for the sheer beauty of it all.

His style, in a carefully measured sort of way, was almost always self-effacing. Blunting the notion that he was the Renaissance man others had called him, he told the same friendly interviewer that he had spent his adult life making sculptures and poems only. "Why this is so," he said, "could probably be explained by a minutely detailed account of the first five years of my life. Because such an account would be excruciatingly boring to everyone but my mother, I will not attempt to supply it." So we are left with the modules.

He was born near Boston Harbor, in Quincy, Massachusetts, on September 16, 1935. What a rare, marvelous year for an American male to be born. The rest of world had been brought to its knees by the Great Depression, but that year's birthdays arrived with a silver spoon from destiny: no matter what else, you could never, by the mere fact of your age, be conscripted and blown apart in any of the three big wars that lay ahead, yet you would be granted sharp memory and experience in the years of your vigor the tumultuous energy of all of them; no other year in the century could bestow quite the same privilege. As a future avant-garde artist, you would be among the first generation of Americans to have grown up in an era in which abstract art had *happened,* and your country would be at the height of its imperial triumph. If you were white, so very much the better.

Carl was the youngest of three children, the only boy. His father's family had come from Sweden, the men usually earning their way in the building or metalworking trades. His grandfather was a bricklayer and his granduncles were blacksmiths. Carl's father, George Hans, was a marine draftsman and a carpenter. He designed and built the family house, down to the hinges and latches on the cabinet doors and the flower beds in the backyard. Carl's mother's name was Margaret. She was descended from Scots. She loved literature and music and was the poet in the Andre home, writing occasional verses for her friends. Young Carl, when he wasn't digging holes in the backyard, heard poetry often, Keats while sitting on his father's knee, Poe from his uncle, who recited it on his way to work in the Bethlehem Steel shipyards, where his father worked, too.

Only through the scrim of Carlish public banter could one perceive any shadow of the familial strife he would later confide to Ana. Asked by an early interviewer how he discovered sculpture and if his family had encouraged him, he replied, "I once drew a saber-toothed tiger on the blackboard in the sixth grade; my parents thought it an aberration." Were there any others artistically inclined in the family? "My eldest sister (of two) had remarkable gifts as a draftsman, but my father insisted she become a secretary."

More often he spoke fondly of his blue-collar father reading poetry aloud at the dinner table, working with his power tools in the cellar, and taking him to the local museum. One of his earliest memories, he told catalogue biographer David Bourdon, was a nighttime image of the large granite prisms from the quarries of Quincy silhouetted against the moon.

Quincy was the historic home of the Adamses, Abigail, John, John Quincy, and their illustrious descendants Brooks and Henry. Henry, a century before Carl's arrival, was raised there, too, and thought it grim, or at least devoid of the "Boston style." He wrote: "Though Quincy was but two hours walk from Beacon Hill, it belonged to a different world." It was a forbidding place, "as everyone knows," he said, "the stoniest glacial and tidal drift known in any Puritan land."

In Carl's day, it had grown into a shipbuilding, granite-cutting, tombstone-making city of about eighty thousand but was no less a severe Puritan land, often covered with snow. "The Quincy of my boyhood," he would say, "was a city of tidal waters, creeks, bays, marshes, islands, and shipyards with their giant girders and cranes and acres of flat steel plates lying in the weather."

He loved the "salty eroticism of the sea," and he would never forget one winter memory of Quincy, of the ever-breaking waters of the bay.

Truth to tell, it was a place to get out of, the sooner the better. At the age of sixteen, the chalk-tiger maker, already writing poetry and memorizing dictionaries, found his talent richly and, as it unfolded, fatefully rewarded. He received a scholarship from the oldest and one of the finest prep schools in the country, Phillips Academy for boys, at Andover. Andover, in northeastern Massachusetts, is also the site of the Addison Gallery of American Art, where Carl, studying under avant-garde painters Maude and Patrick Morgan, could wander with his fancies amid a wide-ranging collection of paintings, ship models, and prehistoric artifacts. There was also Andover's Abbot Academy for girls, which perhaps played a part in a revealed, all-around-boy memory: "Fortunately, I was able to hide in the sumac bushes and make love to my friends."

Carl, when asked, would never fail to credit his teachers Maude and Patrick Morgan as the first of the three primary influences in his life as an artist. "The two of them just set you on fire," was one way he would put it. The other two influences were fellow students, Hollis Frampton and Frank Stella, both one year lower than he. The Morgans were anything but provincial art teachers. Patrick had studied under Hans Hofmann, the most influential godfather of the abstract expressionists, and the couple showed at Betty Parsons, an important New York gallery. Frank Stella would never forget them either. The Morgans, Carl was always quick to say, had taught him that art was for the living, created by the energy of the living, not the dead masters. The second influence, roommate Hollis, a brilliant youth exceptionally well versed in contemporary literature, awakened Carl's sense of "ego energy": not only was it the living who produced art, "it is we who produce art." And from Stella, later in New York, came the crowning idea of the need for the living "we" to affirm what art they were going to do and establish its form and standards.

Hollis Frampton, avant-garde photographer and bedside companion to the ailing and incarcerated Ezra Pound, would become Carl's first, most consulted, and most readable of his biographers, all of whom thus far have been only the flattering kind. In 1969, breezing with wit and affection through the formative years of his "Doctor Johnson," he wrote what must have been a ten- or twelve-page letter to a Dutch curator then preparing an Andre museum exhibition at The Hague. It was published rather obscurely (and sloppily) in the catalogue, but it remains one of the rare accessible independent sources of Carl's pre- and early New York years.

> The events [he began] were boring enough at the time, certainly, but may by now be of some interest to strangers. Carl Andre and I met as schoolboys. We were interested in science and in art. It was customary at that time for young men with diffuse artistic intentions to fancy themselves poets: accordingly, we both were poets. But we took studio courses and painted.

According to Carl, you couldn't pry him from the studio, where finding his "greatest pleasure" he painted, for one thing, a still life of beat-up old army boots, working it into abstract, cloudlike shapes, suppressing every color but gray. Thinking dada was "cute," his first sculpture was a plaster snake sticking out of a painting. When he wasn't molding and painting, he wrote Poe-inspired poems, publishing them in the school magazine, *The Mirror*, though he was now reading Hollis's on-campus collection of Pound.

After the diplomas were handed out, Stella, minus three front teeth from roughhousing in the dorm, went on to Princeton; Frampton went on to St. Elizabeth's Hospital in Washington to cheer up Pound; and Carl went on to trouble at Kenyon College, in Ohio. The trouble, whatever it was, occurred during his less than one semester tenure at the college, a mildly mysterious interlude that would quietly wither away from print and conversation. Frampton, stressing the positive side, told his Dutch correspondent that Carl managed to see the great earthwork Indian mounds before Carl was "asked to leave" by the college. "It would seem," he wrote, "that he lacked what we call in America, 'school spirit.' "

> At any rate [Frampton continued], he went back to his native Quincy, Massachusetts; saved a little money from a job at the Boston Gear Works; went to England for a time (visited Stonehenge and the Parliament), Paris briefly (visited the Eiffel Tower and the Louvre); returned to the States and spent two years in U.S. Army Intelligence.

That was in North Carolina, and though he had enlisted and enjoyed his work as an interrogator, or at least meeting veterans of the war in the South Pacific (who turned his ever-inquisitive eye toward Japan), he did not actually complete the two-year tour of duty. He was discharged three months early because he had been accepted to Northeastern University in Boston, a short commute from Quincy. But Carl, it turned out, was simply not the college-going kind. As soon as his first checks under the GI Bill arrived, he promptly withdrew without even being asked to leave, packed his sack, and took off forever, heading straight for the art world.

It was 1956 when Carl arrived in New York with a serviceable cushion of six hundred dollars and the address of a schoolmate from Andover to look up while searching for a place to live. The schoolmate, later often cited by Carl as another influence and, after Hollis faded away, his closest friend, was cinematographer Michael Chapman, then a struggling writer-painter living with nineteen-year-old Barbara Rose, the future Mrs. Frank Stella.

She was fresh out of Smith College, working on her master's in art history at Columbia on the Upper West Side, which was where Carl found a thirteen-dollar-a-week room at a place called the Viking Arms. Barbara, who would write the first article introducing Carl and his art, went on to become one of his most influential advocates (and the one

to dub him the last Renaissance man). She was, from the first moment,
deeply impressed with the twenty-one-year-old sculptor-poet, or so it
appears from a short memoir she composed a couple of decades later:

> Looking back to the day in 1956 when I first met Carl Andre, I
> recall a young man whose ruddy cherubic face was crowned with
> a stubby crewcut fringe—he had just been mustered out of the
> U.S. Army—a young man of uncommon wit and talent for litera-
> ture and poetry. . . . Coupled with these engaging qualities was
> a great embracing generosity, in particular toward persons of the
> opposite sex, and an ingenuous disregard for the material world,
> or what some might call "reality."

The generosity part, though embracing, may not have been entirely
ingenuous. Another ten years later, Barbara could still remember helping Carl spend his small fortune: "He said [to her and Chapman],
'Here, we all must share this, we must spend this.' We stayed out every
night until we spent it, going to movies, eating out, going to the West
End Café. Then he said, 'Okay, now that you've spent my mustering-
out pay, you must take care of me.' "

Chapman, taking care of him, was working at Columbia University
Press, which was at least a reference for a job Carl landed with the
publishing house Prentice-Hall. He worked as an editorial assistant
from nine to five, and we have it on no less an authority than Barbara
that he wore a tie. In the evenings, in his room at the Viking Arms,
he did semisurreal drawings for a series he called the "adventures of
reason and squalor," and he continued to run around with Chapman
and Rose and an assortment of untold others, upon whom, says Barbara, fortune would smile.

> Together with our little band of insurrectionary young spirits, so
> many of whom have ascended to positions of then undreamed of
> establishment success, we roved through the bars and taverns, the
> movie houses and sleazy transient hotels of the Upper West Side.
> Even in such company, Carl stood out; he was the first and
> possibly the last Renaissance Man I ever knew. He was prolific in

the extreme, producing exotic works in all media. He wrote in many genres: satirical novels, which became ever more abbreviated until they were but a paragraph in length, anticipating the contemporary attention span,[1] as well as concrete poems with words arranged in symmetrical grids, as his metal plates would later tile the ground with neat adjacent squares.

Unshackled by inhibition, Andre improvised cacophonous atonal piano music and conceived of unperformed and unperformable operas and epics. In playful moments (indeed I never knew him to have any others) he wrote lyrics to mock pop tunes with lines like "Art and Nature never goin' to rendezvous so rock with me baby and we'll rock the whole night through." And he was famous as a bearer of such epigrams as "Many are the wand bearers; few are the true bacchanals" or, as a solution to war, "Let them eat what they kill."

Three hundred and sixty-four days later, to hear Carl tell it, he applied for his vacation at Prentice-Hall, but management found him one day short of a full year's service and told him he would not be entitled until serving the whole of the next year. "I told them to screw off, and I quit," Carl would say many years later. By then the episode, known as the day Carl, tearing off his tie, "resigned from the middle class," had already entered the Carlish chronicles by virtue of another biographical letter, this one from Barbara Rose to the same insatiably curious Dutchman in The Hague.

Carl, between it all, continued to correspond with Hollis, getting the latest on the amazing Ezra Pound. At the time, early 1958, the latest was the U.S. government's declaration of the great poet's mental unfitness to stand trial for treason. Pound, more fed up with the spinelessness of his accusers than ever, went back to Italy, leaving Hollis to head for the destination of his choice. It happened to be Carl, now unemployed.

[1]One such opus has survived. "I once wrote a twenty-five-word novel," Carl told an interviewer in 1970, "and the twenty-five words went, 'Manuel corrupted money. He bought the Leaning Tower of Pisa and straightened it.'" There must have been another, slightly shorter chapter, however.

I arrived in New York, to sleep on his floor, early in the spring of 1958. I found him living in one hotel room near Columbia University, forty pounds lighter than my memory [of him], supporting himself by extracting an occasional book index (an activity he professed to enjoy)—and copiously making art. Chiefly he wrote lyric poems. . . . He made occasional drawings. Perhaps poverty first suggested that anything might be material for art. I recall a drawing of a predatory bird, made on a shirt cardboard with a ballpoint pen and A-1 Steak Sauce.

That summer, Chapman, who had already fallen out with Barbara Rose, left the whole group, drafted into the army, bequeathing Carl the few remaining months on his sublease to a cheap apartment on East Fortieth Street. Carl dismantled the walls and made a series of paintings in the latest super-flat, no-paint-above-the-canvas-plane, Tenth Street style. They were rejected by the old Tanager Gallery on East Tenth Street and became Carl's first group of lost works. Unwanted by his landlord as well, he turned now to Hollis, who was living with his friend Mark Shapiro in a tenement on Mulberry Street. Carl was unable to afford his part of the rent, a monthly $19.84, but it remained an unforgettable figure he thought of as "very Orwellian," and Hollis could hardly say no:

I had got a tiny slum apartment in "Little Italy," and the fall of that year found *him* sleeping on *my* floor. The painter Frank Stella whom we knew from school days, had come up to the city from Princeton and was doing his first loose, expressionist stripe painting in a tiny loft near [the] Manhattan Bridge. The three of us began to spend a great deal of time together.

The New York art world into which Frank Stella arrived in June 1958 still toothless, with a three-hundred-dollar graduation present from his father, Hollis and Carl's address, and a yearning to make a new art pronouncement was itself yearning for something, almost anything, new, though that was a closed topic of conversation then.

Abstract expressionism, the coalesced, postwar product of the Tenth

Street, or the New York, school, with all its creative, brainy John Wayneish giants with hard-hitting *K*'s in their names (Jackson Pollock, Kline, de Kooning, Mark Rothko, to cite a few), had established itself as the unchallenged new art, the first purely American art, and some claimed the first *pure* art of all time. The movement had wrested absolute supremacy from the Paris school, from the fauvist, cubist, surrealist moderns grown feeble in their shameless embrace with the decadent European bourgeoisie. In going underground during the worst days of native, thirties-wartime social realism, with its painted legions of muscled, working-class, flared-nostril good guys seen from a low angle, it had also rescued American art—not to speak of the First Amendment—from the tyranny of the American Stalinism. So the giants and their littler companions saw themselves.

These were the first-sung living heroes of unadulterated American art. Never mind if what they painted gave you no clue as to which side was up: they were on freedom's side. Pollock, the insider's James Dean of it all, wrapped his guts (and unsung Edith Metzger's) around a tree, but for nearly fifteen years the whole action-painting rest of them had held sway from their smoky booths in the Cedar Tavern downtown to the smoky salons of upper Fifth Avenue, a vortex into which all things civilized had been sucked.

The Cedar bar, stoa of all the glories, place of court and courtiers, was where Carl, as he would later say, was getting his education, breathing the same boozy oxygen once breathed by Pollock and still breathed by Rothko, de Kooning, and Kline, where art solons Clement Greenberg and Harold Rosenberg handed down the immutable laws of flatness, inscribing in extravagant prose meant to be eternal how utterly marvelous it was, and ladies beware. "The Cedar was so male," remembers Carolee Schneemann. "It was so sacrosanct in that way, even with the implicit kind of male violence, or male importance. Everything was charged with the dominance of the male lair—it was like going into their cave, their hangout where they were what you focused on, and if you were pretty enough and sexy enough they might bestow a little bit of their regal eye or a beer."

This celestial and crystallized state of affairs might have gone on forever, and indeed many had come to believe that abstract expressionism was art in its final form, but as in every tale of perfection worth its salt there was an unforeseen, fatal flaw. The product of the new art, for all its painterly majesty, had proved to be a most un-American commercial flop. Multipage spreads in *Life*, fledgling television coverage, traveling exhibitions, museum shows, and the U.S. government stamp of approval (no small stickum in the coldest season of the Cold War) had done little to move the studio output off the gallery-showroom walls. Famous artists, though their bohemian generation never expected anything more, were still living in cold-water flats and paying their bar tabs with famous but depreciating paintings. Their dealers, who on the other hand had expected the moon, were hard pressed to pay the rent. Museums and patriotic collectors did their duty, but other potential buyers remained unconvinced that, say, a Jack Tworkov canvas, no matter how thick with countless, fulgent diagonal brush strokes, was a better deal than an old-fashioned Ben Shahn social realist painting of Sacco and Vanzetti. People, when they picked up a painting, still wanted to be able to tell which side was up, and the truth was that the American art market was as yet too underdeveloped to sustain its victory over Europe, and Europe, still smarting from the ultimate sins of its decadent bourgeoisie, was a lot poorer. By 1958, dealers, in their heart of hearts, were eager to abandon the theory that abstract expressionism was all there was, and while paying lip service to the theory, were nevertheless shopping around for a newer, as yet unchristened, art, one they could peddle.

By that summer, the newer, unchristened art had in fact arrived, trumpeting itself on the impeccable uptown walls of Leo Castelli's gallery, some of it selling wildly, but who knew it was the new art movement at the time? A couple of young, lean, maverick painters, who were making their nut as window dressers at Tiffany and Bonwit Teller under the shared alias of Matson Jones, had had one-man shows, opening in January and April, that had shaken the foundations of ab-ex complacency.

Five years earlier, in an astounding portent of things to come, one of these Matson Joneses had talked Willem de Kooning, the most venerated of all the abstract expressionists, into permitting him, in the search for a higher abstraction, to erase one of his works of art. Erase it. When he had actually performed the deed, which had required the whole range of rubber and gum and state-of-the-art eraser technology, he framed it as his own work, which it most assuredly was, calling it *Erased de Kooning Drawing.* That was Robert Rauschenberg, and though now both Matson Joneses had become overnight successes, it was the other one who had acquired an instant international reputation and, most auspiciously, a market to go with it. That was Jasper Johns.

The new art, pop art, would not be baptized until a couple of years later, when it had been multiplied and fattened by the Roy Lichtensteins, the Claes Oldenburgs, and the one and only Andy Warhol. Neither would it quite *erase* de Kooning and company, though it would certainly eclipse them (along with the Cedar Tavern), teach them a lesson, and drive one or two of them mad. What it would do was sell and resell, turning over at a healthy, later vertiginous, clip from the very first painting—probably because, beginning with Johns's now priceless canvas American flag, *Flag,* you knew once again which side was up. Unprecedented sales and their giddying accompaniments would in turn outmode and shuck the slow-moving, patched-elbow ways of the old art world, and the reconstruction would offer the usual array of tantalizing possibilities that return with every new shuffle of the deck.

All this was at the moment invisible, of course, and Carl, Hollis, and Frank would never be nor wish to be associated with pop art. But even now—Carl huddled over Hollis's stove burning into little blocks of wood, Hollis tinkering with a still camera, and Frank painting one painting literally on top of another—there was a sturdy connection. Frank had seen the Jasper Johns show, and it had made such a powerful impression on him that he immediately stopped painting in the established abstract style. Along with *Flag,* Johns had shown paintings of numerals and targets. These were not abstractions, but, it had struck young Stella, neither were they pictures of what they were—pictures being the anathematic illusions abstract expressionism had repudiated as a false god. What was wholly new to Stella about Johns was that he had not painted—and one could not paint—a *picture* of the number seven; one could only paint, as Johns had, the number seven. It was what it was, illusion-proof. Johns had achieved a purer form of pure art.

This was what had led to Stella's stripe paintings, which would lead to his black paintings, which, paring everything unnecessary, would lead to his sawed-off, shaped canvases, and one thing leading to another would lead to the next, post–pop art, new art movement, purer than anything before it. It would be inscribed forever in the art-world book of lists as minimalism.

Carl later spoke of the moment before his own enlightenment. Stella and he had begun to develop their boyhood acquaintance at Hollis's. After one long walk over the Manhattan Bridge and back, Stella invited him to see his work:

[H]e took me over to his loft, which was tiny—a walk-up place, a narrow place. It had been a tiny jewelry factory and it had a gigantic safe halfway down the room. Frank showed me the colored stripe paintings, the stripe paintings before the black ones, very beautiful paintings. I looked at them and thought that Frank was a lunatic. I thought he had probably gone off the deep end, because my idea of art was still related to some kind of abstraction from something outside of art—it had to be derived from paintings and have that interior logic, but to me they just looked blank.

The black paintings—black stripes made from dollar-a-gallon hardware-store housepaint—came immediately afterward, that winter, so Carl's conversion to the Stellean vision was equally as fast, though it would take much longer for him to see where he himself fit in. Stella at twenty-three believed that in his black paintings he had achieved what he had been striving for since seeing Jasper Johns's show: Stella's paintings were free not only of illusion, but, unlike Johns's, they were free, too, of symbol and sentiment. Stella's were impersonal images bearing no relation to anything but themselves. They went, he would say, "direct—right to your eye," like the paint in the can when you opened the lid. "What you see is what you see," was the way he would put it in a famous formulation.

Carl, experiencing a "tremendous impression," was a changed man. By that time, Stella had moved to the larger space on West Broadway and had offered Carl a place to do his own work, encouraging him to drop painting and concentrate on sculpture. That same winter, when

Stella made the "prophetic remark" about uncut matter ("Carl, that's sculpture, too"), he began to follow the prophet's way.

For Carl it was a long and painful journey. Stella's success was immediate. His black paintings, still wet, convinced Leo Castelli to give him a comfortable three-hundred-dollar monthly advance against future sales. While the sales were sluggish at first, his allowance liberated him from his bread-and-butter work as a housepainter and catapulted him into the Castelli circle, then (as ever afterward) a kind of seventh heaven for a young artist. He began at once to draw his own circle of museum-class admirers. Carl, trying the same route, wrote to Castelli submitting a detailed, illustrated proposal for a show. He received nothing in return. The young sculptor had neither the space nor the funds to execute his proposals, shortfalls that reinforced the cycle of turndown following turndown.

Unsponsored, broke, and by his own admission constantly overcoming surges of envy of the successes of other artists, he nevertheless found the wherewithal to be as Renaissance a man as Barbara Rose saw him, sculpting, drawing, writing, composing, expanding the studio of his mind.

Carl in that eventful winter of 1959 wrote a short comic novel. With a trace of boyish immodesty, he described it as "Tom Swift written by Dean Swift." Sophomoric at times, it was nevertheless both imitative of Swift's satire and in the vanguard of its day—say, early Lenny Bruce—in humor, portions of it remaining hilarious. It was titled *Billy Builder, or The Painfull Machine,* and affords a rare, indeed the only, glimpse of the range of young Carl's lighter side.

The good Billy Builder is a young, errant scientist who in the company of Miss Mundane Carpenter or Carmen Panacea ("a slip of a girl") cannot keep his Periodic Table in its hiding place (his trousers). He is the inventor of the inexplicably misspelled but mysteriously powerful instrument of the title. The action takes place in the near future. The nation's capital has been transferred to New York (renamed Washington), and the White House (renamed the Presidential Palace), occupied by a "wellmeaning" and "happygolucky" black president named Lafcadio Barker, is now situated on Lenox Avenue. Representing the white military-middle-class complex and introduced to Billy by a burly old abstract expressionist are General Godsend and Admiral Canoe ("Call me Tippy"). Mistrustful of the president, the racist Godsend and Canoe are eager to take possession of Billy's machine— though they have no notion of what it is, other than a black tube carried in a holster—before it falls into the hands of foreign powers. Billy arrives at the Presidential Palace, "a dream of pink neon," in the Borzoi Bus driven by the versatile Malibu Feldspar. He is welcomed by the chief executive and the first lady, Sweetpea Barker, given a sample of the president's pomade, and introduced to the cabinet: Banjo Franchise on bass, Fingers Washington at the ivories, and so on. After a jam session, with Sweetpea coming in on the vocals and President Barker himself playing the "licorish" stick, a crisis breaks out. Billy, drawing the black tube from its holster, is forced to use it on everyone in the room including the president, saving the situation and revealing the nature of the weapon. The Painfull Machine, everyone realizes, is love.

All of the above, even as President Barker removes his "Negroid disguise," is revealed as a vaguely annoying literary deception played on the reader and a rusty device to kick the story up a notch above mere sentiment. But the entire concoction is rich with throwaway esoteric references displaying the uncommon sophistication of its twenty-three-year-old author. Sent off to Grove Press, probably the only publisher that would have taken it then, the fifty-two-page manuscript was rejected as "too long," and Carl stuck it in his beer box full of unpublished writings and unappreciated little sculptures.

Living up to Barbara Rose's image of him as never being less than playful, Carl brought his own Painfull Machine around. The two of them would often meet for lunch in the cafeteria of the Central Park Zoo; one day in the fall of 1959, he showed up with a dark, fuzzy-haired Sicilian, Frank Stella. Barbara, after seeing the black paintings, thought him the most important artist of her generation, and she fell in love. Frank fell in love, too, but his heart was stolen by Barbara's roommate. She was a young poet named Terry Brook, who had already fallen in love with Carl, or at least he with her. Although that was apparently over, Stella, like Carl, didn't get very far with Brook. Everyone went his or her own way until a year or so later, when Stella decided he really loved Barbara and told her she was everything in a woman he had ever wanted: "a blond Smith girl in a camel's hair coat."

Carl, in the second mildly mysterious interlude in his adult life, got married. Like the Kenyon College episode, this one was also leached from memory, and the first Mrs. Andre vanished without even leaving her name. Hollis, barely mentioning it, sounds almost reticent: "In the Fall, he returned to New York [from a summer in Quincy in 1959] and got married. A brief period of quiet followed. He lived in cramped quarters." One of Carl's future lovers would remember seeing a photograph of the bride: "a very attractive light black woman." She wasn't an artist, "an academic or something."

The cramped quarters were in a noisy cold-water flat on the Lower East Side, with broken windows and a constantly flushing broken toilet chiming in. Hollis had gotten a larger place, and Carl worked there, still without luck. After years in New York, his two bodies of work, Hollis tells us, had been "dismissed as pointless." Mrs. Andre was no better off than her husband financially, and marriage, imposing its post-honeymoon responsibilities, drove Carl onto the streets looking for a steady job.

On Saint Patrick's Day, 1960, he was taken on as a freight brakeman by the Pennsylvania Railroad, the blue collar rendering his resignation from the middle class inviolate. For the next four years to the day, Carl would haul himself over the Hudson River to the marshy freight yards between Jersey City and Newark and shunt boxcars and make up trains. He loved it. The long experience of moving, switching, arranging identical freight cars on evenly spaced rails and crossties along endless tracks hugging the ground would become one of the determining influences on his most mature sculpture and the centerpiece of almost every interview. Working on the railroad was also therapeutic; "it was with great relief," he said later, "that I could deal with things I could trust and manipulate. Things that are unthreatening." The railroad knew a good man when it saw one, promoting him to freight conductor, and the whole yard might have been his oyster if it hadn't been for the mistake, a near-multitrain collision that got him fired and sent him home to the unfriendlier art world.

By then, 1964, Carl had all but dropped out of the downtown scene. He had been living in near-seclusion in a one-room brownstone apartment in Brooklyn, and the first Mrs. Andre had done her disappearing act, replaced by the second, Rosemarie Castoro. Yet he had never stopped sculpting and writing his poetry. Since 1960 he had sworn off cutting into his materials, but in 1961, junk sculpture, assembling debris found on the street, caught on, and Carl dabbled in that. He created such unappetizing pieces as "pizza pies" made from patties of Portland cement heaped with broken crockery and bottle shards and scrap wood "polymorphous perverse carpentry." Even Hollis thought them "ranging from prodigiously ugly through downright hideous." His poems, however, which formed the greater part of his creative work at this time, began to reflect the fundamental change that was taking place in his aesthetic outlook. They took on the gridlike forms of the railroad.

With Hollis, he wrote a book, published twenty years later under the title *12 Dialogues*. The dialogues were clattering exercises in which each of them, sitting in the tiny room in Brooklyn, would take turns at a typewriter, pecking a reply to the last thing written. From these short trips to the keyboard, we are left with such early Carl one-liners as: "I have won my women in the face of bad breath" and "Find me a woman indifferent to the shine on her nose," but he would grow out of those old clothes.

Above all, it seems, he read, reading a mountain beyond what he would have been required to read in college, reading himself into a lifelong habit or addiction in which he could barely move from one spot to another without a bagful of things to read. Hollis had steered him to Pound, and Pound, man of every season, had dragged him all over the place, most notably, as only a Pound could, to an unlikely connection between Constantin Brancusi and Confucius. Confucius introduced him to his blessed rebuker (for pride and ambition) Lao-tzu; Lao-tzu and his teachings of the equivalence of somethingness and nothingness took Carl back to Stella's "prophetic remark," which had started with Brancusi.

The whole serendipitous excursion went something like this. Brancusi, carving wood in Paris, had sculpted his first *Endless Column* in

1918, repeating the same symmetrical form one on top of the other. Carl, his interest in Brancusi stimulated, had been carving his own version of endlessness when Stella, observing the untouched part, had said, "Carl, this is sculpture, too." Getting over his resentment and understanding the remark's true meaning took about two years, Stella's impact on his own work being, Carl said later, "slow and inexorable and powerful as a glacier." In the meantime, his gestating perception of matter cutting space was nourished by reading the 2,500-year-old *Tao Te Ching.*

Giving examples of the Taoist virtue of Nothing, Lao-tzu had instructed, "Knead clay in order to make a vessel. Adapt the nothing therein to the purpose in hand, and you have the use of the vessel." Thus, it was written by Master Lao, "what we gain is Something, yet it is by virtue of Nothing that this can be put to use." Giving the whole epistemology, the *wu* and the *yu,* the Not Being and the Being, a twentieth-century bite, Carl, arranging only seven different one-syllable words, would bring it all down to this fun-house mirror phrase: "A thing is a hole in a thing it is not."

He was ready.

—— 15 ——

As an adult, Raquel had become the wilder but frailer of the two sisters. In the seventies, when Ana had already become solidly committed to making art, Raquel was somewhere on a mountain near a Nevada border living in a derelict schoolbus heated by the sun. She was raising two children in a community of quarrelsome hippies, and she was carrying a third child by a new husband she'd met in a Cedar Rapids bar who would bike out of her life before the baby was born, saying, "I want to see the USA on a BSA." Ana thought she was nuts. It wasn't until Raquel met Tom, got her master's degree, and settled into a consummately spiritual family life that she took charge of herself. Since that midnight phone call from Detective Finelli, she of all the Harringtons and Mendietas had seized the reins of a runaway sorrow and was bringing quiet order in its place.

She would always bear a melancholy memory about not having gone with Tom to see Ana's body, but he had insisted, and they both believed it best for their unborn baby, who they feared might enter the world with a grief too harsh and too soon. It was Raquel, however, who was superintending her younger sister's remaining earthly concerns. The job, to be sure, was arduous, leaving only the nights for mourning. She was in her seventh month, still regularly employed as a counselor at a Westchester County prison, though now she had asked for leave. There were, as in any sudden death in a family, unpostponable duties to perform, countless and replete with unforeseen sadness. Ana's affairs were particularly complicated. The police called constantly, as did Ana's many friends—strangers to Raquel. Ana's art, a large but dispersed body of work, was an estate of aesthetic and financial significance that had to be gathered and protected. Uppermost in Raquel's mind, however, was redeeming her sister from the morgue and laying her to rest.

September 11–14, 1985

Raquel knew that Ana, like she, wanted to be cremated. They had spoken of it, making sport of it all, joking about where they would want their ashes strewn. Once, when they were in Cedar Rapids visiting with their mother—Mami, they called her in Spanish—Raquel pointed to Mami's favorite pot as the place where, if it fell to Ana, her ashes should be kept. Mami, a devout Catholic, didn't think it as funny as her giggling daughters, though she had learned in America to tolerate girls being girls. Sometime later, though, when Raquel was at her mother's house again, she found the pot had "mysteriously" disappeared. Instead, the duty had fallen to Raquel and now she searched the New York City yellow pages, looking for nothing less than the "best." That turned out to be a place in Staten Island. For a flat fee of $580, the firm promised to collect the body, cremate it, and ship the residue by air to an undertaker in Cedar Rapids, where the family had decided Ana would be buried.

A complication arose when Raquel received a call from Chief of Detectives Ayers. He had been told, he said, that Carl had asked to view the deceased. How did Raquel feel about it? She had no objections, but when Tom came home and heard the news, he called the Sixth Precinct and spoke with Finelli.

Since their Monday visit to the police, both Tom and Raquel had become particularly sensitive to anything that might help the investigation. In the eyes of the family, the single most outrageous offense that Carl had committed since Ana's death was his failure to call them and give an account of himself. Whatever grounds there were for understanding, and there still were some, were eroding swiftly with the passage of time. To them, the silence of Ana's husband was incomprehensible, an affront to their dignity. It was becoming the dividing line of battle. Tom, having already seen the sorry condition of his sister-in-law's remains, thought this might be an opportunity to get a long-awaited reaction from Carl.

"Is there any way," Tom asked Finelli, "of showing him the whole body? Maybe that will shock him into saying something about what he did."

"No, you can't do that," said Finelli. "They'll only show the same thing you saw, just the face. But maybe that'll be enough."

The family's approval of the request was passed along through circuitous channels. The news of Carl's late-night release from Rikers had not only gone unreported in the press, no one at the Sixth Precinct was aware of it either.

Later that day, Raquel was back on the telephone with Finelli. She had received a condolence phone call from a woman she didn't know, but she had gleaned something from the conversation she thought Finelli ought to pursue right away.

The caller introduced herself as May Stevens, a friend of Ana and Carl's, though she had known him many years more than her. She and her husband, Rudolf Baranik, had had dinner with them on Friday night. The evening had gone through a bad moment. Ana and Carl got into an argument in the restaurant about AIDS. A friend of Ana's had recently died of the disease, and when she'd gotten back to New York, she learned that another friend had been stricken; to make matters worse, Carl could sometimes make thoughtless "quips" about homosexuals. They had gotten loud, Stevens said, and the tension had ruined dinner, but by the time the bill came they had made up. Stevens, also an artist, though rather older than Ana, admitted to Raquel that she had never been able to relate very well to Ana. But that last night, she said, she felt very close to her, almost like mother and daughter, and her feelings seemed to have been reciprocated. When they left the restaurant, the women were arm in arm. She wanted Raquel to know about this final moment of tenderness, she said. It was a measure of her loss and a way of expressing her sorrow.

Raquel thanked her and continued the conversation, but from the instant Stevens had said she'd been with them Friday night, a thought began swimming in her head. After overcoming her hesitation about how the caller might react, she asked, "Did you notice any scratches on Carl's face?"

There was a moment of silence at the other end, and then Stevens replied, "No. He didn't have any scratches on his face."

"He didn't have any scratches on his nose?"

"No, he didn't have any scratches on his nose."

"Well, you know, that's very important that you know that. That's a very important piece of information you have. Would you be willing to say that to the police?"

There was another pause. "Well, I don't know."

"It's the truth, isn't it?"

"Yes, it's the truth, but I couldn't testify against Carl."

"But I'm not asking you to testify against Carl. I mean, you would just be saying the truth of what you saw."

Once again, Stevens reflected for a while. "I guess so," she said at last. "I guess I might be willing to. I wouldn't be doing anything wrong if I'm telling the truth as I know it."

Immediately after they hung up, Raquel called Finelli.

"I think you should get over there right away or call her," Raquel said after relating the substance of the conversation.

Finelli agreed. Then Raquel called Martha Bashford to be doubly sure.

THE FIRST WORDS Carl uttered when he met his new lawyer that Wednesday afternoon were, "I'm innocent."

The encounter took place on Mercer Street, in apartment 34E. Carl's opening assertion, as well as his soft handshake, would make a lasting impression on the man who would defend him now, though his first remark was the sort of beginning the lawyer had heard many times before.

His name was Jack Hoffinger. He was in his sixtieth year, impeccably tailored, slim, gray-haired, much taller than Carl but slightly stooped, with two-thirds of his stomach lost to wounds he believed he incurred on the battlefields of his profession. A keen, surveying light shone from his eyes. A graduate of Yale Law School and a veteran of a five-year stint as an assistant D.A. in the same office where Martha Bashford now worked, Hoffinger had been practicing criminal law continuously since before she was born. He had never heard of Carl Andre and knew little of art—his wife did the reading in his house—but he had infinitely more courtroom experience than Gerry Rosen, and one of his current positions was vice president of the New York Criminal Bar Association. He was on the crest of his profession, a popular lecturer at Columbia

Law School and a recognized master at cross-examination. To represent Carl and place at his disposal the full services of his large Park Avenue firm, Hoffinger Friedland Dobrish Bernfeld and Hasen, he had been guaranteed a retainer of $50,000, payable in advance, and another $50,000 every six months.

Hoffinger had come downtown with a member of his staff, wanting to meet with Carl at his place to get the same feel as the police had, hoping, too, to duplicate the Crime Scene Unit's investigation. But this proved to be only partially possible, since it was clear that the photography and the search—and a thunderstorm that had rained in through the open windows—had altered the tableau. Nevertheless, Hoffinger needed little convincing that this was a piece-of-shit case, and a piece of cake winning it was what it would be, he assured his new client.

In word as in deed, he was a man driven full throttle by the engine of passion. The great-grandson of a Warsaw rabbi, he came out of the East Bronx and Coney Island, playing basketball at CCNY when there was no such thing as jump shots. No other ambition had ever crossed his mind except to become a trial lawyer, learning to talk on his feet, stalking ideas, winding in and out of the loose ends of his discourse before finally tying them all into one. He had no ongoing clientele, purposely rejecting corporate work to maintain his independence. When they pay your rent, they own you. His clients were mostly people in trouble with the law for the first and last time. Some were innocent, some were guilty. He was not a judge. Defending the Constitution of the United States was his job, particularly the Fourth, Fifth, and Sixth amendments—the rights against improper search and seizure, the right against self-incrimination, and the right to counsel. Right or wrong, he believed in this, and he loved to try it all out in a courtroom. It was the whole gestalt, unhinging tough guys, for one thing, the chess game for another, the thrust and the parry—the sex, he called it.

Hoffinger would have his first court appearance in the case on Friday, September 13, the preparatory date set by Judge Sayah for the grand jury action. An initial strategy was worked out now. Carl, Hoffinger believed, had committed the first cardinal error in any defense against the pretensions of the state: he had spoken to the police. A great litigator had once told the young Hoffinger embarking on his career,

September 11–14, 1985

"Be a human being, be a lawyer, be a prosecutor, don't trust the police." One never knew what game they were playing. Carl's statements last Sunday were at the root of his troubles, but they were a long way from fatal. Hoffinger was a great assuager. Is it over just because the cops decide that somebody should be prosecuted? God help us!

The second sin, though he wasn't mentioning names, had been committed when someone talked to the press. Fresh in Hoffinger's mind was a sensational case now in the courts and the media. Nine months earlier, a man named Bernhard Goetz, riding on a New York subway, had shot four young hoodlums who were hounding him for money. Many New Yorkers, including the mayor, applauded his act, and a grand jury refused to indict him for anything more than a weapons violation. He became a media hero as a man who "finally decided to fight back." Three months later, however, when his celebrity as a vigilante had begun to create community backlash, he was indicted by a second grand jury for attempted murder.

The way Hoffinger saw it, you never know whether he got reindicted because he got all that publicity. Who knows? All you know is that he got a lot of publicity, which generated a lot of heat, and afterward he got reindicted. And then there's a lot of pressure on the judge, isn't there? So now you're hoping that everybody operates free of pressure, but who knows? Wouldn't you feel more comfortable if there was no pressure? If you didn't have to worry about whether the pressure unconsciously hurts? Just avoid publicity, that's all. It takes four to tango, right? If the press doesn't come after you and the lawyers don't talk and if the client doesn't talk, you don't get into Bernie Goetz, do you? The press only hurts your case. Press is only good for the lawyer.

"You call the shots," Carl would tell him one day soon enough.

SOMEBODY IN THE family had to speak to Carl. Raquel's mother had remembered that Ana had telephoned her from Rome shortly before her marriage, saying, "I'm making out a will and you're the beneficiary." Carl was writing a will, too, Ana's mother recalled her saying. He was leaving everything to his parents and his two sisters. The way she had understood it, Ana and Carl had agreed they would not inherit anything from each other. She had called some of Ana's Spanish-speaking friends asking if they knew anything about it, but no one did, and when one of them, Liliana Porter, suggested she ask Carl, Ana's mother replied indignantly, "Carl? He killed her."

Like her mother, Raquel wouldn't, couldn't bring herself to speak to Carl, so Tom volunteered. Before mentioning anything about a will, they decided to test his reaction to the subject of Ana's estate. Tom, since he was doing the phoning, had another topic in mind. "I'm going to call him," he said, "and see if he says anything to me about what happened."

Tom dialed Carl's number, Raquel at his side. He had never met his brother-in-law, knowing him only through what he had heard of his courtship of Ana. Until the failure of the marriage, he'd never heard a bad word spoken of Carl. He had even been scolded by Raquel when she had brought home Carl's autographed catalogue and he had scoffed at what passed for art these days. The catalogue had been Carl's gift to Raquel when she had visited them in the Mercer Street apartment last January, just after the wedding in Rome.

Carl picked up the phone.

"Hello, Carl, this is Ana's brother-in-law, Tom Harrington."

There was a pause. When Carl spoke, he gave the first of two back-to-back responses that would curdle whatever compassion the family might have had toward him. He replied, "I didn't do it!"

"Why on earth didn't you call us?" Tom asked, feeling the grip of the family's wrath. "Why did the police have to call us in the middle of the night?"

"I didn't have your phone number." That was the second chilling response.

Tom rolled his eyes incredulously. "Well, what happened?"

"I can't tell you anything. My lawyer says I can't talk about it."

Carl's voice seemed to ring with heartache and distress, but Tom had lost faith in his sincerity. He became cunning now, hoping to trip Carl into saying something, revealing even a small detail that might somehow be used against him.

"You can tell me," he said, reaching for the sound of sympathy. "We're her family. Just tell us what happened."

"I can't tell you. I can't tell you anything."

September 11–14, 1985

"Well," Tom said, unable to get anywhere, "I'm calling you about Ana's personal belongings in the apartment. We were wondering—we would like to have them back."

"Of course. I don't want anything."

"Well, we are going to have to document that legally. If I prepare the papers, will you sign over any rights you have to her belongings?"

"Yes, everything. Get your lawyer to draw up the papers and then meet me in my lawyer's office. I have to meet with you anyway because I have something of Ana's to give you."

Carl didn't volunteer what that something was, and Tom didn't inquire. They made an appointment to meet at Jack Hoffinger's office the following day.

The more Martha Bashford listened to the tape made of Carl's call to 911, the more she wanted to throttle the police operator with whom the dialogue had unfolded. Beyond the drama of it all, there were some curious and tantalizing moments in the two-minute exchange. One was the striking difference in Carl's demeanor between the first and second halves of the call. The unnaturally high pitch of his voice, which caused the operator's early confusion about his gender, did not break up into heartrending distress until a very specific event in the conversation. For about the first sixty seconds, the caller, given the circumstances, was oddly composed, beginning with his very first word—"yes"—which was somewhat jarring in itself.

> Operator: Police. Where's the emergency?
> Caller: Yes. My wife has committed suicide.

Asked to repeat what he had just said, the caller dropped the "yes" and did so word for word ("My wife has committed suicide"), proceeding in a businesslike manner to answer the operator's questions.

> Operator: Where are you calling me from, ma'am?
> Caller: I'm calling from 300 Mercer Street, apartment 34E.

Operator: 34E?
Caller: Yes.
Operator: What floor are you on?
Caller: Thirty-four.
Operator: On the thirty-fourth floor?
Caller: Yes.
Operator: OK, and what's the telephone number you're calling
from?
Caller: 533-2609.

Now, still in this straightforward vein, he gave his account of the
incident, only minutes after its occurrence, in very exacting, terse, and
vivid language.

Operator: OK. Uh, what happened exactly?
Caller: What happened was we had— My wife is an artist and
I'm an artist, and we had a quarrel about the fact that I was more,
uh, exposed to the public than she was and she went to the
bedroom and I went after her and she went out of the window.

After the word "window," there was, it seemed to Bashford, a significant hesitation, as if Carl were about to add something. But the
ineffable breach was quickly plugged—perhaps forever—by the operator, who leapt over the long array of possibilities and volunteered her
own interpretation of what might have happened while Carl was going
"after her" and Ana was going "out of the window."

Operator: She jumped out of the window. How long ago did
this happen?

That was all of it. For the operator, the sorry tale had been told to
the end, and she sailed into the next piece of business. It was at this
point that the caller appeared to be deflected from his hold on the
surfacing thought. In any case, he lost his purchase on reality, growing
more and more disoriented question by question.
The young prosecutor had begun to put together her case for presen-

September 11–14, 1985

tation to the grand jury, and while the 911 tape was still a powerful document, the 911 operator's blunder was not the only gripe she had with the police. The two sets of photographs taken by the Crime Scene Unit, one on Sunday morning and the other on Monday night, did not match. The most elementary rule of the game—don't touch—had been disregarded. Comparing the day shots of the bedroom with those made at night, Bashford detected at least two differences. Some of the scattered clothing had been moved, as well as a lamp on a bedside table—"to get more light," she was told when she complained. This lapse did nothing to undermine the first set, but if the case were to come to trial, any defense attorney, not to speak of a Jack Hoffinger, could run rings around it with a jury, slapping the label of possible contamination on whatever evidence the cops brought in.

Not even Hoffinger, however, could rack up much mileage from the failure to have photographed the body on the Delion rooftop, but this, too, was bothersome to Bashford. The excuse she was given for this one was that the police were eager to remove the naked dead woman from the view of hundreds of apartment windows, but such photographs were known to have sometimes proved useful in determining cause of death.

In the end, she could do little more than shrug. She was accustomed to less than FBI-quality police work, and it was easy to empathize with the local cops, who were understaffed, poorly equipped, and consistently worked to the bone. With twenty indictments and twenty as-yet unindicted cases in her current workload and only one paralegal to assist her, she knew how doors were inevitably left open and how error was always at the threshold waiting to rush in.

Neither did the bad news stop there. Ana was drunk at the time of death. Her brain tissue showed an alcohol content of 0.18 percent. In New York State, the legal definition of intoxication while driving a car was 0.10 percent, and while Bashford thought Ana's reading not that high, particularly for an experienced drinker, she knew it would be harped on to the victim's disfavor.

She had expected worse. Groundless rumors she had heard about Ana included her being "stoned on pills," but tests for cocaine, opiates, and other drugs had all been negative. The laboratory work had also dispelled street gossip that Ana was pregnant. It proved impossible, however, to identify the origin of blood recovered from under her fingernails because it was mixed with roof tar. Nor had the medical examiners been as kind to her as in a recent murder trial, where she had been able to prove conclusively that wrist wounds had been caused by a rope applied to the victim while still alive and not, as the defense contended, during the transport of the body. In Ana's case, among all her massive injuries, the poignant bruise on her eyelid and the cut on a middle finger had been suggestive, but if she had been physically harmed in any way prior to death, the forensic evidence had vanished at the moment of impact.

Nothing in this aggregate of negatives, however, shook Bashford's earlier confidence in getting an indictment. Problems might arise later at a trial, but unless Carl decided to testify, the defense had no seat at the grand jury proceedings.

There was new evidence, too. Bashford had found strong witnesses who would testify about Ana's fear of heights and about her upbeat plans for the future. Dismantling the notion of the victim having jumped seemed uncomplicated. The assistant D.A. had been on the phone with dozens of Ana's friends and acquaintances from Rome to Los Angeles, many of whom had no connection with one another. They agreed without exception that suicide was simply incompatible with her striving and coherent personality, drunk or sober. Bashford's fear-of-heights witness would testify that Ana kept a healthy distance from windows of any altitude, and now that she had the Crime Scene measurements in hand and had herself acted out the whole gamut of accident scenarios, she was certain she would convince the grand jury that the possibility of an unassisted fall was untenable.

The argument for homicide had put on its own weight. In a circumstantial case, where guilt can only be established by consigning any other explanation to the narrow corridor beyond a reasonable doubt, even the smallest circumstance may be as pivotal as the largest. At first, Bashford had not felt completely comfortable with the so-called struggle-scene photographs of the bedroom. She had wished for a lot more struggle from a scrapper like Ana. But in the meantime, she had learned that Carl was known to be fussy about such things as tidiness and cleanliness; a smudge on a wall in a hotel room would drive him crazy, she'd been told, so the photograph of the "attic room"—a pigsty was what she called it—was another welcome addition.

As for the motive, a police search of the Sixth Avenue apartment failed, as it had in 34E, to turn up the photocopies Ana had been compiling, but Bashford was satisfied that the infidelity records seized at Carl's place were sufficient. The missing photocopy file was all but forgotten now. If Natalia's suspicion that Gerry Rosen might have gone off with it was in fact true, Bashford reasoned, he was, after all, Carl's lawyer at the time, and the laws protecting the secrecy of client-attorney relationships would make it nearly impossible to learn anything further. The thought that it might have been removed by someone else did not cross her mind. Besides, Interpol was working on sealing the Rome apartment, so that set of photocopies might yet be recovered there.

She was less encouraged about pinning down either of the Baraniks, Rudolf or his wife May Stevens. Carl maintaining he had been scratched bumping into a door on his terrace was bizarre, to say the least, if only for the conflict with his passport, which showed him out of the country at the time the classic rendezvous with a door was supposed to have happened, but that was a story easily retold, with a memory somehow refreshed and newly tailored chronology to go with it. The Baraniks alone seemed to hold the trump card here. Following Raquel's tip, Finelli had spoken separately to Rudolf and May. Both revealed that they did not see scratches on Carl's face, Rudolf saying that he "didn't notice" any and May expressing even greater certainty that there were none. But that was yesterday, and now both Baraniks were backtracking.

Raquel, Bashford knew, had received a new call this morning from May Stevens. When Rudolf had gotten home last night, May had related, she told him about their conversation, and her husband had said, "How could you have said that? How could you know? Carl has a beard and he has a ruddy complexion and his face was blotchy. How could you notice any scratches?"

"The scratches were on his nose," Raquel had replied, "so I don't see what that has to do with it."

But Rudolf couldn't remember, and she herself no longer knew what she had seen or not seen, so how could she say something she wasn't sure about?

Bashford got them both on the phone. The restaurant had been dimly lit, they told her. They could not be certain of what they saw. In a matter of such enormous import, their consciences would not allow them to ignore their doubts. Bashford, leaving them to their consciences, didn't press them further. Not yet.

RAQUEL AND TOM drove into the city that Thursday afternoon. Once in Manhattan, they separated for a few hours, Raquel to sort through Ana's Sixth Avenue possessions and Tom to keep his appointment with Carl.

Heading for Hoffinger's office on Fifty-ninth Street and Park Avenue, Tom was carrying papers drawn up by his friend Bernie Klein. Klein was a lawyer, though estate law was not his field, and he felt insecure about the document he had drafted. But at least it was something, thought Tom, who saw his job as going in there today, getting Carl to sign, and taking possession of Ana's art for the family. Raquel had a degree in fine arts, and their dream was to do whatever they could to bring greater recognition to Ana's work, though they knew they would need time and a higher expertise than Raquel's. The interim objective was to prevent Carl from having any say in the matter. In their grief, they could not imagine him doing anything but harm to the only thing they had of Ana that was still alive.

Tom felt that Ana's family would have had compassion for Carl if he had come forward with a believable account of what had happened that night—even one in which Ana, who could be so gritty, somehow shared in the blame. But Tom could never believe that she killed herself. About ten years ago, his only sister, then a woman of thirty, had committed suicide. She jumped from a window on Manhattan's Upper East Side. She had been under psychiatric care for years, almost always on drugs, nonfunctional and growing worse and worse. Nothing of this incubus could be further from his firebrand sister-in-law, who had so impressed him from the first moment he met her, when she had bused out to Kennedy to see her sister and her three nieces and him, too, all five of them off to India so Tom and Raquel could get married there. Tom had been taken by Ana's vivacity and her mighty will. He didn't agree with everything she said; more often he strongly disagreed, fighting back, gaining no ground, until Raquel would intervene and say, "Let her think the way she wants." But the way Ani spoke, you were bound to be either with her or against her all the way. Who would not be impressed with that kind of woman, sitting on the edge of her chair with enthusiasm no matter what she was doing?

He had come from a culture far different from the Mendietas'. He was born in Manhattan in 1950, growing up in and out of his alcoholic father's hamburger joint on upper Broadway. When he was eleven years old, his father died; at thirteen his stepfather died, too, and a few years later he was hitting the road on his own. He found his way into carpentry, sawing in the east and in the west for a while, giving his time and craft to ecology groups and a Siddha yoga meditation center in San Francisco. That was where, in 1976, he ran into Raquel and her three little fatherless girls, who he would one day legally adopt as his own. Raquel was completing her master's, doing work-study in a halfway house for people a lot worse off than she. After India, and eight months on an ashram with the girls, they came back and married again when they found out a Siddha yoga ceremony didn't quite count, and traveled for three more years with their meditation teacher and his disciples, running into Ani, who still thought they were nuts. They had a boy, Neelakantha, and there was a child on the way, who would never know his aunt.

Tom knew what Carl looked like, and when he walked up to the glass doors that opened on the offices of Hoffinger Friedland Dobrish Bernfeld and Hasen, he saw him inside. He was dressed in his workingman's blues, a canvas shoulder bag of reading matter at his side, sitting on a sofa in the waiting room. He rose to shake Tom's hand. Unlike Hoffinger, Tom found Carl's handshake strong, feeling it as an extension of the brawny column of his body, and, he thought, Ani was so small. Tom had talked to the police about going to this meeting. "If he says anything, let us know," Finelli had said, but that was all.

They sat, Carl casting his eyes at the floor, shoulders slumped, his head bent over, looking up at Tom only when he spoke, like a timid little boy.

Ana's death was a great tragedy for him, Carl said, the biggest loss of his life.

"I realize this must be a shock to you, Carl," Tom said. "You must be really in distress."

"I can't bring myself to go and look at the body."

"Yeah, it's probably better you don't see it, Carl. It was in such terrible condition. It would be very painful for you to see it."

Carl looked down at the floor.

Tom, hoping to glean something for Finelli, was saying what he thought Carl wanted to hear, pretending, as he believed Carl was pretending, hoping to win the sympathy of the family. Yet, in spite of his attempt at deception, Tom began to feel for him, even as he resisted that feeling. He believed that some people had a power to manipulate others psychically; successful people, great achievers, attained their status because of that arcane power. Carl was a master at it, Tom thought.

"We're going to have her body cremated," Tom said, wondering what Carl's intentions might be about the funeral.

Carl nodded. He reached into his bag, saying he had something of Ana's to give him.

Was this what he had hinted at on the telephone? Ana had owned expensive jewelry, some of it gifts from Carl—Bulgari earrings for one thing. But Carl handed him a cheap wristwatch, a Swatch, along with one of Ana's blank checkbooks.

Carl then gave him a sealed envelope. "Don't open this here, please," he said. "There's a letter in it, but I'd rather you didn't read it until you get home."

Glancing at the envelope, Tom slipped it into his pocket. It had his name on it. What on earth now? he wondered.

After a quarter of an hour or so, Tom and Carl were summoned and ushered inside. It was a long walk through a maze of lawyers pumping legal iron. First in the company name, Hoffinger had the corner office, a spacious aerie flooded with daylight, looking north and west from

September 11–14, 1985

thirty-three stories above Manhattan, surveying Central Park, the boats on the Hudson, and the perpetual comings and goings to and from the George Washington Bridge. The art Hoffinger went in for, at least here, included happy snapshots of his family, Bunny, his wife of more than thirty years, their two daughters, Fran and Susie, and a son, Adam, all of them grown and becoming, or beginning to be, lawyers, too. Like Tom, Hoffinger had come from a broken home, abandoned as a boy by his taxi-driver father, but he had taken another route in life, learning how to be tough and make decisions. That was the difference between him and other people, he believed, but it was all surface. Down deep, life and ten years of psychoanalysis had taught him, we're all afraid of the same things, afraid of dying, afraid of unexpected tragedy. Who knows?

Slick lawyer, Tom thought, looking around as he was shown to a soft chair. Very sophisticated person. Very, very expensive suit. The kind of view you would expect a top New York lawyer to have. Carl had gotten the best that money could buy.

The first thing Hoffinger said to him was, "I want you to realize, Tom, that the reason Carl brought you here is that he's not the kind of man that has a lawyer for his estate and a lawyer for this and a lawyer for that. I'm his defense lawyer, and it seemed appropriate that he would come here with the papers for the estate. I don't even know anything about this kind of thing."

He turned promptly to things he did know about. Three of his associates were suddenly in the room. Two were introduced as lawyers, and the third man, Tom gathered, was a private detective.

All this just to sign some informal papers turning over the artwork? Tom smiled to himself, knowing what was coming next. Carl and the others were silent, but Hoffinger began to probe for information about the police side of the case. In legalese, this was called discovery, learning what the other side had come up with to use against you. It was the defendant's right to know, and sooner or later, Hoffinger would get it all from the prosecution, but the game was to hold out as long as you could. Tom, who knew nothing of this, tried to dodge his questions, but Hoffinger pressed. Fearing the lawyer's slickness, Tom put his foot down.

"I'm not supposed to talk about anything pertaining to the investigation," he said. "Carl said he isn't supposed to be speaking from his position, and the police said I'm not supposed to talk about it either, not at this time."

"Well, maybe later," Hoffinger said.

RAQUEL WAS IN the Sixth Avenue apartment, getting it ready for clearing out. Ana hadn't paid the rent for September, but the landlord, speaking to Raquel, said he was willing to forgo any claim to the $414 if the place was cleaned and vacated within the month.

It was just five years ago, around this time of year, that Ana was full of excitement about moving in. Raquel had come down to the city with Neel, the Harringtons' one-year-old boy, to buy him a baby carriage and visit Aunt Ani. She was living on Sullivan Street then, a few blocks away, making art under a loft bed in a ground-floor space much smaller than this one. She was, as always, brimming with news, this time about a great new friend she'd made, an Indian artist named Zarina, whom she'd met working on the Third World issue of *Heresies*. Carl liked her too, because she made him feel restful. Zarina was in India now, but she'd taken Ana to have her palm read, the palmist freaking her out, saying she'd only live to be forty. She showed Raquel her palms. Short life line, Ana said, both hands, ending abruptly, not tapered, which meant illness, but abruptly, meaning something sudden.

And Raquel, being a big sister, said, "Well, my left hand is kind of short."

"No, no, look at mine. Mine are shorter than yours. Much shorter." Then, abruptly, she went on to the next news, the new apartment.

It had lots of light, she said, rattling on about its virtues. She had been thrilled with Sullivan Street, too, at the beginning, but had since grown claustrophobic in the tiny studio with barred windows on a courtyard and only darkness behind it. On Sixth Avenue, she would have two long windows next to each other and another window on the side, looking south and west from the second floor, and the kitchen, the bathroom, and the bedroom all had windows. It was a sturdy old working-class building, freshly painted white brick, black trim on the architectural flourishes, black fire escapes, art deco glass bricks on the street level. Look out the living-room window or come down the concrete stoop and you had the World Trade Center on your left, the Empire State Building on your right, both views marvelously unimpeded. There was a miniature park right outside the building, a quiet triangle with park benches where old men played chess. At the point closest to Ana, a baby tree was growing out of what looked like a long tin can. And, talk about coincidence, when you walked north on Sixth—the Avenue of the Americas, lined for miles, from beginning to end, with the coats of arms of all the countries of the Western Hemisphere—the very first shield you came to, practically on her corner, was the blue sky and palm trees of Cuba.

Raquel went through Ana's files, finding her sister an avid custodian of paper. She had held on to address books, notebooks, calendars, exhibition announcements, bills and cash-register scraps that might be written off at tax time, stuffing them into cardboard accordions and manila folders. Then there were her writings, reflections on her art, letters perhaps never sent, fleeting thoughts perhaps to build on, poems perhaps never read or seen by anyone but her.

> My art [she had written] is grounded in the belief of one universal energy which runs through everything, from insect to man, from man to spectre, from spectre to planet, from planet to galaxy.
>
> My works are the irrigation veins of this universal fluid. Through them, ascend the ancestral sap, the original beliefs, the primordial accumulations, the unconscious thoughts that animate the world.
>
> There is no original past to redeem: there is the void, the orphanhood, the unbaptized earth of the beginning, the time that from within the earth looks upon us. There is above all the search for origin.

There was a folder of poetry, unsigned and unaddressed but in Ana's girlish hand, and because the poems spoke of making love in the Mercer Street apartment, Raquel understood them to be to Carl.

"To my love (on our second Valentine's Day)," she had written in 1981, after several drafts:

I could give up everything
I could forget it all
except the feeling
we have shared
those certain mornings
that, way beyond sex
we experience the
privilege of each other's
presence

Sometimes she loved him less. "I can not forgive you my love for your poverty of being," she had scribbled on a sheet of paper, "for your incapacity to give roots to my dreams, give ground to our future."

What could the D.A. make of that? Raquel wondered, deciding the answer was nothing.

Toward evening, she got together again with Tom, and they drove back to Spring Valley, Tom recounting every minute of his meeting uptown. She was wryly amused by the Swatch and the blank checkbook. Great belongings. The checkbook would turn out to reveal a money-market account containing $60,000, but Carl had said nothing, and by what Raquel thought of contents of the sealed envelope, it seemed he could do nothing right.

The letter from Carl read:

12 SEP 85
DEAR TOM & RAQUEL—
    THERE WILL BE IMMEDIATE EXPENSES CONNECTED WITH ANA'S DEATH. PLEASE USE WHAT I HAVE ENCLOSED TO PAY THEM. IT WILL PROBABLY NOT BE ENOUGH BUT I HOPE IT WILL BE A HELP.
    ANA FELL & I AM FALLING STILL. PLEASE EXPRESS MY DEEPEST SORROW TO ANA'S MOTHER & TO ALL THE MEMBERS OF HER FAMILY.
    TRULY.
    @ carl andre

There were two enclosures, a check made out to Tom in the amount of $2,500 and $500 in cash.

September 11–14, 1985

Raquel was enraged. Even the way the money was given, part check and part cash, somehow smacked of manipulation. In her mind, he had killed her sister. Now, without a word of remorse, he was giving her family $3,000 in compensation in a cynical attempt to buy gratitude. She would have no part of it. She would cremate her sister with her own $580 and give every penny back to Carl.

On Friday, at nine-thirty in the morning, Assistant D.A. Bashford was back in Judge Sayah's courtroom going face to face with Hoffinger for the first time in her career.

Hoffinger, announcing that he had replaced Gerry Rosen, was flanked by two heavyset men. One of them was a young staff lawyer in the firm named Steve Weiner. The other was Carl. Carl's presence was not absolutely essential, but showing his face was a good piece of defense work. It pleased the judge enough to remark, "I appreciate him coming back, it indicates the condition of the bail." Arriving alone in his blues before anyone else, toting his bag of things to read in a dull moment, he had begun an unvarying routine that would endure throughout his fifty-odd appearances yet to come.

This one, a technical hearing that had been scheduled the previous Monday, concerned the progress of grand jury action and whether Carl would testify, but Hoffinger managed to turn it his way, scoring points in the hide-and-seek game called discovery.

Bashford had come into the courtroom a little unsure about whether, as required, notice of Carl having made written and oral statements to the police had been properly recorded. To be on the safe side, she brought it to the judge's attention. Sayah, as a matter of course, asked her if the defense had a copy of Carl's written statement, to which the author was entitled. She replied that she would furnish it "at the appropriate time." This seemed more or less to satisfy the judge, but Hoffinger, displaying his worth, at least to the cognoscenti, slipped into an almost microscopic opening and stole the initiative—control over "the appropriate time"—from the assistant D.A.

"Are you ordering that it be done today?" he asked the judge.

Today was OK with Sayah. "I'm sure she can go into the office and Xerox it. What else do you need?"

Hoffinger, of course, *needed* everything, but he ratcheted only one stop more, asking for the oral statements, too. This was far less simple. It meant gaining access to police files, since Carl's statements to the Sixth Precinct detectives and the officers who answered the call to 911 presumably were in their reports on the investigation.

Defense lawyers petitioning the courts had to work months, sometimes years, to obtain this kind of material, but something in his day had put Sayah in a giving mood, and he was ready to oblige. Bashford, however, getting up from the canvas, raised a strong challenge to his authority. Sayah was a lower-court judge to whom the case had fallen when Rosen had gone scouting for a place to pitch bail, and she questioned his legal right to order discovery.

Unfazed, Sayah said, "If he made a statement, give it to him."

The prosecutor took an easier route. She would furnish the written statement, but, she said, thrusting and parrying as sharply as Hoffinger now, "I don't know if anything else has been reduced to writing."

"If it has, give that to him also," said the judge.

Suddenly it was all very imprecise, the moment to change the subject, which Bashford did. Hoffinger didn't press his luck.

This first sally into legal foreplay had taken about five minutes, and in even less time they completed their business and adjourned. Hoffinger agreed to notify Bashford next week whether Carl would testify. The grand jury proceedings would begin shortly thereafter.

THE ART WORLD would break into skewed, inimical camps: Carl's camp, Ana's camp, and a small camp of people who would try to cast a plague on every camp, gaining nothing for their efforts but universal scorn. But that fragmentation was only in its infancy; there was still enough time and spirit for everyone to join together and celebrate Ana's life.

Three of her older "aesthetic sisters," Carolee Schneemann, Lucy Lippard, and Mary Miss, had taken it upon themselves to organize a commemoration of the artist and her work. They were amply suited for the job, all of them proud and decorated veterans of the previous, breakthrough generation of women who had stormed the Bastille of sexism in the art world. While the fortresses of the old regime remained a long way from being razed, these women had distinguished themselves, each in her own calling, as being among the originals.

All of them were solid friends of both Ana and Carl. They had known him much longer than her. Lucy and Carl had been lovers in the sixties, and Mary and Carolee had also known him well before meeting Ana. Ana had made friends with Lucy and Carolee independently of Carl, years before she even met him, but she had only known Mary for a short time. Before Ana and Mary had met, Mary had been one of the judges who had awarded Ana the Prix de Rome.

The three women had been in touch all week, questioning one another whether they had heard of anyone planning a memorial. When it seemed that no one had yet recovered from the initial shock of Ana's death, one of them said, "Well, we can do it."

Death, mostly from AIDS, was becoming a frequent event in their circles, and Carolee, who had only recently helped organize an event to honor a deceased painter friend, hauled out that experience as a working model. Ana, someone remembered, had been in an exhibition at a gallery run by the Center for Inter-American Relations, which was housed in a Georgian-style mansion on Park Avenue and Sixty-eighth Street, and they felt that might be a suitable site. The center was quick to offer the gallery space, but when Carolee, who knew the building well, insisted on the exquisite Salon Bolivar, with its crystal chandeliers and Angelika Kauffmann paintings on the ceiling, the trouble began.

The center balked, and a battle for the room was on but quickly overshadowed when word of the plans began to spread among Ana's Hispanic friends. They promptly declared that Ana would die twice knowing that her memorial was being held anywhere near the CIA, the nickname they had extracted from the center's initials to indicate its political orientation. But by now, this too was taking a backseat to something of even greater concern to the organizers.

From conversations with the people who would come to the memorial, Carolee, for one, began to perceive among her women friends the extraordinary depth of the emotions upheaved by Ana's death. When Ana and she had met, they had found their kinship in the common challenge posed by their art, which sought to question what Carolee called "the inherited hierarchies of the male culture." Since then, feminism had made at least some headway. Now, however, Carolee sensed that a deep-seated vein had been severed, and bad blood was gushing to the surface.

Don't you see, women were saying, there's a tradition of male artists losing it, killing their wives and lovers, or trying to. Burroughs had shot Joan dead and Mailer had stabbed Adele in the heart, and Pollock, crushing whiskey glasses in his hands, pissing on Peggy Guggenheim's floor, took poor Edith Metzger with him even as she begged him to let her get out of the car. In the end, everything got sweetened by legend because it was a measure of the male passion, an extremity of the indomitable force of creation. This was all OK in the culture because, anyone could see, the woman somehow drove him to it.

These were the kinds of thorns that were tearing everybody up, Carolee felt, the whole premise of this nightmare being that Ana wouldn't jump. Everyone knew of her appetite for life and, it seemed, of her phobia of heights. Carolee had the same fear, and Ana and she had spoken of it. Lots of artists had it, Carolee told her. Artists concentrating on what the eye was seeing could lose their sense of place, so the vertigo became the brake, reminding you that the eye and body are one. Carolee, as a performance artist, had taught herself how to climb gradually, devising works in which she overcame her vertigo one step at a time, at least for this one time, and she would grow brave and soar, she said. But Ana, who did performances, too, just couldn't learn that. She worked close to the ground.

So Ana wouldn't jump, people were saying. But Carl wouldn't push her, they were told. That was what was going around and around. Carolee decided to try to be neutral, particularly for the memorial. She had been raised as a Quaker, and her suggestion to Lucy and Mary to organize the commemoration as a Quaker meeting, where everyone could get up and have his or her say, was agreed on, although others feared what vein that might open. When the Salon Bolivar was secured, the date was set: next Friday at six P.M.

———

September 11–14, 1985

RAQUEL PRAYED ALL day Saturday. The cremation had been postponed in expectation of word from Carl about viewing the body, but by late Friday, Raquel could not bear waiting anymore. She called the police; Finelli was out sick, but someone else tracked down Carl, or his spokesperson, and learned that he had changed his mind. Once again, the family was infuriated about being the last to know. Raquel made arrangements with the Staten Island undertakers to collect the remains at the morgue on First Avenue and proceed with the cremation on Saturday.

In Cedar Rapids, a mass was said for Ana Maria Mendieta that morning at St. Pius X Catholic Church. It was attended by her mother, her brother, and many of Ana's Iowa friends, but Raquel could not get away and prayed at home. She had her own, special way to pray. She had lost her faith in the Catholic religion that first month in the orphanage twenty-four years ago, uprooted with her sister from Varadero Beach and Havana, shunted through Miami, and, as wards of Catholic charity, dispatched to Dubuque, Iowa, a frigid land whose name they could not say. They were beaten by a nun called the Penguin, beaten by "orphans" who were really delinquent girls armed with scissors and switchblades, girls waiting for space at the Mitchellville reform school. "Motherfucker" was the first English word they learned in St. Mary's Home. "They're going to kill me in here," Ana, then twelve years old, wrote home to her parents, breaking their hearts, their one consolation being that in only a year or so Cuba would again be free. Instead, it was forever.

Two years later, it was the Order of the Blessed Virgin Mary. At five o'clock in the morning, the bell rang, and from the moment you awoke you were not permitted to talk until the bell rang again. You could take your shower now or you could take your shower just before going to bed. So you took your shower or you didn't take your shower, then you dressed. Green skirt, white blouse, green jacket, green beanie, white bobby socks, and saddle shoes. That was what you wore all the time. You went down to mass. You weren't forced to go to mass, but you had to be at prayer after mass was over, so if you didn't go you stuck out like a sore thumb. Then you had to line up for the prayer, Hail Mary, and after that you had to line up again. You marched into the cafeteria, took your tray, got your breakfast, went into the dining room, sat down, and started eating. About halfway through breakfast, three hours after first bell, the second bell rang and you could finally talk and there was one big arrrrrghhhhhhhhhhh!—everybody going wild.

You had to eat everything on your plate. Old nuns and young nuns would come around and check, and you couldn't leave a scrap of food behind. Ana hated oatmeal, but you had to eat your oatmeal. So she figured out a way to get by. She'd take her orange, make a hole in the top of the orange with her spoon so she could eat the pulp without breaking the peel, then stuff all the oatmeal inside, and, when the nun came around, she'd pretend she was taking the orange to eat it later in her room. She got very thin there, going down to eighty pounds.

After breakfast, you cleaned your room, made the beds, and then you went to class. There was another Cuban girl in class and she had come to America alone. You could see that she was on the edge of lunacy. All the girls humored her. She would do strange things, and she refused to speak English. The nun would be talking to her in English and she would answer in Spanish, cursing her no matter what she was saying. If the nun began to bother her and made her stand up to answer the questions, she'd just start unbuttoning her skirt and taking off all her clothes, until the nun would say sit down, sit down, and then she'd be OK. But one day she found out her father had died in Cuba and they had to take her away.

When classes were over, you took a walk around the grounds, the whole school in a row, forty-five minutes every day. After supper, you could either play records or watch television. Everybody watched Ricky Nelson on *Ozzie and Harriet*. That was the thing of the day. And you could only watch half an hour because then it was study time, and you had to be in bed for lights out at eight o'clock.

But when the lights were out sometimes you broke the rules and had fun. You would hide behind this one door so you could see all the nuns take their showers, to see if they had any hair on their heads, to see what they looked like out of their black penguin habits. And very late at night there was one nun who hung out with some girls in a room, and other girls would gossip and make up stories about what they saw.

September 11–14, 1985

Breaking the rules and getting caught got you demerits, a half-hour's labor for each demerit. Ana got into trouble all the time. She had a big mouth. She was loud in the hallways and she talked before the second bell. On weekends, when you had some free time, Ana would be ironing uniforms and polishing shoes and scrubbing floors, working off demerits while everybody else was down at the pizza place having fun.

Now Raquel prayed for Ana's soul, not to the Blessed Virgin Mary, but to the Universal Mother of her belief, of her sister's inspiration, and of all-healing grace.

On First Avenue, however, a clerk at the morgue who couldn't find the paperwork refused to release the body to the undertakers. They went back to Staten Island with an empty hearse.

──── 18 ────

After they had been in a Florida refugee camp a couple of weeks, Ana and Raquel, yet to learn a word of English, decided they wanted to live in Lincoln, Nebraska. They had been separated on arrival and placed in different dormitories. They had heard their fill of rumors of children being sent to hellish institutions in big cities up north, orphanages and even reform schools from which many were running away, some making their way back to Miami to shift for themselves on the streets and tell their terrible tales. Lovely Lincoln, Nebraska, was being touted by the earlier arrivals at Kendall— the town where the beneficiaries of Operation Peter Pan were being held—as *the* place to go. When one of the girls Ana and Raquel had met in the camp was sent there, they reasoned that even if Lincoln, Nebraska, were less than it promised, at least they would have a friend already in place. One day in the third week, they saw their names on a blackboard and found out they were instead going to somewhere they had never heard of: Doobookay, Eeohah, which was the way they pronounced it in Spanish. Panicked, they asked to see the Spanish-speaking social worker, hoping to change someone's heart.

Ana cried throughout the whole encounter, but there was no reason to fret, said the social worker. They were going to St. Mary's Home in Dubuque, Iowa, just for a couple of weeks until the sisters of St. Mary's could find out all the kinds of things Ana and Raquel liked to do and place them with foster parents in an American family just like their own.

"Well," said Raquel, as Ana continued to sob, "I went to a music conservatory, and I have to practice. Will there be a piano there?"

"Oh, yes," said the social worker.

"My sister and I have to be together, you know," Raquel said. "Will we be together?"

"Yes, of course."

Ana kept crying, and Raquel kept trying to console her, but when her patience ran out she said, "Look, you wanted to come here. Here you are. Don't come crying to me."

They arrived in Dubuque on October 5, 1961, frightened during a plane change in Chicago by movie memories of Cagney-style gangsters. After the next four years of growing up with deceit and betrayal at every turn, it would be hard to frighten them again.

Raquel never got to play the piano at St. Mary's. Ana and she were separated on the first day. Nine months of the child-beating Penguin nun and the Chinese nun pounding Ana's head against a doorknob, Raquel screaming for her to stop, kids getting into scissor fights, living with Shirley the Squirrel raped by her stepfather, Marie who was mindless, and oxlike Bonnie who bloodied Ana's nose, being sickened by the blood of the onset of menstruation and the grotesque nunnish reasons given for it, scheming to run away to Miami just like the kids in the rumors, and not one uncensored letter to or from home; nine months went by at St. Mary's before the dirty little Cubans who preferred to watch Bugs Bunny rather than *Sky King* were placed in a foster home.

That was in the old brick house of the Butlers of Dubuque, getting $188 a month from Catholic charity for their trouble: Mr. Butler and his spanking stick hanging on a nail in the kitchen; Mrs. Butler, who would say "I don't care who you were in Cuba—you're nobody in this country!"; little Jimmy Butler, with the spanking-stick buffer of Band-Aid boxes in his back pockets; and his sister Theresa, Ana's age, who got her hair cut off by her father because she wasn't allowed to wear bangs like Ana's and her mouth bloodied when she said *mierda*, the dirty word the nothing-but-a-couple-of-refugees had taught her. Although they never knew when their luck might run out, Ana and Raquel were spared Mr. Butler's corporal punishments but not his seething discontent. He took away their snow boots in winter, told their parents when they called from Cuba what ill-behaved girls they had reared, tried to force Ana, terrified of climbing a ladder, to wash the second-story windows, forcing her to climb and "conquer" her fear, but climbing was the one thing she wouldn't do. Then the Butlers accused her and her sister of stealing twenty dollars from Mrs. Butler's purse, when everyone knew that Theresa was the crook in the house, yet they called Mr. Donleavy, the social worker, as if he were the cops, to take them away. It was back to the orphanage that very day—clearly the better deal the way the girls now saw the world, sixteen months into their exile.

Mr. Donleavy was the OK one, the only one they trusted, so when he called them into his office to tell them they were common little thieves, not so highborn and mighty anymore, and break his promise to let them finish the school year before uprooting them anew, they would trust no adult again, and not long afterward, Raquel, committing what she herself thought was the worst crime anybody could commit, told the mother superior to go to hell. They were sent downstate to wear green beanies at Our Lady of the Angels Academy and tilt at the rules of the Order of the Blessed Virgin Mary. When the school year did end, they burned their saddle shoes in a bonfire. They had received wonderful news. Ana's best school friend in Dubuque, a girl from a well-to-do Catholic family in the dairy industry, had gotten her parents to accept them into their home. It was all arranged. A social worker came to get them, and during the drive north they couldn't have been more joyous, until they realized they weren't going to Dubuque at all. Because of their behavior in Dubuque, they had made themselves *personae non gratae* in that town as far as their Catholic welfare sponsors were concerned. Getting onto the bypass, the social worker made for Cedar Rapids, depositing them at the city-run Children's Home, another halfway house for boys and girls going to and coming from the Mitchellville reform school.

That was the summer of 1963. Ana, going on fifteen, had taken to idling at a mirror, applying deep black eyeliner, mascara, and cakey makeup to her dark complexion. She had dyed her black hair a brassy color called moon gold. When Bonnie at St. Mary's had punched her nose and beat her almost senseless to the floor, the fight had been over possession of a paint-by-numbers set, but that was long before the dawning of her passion for art. This was the period when she dreamed of growing tall enough to become a stewardess, flying off to anywhere but here. It was Raquel who had taken to art, entering "Draw Me" contests, hoping for some sort of redemption, too.

ANA WAS PLACED in a decent foster home that fall, but the demon of displacement continued to bite. Raquel, seventeen, had graduated from high school and was sent to a live-in Catholic college in Cedar Rapids, and though she was just a hill away, it was the first time Ana was truly alone. She lived with a cheery young couple, the Saddlers, and their newborn baby. They had a tidy little house with an old black Ford in the driveway, and they would grow to care for her deeply, providing some ration of the love that had been removed like a vital organ from her being. The new trouble came from Regis High, where Ana, the only Hispanic in a school of adolescents of German and Irish origin, entered her junior year. "Go back to where you came from," was one of the taunts she began to hear when she picked up the phone at the Saddlers'. "Whore" and "nigger" were others. They shattered her nerves. The Saddlers took her to the family doctor, who gave her sleeping pills. Sometimes she couldn't wake up in the morning, and sometimes she fell back to sleep in class. She thought she had a stomach ulcer, a tumor on her brain, and she cried all day long. She met a boy named Dennis Gorman. He gave her his school ring and they dated, double-dated with Raquel, went to the movies, had a pizza, rocked and rolled in a place called the Red Warren, did the Jerk and the Monkey, and parked their car on the local lover's lane, taking slugs from a bottle of Smirnoff's in middle America, 1964. The taunting calls faded away, and so did the tumor, the ulcer, and most of the pain.

THE KNOCK ON the door of the big house in Cárdenas came in January 1965. Two men in plain clothes and shirtsleeves took Ignacio Mendieta away. He was accused of being a major operative in a CIA spy ring, and it was true. His immediate superiors were shot, and he was sent to La Cavaña, a prison in a limestone quarry, sentenced to twenty years. Raquel, Ana's mother, praised God that it was only twenty years. "This is an order," Ignacio wrote to his wife from prison, "this is not for you to think about: I want you and my son to leave this country, because

Raquelin and Ana Maria need you." Over the past four years, fourteen thousand children had been dispatched from Cuba under Operation Peter Pan. Eight thousand had been placed in orphanages and foster homes; many had ended up in ghettos in Miami. Castro was still in power. Kennedy was dead. The CIA, trying to move up from disgrace, turned to rescuing South Vietnam. Redounding failure led someone in Washington to the idea that the Cuban children might be better and less expensively cared for by the parents they had started out with. There was no more talk of Castro falling soon, and he drove another hard bargain. On December first of that year, the Freedom Flights began. Parents of the Peter Pan kids, carrying rum and cigars, headed for the United States. On that day, Raquel, waiting for her exit visa, was allowed to see her husband in La Cavaña and when he heard his name called, he thought he was going to the wall. They sat on either side of a double barrier of chicken wire. The guards cut open the fruit Raquel had brought to see what was inside. Raquel had been told by Concha Mendieta, La Madrina of the Bay of Pigs, not to cry, to show them "we won't cry." She had brought little Ignacio along. He was seven years old. He told his father a story he had made up along the way. He said the first Freedom Flight had crashed.

ANA TOOK ART classes that senior year. Her teacher at Regis High was unable to find one stroke of talent in her work, and she told her so, but what Ana had discovered was independent of local pedagogic opinion. Recalling her teacher's disapproval years later, she would say, "When I made art—whether it was good or bad, or she didn't like it, or whatever—I felt I had a power." Awakened by the power, she was drawn to the local libraries, turned southward to the Latin roots from which she had been cut, her eyes excited by the great Mexican murals of Rivera and Sequeiros, by the sweeping self-portraits of Frida Kahlo, uniting her crippled body with the culture and the soil of the place where she was born.

Ana had taken charge of her life. Her father's imprisonment was being temporarily kept from her and her sister, but a resentment of the parental decision to cast her out so blindly had set in and would continue to grow for years before it receded. She graduated that June.

Raquel had become a problem. She had been expelled from college for unacceptable behavior, particularly staying out late and coming back drunk. The Catholic charity withdrew its support, deciding she was old enough to be on her own. Ana, who had been working part time, had had to give Raquel money until she found a job in a department store. In the fall, Ana went off to Sioux City to Briar Cliff College, where she majored in art. She had dropped the boy named Dennis, dated a certain Dick Penny, and, working in a Kresge's soda fountain that summer, had been won over by Dick's best friend Verl Allen, who would come around every day for a bottle of pop just to tell her how crazy about her he was. She had grown as much as she would ever grow, five feet tall she would always say, fibbing. She had let her hair return to its natural black, and though remaining showy and prankish, she had adopted middle-class morals about what was proper behavior for a girl of seventeen, which, to Verl's repeated frustration, was more fifties than sixties.

IT WAS TWENTY-SEVEN degrees below zero the day in January 1966 when Ana's mother and little brother landed in the Cedar Rapids airport. Ana and Raquel were there to greet them, young women now, bundled against the weather in a way one never imagined in Cuba. Their mother didn't even know it was cold; their brother, who had almost no memory of his sisters, was thrilled by the "smoke" pouring from his mouth and nose. The four of them went to live in a one-room apartment, staying awake cradled in one another's arms until three in the morning that first day, bounding over the years, though the sisters didn't say much about the orphanages, and their mother said as little about their father's prison. The landlord came by the next day and said he hadn't known there would be children. He ordered them out by the end of the month. It was the thirtieth.

Ana had filed the documents required by Cuba for her mother's and brother's expatriation, and now she became the practical one in the stateside Mendieta family. She had been pleasantly surprised to discover that her mother could speak some English, having worried how she was going to support herself. The older Raquel had been a physics and chemistry teacher in Havana, and understanding that an immigrant could hardly aspire to start anywhere but at the bottom, she was happy enough finding a job almost immediately as an inventory clerk, counting hairpins. Ana came back to live in Cedar Rapids after her first year at college. The four Mendietas moved into a two-bedroom apartment. Ana enrolled as an off-campus student at the University of Iowa in nearby Iowa City, which had one of the finest art schools in the country. Later, she would tell a New York audience that by the time she was seventeen she had made up her mind to be either a criminal or an artist. She would in fact never give up a touch of kleptomania— stealing plants from other people's lawns being one of the specialties of her Iowa City days—but by now she had chosen art, and she had chosen it at the beginning of its most exciting moment for women.

BY THE END of the sixties, the avant-garde art scene could barely remember the bipedal, Tenth Street–uptown abstract expressionist juggernaut that had staggered into the decade with the spear of pop art plunged into a seam of its armor. Although the dire news had not yet convinced some of Ana's Iowa City art teachers, ab-ex painting had been Damar-varnished for the last time and quietly museumed. Pop art itself, though still bullish, had been supplanted—along with a midsixties media flurry over illusion-intensive op art—by the new art: hard-edge, expressionless, picked-to-the-bone, what-you-see-is-what-you-see minimalism.

The new art was a rare triumph of the New Left, more specifically of a brilliant klatch of young but post–draft age, loosely neo-Marxist dialectic materialists soaking in a warm bath somewhere between Freud and Jung and railing against the war in Vietnam. Their victory was a revolutionary advance over what one of them, conceptualist Larry Weiner, would shortly be calling "aesthetic fascism," that is, art as private property in the hands of a cultural elite. So stable had this movement become in only five years, one of its stars, Carl Andre, was given a retrospective exhibition at the Guggenheim Museum—a distinction reserved a mere generation back for a lifetime's body of work— at the unheard-of age of thirty-five.

Minimalism at the outset ran into the same problem that brought down ab ex, namely unsalability, but unsalability was minimal art's first principle, which was half the fun, the other half being waving its down-with-the-art-establishment banner. Believing themselves at long last free of the physical and psychological constraints of the system, the minimalists had in the late sixties unleashed or given impetus to a number of unmarketable but suddenly legitimate spin-off movements that were exciting not only a new generation of artists but artists of all ages outside the old main stream.

The minimalists themselves were the first to cross the Hudson River and bring a form of the new art called earthwork sculpture to the hinterland. A 1968 *Saturday Evening Post* trend-watching piece made sport of Carl Andre piling up rocks in Woody Creek Canyon, Colorado, and other minimalists—notably earthworker Robert Smithson—along with their more-minimal-than-thou conceptualist kin digging "artfully shaped holes" in a Nevada desert, carving contours in a New Haven swamp, and burying a cubic foot of steel in Europe ("It's out of sight"). Sticking to their own turf, Larry Weiner and even pop artist Claes Oldenburg joined the earthwork gang. Larry, or rather Alice, his companion (the *Post* preferred to call her his wife), dug "negative space" in their Bleecker Street backyard, which he filled with whitewash. Oldenburg hired two union (the union part being important) gravediggers to do their thing in back of the Metropolitan Museum of Art; as soon as they finished, he ordered the hole refilled. Readers of the article were no doubt as amused as they were bemused, but earthwork was a powerful affirmation of the radical departure from art as a commodity. You could not buy, or hope to buy, say, a Walter de Maria two-mile chalk line in the Mojave Desert. You could only ponder the state of affairs that might have led to such a work and in the process undergo precisely the aesthetic experience the earthwork artists had set out to achieve.

The other major form of this art for art's sake that had emerged at the turn of the decade was body art, with the artist's own body usually being the medium in which the work was executed or performed (hence performance art). In 1958, a French abstract painter and karate expert named Yves Klein had found a way to induce paint-smeared nude women to squirm and wriggle on blank canvases and make "imprints of reality," which he said were the visual equivalents of tape recordings. Four years later, ever-resourceful Claes Oldenburg created a series of "happenings"—fashionable art fun at the time—that consisted of performances involving sound, moving objects, and people, one of whom was a young painter named Carolee Schneemann, who made nude appearances and earned the tag "body beautiful." Carolee would go on to become one of the great innovators in the movement, but these earlier versions were usually exploitive of women, who considered body performance art just another feature of male supremacy in the art world. It certainly seemed like macho business when artist Vito Acconci did a performance in which he "underwent" a sex change; burning off the hair on his chest, concealing his genitals between his legs, and completing the "transformation" by having a woman kneel behind him, his hidden penis vanishing in her mouth.

Women who did take up the genre received "encouragement" from a quarter they least expected. Notoriously insensitive to women participating in the mainstream art world as equal competitors, the same male establishment that had been ignoring their earlier work was suddenly approving of women working with their own bodies, the more attractive the body the better. Nevertheless, the inspiring performances of Carolee Schneemann, who raised a challenge to the insult of sexism by setting out to prove that the body is "more *variously* expressive than a sex-negative society can admit," were in the vanguard of a few female body artists whose work by 1970 had begun to melt the initial reluctance of other women artists. Many women had recently espoused the new feminism and wanted a change in their art as well as in their lives. Others, like Ana, were twenty years old, coming alive in the spirit of their day.

ON HALLOWEEN, 1969, Ana went to a costume party in Iowa City attended by some of the faculty and students from the university's School of Art and Art History. She came as Cleopatra, in a handmade ensemble of clinging orange chiffon, a jeweled band around her neck, a papier-mâché asp in the tassels of her hair, which was a wig fashioned from a mop dyed black. She had wanted her costume to make a statement, the message of which no one can recall, but she could hardly have been more beautiful. A man, coming toward her from across the crowded room, asked her to dance, danced with her all night, the two of them falling in love. Born in 1935, he was thirteen years her senior, married, and an assistant professor of art. His name was Hans Breder, a short, dark, handsome man with an inconcealable glint of devilment in his round eyes and a softly confident voice. He was also an avant-garde sculptor and painter with a New York gallery and a nocturnal life-style given to bohemian excess. Pursuing a deepening interest in the new art media of body, performance, and fledgling video art, he had recently managed to establish a freewheeling, experimental "intermedia" program—the first in the country—only because the university believed it was a conventional course in *intermediate* instruction.

Ana had seen Hans around at The Mill, which was the closest thing in Iowa City to Max's Kansas City where artists and would-be artists could meet and talk and drink and go someplace else when the townies closed the bar. She had heard about his hard-drinking, stay-out ways and stories about him being a gypsy born in Nazi Germany, his mother dressing her dark-skinned boy in black so he wouldn't be hauled away with the gaudy-clothed gypsies and gassed. Of course, everything people said only added to the far-out professor's cachet.

By the time she met him, Ana, going on twenty-one, had fit herself into a fairly average Iowan life. She had gotten her degree in art that year and had gone to work as an art teacher in a Cedar Rapids elementary school. She was continuing her studies at the university, taking evening courses toward a master's in painting, commuting from the little white house just bought by her mother—who was now working as a research chemist—in the North Brook district of town. Routine had not dulled her craving to harness the power of art, and she was as showy as ever, hanging out at The Mill, ripping off plants from a lawn or two, and chasing anything else that was fun. Verl had never stopped being crazy about her, but he had dropped out, burned by his own ultimatum: he had found a girl who would go "all the way," and he couldn't see why he should continue seeing Ana unless she matched the offer. She was dating a medical student now, giving short free lessons in pronunciation to every new midwesterner she met: "My name is AH-na, not Anna."

Raquel remained the one unable to strike an all-American balance.

She got pregnant and married the man, a beery local gun freak named Don Holmes. The baby was named Raquelita, suggested by her godmother, Aunt Ana. The new family lived in Iowa City, where Raquel had gone back to school, also studying art. It was not to be a happy home.

THEY WOULD RUN into each other at The Mill, at university events, at parties to which he had begun to invite her. There was no one in Ana's visible world who was doing anything as remotely exhilarating as Hans, inviting the most avant-garde artists of the day to the university, making ephemeral but startlingly original art, hosting wild-mushroom-hunting parties and goat roasts and vodka parties that lasted until the sun rose above the ridges of the low Iowan hills to the recorded strains of gypsy violins, her eyes meeting his. But he was a married man. Wedlock as a barrier to unfettered expression looked like bald hypocrisy in the Iowa City university art milieu of the early seventies, where going-all-the-way faculty-student relationships were common, and uninhibited sexuality was a touchstone theme of Hans's intermedia, his pace exhausting even the New Yorkers. All of the significant body and performance artists were showing up at Hans's doing their gigs and shtick, as they called them, and when visiting artist Vito Acconci presented a version of his New York gallery performance piece—lying under a plywood platform and masturbating—it provoked no more scandal than a letter of complaint from a parent (promptly reassured by the art department chairman, who replied, "Masturbation can be an art"). Hans's marriage would end in 1973, but the "hypocrisy" had begun to be righted two years or so earlier, when he and Ana had become lovers, the first time for Ana. She kept her secret from her sister, but Raquel would always remember the effect:

I never saw her be with any man the way I saw her be with Hans. She had had other boyfriends, but the first time that I saw her with him she was like this different person I had never met before. She was always driving the guys around by the nose before that. They did what she said or that was the end of the relationship. She was just really in love with him. Loving, surrendered, affectionate in the open. She was madly in love with him and she was willing to put up with anything just to be with him and that was that. She just worshipped him.

Their love would grow stormy over the years—cyclonic, some who were there might say—but only much later, when there could be no going back, would the seemingly endless passion ebb.

IN 1972, ANA received her master's in painting, but by then she had destroyed almost all of her previous work, her art having "exploded off the canvas," as Hans later put it. She immediately enrolled in his program, the only woman working toward a Master of Fine Arts degree. Hans's intermedia, now called multimedia, had attracted national attention and had been vastly expanded by a major Rockefeller Foundation grant, which established the Center for the New Performing Arts. Over the next five years, the time it would take her to complete her studies, she would by constancy absorb the new art into her soul, forging a style uniquely her own. "The turning point in my art was in 1972," she would write, "when I realized that my paintings were not real enough for what I wanted the image to convey—and by real I mean I wanted my images to have power, to be magic. I decided that for the images to have magic qualities, I had to work directly with nature. I had to go to the source of life, to mother earth."

Hans remembers her first body earthwork:

It is 1972—a sunny, humid afternoon, typical of Iowa in the early fall. A group of my students visit my studio. Among them is Ana Mendieta. The smell of freshly cut grass is hanging in the air. Spontaneously, Ana announces that she has an idea for a piece. She undresses, lies on the lawn, and asks one of the students to cover her body with grass. Somebody takes photographs. In the photographs her body blends into the ground. From that point, she blended her body with the elements in innumerable ways.

The use of her own body in hundreds of works would be abandoned within a few years in favor of more universal female imagery, but her clearly stated desire to repeatedly assert a mystical oneness with the earth would receive supernumerary psycho-interpretation throughout the rest of her life—and, by persons least qualified to do so, after her death. Few, however, would succeed in expressing it more clearly than she when she called her life's work a "search for origin." Searching the previous summer, she had gone to Mexico for the first time, on an archaeological expedition sponsored by the university, thrilled to be in a country in whose landscape she saw her own Cuba, whose people spoke as she did, "where everybody was my height and had dark skin." Seeking the power and the magic, she returned to her interest in Santería, going to its African roots and to voodoo as well. Blood and hair, feathers and flowers, fire and water became the materials of her sculpture.

In 1973, a fellow student at the university was raped and murdered, and Ana did a jolting series called *Rape Pieces*, "to bring attention to this crime and all sexual violence," she said. In one performance, students were invited to her room without being told why. Hans, the teacher, went along, too:

> At that time she was living in an apartment house in town. There was this long hallway, and the door was slightly ajar. Nobody knew what was happening. We walked in. She was tied up, leaning across a table, half-nude but nude from the waist down, and the floor was splattered with blood and blood clots and a coat hanger was lying on the floor, somehow suggesting rape.

Assuming correctly that they had walked into an artwork, there was little immediate reaction, but the element of risk, in this case the half-open door into which anyone might have stumbled, gave the series an enduring power. Ana was then working under the impact of male brutality much closer to home. A visit to Raquel had produced a violent confrontation with her husband, who had walked in drunk, brandishing a shotgun and shooting up the house. By then, Raquel had had her second daughter, and Ana, scooping up both children, dragged her helpless sister from the house and called the police. She warned her never to go back to him. Raquel, complying, revealed what she had been too ashamed to admit: that he had been physically abusing her for some time, waking her up after a night of drinking, a revolver pointed at her head, demanding she make him breakfast, and beating her whether she did or not.

Ana took well to Hans's bohemian style. After he left his wife, he moved to an old Victorian house, and Ana spent many of her days and nights there sleeping in a room with heart motifs on its cushions and pictures, but she kept her apartment in town. They never spoke of marriage, but one night in the old Victorian house, when they heard the eerie laugh of a woman they agreed was a ghost, she jumped out of bed and ran through the house, shouting, "There is love in this house!" and because there was love, the love-hating spirit didn't come back again until after Ana had gone away. They spent their summers in Mexico, traveling with other multimedia students, getting naked and making art and sometimes love on the byways and dusty ways of Oaxaca, sometimes running from the *policía*, Ana whipping blood like cream so it wouldn't coagulate, Hans killing one bottle of vodka every day, dancing with whores, and Ana holding her own, getting bitchy and throwing things at him when he got her raging mad.

It is one morning in 1976 [Hans reminisces], as we are planning to visit Yaagul, a Zapotec site in the valley of Oaxaca. Ana asks me to drive her first to the market to buy flowers. She tells me she has an idea for a piece. This is a site that we had visited many times. We walk up to one of the open tombs. She lays in it, nude, and asks me to arrange the flowers around her body, instructing me that the flowers should seem to grow from her body.

She has a *cohetero* (maker of fireworks) in a *colonia* district of Oaxaca make a firework piece in the shape of the outline of her body. One evening, at dusk, we ignite it and watch her form consumed by fire.

During the school year, the multimediaites would go down to Old Man's Creek, or the muddy Dead Tree Area, or the woods on the Petersen farm, Ana carrying her stash of gunpowder to burn out the ground or a tree in the shape of her body, her plywood silhouette strapped to the roof of her VW beetle with the '38 Ford front. Then there were parties, and parties after the parties broke up, when Hans would ask her to do her dance, and if she were in the mood, she would drive home very fast to get her Afro-Cuban records, and the smaller group who had remained would be sobered up by the way she danced. One of Hans's professor friends, Rumanian-born Greek classicist Stavros Deligeorges, remembers it vividly:

> For lack of a better expression, let's call it a voodoo dance. Hans usually would be in tremendous awe of what was going on because it was not just entertainment. This was not something of how the Cubans amuse themselves after hours. But it showed me the dark-continent side of Ana, a thoughtful and meditative side. Ana shook hands with you and would have a tremendous, big smile, and she had a very radiant and projected personality. But this was something that she could sustain, the dancing, without saying a word. And whatever she was doing with her shoulders, with her head especially, the gyrations, was something that showed tremendous self-discipline. Things you couldn't deduce by shaking hands.
>
> Oh, I can imagine the local Anglos, with their tall drinks, etc., just staring and being transfixed. I had another set of thoughts going around in my head. To me these movements were representations of passion, especially the dance she was doing. It was not suggestive dancing. It was not pantomime, but the speechlessness of it struck me as a different language that was coming in. Long black hair, swirling, big, big sweeps before her face, the covering of the face, half-closed eyes, presented a side which is not typical of a Western European: long words, languages, reading, travel, things of that sort. This was the Caribbean—a piece of this continent that I had not seen that close.

Making art became the impulse between each heartbeat. The use of her silhouette to transcend her own body spoke of a unity with nature, not as one woman's yearning or even her gender's, but as a quest of humankind. Similarly, she fashioned a branding iron in the shape of her hand, firing it to burn imprints in the earth. By the time she completed her studies, she had developed as a unique voice in the body art movement, her work beginning to gain national recognition. Lucy Lippard, when she was a visiting critic at Iowa, had met her through Hans, had been duly impressed, and had gone back to Soho to write about her *Rape Pieces* in *Ms.* and in a major piece on women's body art in *Art in America.* Although these works were politically charged (and made good copy), the thrust of Ana's art continued her metaphysical search for origin, and this universal content was what some critics were beginning to see as being original. Some careful courting rewarded her with her first major grant, three thousand dollars, which was just enough money in 1977 to put the boldest dream she ever had inside her head.

"I encouraged her to go to New York," Hans says. "I was the one who said, 'You need this experience.' And of course the idea was that she would be there one semester, maybe two, and eventually we would be back together." Ana was scared, hoping he wouldn't forget her too quickly, knowing she would be desperately lonely, but confident that she would survive. She had met many New York artists through Hans and had every number in her book. Hans drove her to the bus terminal, "to begin life in the art world," he says. They kissed good-bye, and she said she would write every day. She had her branding iron tucked under her arm as she boarded the Greyhound bus.

———— 19 ————

Rumors of Carl having a history of violent outbursts were being passed like a mean virus. One of the carriers was a journalist simply doing her job. Since the day the news broke, a former *New York Post* reporter named Joyce Wadler had been working on a cover-story article for *New York* magazine. She was moving through the New York art world, hanging around the courthouse, making long phone calls, digging into Carl's and Ana's pasts. Her efforts were meeting great resistance. While she found Ana's life a fairly open book, it seemed to Wadler that in the first few days after her death, a solid front of silence had been fielded, protecting Carl. She had never experienced anything like it, and her career as a tabloid reporter had boiled her hard enough to penetrate many tight communities, including organized crime. Ranking dealers, collectors, curators, and artists would not return her calls. She was suspicious. Soho was suddenly looking a lot like Black Rock hiding its dirty secret, and the stranger in its midst was having a long, bad day.

A resident of the Village, she knew her way around the downtown bars. In Puffy's Tavern, an artists' place in Tribeca, a beer pitcher labeled Carl Andre Defense Fund had appeared on the bar. Somebody had contributed a brick, but there wasn't much more to laugh at than that. Although Wadler was many years younger than Carl and the rest of the old hands of Max's Kansas City and St. Adrian's in the defunct Broadway Central hotel, she was picking up stories. Almost all of them were never better than secondhand, but there were memories of Carl getting drunk and picking a fight or ripping up a bar.

Along this route, she became fascinated by his poetry, believing she saw signs of "feelings of vengeance and violence." To her, some of these writings lay balanced "on the thin line between love and rage." Carl was a man of polarized emotions, she felt, with few gray zones in between. He had written, "Every love pretending to be pure must end in solemn compromise," and in one little piece of prose, he declared the material of a sculpture, in this case wood, to be female, going on to say, "Like all women hacked and ravaged by men she renews herself by giving, gives herself by renewing." It would not be easy to make much of all this convenience-store psychology, but going through the artists' "miscellaneous" files in the library of the Museum of Modern Art, Wadler made an eerie discovery. At the age of twenty-two, Carl had written a poem, lugubrious then, but chilling now.

It read:

> The ways of love were
> sometime my revenge when
> I was wronged by something
> done or said & she stood
> naked by the window waiting
> to be struck perhaps where
> her white breasts were
> red. To know that every
> touch will be measured before
> hand is dread worse than
> danger. She turned from
> me & stared, eyes wanting
> tears, with envy at the rain.

When Wadler put this woman standing naked by Carl's window together with the color slide of Ana at twenty-four lying under a bloody sheet on a rooftop in Mexico, she had a double-whammy piece of sensational copy, "a death foretold."

Searching for corroboration for her violence stories, she not only spread them but unearthed new ones. Carl had beaten up a fellow artist in Texas, had ended up in a drunk tank in Seattle, had been abusive in public to a woman in Berlin. "Absolute garbage," was what Jack Hoffinger branded these stories when she managed to get him on the phone, but the worst rumors, those of physical abuse of women, would elude her; the women in Carl's life would remain the most silent of all.

———

THE GOSSIP THAT Carl in June 1980 had been hauled off by the Seattle police and thrown into the drunk tank, which proved to be true, was given to Wadler by the one woman who would become exceedingly vocal, a friend of Ana's named Ruby Rich. She was a compact-sized brawler the same age as Ana, a political activist, organizer, and staunch feminist, a downtown energy station who kept a sharpshooter's eye on the art world, writing occasional and controversial pieces for *The Village Voice*—a willing and made-to-order Nemesis for a Carl Andre.

She didn't like him. She remembered Ana bringing him to the big party she threw for her thirty-fifth birthday, and the guy really seemed like a creep, really antisocial, obnoxious. Ana was dancing and he wouldn't dance, and there were more women than men at the party, so maybe he felt left out, but she had bad vibes. He made no effort to deal with people, and Ruby wasn't inclined to make an effort for him. She was happy they broke up when Ana went to Rome and unhappy when they got together again, thinking, well, people have weird needs. She didn't know why Ana needed to play it out with this asshole, but she did. And maybe Ruby didn't want to know about it. It was that kind of feeling. Like they were probably using each other, she representing to him politics that he never really had and always claimed to have and always aspired to, and he representing to her the legitimacy in the art world that she always aspired to but didn't have. It was just some kind of sinister trade-off, not a cold-done deal, but an emotional S-and-M relationship of torture and need. But she never spoke to Ana about Carl. That wasn't something you did in their friendship. The only thing she really wanted to talk to her about, and had actually been gearing up the nerve to take up with her, was that Ana drank too much, and Ruby was getting fed up with it.

She had not yet gathered that courage when she had lunch with Ana on the Wednesday of that first week in September, and she was off to Toronto the next day to attend a film festival. It was not until her return the previous Sunday, the fifteenth, that she learned Ana had died a whole week ago. She would always regret that absence, believing she would have done something spontaneous and crazy but something that might have paid off, like making up leaflets soliciting possible witnesses and standing on the corner where Ana fell, handing them out for all those nights. The minute she heard the news, she sensed that this was a detective story and thus a question of who held the pieces that when put together solved the crime, people who had seen, heard, or remembered. They had to be out there somewhere.

ON MONDAY, RUBY met with Raquel and three others. Natalia Delgado, the woman who had had the final phone call with Ana, was in from Chicago for pre–grand jury talks with Martha Bashford. Ruby and Natalia were old friends, but Raquel was meeting Ruby for the first time, along with Gary Simon, a twenty-nine-year-old New York lawyer. He was a law-school friend of Natalia's and had volunteered to represent Ana's family. The fifth person was Natalia's sister, Cristina Olsen, in whose Brooklyn home they had gathered.

If there were people holding pieces of the puzzle, Natalia certainly stood out among them. Ruby had met Ana somewhat earlier than she, but no one, not even Raquel, knew more than Natalia about the troubles between Ana and Carl. Natalia, however, was under the strictest admonition from Bashford not to speak of the case. Raquel was too, but Natalia, being a lawyer, was the more rigorous of the two when, almost immediately, they began to speak of Ana. Everyone was eager to learn what both women knew, but with Natalia stopping both herself and Raquel, they did little more than reminisce. Except for their talk on the phone at the Sixth Precinct that Monday, there had been, following orders, no more exchanges between Raquel and Natalia. They were saving it all for the grand jury.

IN HER FILE-CLUTTERED office over the Department of Motor Vehicles on Centre and Worth streets across from the courthouse, Martha Bashford met with Natalia and Raquel. She interviewed them separately to prevent one story from coloring the other. It was the sheer coincidence of being on homicide call that Sunday that had brought the assistant D.A. to the case, but she was at home with tales of domestic strife. Her current caseload was filled with alleged assaults by males on females, fathers and uncles molesting daughters and nieces being popular crimes this year, and what passed for novelty was the case of the EMS man charged with sexually abusing a female patient while rushing her to the hospital.

Natalia's story began in April 1984 when she visited Ana in Rome. That was when Natalia told her friend that she had heard that Carl was having an affair with a woman in New York. This rumor had come from someone who had gotten it from someone else, but Natalia felt that she had to let Ana know. Ana was surprised that she was unaware of such behavior and she was hurt, Natalia said, because she and Carl had only gotten together again a few months before with a host of promises of undying love. Visiting New York that summer, Ana began to investigate on her own. In August, when Carl was away, Natalia stayed with her at the Mercer Street apartment, and Ana confided that she was convinced that the rumor was true, and she had confronted Carl.

He would not admit to anything, Ana said. "Even if it were true I wouldn't tell you," was all he had said. He was angry and wanted to know how she found out. She didn't use Natalia's name, seeking to protect her. She said that it was someone named Lynn and she said to Natalia, laughing, that Carl was so infuriated at this woman Lynn that if he saw her on the street he would probably choke her. When she was on her way back to Rome and Carl saw her to a cab and said something about how lonely he was going to be without her, Ana replied, "Well, why don't you spend time with so and so?" and she shut the door and drove off.

Raquel, speaking to Bashford, revealed much of this, too, and she knew who so and so was. Before leaving, Ana had told her about the other woman, how she had tracked her down by matching Carl's American Express receipts with a restaurant where they were often seen. She was a minimalist artist named Brandon Krall, tall and blond and slim and boyish, who rolled her own cigarettes, drank Scottish ale, had worked that summer as a receptionist at Paula Cooper's and played a lot of chess.

The next time she saw Ana, Natalia told Bashford, was when she came through Chicago in January 1985. She had just been married, seemed very happy, and she brought Natalia up to date. Carl had really matured, said Ana. The Krall woman meant nothing to him, he had told her over and over again, calling her in Rome, sending flowers and postcards and poems, and flying in whenever he could, bearing champagne. Ana, his Tropicanita, was the only woman he could ever love, and he wanted to make a commitment, ringing it in with wedding bells. They had showed their art together in Rome, and her work was going well. She was looking forward to her honeymoon on the Nile, a little concerned, a little amused, about Carl, who was such a fussy, American traveler, wondering how he would fare in the "wilds" of the Third World.

She never saw Ana again, but they had been in touch by mail; Ana was in New York part of May and June, and they were often on the phone. The marriage was not going to work. He was back to screwing around with Krall or maybe someone else, or maybe both, Ana revealed. Worse, there was a new woman, some jerk in Berlin named Rita Sartorius, who sent him cutesy postcards about dreaming how she "ends up in CA life oui sir" and gave him photographs of herself, which, as Natalia understood it, were nudes. Ana rummaging through Carl's things had garnered proof, making photocopies of the pictures, the postcards, telephone bills, check stubs—all safely stashed to use against him.

She was really pissed, she told Natalia, and had concocted a daredevil scheme to strike back. Natalia and she would catch Carl in the act. They would disguise themselves, Ana said, follow him, and photograph him together with this woman. The best fun of it all, the most satisfying part, would be to rip off their disguises so that he would know she had him cold, but, Ana said, "We would have to take off running because he would really blow his top." Natalia said, "Ana, you're crazy!" She wasn't sure if her friend really meant it or not, but suggested she hire a detective. That was when Ana went to Abramowitz about getting a divorce.

It was just before Labor Day when Natalia heard from Ana again. She was back in New York once more. The situation had deteriorated and there had been a disastrous trip to Spain in the meantime, Carl meeting Ana's mother for the first time and traveling with them. It was all a stressful charade, Ana said; luckily, her mother was so out of touch that she didn't see that they were not getting along. But she hadn't wanted to say anything to her. "You know my mother," she said, "she's wanted me to get married for so long and I felt that this would give her a lot of comfort now that I'm married and here it's not going to work out. It's going to be a big blow to her and she's been through so much."

Natalia told her to come out to Chicago for the Labor Day weekend jazz festival, but Ana said she had a lot of work to take care of and didn't want to leave. And then during the week, Natalia tried a couple of times to get hold of her, but she either wasn't in or they couldn't speak very long for one reason or another. So that Saturday night she called after midnight, knowing they were always up late, and she got Ana in New York.

Again, a great deal of this corresponded with what Ana had told Raquel, who now had other details to add. About the trip to Spain, for example; Raquel knew from her mother that she had not been completely taken in, but she had held her tongue so as not to interfere. She had also seen the material removed from Carl's apartment after it was searched by the police, and her sister's suspicions about still another New York woman in Carl's stable, while not corroborated, were not contradicted. Ana had been jealous of Nancy Haynes, the other tall-and-slim type whose paintings Carl had bought and hung in the living room, and the "infidelity records" taken by the police included notes from Haynes as well as Krall—though the content revealed nothing improper. The letter in the same group of papers that ended in "hugs and kisses" was from Sartorius, and it began with "Dear Arc-en-ciel," or "Rainbow" in French.

Both Raquel and Natalia recounted their final conversations with Ana, as they would again and again, but only much later would Natalia perceive something she believed Ana was trying to tell her so near to the end of her life, an incandescent flare sent up from her heart but had passed beyond the horizon of Natalia's imagination.

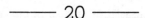 20 ⎯⎯

When Carl was courting Ana in Rome, he wrote her three love poems for her thirty-sixth birthday. Sometimes, usually to make up, he gave her nine roses and nine postcards; the search for higher forms of harmony was his way of love as well as art. Thirty-six, he told Ana in one of these birthday poems, is an exceptional number. It formed both a triangle and a square, which he drew making thirty-six little circles:

O

O O

O O O

O O O O

O O O O O

O O O O O O

O O O O O O O

O O O O O O O O

                 O O O O O O

                 O O O O O O

                 O O O O O O

                 O O O O O O

                 O O O O O O

                 O O O O O O

HAPPY BIRTHDAY ANA!

ALL MY LOVE @ 18NOV84

Another pattern poem spoke of Ana dreaming about Egypt on her birthday morning; in the third she was already there, and beyond his love, birthday wishes, and his @ sign, he wrote something that only she would fathom: "One of Ceasar's cats has false teeth."

Ana had had a dream that she was in Egypt and she was a cat with a huge pearl on her tail and Caesar was her master. She also had one false tooth; as for the misspelling of the great conqueror's name, that was Carl using his poet's license. Thirty-six, however, rare as it may be, was not her lucky number. She didn't live out that year and was finally cremated on Monday, September 16, Carl's fiftieth birthday. The dead hand of arcana was going to hold on for a long time.

WHENEVER HE ASKED someone to one of his vernissages in Rome, Gian Enzo Sperone always sent an invitation with a simple elegance unmistakably his. It would arrive in a hand-addressed envelope, the off-white rag-fiber card tucked inside that stated nothing more than the name of the artist whose work he would show, the gallery address, and the day the event would be held. If you were on Gian Enzo's invitation list, you knew the time. His season-opening invitation that year, which had gone out to perhaps a hundred people in Rome, read: *Martedì, 17 settembre 1985*, Carl Andre.

Modern Rome was to the art world what the whole outer world had once been to Imperial Rome: a provincial domain. True, a Roman school of neoexpressionist painting was making its mark on the New York scene, and the Pasta Factory lofts were turning out Soho-quality avant-garde work, but Romans were notorious noncollectors, and to run a gallery there without being well connected elsewhere was bound to be a passing labor of love. Of all the thirty or so dealers showing contemporary art in Rome—most of them in a narrow baroque quarter of grand palazzi between the Spanish Steps and the Piazza del Popolo—none was better connected than Gian Enzo. Above all, he was well placed in Soho as a partner in the Sperone Westwater Gallery on Greene Street, affording direct access to the New York market.

A man of about fifty and a native of Turin, Gian Enzo was a paradigm of the handsome, debonair northern Italian, the black hair and beard slightly silvered and carefully groomed, the radiant tan soaked up at Porto Ercole, and the kind of tailoring that allowed no wrinkling. One did not think of such men as being easily unnerved, but Gian Enzo was extremely anxious about this opening. By now, not one of his invitees would be unaware that Carl had been accused of murdering Ana.

The news, though it failed to interest the local press, had spread through Rome almost as quickly as it had in New York. Both Ana and Carl had been expected back last Thursday to be present at Carl's opening at Gian Enzo's; by then, all their Roman friends knew that this was not to be, and the shock had crossed the ocean untempered. In the two years that Ana had lived there, with Carl in and out countless times, the Andres had cut a striking figure at some of the

smartest places in town. On her own, Ana had staked out and con-
quered a certain part of Rome.

Gian Enzo was one of the last to see them together there. It had
been a pleasant mid-August evening just before they left. They had had
dinner in the piazza around the corner from their new apartment, and
he had been surprised to hear that Carl had paid a year's rent in
advance on a three-year lease. It seemed out of character for the Carl
he knew. The sculptor had spent his whole life opposing himself in
dress, manner, and every other way he could think of to being bourgeois, but the newly renovated apartment, though situated in one of
the choicest parts of the city, was quintessential middle class, the best
chrome and plastic with a view that money could buy. Gian Enzo
imagined that Carl was doing it all for Ana.

Since coming into his life, Ana had had a remarkable effect on Carl,
Gian Enzo thought. He had known Carl since the late sixties, when
he was with Rosemarie Castoro and then Angela Westwater, and the
contrast between then and now was sharp. In all the years he had
known him, Gian Enzo had never seen Carl as happy as when he was
with Ana. She had made him *docile;* she had tamed him.

Carl and he had never really been friends; rather, the way Gian Enzo
saw it, they were friendly "enemies," the merchant and the artist,
dealing man to man. He had given Carl his first show in Italy, in 1969,
and he, the merchant, was taken by the artist's noble ways—asking for
nothing, above discussing the pricing of his work, the outcome of the
sales, and the money due. When Gian Enzo had finally gone to him
and asked him how he wanted to be paid, Carl said, "Pay me in
copper." He wanted copper ingots, with which he planned to finance
the new work in his 1970 retrospective exhibition at the Guggenheim,
using a store of copper to barter with the suppliers of metal plates, the
material for the "carpets" he was using to cut space then. It was his
way to remain unbeholden to dealers and collectors eager to sponsor
a Guggenheim-class sculptor not yet thirty-five. That was the Carl he
knew, the man of simple kindnesses who, when he began to go with
Ana, had come to him in New York, wanting him to see her work. "You
should look at this," Carl said, "she's a real artist." And when Ana came
to live in Rome, he looked, but he wasn't sure. Not that he worried

about whether her work would sell; out on the cutting edge you didn't think that way. He had once sold a hole in the wall. You could never tell, so he had not said no to Ana, and she was like Carl, asking for nothing.

Now this tragedy. After that first show, Gian Enzo held a reception for Carl in his apartment in Turin. There was a *stregone* present among his guests, an old man who could read palms, and he took the artist's hand, looked down, and suddenly darkened. Carl had a *destino contro,* the old man said; ill fate awaited him; he was a *disgraziato,* a poor soul. Somehow, Gian Enzo felt, Ana's death had something to do with Carl's place on Mercer Street. The only time he had ever been there, some time ago, he had been struck by the way it was furnished, so sparely, the way you would expect it to be, antibourgeois. Gian Enzo had had a fever that day, a bad cold, and when Carl showed him the view out on the terrace, he got dizzy, wanting to sit down, but there was no chair, not one in the whole apartment. Something like that, but so much worse, must have happened to Ana. Carl would never lie. It was not in his nature, not the Carl he knew. It would be middle class, stooping.

They had spoken about the show during that last dinner in Rome. Carl had said nothing about the work, only that he would do the installation on his return. When the terrible news came, the invitations had already gone out, and Gian Enzo had no idea what to do with the raw materials Carl had selected and stored in the gallery warehouse, but it was unthinkable that the show would be canceled. It would have broken the continuity of the artist's career, Gian Enzo believed; it might even signify that Carl Andre was finished. Then Carl's jailhouse message detailing how to install his work was relayed from New York. To Gian Enzo, it was also a message of concurrence, a sign to go forward.

Fifty-three cubes of travertine—the most Roman material of them all—were stretched out on the gallery's terra-cotta floor. Following Carl's instructions to the letter, four groups of thirteen cubes were placed end to end, extending in a straight line from each of four opposite sides of the central fifty-third cube. When all the polished white cubes were so aligned, the arms reached across the entire gallery floor space to all four walls, forming an imposing *crux quadrata*, a perfectly symmetrical cross.

Consulting with another of Carl's dealers, Gian Enzo learned that the price would only be about six thousand dollars; if he couldn't sell it, he thought he might buy it himself.

ONE PERSON WHO was on Gian Enzo's invitation list was a freelance art critic named Edith Schloss, who covered the local art scene for the *International Herald Tribune*. An artist herself, she had spent the summer painting on the Italian Riviera and did not get back to Rome until a day or so before Carl's opening. She lived in an old palazzo in Via dell'Orso. It was a cluttered loft at the top of four or five flights of stairs where she did her writing and turned out naive pictures limned in bright and happy colors, sometimes sharing the space with her lover, avant-garde composer Alvin Curran. The invitation from Gian Enzo was in the stack of mail she went through on her return, and catching up with a friend brought the news that the sculptor was in the hands of the law, charged with killing his wife.

Edith, lined and gray and full of middle-European sorrows, was in her sixties, a refugee from Nazi Germany and a lifetime of rough edges, so she was not easily shocked. Sometimes, when people she knew died, she was pleased to see them go and not afraid to think so, but Ana's death made her sad. She had become fond of her in the two years Ana was in Rome, having changed her opinion completely from her initial dislike. Ana, to put it bluntly, was vulgar and pushy, but that became for Edith part of her appeal. She was so tough, yet, she discovered in moments when they were alone, so tender, treating Edith, who could and did review her work, like just another woman, not wanting anything from her.

With Carl it was the other way around. She recalled him being in Rome during the summer of 1973, long before he met Ana. He had installed a piece in an outdoor exhibition in the parking lot of the Villa Medici, and during the opening, a woman ran out of the villa, screaming that an "artist with a beard" had tried to rape her. The artist with the beard was Carl Andre. The police were called, but only to restore order, Carl denying wrongdoing and the woman backing away from her allegation as she regained her composure. To the onlookers it all seemed rather hysterical, Edith thought. Long ago, she herself had been chased around a studio by a famous artist and then as now found the situation somehow comical; in this case, she was amused by the "victim" having apparently concluded that because her "assailant" was bearded, he was an artist.

Since getting to know Carl with Ana, however, Edith had grown to feel uneasy in Carl's company. He was not a nice person. He was somehow threatening, in manner and appearance. It was the first time she had ever met someone in the art world who had what she thought of as a streak of violence, who made her a little bit scared. Whenever she and Alvin went to dinner with them, Carl and Ana got roaring drunk, and Carl was always so violent. One night, they went to Da Francesco, a pizzeria in Piazza del Fico, and it got to a point where he picked up a bowl of pasta, held it over Ana, and said, "If you don't shut up, I'm gonna smash this over your head!" He seemed very serious. Ana shut up. She, too, was a little bit scared of him, Edith thought, but she really loved him. She could tell from the way Ana spoke of him. New York was the standard by which Ana measured everything, and Carl was royalty there. Edith called him the Prince of New York and Ana the Little Orphan, and when she married him it was like she had married Prince Charming and would live happily ever after. Edith gave them both a big hug after the wedding. That was at the opening of their joint show in a Roman gallery on the day of their marriage, Carl in his custom-made overalls and a military greatcoat, Ana wearing a gray knit dress and pearls, overjoyed and absolutely glowing, all of Rome's art crowd wishing them happiness. When they came back from their honeymoon in Egypt, Edith got the impression that they had never left their cabin, since they couldn't really talk about what they saw. Ana brought back Egyptian earrings made of teeth.

When Edith and Alvin found out that Carl was going to exhibit a cross, they grimaced. There were certain openings Edith never failed to attend because you could count on seeing people you wanted to see and it saved you a dozen phone calls. An invitation from Gian Enzo Sperone meant that kind of opening, but this was a Sperone event to which she would not go. Alvin said he would "boycott." Nobody was going to go, she thought.

EIGHT O'CLOCK IN the evening, a little earlier or later, was the proper time to get to one of Gian Enzo's vernissages, and Carl's opening was no exception. Rome in the third week of September was, as almost always, sticky and hot, and the people who attended the show, after a glance at what lay on the floor, gathered in the narrow Via Pallacorda outside, seeking a breath of cooler air. Gian Enzo seemed nervous. Although some people had probably still not returned to the city, the crowd was thinner than usual. They stood on the street in the light cast through the gallery windows, speculating in hushed tones. There was hardly anyone there who had not known Carl and Ana, and a few had gotten to know at least Ana well. The sense of affliction and, to some, distaste, may have been heightened by that peculiar, passing stillness of the old part of town when the shops have rung down their shutters and the Roman night has yet to begin and you can hear the sound of footfalls on the cobbles.

Terrifying was the way it all felt to Daniela Ferraria, who, like everyone else, she thought, found Carl's travertine cross shocking, to say the least. She ran a small contemporary-art gallery a short walk away, often showing minimalists and dealing on one occasion as a go-between for Paula Cooper, who had wished to remain anonymous. Ana would drop in now and then, sometimes dragging Carl along. She was a little too forward for Daniela, even aggressive, but she was full of *grinta,* gutsy. The Andres had established themselves as a meteoric presence, dazzling the phlegmatic local scene with an unheard-of five well-received exhibitions in less than a year. Ana alone had been in three of them, plus the wedding-day show with Carl, which many of the people present now had also attended.

Among the group at the opening were three Romans who had been directly responsible for that suddenly unforgettable event only eight months ago to the day. One was a fine-arts printer named Romolo Bulla, who had spoken to Carl since his release from Rikers Island. He was standing on the street at Gian Enzo's with his sister Rosalba. The

two of them were the proprietors of a small printing plant they ran in
Via del Vantaggio a few blocks away, servicing artists and living above
the shop. The third person was Francesco Moschini, the dealer in
whose gallery, a couple of doors down from the Bullas, the gladdest-day
opening had been held.

Romolo Bulla had been the best man at the wedding that January
afternoon. He had known the couple only a short time, but it had all
been sweet. He met Ana first, on one of her sorties coming down in
her VW bug from the Academy hill. Both he and Rosalba took to her
at once. She was so full of life. People who didn't really know her
thought of her as aggressive, but maybe, Romolo felt, she used that
posture to cover up her timidity. She was never aggressive with him.

He knew Carl Andre by his work and reputation long before Ana
brought him around. One day, the three of them were together in the
print shop, and how it came up Romolo didn't remember, but Carl
said, "I'd like to do a book with you," and he was all for it. First it was
to be Carl alone, and then Ana, too; they were going to do it one side
Carl Andre one side Ana Mendieta, like those books you turn upside
down and it's another book, but in the end it was just a conventional
book of twenty lithographs, half Carl, half Ana, titled *Pietre e Foglie—
Stones and Leaves.* Carl had worked with one greased, little squarish
stone, turning it this way and that into the lithographic plates, making
orderly motifs that brought to mind the basalt Roman paving blocks
of the Appian Way. It didn't take him more than a few hours one
morning, from about eleven o'clock to one. Ana worked at it much
longer. She would come with a little bag full of leaves picked from
different plants at the Academy at different times of the year, working
off and on between March and October 1984 at a table in the Bulla
stamperia.

That was how they all became friends, despite a language problem.
Carl or Romolo would say something and Ana would translate. When
Carl was in town, they'd go out to dinner or—because Carl insisted on
paying the bill and that bothered Romolo—they would eat in upstairs,
Rosalba making pasta, Romolo pouring wine. Ana and Romolo would
go out alone when Carl wasn't around. Once, she got so drunk, he had
to put her in the VW and take her to her little house in the Academy's

backyard. She was angry at him for being so male and thinking she couldn't drive herself home, but he had had to do it.

It was in one of those three-way conversations in Italian and English (so he didn't know which of them it was) that he was asked to be best man at their wedding. They got married at the Campidoglio, the Capitol, "the head of the world, where the consuls and senators abode to govern the earth," it was written, and Romolo was there with his girlfriend Francesca and maybe five or six others. After the wedding ceremony, they went to Ana's cottage at the Academy for the reception and that evening to the opening, exhibiting the book at Moschini's gallery. They had printed forty copies, each numbered and signed by Ana and Carl. Carl had had the idea of putting forty numbered scraps of paper in a hat, each of them—Ana and Carl, Rosalba and Romolo— drawing ten, so that there would be a random division of the copies; not that number one was better than any other, although some people considered it more valuable. Romolo drew number one, one and two, to be precise. He didn't charge them for the printing, and they asked nothing from him. Moschini priced the books at $1,500 a copy, but didn't sell any. When the opening was over, the wedding party went to dinner at Il Galleone, the big-English-menu place in Piazza Cosimato, Carl's favorite. The bride and groom seemed so happy—just as they always did whenever Romolo saw them, never a hint of tension, and Carl was so loving toward her.

Strange "news" was reaching him now. Carl had a lover, an artist in New York. Ana had had a lover, a German, and he'd made her pregnant. Carl wanted to get rid of his lawyer and defend himself. Romolo spoke to Carl in New York as soon as he could get him on the phone. Someone translated. Carl said to Romolo, "Don't worry about a thing. Everything is OK."

—— 21 ——

Raquel had been letting her hair grow long all summer. She didn't look very much like her sister. She was taller and fairer, and though she was as easy as Ana with a smile, the keel of her temperament was more even, her look more contained. She had reddish brown hair that fell below her shoulders, but now she cut it short, almost crew-cut short, surrendering a part of her as her own way of mourning.

She wore a gray maternity dress to the memorial service on Park Avenue. The dress was made of cotton and had long sleeves and a pattern of little white flowers. The Mendietas and the Harringtons went in two cars, Raquel, her mother, and her aunt in one, Tom and the children in the other. They would be meeting Ani's friends for the first time. She had a horrible feeling in the pit of her stomach. Lucy Lippard, one of the three organizers, had called and said, "I don't know if Carl is going to come, but we thought we had to ask him, and you should expect that maybe he'll show up." So she told her mother and her aunt, to warn them, and they were all hoping it wouldn't happen.

Her mother was under still another strain. She had flown in from Iowa, where only yesterday she had buried her daughter's ashes in a narrow, uncharted piece of earth between her husband's grave at Cedar Memorial and the plot reserved for herself. Beyond everything else she had had to abide ungodly cremation and now this secular memorial added one more impiety to her tribulations.

Lucy had asked the family to get there early because some people would be coming straight from work and would probably be there before six o'clock. To oblige her, Raquel left a half-hour before Tom and was one of the first to arrive. When they went inside, Lucy introduced herself and said, "Carl is coming."

Raquel's mother turned ashen, and Raquel said, "We don't want to see Carl."

"You won't have to see him," said Lucy.

What to do about Carl had been uppermost in the minds of the organizers all day. When Lucy, Carolee, and Mary Miss and other volunteers had gotten there some hours earlier to set up the space, one of the women said she'd heard that Carl was indeed coming. Lucy remembers "freaking and thinking, 'Oh, my God, we're going to have them sitting across from each other here.'" Everyone fretted, wondering how to rearrange the layout to form a blind between the family and Carl. To their good fortune, the Salon Bolivar was a perfectly L-shaped room with two entrances and one short stretch of wall to hide behind. You came up a stately flight of stairs, and if you went through the secondary entrance, you would be in the smaller, horizontal part of the

L. If you stood or sat in the corner where it met the vertical part, you couldn't see who was standing or sitting just around the bend. This was the corner where they sat the family, because the truth was that Carl was already there, sitting completely alone just around the bend.

The room had been laid out with that "solution" in mind. Whatever was going on in the bigger part of the room was also happening in the smaller. More than a hundred chairs had been lined up here and there, two slide projectors were casting images of Ana's work on screens in both sections, and there was a table with flowers and candles for this side and that. There was a plenitude of wine. The setting was opulent: the ornate gold of Spanish colonial, the blue of the Angelika Kauff-manns on the Adam-style ceiling. The flooring was made of wood from the forests of Brazil. Until 1965, the mansion had been the headquarters of the Soviet Mission to the United Nations, and a developer, who had bought it that year from the Russians, was ten days into tearing it down when it was rescued by a Hispanic dowager.

For a while, nobody else seemed to be coming to the memorial, and there were few more people other than Carl sitting back to back with the Mendieta clan and the reception committee feeling and looking awful, trying to keep busy shuffling slides. Someone came up to the family and told them where Carl was and asked if they cared to say anything to him. No, they did not. Each of the three organizers, aware of the threat of disturbance that Carl's presence posed, had agreed to keep their eyes peeled in different directions. Lucy's job was seeing to Carl, and when she discovered that there were two reporters present, she asked them to leave, but they refused. Lucy grew angry and an argument ensued. Eventually, they left.

Another early arrival was Lowery Sims, the curator at the Met who had bought Ana's drawings. There had been a last-minute scramble when it was discovered that no one seemed to have very many slides of Ana's work. Carl in fact had brought some of his, but Lowery had an up-to-date collection that saved the day. The moment she walked in, she sensed that the room was somehow tensely drawn; when one of Ana's friends, painter Juan Gonzalez, rushed up to her, saying, "Carl's here," to her utter astonishment, she understood why, wondering where it might lead.

Suddenly, people began arriving in droves. Marsha Pels found the atmosphere strangely irreverent. "All the art-world people were talking to the art-world people. It was like an opening. Everyone was networking. Mary [Miss] came up to me and said, 'Hi, how are you doing?' I said, 'Not too well, Mary.' . . . It was like a real art gathering, and the family was way off in a corner, and no one was talking to them. My main reason for being there was to meet Ana's family, so I went over and introduced myself to her sister and her mother. And then I kind of stood by myself. I was not making the scene. I was just in my own turbulent world."

To her art-world friends, the ethnic part of Ana's life was a piquant slice of Latino exotica, and many of her Hispanic friends had been deeply offended not only by the peremptory choice of the "CIA" as the place for the memorial but by what some of them perceived as a racist slight. Many had been simply overlooked when it came to the invitations, and others refused to come. Ruby Rich, though not Hispanic herself, spoke Spanish fluently and was one of the few who moved easily in both circles. She was as irked as anyone else when she returned to New York and found out about the arrangements, but she had been on the phone since, trying to get as many of Ana's Hispanic friends to come as possible, trying, she hoped, to make some difference in the way the service would unfold. Now her efforts were paying off. The Cubans came with a record player, putting on records of the old Afro-Cuban music that Ana used to dance to often late into the night. Unless you knew this part of Ana and spoke with her in Spanish, some would say, you didn't really know Ana. Others came with mixed flowers, individual compositions expressing different kinds of affection.

The people were suddenly overflowing out into the hallway and down the staircase, three hundred, perhaps three hundred and fifty people jamming every corner except one, Carl's. This moment of coming together was so inflamed by burning sorrow and rage that memories would bend instantly and grotesquely, like concrete and steel in a meltdown. Yet there were some episodes, refracted, to be sure, by the eye of the beholder, that would be recoverable.

No one would forget the sight of Carl. Sheathed in his coveralls, he sat against a wall, brooding on a gilded chair, comforted now by an artist named Brenda Miller. Miller had been his disciple and lover, and like many of the women who had loved him, she remained at his side. Some would go up to him and offer their hand in consolation, but more would look away, and some would whisper *he came with his girlfriend.* Word that Ana had discovered other women and that Carl had never called the family was widespread by now. Perhaps because Ana's friends attending the memorial far outnumbered his, people had hollowed out a void around him. While there was standing room only, he sat alone with Brenda Miller in a row of empty chairs.

Carolee had taken on the task of keeping a watch on the people who she sensed were ready to bite and claw, and at this point she began to spot simmering trouble. "There was a group of women," she would later recall, "who just wanted Carl not to be there. They were ready to tear him to pieces. They said, 'The murderer has dared to appear here.' They said it to each other, but loud. . . . Yeah, it got like a little village in a foreign country, you know, with local justice about to be enacted. I tried to calm that down, move people around a little bit."

This was not one woman's impression. "The thing that amazed me," Lowery Sims recalls, "was that there was a moment where there might have been some kind of explosion because it was a situation that had a heavy feminist take on it, and I could think of similar situations where there would have been a confrontation. . . . I was really blown away that he was there. I said, Wow! And a lot of other people felt that way, too."

"There was a lot of tension," says Mary Perot Nichols. "Carl sat in one corner with only about three people speaking to him, and everybody else was on the other side of the room. I was waiting for somebody to go up and swat him or something."

Artist Ann Minich remembers it this way:

His girlfriend . . . would walk across the room and get him coffee, or whatever it was, and she would bring it back, and he sat like a bump in this place, and he was like a specter. He sat over in the corner and a lot of people—he's a very powerful man—went over and said how they felt very bad for him, and for the others, it was probably a little hard to take. There were women, for instance, who were considered feminists who were rushing to his comfort.

This is all my cynical side or all my something but the feeling was, let's not make an enemy of this man. And, yes, I had a real sense of anger at this woman, because here she was with this power—she was such a beautiful, absolutely gorgeous woman, bright, motivated, talented—and she put herself on the tracks this way and got run over.

Critic John Perreault, a longtime friend of Ana's, observed it from another perspective. He was in the overflow with his friend Jeff Weinstein of *The Village Voice*.

We just stood in the back. I was leaning on the staircase. I felt very uncomfortable. I didn't have my art-opening hat on, and far too many people for me were behaving as if it was an art opening. I mean, nobody actually pushed an invitation on me, but there was that feeling that this is an art-world event, not an event about mourning. And then I got a glimpse of Carl, who was sitting in the main room, where the chairs were. And I just felt nauseous and sick and angry and I couldn't go into that room. I thought it was in very poor taste for him to show, incredible bad taste that he was there in the same room with the family, who for whatever reason blamed him for it. It was really unfair to them to have to be with the man who they thought was the murderer of their daughter.

There were cooler heads, of course. Painter Leon Golub, with his wife, Nancy Spero, an artist, too, had been to dinner with Carl and Ana two nights before her death. The Golubs had known Carl since the sixties, and Nancy, feeling rather uneasy about it now, had introduced him to Ana. She sensed that people were very uncomfortable about Carl being there, but Leon saw it differently: "He carried himself with quiet demeanor. People were very polite. They were aware of him, but they didn't make a big thing of turning heads. It was like he was just one amongst the others. There was nothing special. People tried very hard not to notice him. We did, too. I tried very hard not to stare. But we did nod hello."

The organizers had an agenda and moved it along. Someone felt that the family was being lost in the "back room," and they were asked to go into the larger part of the L. "You can't sit here because nobody knows you're here," Raquel remembers being told. Overwhelmed by the press of so many people, the event was little more than a blur to her by now, and her mother and aunt and Tom and the children were faring no better. They rose and followed along blindly, coming out from their place around the corner, knowing without looking that they were being ushered past Carl, and seeing him anyway from the corners of their eyes sitting with this woman, this *girlfriend.* At last they landed in a row of chairs placed as far away from him as space would allow.

None of the organizers were sure about who did what to get the service going, but one of them, either Carolee or Mary Miss, explained to the gathering that everyone was there to remember Ana and to build that remembrance together, "to consecrate our feelings about Ana and to say whatever you are moved to say." Raquel was then called upon and asked if she wished to speak first.

"Well," she said, her heart racing, "I have some poetry of Ana's that I'd like to read."

There was a lectern in the center of the main part of the room. Raquel, sitting now in the right angle at the top of the L, approached it, her head turned away from Carl, sensing him close by, catching sight of him *right there.* She read a poem she had found among her sister's papers at Sixth Avenue. Ana had written it four years earlier, some months after returning from a trip to Cuba she had made with Carl. Raquel looked out at her audience. Full, full, packed full, she thought, feeling she didn't know what was going on, reading the words.

> Pain of Cuba
> body I am
> my orphanhood I live.

> In Cuba when you die
> the earth that covers us
> Speaks.

> But here,
> covered by the earth whose prisoner I am
> I feel death palpitating underneath
> the earth.
>
> And so,
> as my whole being is filled with want of Cuba
> I go on to make my mark upon the earth,
> to go on is victory.

To some, it sounded like a cry for justice, and when the floor was thrown open, so were the valves of passion. No record was made of what was said, and people who spoke would be unable (or in a few cases unwilling) to recall their words. Indeed, some—Marsha Pels and Nancy Spero, for example—would in all sincerity have no recollection of having spoken at all, while others would be almost certain they had. What many would agree on, however, was that all of the issues that would become part of this case stirred here for the first time: justice and the absence thereof, power and its abuse, race and gender and who holds sway over whom, all of those wicked, malodorous little no-nos, little because they were kept stunted under a sanitizing sand of proscription, that would surface, reek, divide, haunt, and in the end reshape Ana's world.

Some people couldn't stand it. Ted Victoria, one of Ana's oldest artist friends, was one of them. He had known her in Iowa and later in New York, where he had helped her furnish her first apartment. She would jog to his loft on Greene Street to cook him a meal and cut his hair. Like many who came to the memorial, he was stunned and left somewhat incredulous by the size of the turnout, particularly the large number of Hispanics, friends of Ana's he was surprised he knew nothing about, but he certainly knew many of the people present.

It was funny, I was sitting there, and these people would get up and say things and I was thinking Ana used to call her "bitch," and then somebody else, and I was thinking, Ana hated her. One of the things I didn't like about it is that some of the Latinos turned it into a very political thing, and I felt that was wrong to do. I remember this one guy, I didn't know who he was, and he gets up and says, "I was like a little brother to Ana," and then he started talking about how difficult it was for Latinos to make it in the art world. I thought it was bullshit and I walked out after that, and I saw Larry Weiner walk out, too.

In the beginning there were some people who got up, Lucy, and others, who said some very real things, very poignant, very nice things about Ana. I had something I was going to say. It was kind of neat. The night before Ana left for Rome for her Prix de Rome, I gave her a big party and all her friends came, and she wore this sequined dress, this tight, tight, tight old dress with these pink sequins that she found somewhere. She had this cigarette holder and she was dancing till three o'clock in the morning. And it was strange that even two years after that party, every once in a while I'd find sequins on the floor from all that dancing. But there are people in the art world that can take anything and veer it, and all these people got up and said, "I'm Ana's best friend"—"I'm Ana's little brother"—"I'm Ana's big sister." Christ, this Ana knew a few people! No wonder every time I called her, her line was busy. So when this guy got up and started talking like that, I just walked out.

There was a feeling shared by some of the inner circle that there were outsiders present, some of them interlopers who had come to be seen, for whom being there was being there on business, some of them art-world curiosity seekers who spent their Saturdays in Soho and had come so that they could talk about it for the rest of their lives. That was only one way of seeing it, however. "It was amazing to me what a wide swath she had cut through the art world," Lowery Sims says. "I also got the feeling that they didn't come because it was a scene. They came because they cared about Ana or they cared about what she represented as a person."

Ann Minich was decidedly one of these last mourners. She was attentive to the substance of what was being said: "People would come up into this area and speak. It wasn't only women, but the effort itself was very female oriented. There were people making a huge amount about Ana's involvement with Third World women and issues like that. You got a real sense of how these women were willing to pull behind her."

Lowery remembers what she said:

I got up and started talking about seeing Ana so periodically and how you came to measure the year because she always showed up about the same time. So it was like this kind of welcome, rhythmic thing like the return of the birds or something. I was just sort of thinking out loud about how this time next year I'd be sitting there waiting for her to show up and she wouldn't be coming, and I couldn't even finish because all of a sudden I just broke down and cried. I really couldn't continue. So some friends sort of helped me and some other people got up.

Ann Minich continues:

Some of it was very emotional, but the general tone was really, this woman was positive, this woman was up, this woman was working. There were a couple of people, a couple of women, who blew it. They got up and made long impassioned speeches that would have been better not made, but apparently most people had, whether they talked to each other or not, agreed that there was no way this lady committed suicide; this was certainly the overriding thing. It came out that Ana was a difficult person, but it gave the thing a reality. In other words, we were not memorializing a saint who was being assumed into heaven.

The family—even Raquel—were hearing things about Ana they had never known, and some things, especially her leftist Cuban politics, they didn't believe were really true. In spite of it all, they were profoundly moved.

All those hundreds of people, Raquel thought, it showed how they cared, how Ani had touched so many lives in one way or another strongly enough to make them come and pay some kind of homage to her. That felt good, and her mother, though never losing sight of Carl in his corner, felt real good, too, glad that she had come. Tom, who would sit with Ani in the kitchen in Rockland County arguing himself blue about some of her opinions he didn't care for, saw now that, like him, so many of her friends respected and admired her just the way she was, and he was very proud.

Suddenly, three or four hours had gone by, and after Raquel had read some more of Ana's writings, it was over, people getting up and waiting for a turn to embrace her and her mother. Carl got up, too, gathering his things, Brenda Miller coming down to the crowded side of the room, working the waiting line, saying, "Don't you want to say hello to Carl?" Shortly afterward, when some people had said hello to Carl, he slipped out in silence.

Many of those obliquely focused eyes that had tried so hard not to stare, diverted in wonder of what he was thinking and what he alone knew, didn't even see him go.

 22

The community undergoing this ordeal was small. If there were 350 people at the Park Avenue memorial, it was a congregation of probably more than 10 percent of the entire New York contingent of avant-garde artists, dealers, critics, curators, and collectors. The New Yorkers accounted for about a quarter of the entire contemporary art establishment—an extended cultural kinship made up, for the most part, of intensely serious but fun-loving and glamour-hungry urbanites dwelling in less than a dozen hip, fat cities of the Western world.

These were people, apart from the collectors, who usually lived and worked together, ascribing in varying degrees to beliefs in ever more highly rarefied doctrines while maintaining a fiercely individualistic and competitive manner. Year after year, conforming to a rigid, hierarchical order, they created, produced, and marketed a time-honored product, making minor style changes more or less annually and a radical restyling every five years or so—a small line of merchandise whose aesthetic and

economic value was, in spite of constant outside scrutiny and fascina-
tion, as hard to comprehend as was the seemingly nonconformist life-
styles of the creators.

Critic Harold Rosenberg, laying out what he saw as the profound art
crisis of his epoch in a 1973 essay, complained that the nature of art
had become uncertain. "No one can say with assurance," he wrote,
"what a work of art is—or, more important, what is not a work of art.
Where an art object is still present, as in painting, it is what I have
called an anxious object: it does not know whether it is a masterpiece
or junk."

With the radical restyling of the early eighties and the spectacular
rise of the neoexpressionists, any hope of comprehending which art was
and which art wasn't good for your soul without receiving the faith and
communion of art-establishment doctrine was a hope against hope.
The anxious art object, if ever indeed it had been, was anxious no more;
the anxiety was all in the beholder, which was what made the art world
turn.

The present hub of this industrious and rather devout society lay in
the paved lowland between the skyscrapers of commercial midtown
rising to the north and the skyscrapers of the higher commerce in the
financial district at the south neck of Manhattan Island. Long before
its discovery by artists in their endless quest for north-lit lebensraum,
it had been named SoHo by bureaucratic planners as their acronym for
a forty-three-block light-manufacturing area, the South Houston district. Soho, and its satellite community north of Houston Street,
dubbed NoHo, was now a rezoned entity unto itself—the upper case
H's dying hard but dying. It had taken shape only in recent years in
a climate of political turmoil and explosive growth in the art, real estate,
and stock markets. By 1985, it had a resident population of about
forty-five hundred, mostly certifiable denizens of the art world.

The producing class of these people, the artists, was regulated by a
kind of oligarchy with a few hallowed dealers on high. Class, however,
was not the operative word to describe the system. The contemporary
art world, in spite of its ceaseless, spellbinding tango with bohemia,
tangoed no place else but in one of the better-appointed ballrooms of
the middle class, to which it grudgingly belonged. Few other human

endeavors have gone so far to feign aloofness while spending so much energy in educating the manners, easing the stress, warming the hearts, brightening the environment, guarding the heritage, protecting the future, abiding the caprice, stroking the conscience, feeding the fantasy, sharing the dreams, and consuming every crumb of largess of the object of its disdain.

Barbara Rose remembers the day in the late fifties when Carl threw off his tie and resigned from the middle class, and it was not too long afterward that he began to call himself an artworker, dress accordingly, and conspire in the back room of Paula Cooper's gallery to unite and overthrow the art world. But Carl, along with his and the next generation, and unlike the one before them, would forever owe the wellness of his being to the latter-day bourgeoisie.

The flight from the pure bohemia of, say, Greenwich Village in the earlier part of the century is another story, probably having a chapter in which those genuinely bleeding hearts making art for art's sake, who found spiritual emancipation in the crucible of a marvelous hatred of the middle class, suddenly began to turn a profit. In any case, by the early eighties, the peace treaty between the avant-garde, or what little was left of it, and the two-hundred-year-old archenemy had been signed, framed, and all but hung in every gallery for easy viewing.

In an astonishingly short span of time, from the midseventies and the mideighties, many malnourished artists, with Winsor and Newton paint caked in their ponytails and beards, who hadn't been able to move a single sample of their oeuvre out of their lofts and *still* couldn't, suddenly found themselves with half-a-million-dollars' worth of mortgage-free real estate to protect. For some, seeing the cold stare of rejection in a different, who-needs-this-crap light, it turned out be a first-class ticket back to the comforts of middle America, where a man and his oeuvre and a half-million in the bank could absolutely count on being judged more kindly. For others, especially the more successful artists—some of them holding deeds to entire loft buildings that were now being written up and pictured in the trend-watching media—the emergence of Soho had transformed them into entrepreneurial landlords. Still others, the most successful, some with waiting lists for their work—whether they had bought into a building or not (Carl apparently being one of the rare ones who hadn't)—the boom and the neomania in the Soho-generated art market made them rich and famous whether they liked it or not, though they all grew to like it in their own, newsmaking ways.

Success and failure, the process by which a work of art was given credibility, was, however, firmly if not entirely in the hands of the managers, and the manager of managers was the dealer. It was he or she who imparted the breath of life without which there was nothing but a long, blue oblivion lying somewhere over the mainstream. From Paula Cooper to Mary Boone, from Leo Castelli to Joe Helman, the dealer, screening or screening the screenings of the slides or the actual work of hundreds of unknown artists each month, had by default become the arbiter of what was a masterpiece and what was junk and where to consign everything in between. The art critics, the museum curators, and the art bureaucrats holding the governmental purse strings had long ago chosen the comfort of the clubhouse from which they could watch the dealers' latest workouts to better tout whom to back.

Dealers who did not have an aesthetic sixth sense would soon be using the standard set to hunt for a new line of work, but what they were looking for in all that constant sifting was not merely a new imagery but a new ism, something packageable as a new movement, and in its highest form, The New Art of the Zeitgeist. It was simply good business sense to work toward a consensus, which inspired confidence in collectors, attracted media attention, and roused the ichor of the critics and the museums.

There were very precise tactics to develop this strategy, and they were particularly effective in the more powerful galleries. A minor common tendency discerned in the work of three or four artists could be encouraged, nurtured, given an original but not too original name (as in postminimalism), exhibited, hyped, and finally parlayed, as lesser dealers, who were the first to prick up to what was happening and could be counted on to be eager to get in early, drew their own artists into the "ground swell." The artists who didn't join in were separated by a cataract, and before you knew it, everybody was doing it, whatever *it* was, some more ingeniously than others, and one day you woke up and saw it in your copy of *People* and the *New York Times*, geniuses and all.

The unmentionable strategies and tactics, often brutal but always impersonal, served an unmentionable purpose. Thousands dreamed of glory, but the new market was structured so that only a few artists from each new movement could rise to the top.

The conservatism of the critics, museums, and foundations had given the collector the Medicean privilege of bestowing legitimacy on the new art. By the agency of the dealer's first touch, the avant-garde artist was certified as collectible by the vanguard of the middle class. But the collector, too, had first to be anointed by the dealer. The dealer advancing the new art (who was almost always a collector, too) was engaged in nothing less than unregulated, unmonitored, and perfectly legal market fixing, and his or her major collectors, knowing the wink of insider trading when they saw it were given the chance to buy first, while everyone else queued up. Smart collectors did not have to be told that they, too, had an interest in subscribing to the consensus and promoting their dealer's new art among their fellow collectors, with whom they often socialized. The new, unknown collector, drawn from the new rich and often as ignorant of art as of the art business, was automatically shunted to the less profitable end of the line.

Why collectors, who came forward with staggering sums of money, went in for this treatment was easily explained, though not often in polite company. Robert Hughes has cast it in vivid terms. "There is a crack of doubt in the soul of every collector," he says. "In it lurks the basilisk whose gaze paralyzes taste: the fear that today's klutz may turn out to be tomorrow's Picasso. Thus nothing except the manifestly out-of-date can be rejected with impunity."

Nevertheless, everything about the art world—except for one startling difference—was not greatly dissimilar from the American way of business, especially in the field of cultural activity. Broadway had its courtly angels, Hollywood had its modern-day moguls, and market manipulation, price fixing, kickbacks, skimming, and tax sheltering did not originate in Soho, even though they were practiced there. But unlike the stage, film, publishing, broadcasting, music, records, video, sports, advertising, cabaret, and sidewalk-fiddling, the public—the tens of millions of people who spent tens of billions of dollars every year on whatever someone could dream up to get them out of the house—had virtually no say about art.

The unregulated art world was its own world, a tight, elite world that did not depend on public acceptance for its existence. Popular culture gave us James Dean, the Beatles, Pete Rose, Bill Cosby, and the enchanted legion of others who earned, as they had to, the public seal approval a thousand times over—principally for interpreting popular taste shiningly and giving life to people's dreams. But when Leo Castelli gave us pop artists Jasper Johns, Robert Rauschenberg, Roy Lichtenstein, Claes Oldenburg, and Andy Warhol (whose work, by the way, was said to be the apotheosis of popular culture), the public merely scratched its head, bought a few posters and T-shirts to alleviate anxiety, and changed the channel. This was just fine with the art establishment, as it would be for any other enterprise that never had to worry about being held accountable to the public.

With a hundred collectors literally begging to pay hundreds of thousands of dollars for admission to the salon, who needed kibitzing from the unwashed, unenlightened public? The collector who, on the day the news of Carl's arrest hit the stands, called a curator at the Museum of Modern Art and asked, "Should I buy or sell?" was either very nouveau or incorrigibly naive. The new art was made like the old art of illuminated manuscripts, monastically, ecclesiastically, hermetically, beyond the purview of the vulgar laity that couldn't tell the difference between a solid black painting by Ad Rheinhardt and a solid black painting by Frank Stella, that couldn't tell a Carl Andre from a row of bricks. A movie star, a literary lion, or a football idol could claim his due in fame, money, and beautiful lovers, but he claimed it by the grace of his public and one false move in performance or personal conduct could send him to the Sheol of where-are-they-now. But the hero-artists were ordained by their own kind, announced by a herald to the outside, and, by the grace of the lords of West Broadway, given an irrevocable license to stray.

This fundamental difference had clearly negative consequences. Like most closed societies, the art world lagged when it came to fair play. The establishment described thus far—the makers, exhibitors, promulgators, and consumers of the new art—was overwhelmingly male, white and Anglo-European and was a jealous guardian of power, privacy, and privilege. Wearing a politically liberal label in all the major issues since the sixties had not driven out the unreconstructible gremlins of elitism, sexism, and racism, though it had taught them to keep their mouths shut. Women artists and women in the art field, putting up and sustaining the usual frustrating struggle, had made advances in the seventies and early eighties, but the statistics continually showed them trailing far behind their female counterparts in national trends and in some instances falling back. Blacks, Hispanics, and other minorities, despite their own battles, were in more outlying and dimmer regions, circling somewhere around Pluto. There was in the end a Frank Lloyd Wrightish, Solomon Guggenheimish spiral paved with the slippery, moss-covered, nasty-going stones of status. It separated one part of the art world from another. One was Carl's part, one was Ana's, but they were all in it together.

Insiders, as insiders always do, saw their world through different eyes. Many of them would agree that the art establishment was run in grand old-boy fashion, women players notwithstanding, but they rarely failed to fall in with the old boys and girls themselves in taking umbrage whenever "outsiders" like Tom Wolfe and Robert Hughes came downtown to poke fun at their foibles. When the *New York Review of Books* published Hughes's "The Sohoiad; or, The Masque of Art, A Satire in Heroic Couplets Drawn from Life" in 1984, he flogged the five estates of the art world—artists, dealers, critics, curators, and collectors—with equal Swiftian derision. Soho was the playhouse where the mummers of greed, fraud, and hype performed their masques for a new aristocracy of "mild stockbrokers with blow-dried hair" and their ilk:

> Who are the men for whom this culture
>   burgeons?
> Tanned regiments of well-shrunk *Dental*
>   Surgeons.

Soho, to be sure, was not amused. Hughes's lampoon was seen, as insiders often view effective criticism, as promoting stereotypes, debasing genuine artists, and servicing the fancies of outsiders who like to feel superior to things they do not understand. The progressive wing of the art community preferred to raise the banner of its own twenty-year war against art as a precious object to be bought and sold in a marketplace. They looked back at the seminal minimalists who refused by self-definition to make such an accommodation and spawned object-free conceptualism, unmovable earthworks, ephemeral performance and body art, and an egg-throwing, Tampax-ripping radical movement that was tearing down the barricades of prejudice. If the art world was currently being ravaged and disgraced by a few fashion-conscious hucksters and flash-in-the-pan neos, it was far better to rally around the movement than to cast disdain on the entire culture. The insiders, behaving once again the insider way, saw the best chance for change and renewal as coming not from the dithyrambs written on the outside looking in but from hard and honest work within the system. Here they were probably at least half right.

A system like that, however, structurally insular and emotionally sodden by neurotic feelings that it could not be understood by outsiders and would therefore remain misunderstood forever, inevitably grew more and more distrustful and suspicious of the Other—the art world's name for anything lying beyond the epicenter. This, in any situation, had to be an unsalutary predicament; in moments of particular stress, it made it dangerously easy for the masters of the house to pull in the shutters and putty up the cracks in the doors.

—— 23 ——

The assistant district attorney stood in the pit of one of the little amphitheaters in the back ways of the Tombs, shielded from the eyes of the public. She addressed the grand jury.

"[This] is not a trial presentation," Martha Bashford said. "Your duty, therefore, is to make a decision as to whether or not an individual should be charged with an offense, not [if he] is guilty of that offense beyond a reasonable doubt. The finding of an indictment, if that is what you find, is a finding that there is sufficient evidence to continue the case in the criminal justice system. It is a step toward the trial of any defendant."

That step had begun on Monday, September 23, with the first chill of autumn in the air. While Gerry Rosen had savored the idea of advising Carl to swear in and bare his soul before the grand jury, there was never any question in Jack Hoffinger's mind about allowing him to get anywhere near the opposing team's ballpark, though he didn't let on until he had to. Whenever a defendant took the stand, Hoffinger knew and taught every day, there was a subtle shift in the burden of proof. Even a defendant with an airtight alibi was more often than not disbelieved. All the prosecutor had to do was ask the jury whether the defendant had an interest in lying, and the jury could only conclude yes. Louis Nizer, the "great trial lawyer," once called and asked if he thought his defendant should take the stand, and Hoffinger gave him his rule of thumb: each case was different, "you gotta ask yourself whether this testimony puts me ahead or sets me back."

Bashford wanted the grand jury to consider indicting Carl on two counts: one, that he had intended to kill Ana, and two, that acting with "depraved indifference" to human life, he had "recklessly engaged in conduct" that put her at risk and caused her to die. Either count carried with it the charge of murder in the second degree. The depraved-indifference and reckless-conduct phrases were the standard formulations of the second count.

Since a 1977 decision eliminating the death penalty in New York State, second-degree murder was the state's most serious crime, a class-A1 felony. Conviction, even on the depraved-indifference count alone, brought a mandatory maximum sentence of life imprisonment and mandatory minimum of fifteen years. The minimum sentence excluded any possibility of a reduction in time served; there was no going home for good behavior.

Over the past few days, Bashford had "prepped" her witnesses. It was, of course, unlawful to tell your witness what to say, and Bashford was a conscientious prepper, which was the sensible way to be; a witness was not necessarily on your side, and though the sessions were unmonitored, he or she could one day be turned by the opposition. Still, the old lawyer's saw about never asking a witness a question to which you didn't already know the answer had to be observed, and here was the place that was done. "This is the question I'm going to ask you," she would say and ask it, and if the answer were problematical—a wrong date, a non sequitur, a contradiction—she would prompt, "Are you sure?" This was also where witnesses learned to say phrases they had never spoken before, like "to the best of my recollection" and "yes, there came a time."

The so-called Fourth September–October 1985 Grand Jury of the County of New York heard Bashford's presentation of the case in installments. This was the custom in more complex cases, and the Andre case required five sessions spread over the next three weeks. The case of *The People v. Carl Andre* rode on the same train as those of *The People v. Wai Hong Leung,* aka "Big Hero," *The People v. Frank Mitchell,* dubbed the "short/tall" stabbing, and several other nefarious affairs of recent allegation.

Scolding Bashford at Carl's bail hearing, Judge Sayah had said that the grand jury was not a rubber stamp, but a more picturesque and better known epigram once uttered by Judge Sol Wachtler of the state court of appeals had it that a grand jury would "indict a ham sandwich" if that was what the prosecutor wanted. As usual, the truth lay somewhere between two dictums.

There was, however, something gladiatorial about the process. Twenty-three citizens served month-long terms—but only a majority needed to be present—sitting in secret sessions and thumbing up or thumbing down, but more often up, the performances of prosecutors tilting at rarely seen and always unarmed opponents. Nevertheless, the procedure, when it worked right, was the defendant's best protection against a crooked or overzealous prosecutor, and even when it worked wrong, there was ample recourse.

PURSUING HER STRATEGY of dismantling the suicide and accident hypotheses, leaving murder only, Bashford had assembled twelve witnesses. She was laboring under a handicap. One of her most important witnesses, Detective Finelli, was ill. There would be no trip to Rome, no more smoking either; a week before the grand jury met, he learned that he would have to undergo surgery for lung cancer. Detective Nieves would fill in, but Ron Finelli, who had spent all those first hours with Carl, was the old pro she had been counting on.

She tried to knock down suicide first, but here, too, she had been stymied. She had hoped to bring in one or two art-world authorities—selected from the foundations that had given, the museums that had bought, the critics who had sung—to testify to the indisputable: that Ana's career was thriving. But the authorities, or those to whom they were beholden, were among the people who were choosing and counseling silence, the higher up the more buttoned up. Although one did not easily say no to the D.A., none had said yes, preferring either to ignore messages received, refer her to someone "better suited," or be called out of town. A few authorities, choosing the better part of valor, used all three tactics.

Instead, Raquel's and Natalia's testimony regarding Ana's high spirits about her life and her art was backed up by three other persons, less for the details they added than for their status as relatively disinterested parties. Bashford summoned Joel Bernstein, the lawyer who had settled Ana's problems with her subtenant. He told the grand jury of Ana's forward-looking plans, hoping the apartment would go co-op, for one. Craig Vaughn, an officer of the Bank of New York, disclosed that on the last business day before her death, she had opened an account with a sizable deposit, $3,900, which seemed hardly the sort of thing one might worry about in one's final diurnal cycle of life.[1]

Following Vaughn's testimony, Bashford introduced a letter she had discovered only recently. Written in Ana's own hand about ten hours before her death, it was addressed and mailed to Los Angeles early Saturday evening, almost certainly when she went out to jog. It concerned a conversation she had had that afternoon with Al Nodal, who was in charge of her commission for the sculpture in MacArthur Park. He had solved some shipping problems that had been on her mind, and she wrote to thank him, glowing with happy detail about her project and all the things she planned to accomplish in the next few months, beginning as soon as she got back to Rome. She had signed it "Tropic-Ana," a signature she had taken to lately, reserving it for special friends.

Mopping up her assault on suicide, Bashford called Mark Coler, the neighbor in 34D. He not only recounted hearing the two heated arguments that final week, but he remembered a pertinent conversation he'd had with Ana. They were in the elevator remarking about it being "a long ride down," and when that led him to ask if she was afraid of flying, she revealed herself as being knowledgeable about the safety records of American and foreign airlines and thus very particular about the airlines she flew.

Bashford brought in a Cuban friend of Ana's, Modesto Torre, to testify about Ana's fear of heights. He related an incident in which she had been unable to look out at the view from his closed, fifth-floor window. Coupling this episode to the Crime Scene Unit's measurements of the bedroom window in 34E, with its chest-high sill and intruding radiator, Bashford argued that if Ana couldn't look out of a closed fifth-story window, what would she be doing behaving acrobatically on the brink of a wide open one on the thirty-fourth floor?

---

[1] In the same vein, two days earlier, she had gone to a dermatology center to have a minor skin growth (sebaceous hyperplasia) removed.

But what was most damning to any accident theory, the prosecutor pointed out, were the words of the defendant himself. Playing the 911 tape for the jurors, she underscored the part where Carl told the police operator that in the course of an argument she went to the bedroom, he "went after her," and "she went out of the window." He had thus cast himself as an eyewitness to what had happened and had not described what he saw as an accident but as the result of an act he called suicide.

Bashford, dutifully revealing Ana's 0.18 alcohol level, nevertheless asked the grand jury to reject any likelihood of an accidental fall as unreasonable.

This was one of at least two wholly circumstantial cases currently before the grand jury, and consequently, the jurors were given a lesson on the law of circumstantial evidence. Later, that famous but fuzzy phrase, *circumstantial evidence*, would prove to be so equally confounding to both Carl's friends and his enemies that many of them in both camps would equate it with no evidence at all. Experienced trial lawyers were well aware of the public's misconception about the nature of circumstantial evidence as opposed to direct testimony or so-called positive evidence. When it worked to your favor, you muddled it further; when you were on the side with the burden of proof, you hammered away, trying to correct it. Thus, here was the plain truth at the outset, and though it fell on the ears of the jurors only, any desk reference book states it more or less the same way.[2] It is a legal axiom that a well-connected chain of circumstantial evidence is equally as conclusive as the greatest array of positive evidence. Indeed, jurisprudence recognizes circumstantial evidence, which is the bulk of all evidence anyway, as potentially more powerful and always more objective than direct testimony, confessions of guilt and eyewitness accounts being notoriously unreliable. Finding the butler's fingerprints on the

---

[2] *Webster's Third New International Dictionary:* "circumstantial evidence *n:* evidence that tends to prove a fact in issue by proving other events or circumstances which according to the common experience of mankind are usu. or always attended by the fact in issue and that therefore affords a basis for a reasonable inference by the jury or court of the occurrence of the fact in issue."

murder weapon may be circumstantial, but it can travel a lot farther
in a court of law than someone with an interest in lying claiming to
have seen the butler do it.

By the time the jury received this bit of enlightenment, Bashford was
well into her explanation that Ana was pushed to her death, and since
Carl had made no claim that someone else was in the bedroom, she was
pointing her finger at him. The discrepancies in his stories were irrecon-
cilable. No matter which version he had offered, he was left stranded
with at minimum a ninety-minute gap in which Ana was still alive and
unaccounted for. These facts, as well as the scratches observed on his
body, the overturned chair at the foot of the disheveled bed, and the
chaotic bedroom, were attested to by Officers Connolly and Rodelli
and Detective Nieves. Ed Mojzis, the doorman, related his experience
of hearing a woman repeatedly crying "No" and pleading, "Don't."
But Bashford worked hardest at trying to establish a motive.

Raquel, taking the stand on the first day, and Natalia, testifying later,
were led by Bashford down the now familiar path of all they knew about
Ana believing Carl had betrayed their marriage and her plans to divorce
him. The prosecutor had gone over the details with them many times,
but in interviewing Natalia only days before the grand jury first met,
she had perceived something in Natalia's recollection of that last phone
call that seemed crucial to understanding the motive.

At a certain point in their postmidnight conversation, when Ana had
begun to vent her anger at Carl, Natalia grew concerned that she might
be carried away into saying something unwittingly that she would
regret. Natalia told her to speak in Spanish, and Ana did. But Ana
continued to speak about *divorcio* and hiring a *detective*, a word used
in both languages. Besides, Bashford reasoned, when you live with
someone who speaks Spanish, you pick up words, so he could easily have
known what was going on. Since the women's conversation had ended
with Natalia urging Ana to tell Carl what she had on him, Bashford
had become convinced that Ana had indeed done so. That, and not
some abstract discourse on the public exposure of their art, Bashford
believed, was what their last fight was all about, and he "went after her"
and "she went out of the window."

Little of Bashford's own working model of what had happened that night was revealed to the grand jury. Natalia's and Raquel's conversations with Ana remained hearsay under the law, and the only way they could be introduced was by way of the well-established state-of-mind exception to that law, in this case, as she explained to the grand jury, to show Ana's lack of suicidal behavior. According to Bashford, Ana collecting her evidence, consulting a divorce lawyer concerning her legal options, and wanting to hire a detective to build her case was a wholly positive reaction to her suspicions of Carl's infidelity. Far from portraying a depressed potential suicide, it completed a three-dimensional picture of a woman actively planning for her future. If it also helped the jurors understand what may have driven the defendant to murder, so much the better.

24

Against the advice of his attorneys, Carl was suddenly making an effort to establish contact with the family. Freed by counsel from testifying before the grand jury, he had spent part of the first day composing and posting a registered letter to Raquel. This had come after repeated attempts to call. The phone would ring in the little house in Spring Valley, and the mellow voice at the other end would say it was Carl and could he speak to Raquel.

Once or twice it was Raquel herself who had answered, but she had passed the phone to Tom, refusing to talk to Carl. Their lone encounter, in which he had given Tom three thousand dollars toward Ana's funeral, still rankled. Since then, she had remembered something Ana had said to her in the phone call the day before she died. It had returned to her in these words: "I have come to realize that Carl doesn't love me or anybody. He's never loved anybody. The only thing that he cares about is his money. And he feels that he can do anything to anyone as long as he repays them financially."

A question of a sizable amount of money, Carl's and Ana's, would arise later, but if money was what Carl had wanted to talk about now, he was having a hard time putting it across. Tom, from his earlier experience, his knowledge of the case, and Carl's ossified position of refusing to offer an explanation of what happened to Ana, had concluded that there could be no further dealings with his brother-in-law that would not be part of Carl's design to save his own skin. By now, the matter concerning Ana's estate had been settled, Carl having signed a more complete set of papers than before, which had been drawn up by Natalia's lawyer friend Gary Simon. Tom, when Carl had gotten him on the phone, had told him that Gary was now representing all of the family's interests and that in the future he should address himself to him.

In the latest call, Carl said he was not supposed to be revealing anything but he had information about Ana that the family didn't know.

"Fine," said Tom, his curiosity piqued but his resolve still firm, "give it to Gary and he'll give it to us."

And Carl said, "No, I have to give it to you."

And Tom said, "No, give it to Gary." Finally, he said he didn't want Carl to call anymore.

Now this registered letter. Raquel signed for it, looking at the envelope with a mixture of apprehension and some puzzlement. Carl had addressed it to "Raquel Mendieta c/o Harrington," which seemed more a letter to her mother than to her. The legal Raquel Mendieta was back in Iowa, but Raquel Harrington opened it anyway.

It read:

23 SEP 85

DEAR RAQUEL,

THE SORROW OF ANA'S DEATH IS HEAVY UPON ALL OF US. IT IS A GREAT TRAGEDY THAT A WOMAN WHO SO LOVED LIFE IS LOST. THE STATE HAS CHOSEN TO ADJUDICATE THE CAUSE OF HER DEATH. WE CAN DO NOTHING IN THAT MATTER BUT AWAIT JUDGMENT.

BUT THERE IS MUCH THAT MUST BE DONE TO HONOR ANA'S NAME, HER MEMORY, HER RICHLY PRODUCTIVE LIFE, & THE GREAT BODY OF CREATIVE WORKS WHICH SHE GAVE TO THE WORLD. THE ONLY CLEAR PURPOSE REMAINING TO ME IN MY LIFE IS TO SO HONOR ANA.

THERE IS NO QUESTION THAT ANY BENEFITS ACCRUING TO ANA'S ESTATE SHOULD BE ASSIGNED TO YOU. HOWEVER, I CANNOT WAIVE THE RESPONSIBILITIES WHICH INEVITABLY FALL UPON ME AS ANA'S

HUSBAND. FURTHERMORE, THE SKILLFUL REPRESENTATION OF AN
ARTIST'S LIFE WORK IS A VERY DIFFICULT & DELICATE MATTER.

I FEEL IT IS IMPERATIVE THAT WE MUST MEET TO SHARE OUR
SORROWS & TO DISCHARGE THE DUTIES THAT WE OWE TO ANA. BE
WELL

    Carl Andre

No matter how many times she read it, the letter remained ambiguous. The voice seemed addressed to her, but Carl, having signed the waivers, knew that the sole beneficiary of Ana's estate was her mother, so what kind of benefits was he talking about? Furthermore, Tom had already told Carl bluntly that the family, though no one presumed to know half as much as Carl did about art, wished to exercise complete control over its future exhibition. So what was he, with all this flowery stuff, up to now? Raquel wondered. With her mother's blessings, she turned the letter over to the D.A.

CARL HAD NO way of following the deliberations of the grand jury, and the uncertain days turned into weeks of waiting. He had moved back to Mercer Street. After the Deauville Hotel, he had gone to stay at Claes Oldenburg's Broome Street place on the west side, but only a few days later he went home to the mess trapped in that terrible moment when time stood still in 34E.

He had gotten an unlisted phone number, and he made a lot of calls and sent a lot of postcards to let people know his new number. For many, this would be the last time they would ever speak with or hear from him again.

The perversity of Carl's behavior following Ana's death was not yet at great issue in the community. The case being laid out before the grand jury was still secret, and, to the extent that some of it was afloat as rumor, people who knew or thought they knew Carl best and were accustomed to his quirks preached forbearance. With time and sympathy, they felt certain, he would find his way, and the whole truth of what had happened would be forthcoming from Carl himself.

There was something in Carl, an elixir of charisma and a certain constancy, that inspired faith, whether you liked him or not. Marsha Pels, who was decidedly among the latter, believing that she had long ago seen through the curtain of his wizardry and had found an "effete hypocrite" at the controls, had had that faith nonetheless, though by the time he had answered her letter of condolence, she felt taken in. "Just after it happened," Marsha says, "I felt oddly close to him, and I sent him a note saying that I was grieving and I felt very terrible for him. I believed that he was grieving, too. At that point I wasn't angry, because I thought that he would come through and say, 'Look, this is what happened.' I didn't realize what a complete asshole he was going to be, not to act the way a normal, decent human being would act."

Others located his persona in a higher region of his body, his mind as the altar of his art. Throughout the ranks of the community, few had failed to be impressed by the daring purity of the early minimalists, of which Carl's work had remained the purest of them all. To the paradox that Ana wouldn't jump and Carl wouldn't push, these people added, Carl, in any case, wouldn't lie.

Younger painter Christian Haub, who knew Carl and Ana, was one of these people. He had spotted Carl walking on Mercer Street a few days after Ana's death, and he surmised, from the way Carl looked back, that he would have been happier just to walk by, but Chris felt he had to cross the street and say something. He was choked with sadness by the time he got to Carl's side, and he could do nothing more than put his hand on Carl's shoulder, neither of them saying anything, walking it through. All Chris had thought of was that Carl had lost Ana, not about how. Because of the kind of art he did, Chris felt, because of the way he was, he expected Carl to present a plausible explanation. He expected that he'd get the truth, that if Carl had done it he'd say, "I did it. This is how it happened. Punish me. But it's not first-degree murder. It's like drunken driving. I'll take three to five years or whatever it is. I'm responsible, but I didn't set out to murder her."

Everyone waited for the revelation, some with fundamentalist devotion, some giving up, some giving up on Carl. Gian Enzo Sperone, in from Rome, was one of the very few who couldn't wait, perhaps because of the seasoned timber of their long man-to-man, merchant-artist dealing. He had brought his condolences when Carl was still at

Claes Oldenburg's. He hadn't sold Carl's travertine cross, and he hadn't decided whether he would buy it himself, but that was not what was on his mind. At a certain moment, he did what was a properly upper-middle-class Turinese thing to do: he simply asked him.

Did he remember the *stregone* who had read his palm long ago and had seen a terrible destiny waiting?

Carl didn't remember.

Did he remember what happened with Ana?

"I loved her," he would recall Carl saying. "It's impossible," meaning he would never have harmed her. Then he added: "But I was drunk."

That was enough for Gian Enzo. Carl would never lie.

OF ALL THE people who night after lengthening night yearned to know *what happened*, who stopped in their tracks to crane at the light burning late from that poignant window high above Waverly Place, rerunning Ana falling again and again (how many times must she have fallen!); of all those people, not many were as near to Carl and the hidden, fortress harmony of his mind as Lucy Lippard. She remembered becoming lovers. He had an apartment, or maybe it wasn't his apartment, over those columny buildings on Lafayette Street. She was writing about the dawning minimalists and their art whose time was coming, she and Barbara Rose, with whom she'd gone to Smith, but who was already known. Lucy was only just starting to write. It was 1964, a vital time. She was twenty-whatever, married to a minimalist, and Carl was one of them too, one of the first. It was something in the air, and a lot of people began to do this kind of work at the same time, and she was there, so excited to be sort of living in the art world, being in on the ground floor of this thing, which you hadn't known was a thing until everybody else picked it up, too. And Carl was every bit of this to Lucy: very charming, extremely articulate, very, very smart, very poetic, flamboyant, yet a very gentle, tender kind of person on one side.

But over the years, her marriage gone, Carl being with everybody in town, she'd come to know the other side, this other business, she would say, of Carl as the world's most obnoxious person, angry, vicious, verbally violent, an absolute horror, who, goading, sent you to the edge and could drive anybody to anything. Lucy put up with him, trying to deflate the truculence, because of the engaging complexity of it all, because of that sympathetic something about him that made her— even after she had fallen away—never stop loving him around some bend of her heart.

She was torn. She loved Ana, too, and Ana used to say to her when she'd be in from Rome and before going back, "Now, be nice to Carl, he wants to see you, have lunch with him, you know, he needs to see people." Ana was always making excuses for Carl's ridiculous behavior. She had a tremendous vitality to her. Sometimes she was obnoxious, too, the two of them just such a crazy combination. Lucy didn't ever think that relationship was a good idea. Years back, in fact, she had told somebody that it was a lousy idea, and when they broke up, Lucy thought, well, that's not so terrible. Then they got back together again, and Ana said Carl was just not adult enough to deal with this relation- ship, and Lucy thought, yeah, that's probably true. Sometimes they were lovey-dovey and sometimes they were nudging at each other, like all couples, except they drank more than most people in public so you got a little more view of what it was like when it was bad. But when it was good, you saw what that was like, too. It never occurred to Lucy that anything like this would happen—but she could just see the two of them putting each other through a certain amount of stuff.

Now, there were women who wanted to lynch Carl. If he hadn't done it, Ana would want her to be nice to him, but why wasn't he getting his act together, coming forward and telling *what happened?* Women, comrades in the movement, got angry at her, but she went on speaking to Carl, presuming his innocence until proved otherwise, which was simply the decent thing to do and to fight for as well. Down at *Heresies,* clashing with Ruby, she had used the force of her status to keep the troubles with Carl out of Ana's obituary. The collective, mostly women younger than she, went along, but Ruby challenged her. Ruby was furious. Ana had been a part of *Heresies,* she said. The magazine ought to be holding the line; instead, here was this wimpy obit.

"You can't put in anything," Lucy told Ruby and the rest of the collective, "because he hasn't been brought to trial."

"That's fine," said Ruby. "Then you put something in saying that Carl Andre has been charged with her murder. That's a statement of fact."

Lucy had it her way, but it was a hollow victory. She refused to condemn Carl because, she thought, if he didn't do it—and, maybe, even if he did—Ana would want her to be nice to him.

In all these years, she had never seen him get physical; she thought of him as a coward that way. But like everyone else, she was hearing the same crude stories racing around, and even before all this she had heard of Carl in Europe being hauled off drunk and abusive, maybe even hauled off by the cops. Nothing was impossible, she thought, and she wanted to know if those stories were true, but it all seemed out of character for the Carl she knew. Whether he did it or not, she felt, the Carl she knew was smart enough to know he was in trouble, like when you're a kid and you've sort of done something and you sort of haven't, but you figure you'd better lie about it because they might think you actually did. So maybe he wasn't going to tell, after all, and she would wake up in the middle of the night in her Prince Street loft seeing or having seen *what happened* in a hundred horribly different ways. Finally, though she dreaded the thought that she might become the person who was told, she asked him.

Did he know what happened that night?

"I don't want to know so much as I want to know what you know," Lucy said to Carl. "Because I think you're going to need to deal with that at some point—whatever went on."

And Carl, who looked a mess, said no, he just didn't know.

Lucy, like so many others, was unaware what a distance he had traveled since the dark morning of the 911 call.

THE NEW YORK galleries, kicking off the fall season in October with their customary hundred one-person-show openings, were the art-world bathhouses of social intercourse. This year, the habitués got sick there, and it spread, people getting sick of one another, men sick of women, whites sick of blacks, ins sick of outs, and vice versa. And a few men and women got sick of their own kind.

The closing months of the previous season, last spring, had seen one

sensational scandal involving a dealer and another high-profile, generally unfavorable story about a hero-minimalist. Both incidents had
broken through the membranes of the art world into the glare of *New
York Post,* Channel 5 publicity.

The scandal concerned the May arrest of Andrew Crispo, the forty-
year-old voguish-roguish uptown dealer who had recently volunteered
to help raise Carl's bail. Crispo had been accused of kidnapping, tortur-
ing, and sexually molesting a young man in his East Fifty-seventh
Street gallery and was a suspect in what even the *Times* was calling a
"sadomasochistic slaying" of another young man. Crispo was harming
the reputation of the whole art world in public, but he was as distant
from avant-garde Soho as Greenland. His case could never be more
than a passing bruise, and Soho was having as much fun as anyone else
reading about Crispo's rough-trade, Nazi-clothing, necrophilic night-
life. What had been far more disturbing that spring and much closer
to home was an unheard-of public outcry against one of Soho's own.

Early in March, a three-day federal hearing—artists were calling it
a Stalinist trial—was held in a packed lower Manhattan courtroom. On
"trial" was a massive piece of sculpture fashioned in the postminimalist
conceits of Richard Serra, a surly, egocentric, humorless, forty-five-
year-old art-world Olympian who always dressed in solid black. In 1981,
commissioned by the United States government, he had installed a
12-foot high, 120-foot long unmodeled expanse of steel in a public plaza
downtown in Foley Square. *Tilted Arc,* as the artist had named the
work, was instantly loathed by the very people whose lives it had been
meant to enrich, the thousands of civil servants employed in the lack-
luster forty-one-story building towering above it. The sculpture cut
through the plaza like a Berlin Wall, which was what it was predictably
nicknamed, and, predictably, it soon took on a patina of flaking rust,
graffiti, and, at the base, shades of man and dog. Before long, the least
grateful workers had circulated a petition to move it to another home,
and this had led to the public hearings.

The art world, collecting three times as many signatures as the civil
servants, flexed muscle, particularly the Carl Andre generation that had
overturned the postwar abstract expressionists and was now getting a
touch of paranoia about being displaced by the neoexpressionists of the

early eighties. Carl himself was traveling in Europe at the time, but the courtroom was crowded with other art stars and satellites, the Castellis and the Oldenburgs on one end and the two Gerrys—Rosen and Ordover—at the other, all trying to save America from every evil from the loss of artistic freedom to the loss of Richard Serra, who, claiming betrayal by his country, had threatened with Solzhenitsynian rancor to go into exile.

It was not, however, a great day for democracy. Claes Oldenburg, for one, came forward to denounce "vigilante-type" know-nothings who were trying to "override the opinions of better-qualified persons." Inevitable invidious comparisons to Philistines, witch-hunts, and book burning were dredged up, but that failed to impress anyone except Serra and the rest of the dredgers. There remained some thoughtful people in the art world who were wary of kicking the heroic sand of avant-garde art in the eyes of the mass media.

But for the most part, the freedom-fighting ex-artworkers of Soho, when it came down to it, were unable to distinguish a horde of Philistines from ordinary workers whose federal income taxes had gone toward paying Serra in the first place and whose minority testimony revealed the touching sincerity of their protest. They had simply grown fond of the uncluttered plaza as a place to have their lunch, read a book, and watch the lunchtime people going by, none of which could be enjoyed any longer. Shortly afterward, the government ruled in their favor, though the actual removal of the sculpture faced many additional hurdles. In the meantime, Serra, looking like a defiant refusenik, posed for *People,* saying he couldn't stay in a country that "wantonly and willfully destroys" his work. A month later, the Crispo story broke, so the rest of the art world and *People* had something hotter to follow.

The Serra affair, however, was infinitely more revealing. The entire singular exercise in town-hall debate demonstrated how alienated and insensitive a cultural activity such as the one conducted by the New York art establishment could become when it lived beyond the auditing powers of public approval.

THE RESTORATIVE AIR of summer in the Hamptons, on the Cape, and in the hills of Tuscany normally returned the art crowd dark of skin and light of heart, full of fresh, impatient ways to outclass the old and usher in the new. In Soho, by definition, nothing was as new as the new season, so Serra and Crispo would have been passé even without Carl and Ana. The rest of New York may have been talking about the discovery of the *Titanic*, the space walks off the shuttle, the new guy Gorbachev's first interview in the west, *The Mystery of Edwin Drood*, Yeager and Iacocca, but down in Soho, when you went to an opening, you talked about Carl and Ana and got mad doing it.

"Every opening you'd go to," Annette Kuhn remembers, "that would come up. You went to the opening and everybody's first question was, 'How are you, how was your summer?' And then, 'What do you think of the Andre thing?' That was *the* topic. Any group that you were talking to would instantly split into two camps. Five people standing in one of these little chat circles—three would say one thing, two say another, everybody getting vehement, and there was no way of convincing one or the other side. Just a total split."

The coming together of, say, a hundred people, each of them knowing a hundred people making different rounds of the hundred openings, added up to a kind of steam engine propelling every bit of gossip and rumor, and by the time you ran into the same faces again, you'd gained a few more enemies.

"It was the most horrendous situation," says Larry Weiner. "You can imagine the kind of stories about Carl's behavior. . . . It's that funny kind of thing. It's the press. It's let's jump on. It's fashionable to have an opinion about something. I mean, if they had ever known the truth they wouldn't have known what to do with it. They acted like pigs. Both sides running around slandering either one of the people." He continues:

> You had to make a decided moral decision whether you believed the male in the situation when he said he did not know what happened. Or whether you didn't believe him. And I don't hold anything against some acquaintances who genuinely did not believe him. A lot of people would not say certain things to me. The snide jokes, the snide comments, I would hear about them, but

they wouldn't say it to me because my position in the situation was pretty aboveboard from the beginning, from the first night. I was in a difficult situation, I was friends with both people. I also had no opinion other than the fact that I just could not believe that Carl was responsible. My affection for both of them was pretty well known.

Sometimes people would scream at you on the street, taking an a priori assumption of what your position was. It was quite a confrontational thing. And it must have been absolutely sheer hell for Carl. But it was an absolute confrontational situation. People saw this as the demarking of a feminist issue. When, in fact, it was more demarking of a life-style issue. Maybe the life-style we lead is not that healthy.

Carolee Schneemann witnessed much the same phenomenon. She had refrained from forming an opinion, wanting, above all others, to get this one right. "My sense was that I just had to stay in neutral. Everybody around me was championing Carl and saying, 'We've got to protect him from this awful accident or this dreadful thing that *she* did, this wild, destructive creature.' That was coming mostly from male associates of Carl's, with the women saying, 'He lost it. He went berserk. He has to be made to realize what he did.' So I was threading my way between all that, saying, 'We weren't in the room.' "

THE GRAND JURY completed its term on Friday, October 18, having been once extended. The short/tall stabber had already been trans-ported and dropped off at the next way station of justice, indicted. Big Hero had been sent there, too. Carl had remained a last piece of business. Bashford stood before her jurors and said what assistant D.A.s always say at the end. Are there any questions regarding the law? OK, seeing no questions, I'm going to withdraw for your vote. I'm going to remind the grand jury that only those members who have heard all the evidence in this case should vote. Thank you.

Bashford left. The jurors voted. It went fast. They accused Carl of the crime of murder in the second degree, indicting him on both counts. Their job was done, and thank God it was Friday. The Fourth September–October 1985 Grand Jury of the County of New York went home.

 25

"It was a planned murder," said District Attorney Morgenthau in announcing Carl's indictment. Beyond that, he had nothing new to offer, and the press treated the story accordingly, with neglect or bare mention. This silence was welcomed by Carl, but he had been clinging to the hope of not being indicted at all, and he reacted with resentment toward the family, abandoning his attempts at personal contact and passing a message of his dismay through Lucy ("Carl is very upset"). He also renewed his anger against, of all people, Gerry Rosen.

Rosen had billed him a flat three thousand dollars for his services, and Carl wrote him a long, nasty letter the day after his indictment, telling him he hadn't been worth half that. Rosen, Carl said, was inexperienced by his own admission, had, it was true, won him bail but failed to raise the cash, and had actually impeded Carl's own jailhouse efforts by not following his instructions to bring him his portfolios that day at Rikers. Carl then rewrote the bill submitted. He determined Rosen's hourly rate to be a bargain-basement $50, told him he couldn't possibly have worked on his case for more than a third of the seventy-two hours of his tenure, and threw in $300 for expenses. He sent him a check for $1,500, along with a note expressing his belief that Rosen's "extralegal activities (statements to press, etc.)" were less than helpful, and if Rosen didn't like it, he could go to arbitration.

A few weeks later, the old hippy lawyer replied, refusing to quibble over the points Carl raised, saying that doing so would be unseemly, but feeling very glum and stiffed. But since no self-respecting New York lawyer would work for $50 an hour, he suggested Carl ask Hoffinger what *his* hourly rate was—never dreaming of anything near the amount his colleague was in fact getting—and make up part of the difference. That was where it ended, "forgotten" even two years later when Carl would need Gerry again.

October 1985–April 1986

IT WAS A forlorn, tortured countenance that Carl showed in public when, on October 29, carrying his tote bag of reading material, he arrived at 100 Centre Street to respond to the indictment, as usual alone and too early. He had shed several pounds of pot belly and shortened his beard. He waited outside the locked courtroom for half an hour before his lawyers arrived and the judge returned from lunch.

Carl pleaded not guilty. Hoffinger and his staff were already at work, preparing a challenge to the indictment. Pending trial, the case had gone at random to Judge Carol Berkman, the so-called "up-front" State Supreme Court justice who would in fact decide whether to send it to trial or not. Berkman, who wore her hair like a motorcycle helmet, ran a no-nonsense operation with a jutting jaw and a sarcastic tongue to go with it. She had a downtown reputation of being tough on both women D.A.s and women lawyers, especially young ones; yet, from the defense's point of view, Berkman was after all a woman, and this was a "woman's" case, so no one at Hoffinger's shop was doing anything less than his best.

By the first week in December, Hoffinger had fielded his offense, bombarding Judge Berkman and Martha Bashford with the first of a series of motions requesting and demanding discovery and suppression of evidence real and imagined, complaining and foot stomping about the shortcomings of the D.A., and soliciting above all dismissal of the indictment, along with "further relief as may be just and proper," as the boilerplate saying went.

THAT WAS THE same week that *New York* magazine hit the stands with the biggest count-the-cracks-in-his-lips close-up ever taken of Carl Andre on its cover.[1]

---

[1]The unique photograph had been taken fifteen years earlier by Gianfranco Gorgoni, who has recorded the circumstances: "Andre was against having his portrait taken, but after we had known each other for a little while, and I had made many photographs of his pieces, I ran into him on the street one day when I had my camera. 'Don't worry,' I told him. 'We won't take a big picture, just a little one, like an identification picture.' He said OK, but after just two shots he said no, no, no and held up his hands. He wanted his work to represent him, not a picture of his face. But I had two shots, and one of them was pretty good."

"A DEATH IN ART" read the blue headline on the canvas-white cover, with Carl, looking like Svengali, staring out hairy, life-size, gloss-eyed above an album-type snapshot of Ana and a good-looking question:

DID CARL ANDRE, THE RENOWNED MINIMALIST SCULPTOR, HURL HIS
WIFE, A FELLOW ARTIST, TO HER DEATH?

The initial *D* was outsized and bloodred.

THIS WAS THE second art-world scandal cover story in *New York* in less than six months, "the shadowy world of Andrew Crispo" making it back in June. It is hard to know what impression either article had on the magazine's general audience, but while the Crispo story made for fun summer reading in the art-world vacation haunts splayed on both sides of the Atlantic, the Andre piece hit Soho like an ax.

The division into camps that was taking place in the fall gallery-openings arena had until then been the outcome of strong personal loyalties or emotion but poorly supported by facts. The article, however, had bared a great deal of what was then known about the prosecution's case. Insiders were already aware of many of the details, and some could see that it had been garbled here and there, but not one of them could have known it all. Only now did it become public, for example, that Ana had a hale and hearty state of mind, that she had a documented fear of heights, that she was furious about Carl's other women, that she was planning a divorce, that she had discussed it in a late-night phone call before her death, that the "signs of struggle" and the screams heard by a passerby alluded to in earlier reports were replete with detail, and that Carl had told the police they had had a fight that night, then had taken it back, adding and subtracting holes and contradictions to his stories.

The article, however, pleased no one downtown. It appeared slanted against Carl, but Ana fared no better. If Carl had but two extremes to his personality, Ana had barely more than one. Their marriage was a joining of opposites: "detached New Englander" weds "impulsive and outspoken young woman from Havana." All three photographs of her as an adult show her partying; in two of them, including the one on the cover, a total of four bottles of wine and champagne are within reach in the foreground, one in her grasp.

The creation of stereotypes and the journalist's failure to "understand" the art world exasperated the hostile divisions in Soho, but the effect of the article went far beyond that. It had not only managed to deliver an array of the disquieting facts, it had also set the agenda for what would be fought out. Wadler, reporting on the deep rift in the art world and the silence she had encountered, singled out a statement by one of her anonymous sources, "a woman in the art world," that ran deep. There was, her source declared, a division between Carl, "a white, supersuccessful artist, and Ana, who was a rising, though not too successful, female Hispanic." The art establishment, her source said, was coming down on Andre's side. "There is a whispering campaign: 'Here's this loony Cuban and what can you expect?' "

The article did not explore this claim. Lowery Sims, however, was among many who witnessed the same phenomenon. She also noted how strongly the article affected the community. "The *New York* magazine story really polarized the whole thing," she says. "Journalistically it very clearly set up the kind of race and gender politics that the art world would never have admitted to—because it tries to skirt around those issues and say, 'Ugh, we don't participate'—but the article set a lot of the tone for what went down subsequently in terms of people's attitudes." She goes on:

> I remember being shocked how people felt that they had to take sides. . . . In the ensuing months, many people who one wouldn't have thought would have been so strongly ideologically attached to Carl were just doing character assassinations on Ana, because they felt they had to make a political statement in support of Carl. I couldn't see how that was necessary. I remember being at the Palladium for something big—it might have been like Leo Castelli's eightieth birthday in the Mike Todd Room—and [a couple who were friends of Carl's and Ana's] launched into a whole thing about how Ana drank, and the whole you-know-how-she-was

thing, and I had heard as many stories of Carl drinking and beating women and all this kind of stuff, so I was really very shocked by that.

The article had not said a word about Carl physically abusing women, but as the strife thickened, so did the arrows fly.

HOFFINGER HAD REFUSED to comment on the case when Morgenthau was going on in the press about a "planned murder." Privately, however, he did not believe that the D.A. was up to anything other than doing his job. Morgenthau's office was about the best you could get, he felt, but still a bureaucracy where no one had the courage to make a decision. Few cases actually went to trial. You sat down with the D.A., eye to eye, you made a deal. You lived in a small world; you had to work with the same people over and over again. But this case was different, cover-story class, and once the machine had been put in motion, once the original arrest had been made, nobody was going to take the responsibility of stopping it all. It was, he sensed, going to be hard fought all the way, and he was ready for it, working late, writing his briefs, writing them himself, not turning them over to his staff, because there was no guarantee that the system would work. If it were guaranteed, he never tired of saying, we wouldn't need lawyers and judges, would we?

On December 30, he and his staff went into Judge Berkman's court initiating his four-month counterattack against the indictment.

"This is a homicide," he declared, "that exists only in the minds of crime-oriented law-enforcement personnel." They were pursuing his client with an ardor "fanned by the scent of notoriety attendant upon the prosecution of an established artist and public figure."

He railed against the People, meaning Bashford. On November 7, he complained, he had served her by hand with a bill of particulars, demanding she produce evidence to which the defense was legally entitled. All he had gotten so far were "assorted bits" and nothing listed in the bill itself. He still hadn't even been given the reports on Carl's oral statements to the police, promised more than three months ago.

In any case, he asked the judge to declare these statements inadmissible evidence on the grounds that they had been coerced.

Striking at the very language of the indictment, he demanded to know what the assistant D.A. meant when in both counts it was said Carl "forced" Ana out the window. Did it refer to *physical* force? If so, what was the nature of the alleged contact? If not, what kind of force was it and how was it manifested? The second charge spoke of "reckless conduct," but what was the substance of the conduct? Hoffinger wanted facts, not "conclusory terms," by which he surely meant he didn't want generalities.

He also wanted to see the grand jury minutes. He had no legal claim to these, and only Judge Berkman could grant access, so he was only requesting, and doing so respectfully. But how else could he know if Bashford had properly instructed the jury, particularly about circumstantial evidence, and more important, if the evidence presented was sufficient to support the charges? Then, in virtually the same breath, he asserted that it wasn't.

"Ordinarily," he said in explanation, "defense counsel can only guess at the evidence presented to the grand jury. In this case, however, the People have made numerous statements both in court and to the press." He then went on to argue from what he had made of Carl's versions, the "assorted bits" Bashford had supplied, and his newspaper-clippings file, moving that the case should be dismissed. Short on data, he went for the kindness of Berkman's heart.

"It is an outrage," he said, "that the husband should be forced to undergo the shame of accusation and the tribulation of a public trial. Carl Andre has already suffered from the tragedy of Ana Mendieta's death. He should not casually be asked to suffer further." And, perhaps in keeping with the holiday spirit, he ended his plea saying that he "respectfully prayed" that the relief he sought for his client be granted.

Berkman, who wasn't often persuaded by being prayed to—and Hoffinger, at least in this case, would drop all forms of praying from his courtroom vocabulary—denied the motion. Nevertheless, she did answer part of his prayer. In the absence of opposition on Bashford's part, she gave him the grand jury minutes and time enough to ponder.

In a general exchange of Happy New Years, she ordered everyone back to court in February.

26

The new year rang in with the baffling episode of the keys. It was in some way connected to the earlier mystery of the information about Ana that Carl, ignoring Hoffinger's admonitions, had insisted on disclosing only to Tom or Raquel.

Giving up on getting through to the family, Carl finally had called their lawyer, Gary Simon, sometime during or shortly after the grand jury proceedings. Ana, he said, had $10,000 in cash in a vault at the American Academy in Rome. There was another $10,000 in German currency in the same box, but that belonged to him. This came as welcome news to the family, because Ana, they knew, also had an estimated $13,000 in jewelry, some of it family heirlooms, which had yet to turn up. The Academy had made a meticulously documented inventory of the contents of Ana's studio there, and while it catalogued a multitude of items—ranging from her latest works, four six-foot sculpted tree trunks, down to a bag of sand from the Red Sea, a tin cookie box containing gunpowder, and her Walkman—there was none of her personal valuables. The jewelry, Carl said, was in the vault, too.

There was something else. Did Raquel have the keys to the apartment in Rome? There was only one set, he said, and not even the landlord had duplicates. The police had removed Ana's purse when they had searched the Mercer Street apartment, so the keys had to be there. The Rome apartment was his home, and the keys were his, and though he was unable to leave the country, he wanted what was his. Raquel, however, had seen the contents of Ana's purse, and there were no keys at all.

She was quite suspicious of the business about the keys. By now, to be sure, the family was categorically distrustful of anything Carl said, and they had taken to keeping a mental black book, writing off anyone suspected of being less than on their side. But there was nothing paranoiac about wondering why the sudden interest in his unvisitable residence in Rome. It was after all the repository, according to Natalia

Delgado, of the other set of photocopies Ana had been collecting to use against Carl in the divorce. Who knew what they might show or what else Ana might have stashed away? The matter, however, was not something that caused Raquel any concern. The apartment, she had been assured by Martha Bashford, had been sealed by the Italian police, and when Carl failed to call about the keys again, it fell to the bottom of her worry list.

It rose again, however, when Carl, after months of silence, called Simon in early February to say that he was no longer interested in the apartment and would make no claim on anything in Rome except for his German marks in the Academy safe. That was acceptable to the family, but shortly afterward, Simon got a call from the landlord, which sent Raquel's suspicions soaring. The landlord, a man named Joseph Golan, was a non-Italian who spent part of the year in New York and very little time in Rome, renting out his flat to foreigners at exorbitant black market prices, as was the practice in that city, with its excess of warehoused apartments. He was losing money, he told Simon. He had spoken to Carl and his lawyers and nobody had the key. He wanted in. Ana had left a window open and it was raining in, ruining the floors and damaging the flat below. Worse, the rent hadn't been paid in months, though if the apartment was cleared out immediately, he wouldn't sue, but he was talking *immediately* or the whole Andre household was going out on a Roman street.

Ana, ecstatic about her new apartment, had told not only Raquel and Natalia that the rent had been paid in advance for a year—from July through the following June—but others as well, expressing some amazement about it all ("I don't know how we can afford it, but Carl says we deserve it," she told one friend in Rome). The year's rent was, of course, the prize she hoped to win in a divorce settlement with Carl, so she clearly believed it, as did Raquel. And whether or not the rent had been paid, how could her dead sister's belongings be moved if they were under police protection?

That was when Bashford told her about the bureaucracy. All the paperwork had been done, said Bashford, and she had thought that was all there was to it, but it had proved to be too complicated. The Italians, for reasons no one, probably not even the Italians, could hope to fathom, would have had to seal off the entire city block, or so Bashford had been told by Interpol. Whatever evidence Ana might have kept there was suddenly at the mercy of a landlord losing money by the day. Without the cooperation of the Italians, there was nothing short of trying to mount an American expeditionary force that Bashford could do. Raquel and her mother made plans to fly to Rome.

PEOPLE HAD DREAMS. As might be imagined, they were mostly women, but some men, too, waking up in the middle of the night, seeing *what happened.* Ana was a very active dreamer herself, or at least she was unusually voluble about it to friends, leaving a trail of graphic scenes from her dreams remembered by others as if they themselves had dreamed them and jotted them down. It may have been her passion for the arcane that drew attention to the stuff of her dreams, and some saw it, or her, as psychic. An Iowa art-school friend, Warren Rosen, would never forget Ana's dream on April 8, 1973, related to him only hours afterward. She had dreamed that Picasso had flown her to New York, taken her everywhere, introduced her to everybody who was anybody in the art world, giving her a wonderful time, and when she woke up that morning, Ana told Warren, she heard on the news that Picasso had died in Paris—the time of his death being around the time of her dream. She would speak to others of her dreams as a child, voodoo nightmares was what they were, she said, flowing from the scarier stories of Santería she had heard from the maids. She had powerful sexual dreams, wet dreams, she called them with Hans, and she would tell a friend how her heart would pound in the dreaming of the feel of his hands on her skin, and years later, sleeping in a house perched on a cliff outside Rome—after a bout with acrophobia—she dreamed an "incredibly sexy dream." Carl was a pharaoh and she was his queen and there were thousands of good snakes and bad snakes as the royal couple sailed down the Nile.

Marsha Pels, to whom Ana had told the snake dream only weeks before her death, began to have recurrent dreams not long after Ana's memorial. "I dreamt them for about six months, and I had a dream at least once a week about Ana, that she was alive and that she was telling me what had happened. I really became somewhat obsessed with it. I really felt that she was alive, her ghost was with me."

Mary Beth Edelson had her own snake dream, a huge, ugly snake approaching her after she had been exhausted by an ecstasy. She made a gesture to scare the beast away, and it turned into the shape of a goddess, transforming into one goddess shape after another. "The energy from these goddess figures was not peaceful. It was restless and agitated. I said out loud—'Oh, my God, it's Ana Mendieta.' "

An Italian friend whom Ana met in Rome, Ida Panicelli, had moved to New York to take up the job as editor of *Artforum* magazine and had gotten an apartment on Waverly Place down the street from Carl's building. She walked past the Delion rooftop every day on her way to her Bleecker Street office, and she always thought she would run into Carl. She developed a recurring dream of Ana falling, continually falling. "I talked about that with my therapist, and he told me, probably to make me feel better, that in cases when you fall from such a height you die before you land because you suffocate. You cannot breathe." She didn't believe it.

Zarina Hashmi, the woman who had taken Ana to the palmist who had so upset her about her short life line, was "converted" by a dream. She had refused to believe that Carl, who had always been so kind to her, could have harmed Ana. "I'm Indian, of course, and I'm into dreams. I'd look for something [about Carl] and I was very confused. . . . I said, I have to think about it. Blood and violence. I said, he can be so nice. What happened? So I had a dream. This might sound crazy. Yes, I had a dream and I saw Ana in her usual way, and I said, 'Ana, what happened?' And Ana said, 'He picked me up and pushed me, threw me out of the window.' She was not unhappy."

Carolee Schneemann, who, like Zarina, had wanted to remain open-minded until she got it right because she wasn't in the room, lost her neutrality on a cold winter's night in January of that new year. She had been under pressure to come up with a body art piece. She had agreed to participate in a memorial exhibition of thirty women artists showing works created with Ana's life and art in mind. The show was due to open in the East Village on February 5, and the gallery had been calling

every day. To get away and think, Carolee had gone to her house in
upstate New York, and she had a dream.

"It was very cold, and I had a dream of snow, snow falling, big snow,
snow landing, and a kind of visceral transposition of ashes . . . ashes
and blood and something like, something else pink, and then my body
would be embedded in this painting in the snow."

She awoke in the darkness, saying to herself, "I see it. I have to try
this. I don't know what it's going to be, but I have to try it." She ran
outside in her nightgown, ready to paint, wakened anew by the bitter
cold, standing in the black of night without any paint, and knowing
even if she went back and got it she couldn't paint her dream in the
snow. She began to paint inside instead, letting paper represent the
snow. Using red paint for blood, she made a sequence of images, laying
her own arms in what she was painting, this hand above, that hand
below, left arm, right arm, but the dream and now the work, painting
until the day broke, continued to elude her.

"There was something filmic about it. I didn't get it. I went down
to have breakfast with my friends, all covered in red paint, and I said,
'I think I've got the good idea for a work for Ana.' They said, 'Great,'
and then we went upstairs to look at what I'd done, and I thought, Oh,
my God. Oh. I was just torn apart. I just had a completely different
feeling about her death. I felt that she was inhabiting me to make it
very clear how she had died. And what I saw I was painting was her
arms falling through space, clutching at space. . . . I felt that she was
communicating her murder to me, by situating it in my own system
so that I could be clear. Yeah, and that wasn't what I really wanted to
assume."

THE WOMEN ARTISTS' Homage to Ana Mendieta show at the Zeus-
Trabia Gallery was called "an antidote to the obscene New York magazine cover story," by critic Judd Tully. It stripped away the "gory hype
surrounding Mendieta's death," he wrote. Many of the works on exhibit recalled Ana's own work, employing earth mounds and fetish
figures made of feathers and bleached bones, belying the loony-Cuban
theorists and their rhetorical, ineluctable what-about-those-pieces-
where-she-seemed-to-be-killing-herself question. Tully praised the cura-

ANA MENDIETA IN THE LAST YEAR OF HER LIFE

Cooking penne all'arrabbiata, *a hot pasta dish, in her Rome apartment on a hot day in August three weeks before her death* (photo courtesy of Marsha Pels).

In Brooklyn on a spring day in 1985 (photo by Dawoud Bey).

In her Rome studio with a 1985 untitled sculpture, a wood slab carved and burned with gunpowder (photo courtesy of Raquel Mendieta Harrington).

In Los Angeles in the fall of 1984
for conferences on her unexecuted
sculpture planned as a permanent
installation in MacArthur Park
(photo courtesy of Joy Silverman).

Ana and Carl falling in love in
New York, circa 1980 (photo courtesy
of Raquel Mendieta Harrington).

Ana and Hans falling out of love (slowly), Oaxaca, Mexico, circa 1979 (photo courtesy
of Raquel Mendieta Harrington).

Ana executing an early performance work she called Los Danzantes, *in Monte Alban, Mexico, 1973* (photo courtesy of Raquel Mendieta Harrington).

Batwoman and her niece-goddaughter-pupil, Raquelita, on Halloween in 1974, outside the Iowa City elementary school where Ana taught art (photo courtesy of Raquel Mendieta Harrington).

Ana's graduation photo from Regis High School, Cedar Rapids, 1965; in the fall she went off to Sioux City for college and a major in art (photo courtesy of Raquel Mendieta Harrington).

A five-year-old mariposa, or butterfly, Varadero, Cuba, 1953 (photo courtesy of Raquel Mendieta Harrington).

CARL ANDRE ON TRIAL, NEW YORK, JANUARY-FEBRUARY 1988

The defendant in a customary mien (photo by Sylvia Plachy).

New York State Supreme Court Justice Alvin Schlesinger – the "one head" judging Carl after the accused waived his right to a jury (photo by Sylvia Plachy).

Prosecutor Elizabeth Lederer doing battle with Chief Defense Attorney Jack Hoffinger (second from right) (photo by Sylvia Plachy).

The defense team with their client during a break in the proceedings (photo by Sylvia Plachy).

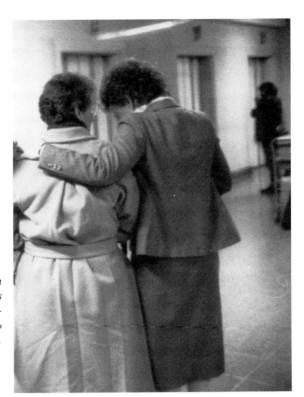

The prosecutor with her "client," Ana's mother, in the court-house corridor (photo by Sylvia Plachy).

Carl walking out of Schlesinger's courtroom (photo by Sylvia Plachy).

Ana's mother and sister in New York a few days after the trial (photo by Niki Berg).

300 Mercer Street seen from the corner of Waverly Place and Broadway; Ana and Carl lived in the apartment that adjoins the balcony on the next to the last floor at the right side of the building (photo by Niki Berg).

Carl Andre: Lead-Magnesium Plain *(1969), described in 1990 by the* New York Times – *the title of the piece notwithstanding – as looking like "a silvery . . . nighttime lake."*

Carl Andre: untitled and undated aluminum squares; the artist donated the work for a National Emergency Civil Liberties Committee fund-raiser (from the collection of Carole Rosenberg; photo by Niki Berg).

Ana Mendieta: Iyare (Mother) *(1981), one of a series of rock carvings in the mountains of Jaruco, Cuba* (photo courtesy of Carlo Lamagna Gallery).

tor, Quimetta Perle, for giving the show its meditative air without censoring the underlying angry currents. There were more than currents, however; there was a transcendental accusation. "I can not forget this death," artist Betsey Damon wrote on a card on display with her sculpture. "I can not forget the dehumanization of men that causes the brutalization of women. I can not forget that I am a female and weaker. I can not forget the inhumanity of a society that will not recognize that the oppression of one member of that society by another hurts us all. I can not forget that this is what we fear every day."

Such were the propositions that fired the internecine animosity of artists on both sides.

THE EAST VILLAGE show had been up one week, with two more weeks to go, when the case rolled around again in Carol Berkman's court. Hoffinger had had more than a month to read and reflect on the 120-page grand jury minutes, and he told Judge Berkman that she had been more than justified in giving him the transcript because it confirmed that the evidence presented was "patently deficient."

In a lengthy memorandum of law to support dismissal of the indictment, he sought to pick apart the prosecution's case stitch by stitch. He attacked the evidence first.

- The inference that the scream heard by the doorman was Ana's voice and that she was pleading for her life required an impermissible leap of logic and was sheer speculation.
- The scratches on Carl's body did not compel the conclusion that he forced Ana out the window.
- As for the overturned chair, there was no evidence to indicate when and by whom it had been displaced.
- Ana's future plans, offered to show she was not suicidal, were "of no consequence" because she was "given to irrational outbursts over minor occurrences" and was probably "distraught" over the failure of her marriage.[1]

[1]To support this allegation, Hoffinger cited the grand jury testimony of next-door neighbor Mark Coler. He had heard a woman crying and screaming in the hallway over

- Ana's purported fear of heights, even if accepted, described only sober behavior and not how she would feel when intoxicated and released from inhibitions.
- The 911 tape showed that Carl called the police immediately after Ana's death, and his later conflicting statements to the police represented a confused attempt at both reconstructing and "subconsciously blocking out the memory of the traumatic experience."

Hoffinger's second major point was that what little was left of the evidence was inadmissible, prejudicial, and irrelevant. Hearsay had been presented to show Ana's state of mind, but that was mere sleight of hand used to construct a nonexistent motive. The grand jury had been led to believe, Hoffinger argued, that the hearsay testimony of Raquel and Natalia was true, and the jurors were then encouraged to jump to the conclusion that Carl had eavesdropped on Ana's conversation with Natalia, had heard the Spanish words for "detective" and "Berlin," and had decided that his wife was plotting against him and that Ana had acted on Natalia's advice to confront him, which was why he killed her. This was an unacceptable string of inferences and "grossly improper."

In a final argument, he assailed the prosecution for failing to instruct the grand jury on certain points of law, contending further that the instructions actually given were purposely misleading. The memorandum concluded on a note of indignation. On that terrible Sunday last summer, Carl had experienced the double tragedy of his wife's death and his arrest for her murder. He had been put to public shame by suspicion and conjecture orchestrated by a prosecution out to force him

---

something that had spilled on her sweater. Assuming it was Ana, Hoffinger interpreted the event as the behavior of an individual "whose fury was unleashed by a trivial mishap—quite different from the 'upbeat' person the prosecution tried to paint." A moment earlier, however, he had dismissed Coler's account of a man yelling in the Andre apartment a few nights before Ana's death, in part because one had to assume that Carl was doing the yelling. It was, according to Carl's lawyer, the "emotional turmoil existing within Ana Mendieta [that] cannot be ignored."

to trial. "Carl Andre's nightmare should end," said his lawyer. "The indictment should be dismissed."

Martha Bashford had been served with Hoffinger's brief days earlier, and she came to court with her own opposing memorandum of law. It was a detailed account of the case she had submitted to the grand jury—homicide as the only viable explanation of Ana's death. She cited numerous legal precedents to support the propriety of her actions. She hammered at Hoffinger's offhanded treatment of the defendant's conflicting statements to the police. To claim they were immaterial, Bashford said, was "ridiculous." When two people are alone in an apartment, she argued, and one dies in suspicious circumstances, contradictory statements by the other as to how the person died were crucial. Carl Andre, she concluded, "should be held for trial for the brutal murder of his wife."

Hoffinger was given a final shot at Bashford's memorandum, and he came back into court a few weeks later trying to prop up the suicide and accident theories. Her "so-called fear of height" was "irrelevant," while multiple references to her being "thoroughly intoxicated" were raised in support of a brand-new theory: "the reasonable possibility that Ana jumped onto the radiator and windowsill and fell to her death, either accidentally or by design." The aerodynamics of such a drunken feat were left to the judge's imagination.

It was part of Berkman's courtroom style when listening to a plea to stare impassively over the top of her reading glasses, her strong chin resting on the palm of her hand. Now that she had heard it all, she sent the lawyers on their way, promising a decision in April on whether Bashford's indictment would stand or fall.

— 27 —

A third person in whom Ana had confided the intimate details of her failing marriage turned up in early April. Ruby Rich had never quit playing girl detective, as she called it, snooping and stalking clues. The police investigation had come to a near standstill after the loss of Finelli, so Ruby's prying was welcomed by Bashford. The two women maintained frequent contact, Ruby feeding the assistant D.A. with bits and pieces of information plucked from here and there. By coincidence, Ruby's office, where she ran the film program of the New York State Council of the Arts, was in the same building as Bashford's, making the operation that much smoother. Circulating among Ana's Hispanic friends, Ruby discovered that Ana had made a two-day trip to Miami during her May-June visit to the States before the one-way return in late August. She would often pass through Miami, craving things Cuban, needing and getting a cultural fix in the ghetto. This time she had stayed with a painter named Carlos Alfonzo.

He was a Cuban émigré who lived in Miami and had gallery representation and some success in New York. They had met in 1980, months after his flight from Cuba. They were political opposites, and kept away from that subject, making an enduring friendship of their common passion for art and Santería. Ruby interviewed Alfonzo by phone and wrote the following memo to Bashford:

> Ana talked to him extensively about the problems she was having with Carl. She was very jealous of the girlfriend she had discovered he had in Germany. She felt very betrayed, was depressed about it, and was talking about divorce. She was gathering together the telephone bills with the calls he had made to Germany as evidence. Alfonzo advised her to just go ahead and get a divorce, but she said, "No, no, I have to keep trying. I've been with him for so many years." He advised her not to say anything to Carl but just to gather the evidence until she had enough information for a divorce case. Alfonzo said to her that she'd been with Carl for so long, "I think you deserve a piece of the pie."

This was powerful corroboration of what Natalia and Raquel had been saying, and Alfonzo was willing to testify. Legally, however, his story added only additional hearsay, and hearsay was Bashford's biggest problem at the moment. Moreover, Ruby's memo went on to conclude with a jarring bit of news that could readily be turned to grist in Hoffinger's mill.

"On this same day," Ruby reported, "Ana said to him, 'Carlos, I think I'm going to die very soon.' " Ruby, pressing him further, was told that Ana had never mentioned a word about suicide and was in fact "full of energy about her work. She lived for her work." Later, confirming Ana's premonition of death, Alfonzo would nevertheless remember her during her stay as having been "radiant" and "so happy with her new projects." She had come to Miami bearing a painted fossil as a gift to Eleggua, the messenger of the gods without whom nothing could be accomplished. The next day, at dawn, they had gone out as *santeros* to gather magic leaves to be hung and bathed in sunlight, the premonition gone. But none of the parties now acquainted with Ana's Miami episode in clairvoyance was aware that while in New York on this same trip home, she had spoken of the disturbing feeling to someone else in more detail.

ON APRIL 6, Ruby held a meeting at a friend's loft to see if anyone could come up with useful leads. There were about a dozen women present, including Raquel, Nancy Spero, and Martha Bashford. Little more than the latest anti-Carl gossip and how it might be checked out was discussed. These rumors had multiplied and had grown more serious than the earlier stories of barroom fisticuffs.

There were people in Soho who claimed to have seen Carl being violent with women. Critic and painter Jeff Perrone, who ten years earlier had written a rare, scathing attack on Carl as some sort of art con man ("Carl Andre: Art Versus Talk"), had no qualms about saying he had seen Angela Westwater, during the years she was living with Carl, walking around battered and bruised and saying she'd bumped into a door when everyone knew it was Carl. Perrone insisted he disliked Ana as much as Carl, presumably to heighten his credibility, but such testimony fell far short of courtroom proof. Even gallery owner Max Protetch's much more cautious avowal that he had actually seen Carl strike Angela, wouldn't go very far. The incident was said to have occurred on a street in Washington, D.C., when Carl had a one-man exhibition at Protetch's gallery there. That dated back to 1973, which happened to be the same year he was in Rome, momentarily accused as the rapist artist with the beard. But Angela was an active player in this unruly game. She denied the story to whoever cared to listen, telling Paula Cooper, for one, "I've been beaten around by plenty of men in my life, and I'll tell you Carl wasn't one of them." To writer Susan Cheever, she said she had been in every possible worst-case situation with Carl and he had never gone beyond verbal abuse.

At Ruby's meeting, people reached even further back to the sixties. Rosemarie Castoro, Carl's second wife, was an art student at Pratt Institute then, and she, like Angela, was purported to have been seen coming in welted "the morning after." Someone said that Bashford should try to find the man who had been Rosemarie's boyfriend after Carl ("some guy named John"); he knew all about it, and there were people who had to know who John was.[1]

Ruby, having heard it from the victim herself, knew that Carl had sent a series of anonymous pornographic postcards to avant-garde dancer and choreographer Yvonne Rainer, later telling her he was the author. But that was ancient also, dating back to a time in the seventies when posting serial, sometimes anonymous, unexecuted whimsies and desires was on the cutting edge of conceptual art, and Carl himself had done several signed "mail pieces." There were recent tales, too. Carl, it was being said, had pushed a woman down a stairway in Germany, another woman out of a car on the autobahn, another woman out of a taxi in New York, breaking her wrist, and had shoved women around here and there—somehow always *throwing*. It was probably mathematically impossible that even a fair amount was true, and not one of the brutalized women in the stories had yet come forward. But the cumulative effect was as mighty on the streets as it was further inadmissible hearsay in a court of law.

There were some women who refused to attend Ruby's meeting. Liliana Porter declined, saying, "Carl has suffered enough." Liliana was one of several women and men close to Ana who appeared to both camps to be trying to keep one foot anchored in each. Of the three staunch feminists who had organized the Park Avenue memorial, only

---

[1]The John in question was located three and a half years later through a person mentioned at Ruby's meeting. He had been the boyfriend of an artist named Rosemarie at the time, but not Rosemarie Castoro.

Carolee had given up the straddling position, which grew more painful as the camps moved farther apart. Lucy, though she was said at the meeting to be upset by Carl's stories not adding up and his failure to show emotion, was given low marks for supporting him anyway. Mary Miss was seen as another waffler, and May Stevens, the woman who had told Bashford of her hardship in testifying that Carl had had no facial scratches the night before Ana died, was regarded as a potential traitor to the feminist cause. The artist who so conspicuously attended Carl at the memorial, Brenda Miller, was relegated somewhere over the Styx.

Get-togethers such as Ruby's, however, were being pointed at by some as feminist cabals out to get Carl. Other women, Mary Miss and Wendy Evans among them, regarded the behavior of feminists like Ruby as a form of hysteria. "The feeling among people like May Stevens and Brenda Miller," says Liliana Porter, "was why go after Carl the way the lesbian feminists wanted? Ana was dead, and now, no matter what had happened, Carl needed their support."

Art worlds were colliding.

Golan, the landlord, called Gary Simon, the lawyer, screaming again. He no longer wanted the key. He had the key. He was in Rome. He had been in the apartment because Ana had left something in the refrigerator that was stinking up the whole building. He was going to sue for thousands of dollars in back rent and damages. No more Mr. Nice Guy. The apartment had to be vacated by the end of the month. Period. That was in March. Raquel and her mother were unable to leave for Rome until sometime in April, their lawyer screamed back. He had been put to some difficulty trying to trace the allegedly missing, one-of-a-kind set of keys, on the phone with the police and Carl's lawyers, worrying with Raquel and the rest of the family about Ana's possessions. He wanted to know how the landlord got it. He got it from Carl, Golan said, through Hoffinger. Simon, enraged by it all, called Hoffinger. What was going on? Hoffinger shrugged it off. Carl had the key all along, couldn't find it at first, and found it later. The landlord had to get in because "a pipe broke or some such thing," so they gave him the key. There was nothing more to it.

N A K E D   B Y   T H E   W I N D O W

2 1 6

Raquel, along with Bashford and Simon, imagined much more to it. They knew that Carl's defense team had hired a private detective, and now they wondered if he had been sent with the key to Rome. Carl's early claim of not having the set of keys suddenly looked like a cover story, unmasked solely because of a landlord's implacable greed. Hoffinger's demand for a copy of the search warrant and an inventory of what was seized in Carl's apartment—items on his discovery shopping list—had still not been fulfilled. Even if it had the specific mention of the unfound Xerox copies would not in itself reveal the possible existence of a second set in Rome. But that, or something like it, was not very hard to deduce from known facts, which now included the grand jury minutes with references to Ana "collecting evidence." In any event, prudence would suggest that a little look around might be worth the price of the airfare.

If that were the case, all hope of recovering the second set of papers seemed gone, and Raquel now regarded the trip to Rome with less urgency. Through Simon, she hired a lawyer in Rome to represent her there, and when the American Academy agreed to store the contents of the apartment along with the things in Ana's studio, she yielded to the landlord and had everything moved out.

RAQUEL AND HER mother had reservations to fly to Rome on April 18, but on the tenth, Carol Berkman threw the case out of court, dropping all charges against Carl.

In a four-page opinion, Berkman agreed with almost every point of law raised by Hoffinger, often adopting his own words. Bashford's performance had been "woefully inadequate." Because of her, the "integrity of the Grand Jury process was severely impaired." She had allowed the grand jury to hear "a large amount of both inadmissible evidence and highly prejudicial evidence" and this was made "all the more egregious" by her failure to properly instruct the jurors. Using a "cryptic explanation" about the state-of-mind exception regarding hearsay, Bashford had broken the rules of evidence, inducing the jury "to leap logical gaps."

As examples of Bashford's failings, Berkman cited Ana's statements about Carl as recollected by Raquel and Natalia. Legally, to show Ana's state of mind, it was correct to introduce testimony that Ana was planning ahead and one of her plans was to divorce her husband, but to give reasons such as his unfaithfulness or other past incidents was using hearsay to establish a motive and thus should not have been allowed. Finally, the jury's instruction on the nature of circumstantial evidence had come too early in the piecemeal presentation of a case as complex as this one and should have been made at the end. "The indictment against the defendant," Berkman declared, "is therefore dismissed."

The judge, however, left no moment for a cry of either victory or defeat. Berkman had a lesson in humility for everyone. In addition to her many misgivings about Bashford, she had one major difference with Hoffinger. Although it wasn't the judge who had heard him use those words, this was, by her very next sentence, not a piece-of-shit case. It read: "The court does not rule at this time on the sufficiency of the evidence." This was, she said, "what can only be described as a close circumstantial case." It appeared to her, she explained, that even eliminating the inadmissible part, "there may remain sufficient evidence" to send Carl to trial. Warning the prosecution that her "caveats" be strictly observed, she granted "leave to re-present." This meant that Bashford, if her boss chose to give her the go-ahead, could try once again to get Carl indicted and make it stick.

—— 28 ——

Boom times and Paula Cooper spurred the uptown art-world family to migrate to Soho, but Mickey Ruskin—the rabbi of the demimonde, Carl would call him—initiated the long wedding party of uptown and downtown a couple of years earlier with the grand opening in January 1966 of his Max's Kansas City.

No one had ever seen a place like Max's before, and after it was gone, eight years later, everyone would dream, but have no hope, of seeing the likes of it again. The five-bar, upstairs-downstairs, red-velvet, wet palace on Park Avenue South, territorially nowhere at the time, but midway on the old uptown-downtown axis, would live on instead in the daily discourse of artists and writers, outliving many of them, as an extended metaphor for everything that burst on the culture scene in those Max's Kansas City years.

Max's, says writer Ronald Sukenick, who lived it and tells it best, was the result of several art upheavals happening concurrently. "It was the change in the gallery scene, from Abstract Expressionism to Pop, Op, Minimal, Conceptual, and Color Field painting, at the same time pop music tastes were changing out of folk music, jazz, and blues into a new kind of rock 'n' roll, when fashion was going through important changes in exhibiting the body, when there was a strong underground film scene, when Off- and Off-Off-Broadway theater was exciting, when the antiwar movement was gaining momentum and the civil rights movement was important. There couldn't have been a better time to open a very large bar where all these elements were welcome, the more so since the Cedar, down University Place, had been closed for a while, and had moved."

Not even Sukenick knows how Mickey Ruskin—a taciturn, dropout lawyer who every night fed goldfish to his piranhas to the cheers of the crowd at the entrance bar—picked the right moment to go into café bohemianism supermarket style. La Coupole was far larger but long established on boulevard Montparnasse, far from the gray-flannel, insurance-company-town of Seventeenth Street and Union Square.[1] The old-timers credit Mickey's instinct, Carl likening him to an artist in his own right, but he had already built up a clientele of artists in previous places by letting them pay their bar bills with their work, and they followed doggedly wherever the vicissitudes of enterprise took him. With all the new art setting the cultural pace and more so fashion trends, Mickey's stalwarts were suddenly drawing everybody from Hollywood celebrities to teenyboppers from the Bronx. Even de Kooning switched and the list of the regulars among the new greats ranged wide, the minimalists holding court in the red alcove out front, the Warhol and Edie Sedgwick Factory bunch in the back room—"arena of prancing frenzy, almost carnivorous," in Terry Southern's phrase—the von Fürstenberg fashion crowd somewhere in the middle limbo, the music scene upstairs, with the first rock disco and the beginnings of glitter and punk, Janis Joplin, Jimi Hendrix, Jim Morrison, Mick Jagger, Willie Nelson, Bob Marley, and young Bruce Springsteen either hanging out, whacked out, or starting out, and Jane Fonda, Faye Dunaway, Cary Grant, Mel Brooks, Bobby Kennedy rubbing shoulders or the shoulders of shoulders rubbed with Abbie Hoffman and Jerry Rubin and garden-variety gawking out-of-towners, going up and down to the upstairs Siberia, and, when the out-of-towners weren't gawking, people on speed or not, dropping acid, smoking dope, shooting up coke, and having a sexual revolution funny or straight in the phone booths, in the bathrooms, in Mickey's office upstairs if they were somebody special, and who but the ultimate insiders knew what and who went down under the tables? There it was at Max's: while squares in minks and ties waited in a tight line on the street outside and artists and homeless-looking future homeless freaks were shown right in; the whole big vanguard middle-class tango of art patrons as art pals, reeling with the

---

[1]A major reason for the location was a contractual agreement with a former partner not to open a place in the Village—a condition that also gave rise to its name. It was bestowed by poet Joel Oppenheimer; anticipating Saul Steinberg's map of the world, he saw Max's as being about as far away from anything else as Kansas City.

New Bohemia, playing on or boosting the Max's Kansas City traveling softball team; there it was, fusing in the heat of the sheer, plucked-and-skinned desire not to be one of *them;* creating before *their* very eyes and coats and ties what Sukenick calls the Hipoisie.

CARL MIGHT HAVE missed everything, or at least having his front-row seat, if it were not for a revelation he had experienced the summer before Mickey opened the portals to it all.

Minimalism, though nobody would be sure what to call it until 1967, had been on the rise all through the decade, long before any of the other pioneers, not to mention Mickey, had ever heard of Carl Andre. His fellow founding fathers, future art-world household names such as Donald Judd, Robert Morris, Dan Flavin, Richard Serra, and Sol LeWitt, were becoming increasingly well known as the movement began gaining ground, particularly at the Green Gallery uptown. They all knew one another when Carl was still watching through the plate-glass windows. Fired from the railroad and broker than ever, he was dedicating himself almost exclusively to writing, working on his first shaped poems, stacking hard-edged Anglo-Saxon nouns and conjunctions, as in "bird and bone" and "wing and womb," in alphabetical order. He was still spending his time at the evanescent Cedar and another old art bar called Dillons when, in 1964, a critic named Eugene Goosen showed up one day with a nifty proposition.

Goosen was putting together a show at the Hudson River Museum in Yonkers, New York, to feature young artists practicing the unchristened new art. He remembered having seen one of Carl's sculptures in Hollis Frampton's old apartment four years earlier. It was a man's-height piece made of unjoined two-by-four lumber notched log-cabin style, and would Carl, if he were still in the business of sculpting, care to be included in the exhibition?

Carl had never shown his work publicly before, and this was a capital beginning. The trouble was that the person who had taken over Hollis's place, art dealer Richard Bellamy, had broken his promise to let Carl store his sculpture with him. Bellamy, in a season of discomfort in the large cold-water flat, had used the convenient two-by-fours for firewood, adding to more than subtracting from the story.

Carl, the young artist looking forward only, made a reconstruction of a similar piece with Stella and Brancusi somewhere on his mind, and when it was shown, his positive nature was rewarded. Somehow the work caught the eye of John Myers, who ran the Tibor de Nagy gallery uptown and found "delight" in what was being called simply "minimum." A few months later, in early 1965, he put Carl in a group show of the new "Reductionists," which was what a critic in search of a stickier name that might also adhere to his own dubbed them now. Among the others in the group of ten were Donald Judd and Robert Morris, so Carl was at last mingling in what would prove to be the very right company.

In April of the same year, Myers gave him his first one-man show. Not quite sure what to do, Carl filled the gallery's Seventy-second Street "negative" townhouse space from floor to ceiling with those marshmallow-white Styrofoam slabs, unsettling a few claustrophobic visitors at the opening but giving his friends the Smith girls, Barbara Rose and Lucy Lippard, something to work into their periodic essays in the art-press slicks.

Lucy, trying like everyone else to come up with a name for the new art, discarded "reductive" and even "minimal" as "rather insulting." She proposed "rejective" (because the universal rejection involved went beyond "paying the compliment" of mere reaction against everything in art it sought to displace); she called its practitioners "structurists." She lifted Carl from the obscurity of the "and others," tacking him on for the first time in print right after Judd, Morris, Flavin, and Robert Smithson. "Rejective" was promptly forgotten, but she had guessed right about Carl. By the time her piece was published in 1966, Carl had already had the legendary revelation and had begun to show the results dazzling a certain part of town.

David Bourdon, soon to become Carl's biographer, heard it early, straight from Carl, and was the first to write about it:

> During the summer of 1965, Andre experienced a revelation while canoeing on a New Hampshire lake. He had long wanted to break away from the vertical in his sculpture, and it now suddenly occurred to him that his work should be as level as water. He

wondered how he could go about putting the equivalent of Bran-cusi's *Endless Column* on the ground instead of in the air. His initial—and instantly controversial—solution was *Lever*.

The problem of verticality in sculpture, if there ever was one, had already been tackled by Judd and Morris, and even before them, but no one had gotten much further than getting rid of pedestals, getting lower, or making inchoate attempts to sprawl. Carl, however, solved the whole conundrum in his canoe, at the same time accomplishing what every artist since the Paleolithic sculptor of the Venus from Brassem-pouy has set out to do, saying it or denying it, namely, making art sexy.[2]

Lever, taken both from the name of the rigid tool and the French verb "to raise," was put on display at the Jewish Museum early in 1966, one of the more humble works among the cubes, rectangles, and cones of forty-one other young structurists in a show called "Primary Struc-tures." Carl's piece consisted of 137 freestanding common fire bricks. Brand-new and rosy, they were lined up on the floor face to face in a straight, thirty-four-foot, six-inch row, starting from a wall and ending just short of the opening of a doorway. It was hard to see the sexy part,[3] but Carl had a theory (and an enthusiastic publicist in Bourdon) to propound it: "Most sculpture is priapic with the male organ in the air," he observed. "In my work, Priapus is down on the floor. The engaged position is to run along the earth."

Since there could be nothing more sexy, or at least sexual, than "the engaged position"—the engaged position of Priapus, fertility god of the biggest phallus, son of the god of wine, his mother a local nymph, patron also of men in need of good luck—the message or the medium seemed bound sooner or later to heat up.

That would take some consciousness-raising, an activity, by a stroke of luck, on the move at the time. Carl, perhaps starting the process, denied emphatically (to Bourdon) that his *Lever* had even implicit

[2]In a rare expression of a "great resentment" of his Puritan upbringing, Carl in a 1972 interview would speak of its objection to art as having something to do with sex. "Art is sexy in its basic root," he said. "It is about an erotic relationship with the world."

[3]Carl had wanted it to actually penetrate the doorway and enter the next room, but the museum needed the space for others.

sexual meaning. Moreover, people who were actually on the scene, including Carl, were, as is often the case, unaware of history being made, and art dealer Alex Rosenberg remembers little more than stubbing his toe.

For the most part, Carl's brick organ jarred, bewildered, and irritated, when it did not insult, its audience, but critics, sensing perhaps that minimalism or whatever it was had arrived, picked it out as one of the key works in the show. Its audacity forced many people proud of their open minds to rethink the received notions of what sculpture was supposed to be. The other minimalists, in rejecting sculpture as form, had ushered in sculpture as structure, but Carl, some discovered, had suddenly taken it all a step further. Engaging his *Lever* with the doorway implied incorporating the room itself into his sculpture; though no one yet had a durable name for that either, it was "site-specific."

Art-world pundits, who were not of a mind to rethink, dismissed it all as hopelessly dated dada, bricks as Duchampian urinals and bicycle wheels, one unsung wag calling it the emperor's new sculpture. The rethinkers looked for and found a qualitative leap forward and a comeback: a urinal is a urinal is a urinal, but bricks were the building blocks of dreams; given enough of them, as with Brancusi's *Endless Ladder*, one could build a stairway to the stars. The final, Fifty-seventh Street–smart analysis was, however, but will it sell?

As yet unconcerned about sales, Carl wrote a "poem-essay" in the catalogue to accompany the piece, titled "L E V E R   W O R D S." Part of the first stanza read, or rather appeared, this way:

> beam
> clay beam
> edge clay beam
> grid edge clay beam

By the addition of a new noun on the left margin, every line stuck out that much further. The second stanza as well as the third and the fourth had different four-letter bricks but looked like more of the same—a stack of lengthening (or shrinking) levers.

People laughed, but not last and they didn't make friends downtown.

Carl never looked back. He could not have known at the time that he had struck so rich a vein, but he surely whiffed it coming into his next public appearance—a month or so later in his second one-man show—bearing 960 freshly kilned white bricks. In the tradition of his father's father, he set them out, knees bent, on Johnny Myers's floor—Myers nervous about the weight—in eight different arithmetic combinations of 120 bricks each, a square and a rectangle here, a square and rectangle there. He titled the series *Equivalents,* meant to recall literati to the work of Stieglitz, a kind of patron saint of derided artists, whose post–World War I "Equivalents" were hundreds of dramatic photographs of clouds evoking every emotion, so sex was present by definition.

Leon Golub remembers the opening, Carl in a dark suit, a ruffled shirt, some sort of tie, looking like a "dandy," the spectators unsure of it all, a certain tension in seeing art not on the walls but on the floor. Paula Cooper thought it was "fantastic, really, I couldn't leave the show, and he was so polite and so nice." Somehow Paula and Carl ended up being interviewed together on a public-radio talk show, and somehow the art world began to absorb what was in and on the air. There was a trend, a new art movement, which meant a new art game in which you either played or you didn't, but it could end up the only game in town, so there was a compelling logic in playing, though the logic was not yet commercially driven.

Myers couldn't give the work away, not even back to the artist, and eventually he had to pay seven hundred dollars to haul them away, the glorious bricks regaining their plain old selves like Cinderella. But it was cover-story time for the bricklayer, and he was strategically, though not tactically, prepared. *Artforum,* going to press with a photograph on the cover of 137 bricks identical to and lined up precisely like *Lever,* had to kill the artwork when Carl impugned its authenticity, since he hadn't been the one to lay them. Nevertheless, the accompanying article-review by Bourdon ran as uncensored as it was fulsome, his subject's "astonishing" display of bricks on the Tibor de Nagy parquet floor likened to an "archipelago of Euclidean isles." Bourdon didn't know what to praise higher, Carl's brick sculpture or his brick poetry, and the unpolished observations of the young sculptor were patently self-serving ("Actually, my ideal piece of sculpture is a road"). When, alas, space ran out, Bourdon ended in wide-eyed wonder at what marvel the artist might accomplish next—getting in a ten-second spot to the wise that Carl but "awaits commissions."

Lucy, writing in *Art International,* came out at the same time with praise more muted and probably more effective. Doing his part, Carl went shopping for new kinds of bricks, chiseled away at his media style, and switched to a hipper gallery with a stronger floor. In his next show, at Virginia Dwan's, he covered her entire floor with some twelve hundred concrete coping stones, now inviting his still-timid viewers to walk on the slightly wobbly sculpture, to hear it crunch and feel it through the soles of their shoes. That added a dash of much-needed humor, and over the next year or so, with the word "minimalist" finally taking root, a throaty chorus of art writers and the minimalists themselves, plugging one another, joined in, and there was nothing minimal about it. Barbara floated the word "Renaissance" in connection with the movement, if not yet the man ("Shall We Have a Renaissance?"), Lucy capping it all with an *annus-mirabilis* piece in the *New York Times* titled "Rebelliously Romantic?" With credentials like that, Carl along with everybody else high in the movement, earned his own table and check-writing privileges in the red alcove at Max's.

THE TAN-COLORED walls at Max's were covered with the new art as well as the art it had elbowed aside, Mickey sallying out to his debtor-artists' lofts and choosing the work himself. A John Chamberlain abstract expressionist sculpture was the first thing you saw when you walked in and faced the bar, and if you were in the Andy Warhol crowd, you took your back-room pleasures in the voluptuous red light of Dan Flavin's plugged-in fluorescent minimal piece. Mickey had ecumenical taste, but the artists at Max's stuck to their own religion, and sometimes there was intolerance. "It was like, 'You're ruining art, I want to punch you in the nose,'" says conceptual artist Joseph Kosuth.

Five times as much was happening ten times as fast as it did anywhere else, according to Sukenick, and five hundred seems to be the number of people who came and went every day seeking the jukebox gospel of liberation. But it wasn't all gladness, and the life span of the regulars, when you count up the ODs, DOAs, and other anticlimactic endings, may have been twenty times the rate on the outside. Max's, unlike the Cedar, couldn't get its fill of women, but the Cedar macho air had moved in with the artists, hanging out front like them, and it was still ladies beware. To get to the Warhol room, you had to walk through the same Cedar-like "male lair" described by Carolee. Critic Peter Schjeldahl remembers making the Andy-bound journey: "It was like walking through heavy metal to get to strawberry shortcake."

"Everyone was macho then," Paula Cooper recalls. "Yeah, it was a real scene. You'd have a certain gang who were always at the bar, and they were really drunken and macho, Neil Williams and Chamberlain and the macho guys. And then there was Bob Smithson and Carl, who would really be the more intellectual, you know, they would be arguing about art and life."

John Perreault, who was one of the first to write about Carl's break-through art, saw a difference between Carl's and Smithson's argument styles at Max's. "[Carl] was always quite cantankerous and I admired his spark, but he was a quite dogmatic fellow. There was only one art and it was his. I was much more friendly with Robert Smithson, who was also very argumentive, but at least there was something to argue with him about. You didn't have to argue about entropy or science fiction with him. Carl was just, 'I'm right, and you're all a bunch of shits.' But he could be amusing."[4]

The whole minimalist group made for "quite a team," to hear about it from Kosuth. "You would sit at their table, and would just be absolutely, you know, wiped out, like fastest-guns-in-the-West art conversations, you know, real pricks, real killers. Carl Andre, Smithson, and Serra. I used to give them a fight, but on the other hand I thought a lot of it was macho posturing, and not really that productive. But of course if there were, you know, attractive young ladies around, our masculinity was on the line, so we would have our art battles."

---

[4]Perreault may not have liked Carl's debating style, but his memory of one of the topics certainly remained unclouded. Many years later, in a diary Carl kept in early 1985, he looked back fondly on the countless hours he'd spent with Robert Smithson in drunken argument over whether Carl's or Smithson's notion of entropy was more valid.

Some women had taken to coming to the lair less interested in the male art battles than their own. Perreault remembers Nancy Holt, Smithson's wife, and Carl's lover Brenda Miller, showing up one evening with a group of women only. "There was a show that included an unusual number of women artists, and after the opening, they went to Max's Kansas City and had their own table. It was just virtually unheard of and—who was the guy [who made sculpture] with the crushed automobiles—anyway, he was roaring drunk and was insulting them, trying to get them to get out of the bar, saying that women didn't belong there."

Sometimes, however, it was OK with everybody, Carolee arriving at Max's with a group after a performance: "We'd come in, ten or eleven of us, almost naked, with greasepaint and glue and the performance would be sticking to us. I remember being wheeled in there once in a grocery cart that was a prop left over from a BAM performance that we did. And that was just fine, to have me naked in the grocery cart being wheeled up the aisle."

Women artists came to Max's for still another purpose, according to Perreault, "to be in on the action," which meant business more than pleasure. Sukenick saw the same phenomenon. "At that point in the culture business, art was where it was happening." He continues:

> The stakes were high, and maybe they weren't the right stakes, but for a young artist to be at Max's, where there were plenty of collectors hanging out as well as painters, to be seen at a table with Larry Rivers or de Kooning was a good move. . . . So some young artist comes over to sit at, say, Carl Andre's table, knowing that Andre . . . has a reputation for being strict about who sits with him, and you can imagine how much guts it takes and how much is at stake. And there might be eight people at the table and Andre says, "You can't sit here."

"It sounds petty," Sukenick goes on to quote gallery owner Joe LoGiudice as saying, "but under the pressure of the times, the availability of fast fame even for some mediocre talents, that kind of putdown was a major setback."

One newcomer was minimalist painter Jeremy Gilbert-Rolfe, who would later show at Paula's gallery and befriend Carl, but not yet. He had arrived from England and was thrilled by the New York art world, but when he showed up at Max's, seeing his idols popping the ubiquitous chickpeas with their beer gave him a closer look at the scene. "These people who didn't know who the fuck I was and had no reason to know who the fuck I was would as often as not sort of brush me off with some use of Wittgenstein or Hegel or whatever, which was incredibly illiterate, you know: 'What you have to do is read Wittgenstein'; he said thus and thus. I happen to know Wittgenstein quite well. It would be a gross misunderstanding of what Wittgenstein was about. So there was this double thing: these people whose work I really liked would call me shit, and at the same time I didn't like them that much. [Max's] was exciting but a tremendous amount of bullshit."

Some amount of it seemed worth fighting over. Suddenly the arguing would stop, John Chamberlain, Brice Marden, and Neil Williams going at each other flying over tables, Western style, blood streaming down Robert Rauschenberg's face, a bottle crashed over his skull, somebody going through a plate-glass window, a bottle of beer dumped on Andy Warhol's silver wig, maybe not all in one night, but there were survivors to tell the tales. The "real pricks," however, may have been all talk. Paula vouches at least for Carl, "Of all the [physical] arguments and things at Max's Kansas City, and there were plenty of brawls and fistfights, I don't think he ever was involved in any."

IT WAS NOT all play. There was a dirty war going on in Southeast Asia, and what looked like a civil war at home. The new art was a rejection of not only the art of the Tenth Street school but its politics, of which, now to its shame, it had none. By 1969, with opposition to the war in Vietnam, the civil rights movement, and the "answers" blowin' in the wind as hard as they ever would, Carl had become one of the leading exponents of an anti-art-establishment struggle called the Art Workers Coalition. Fame, money, and beautiful lovers came, at least in the sixties, with social responsibilities, and the many minimalists and their conceptualist comrades obliged. The sympathies of the Art Workers lay with the Black Panthers, the Chicago Seven, the peace protest movements, and, being a coalition, with almost anything this side of the Abominable System from Che to Ho, but it concentrated its energies on trying to change the art world.

Much earlier in the decade, Carl in his *12 Dialogues* with Hollis Frampton had said it was important "not to become a weapon in the hands of those we despise." Now, though he still hadn't found the right costume, he let out his hair and his beard, dark brown locks covering his shoulders all around, and took the cause of the common artworker to the barricades. Abstract art, including his own, he said, had been manipulated by reactionaries for the last twenty years in the service of the cold war. They had exalted freedom of expression over imposed Soviet "tractor art" as long as nothing was expressed. Art was political by nature, and though he had nothing against abstract art, the new generation of artists would no longer acquiesce to the "dictatorship of the bourgeoisie."

Never having cared much for Wittgenstein, Carl, like many of his contemporaries, had rediscovered the incomparable antiestablishmentism of Karl Marx, and it fit this moment like a peg. The goals of the Art Workers were basically middle-class trade-unionist. Most of the artists, while mongering racial and gender equality, were, unless they were black or female, more interested in somehow obtaining higher earnings, pension plans, and health care than other items on the AWC agenda. A year of weekly meetings, slapping up posters, and picketing the Museum of Modern Art had produced only intramural strife, and some like Carl saw racism within the AWC itself. He and others viewed the struggle as futile without a classic, hold-the-line solidarity of the downtrodden.

In a memorable AWC meeting on October 20, 1969, he castigated the leadership for failing to convince the Art Workers that the mere recitation of injustice was worthless, that art was not a career "but a constant witness to the value of all life," and that the "essence of art is inspiration and not petty ambition." As the AWC went into its second year, he proposed a writ of demands with the dignity of the artist as the central issue of any struggle.

The other "Marxists" did what they could, but Carl had acquired an influential voice in the art world, and he raised it selflessly and courageously in the media and on the streets. The powers in the art world, the museums and galleries, were using the "fascist lie of quality," said Carl, in the service of old-style elitism, racism, and sexism. The art world was "one of the most thoroughly segregated communities in New York." The art-loving trustees of the museums, while claiming to be apolitical, were the same people, man for man, sitting on the boards of the biggest corporations and foundations, devising American foreign policy, supporting when not waging the war of "punitive oppression" in Vietnam, and "suppressing politics among artists." A "crisis of freedom" was at hand. "If freedom has to be at the expense of other people's lives, it isn't worth having at all." With his retrospective coming up at the Guggenheim, this was not the best way to ingratiate the museums, and he had more to lose than his chains. There were indeed those patrons, feeling the bite on the proffered hand, who recoiled in indignation, and there were fellow artists equally hostile to Carl's challenge to complacency. But many saw him defending a purity of art with a purity of soul, and he won enduring respect in the art community, from friend as well as foe.

THE START OF the seventies brought the United States' invasion of Cambodia, the Kent State killings, the Jackson, Mississippi, murders of civil rights workers, more national revulsion and protest, and, in the art world, the New York Art Strike against Racism, War, and Repression, with artists closing and sitting-in on the steps of the Metropolitan Museum, Carl preaching to hundreds of artworkers. But most artists, like most Americans, stayed home, worrying more about number one. Writing a year-end lament in *Studio International,* Lucy threw up her hands, saying how sad it was that "the majority of the art world is afraid to take its bullshit out of the bars and into the streets." While a very few like Carl remained courageous in the face of the "mud-slinging," she wrote, his colleagues preferred to "wallow in suspect patronage . . . content to be a waterboy to a critic or a mascot to a collector." They were a craven bunch, these artists, afraid of losing purchase on the ladder to the top, and there was nothing worse than the "man who hates himself for compromising and is having the fruits of his ass-kissing taken from him too."

THE WAR, OF course, ended. The warriors, from scapegoats to Nixon, got a measure of their due, the issues shifting back from guns to butter, ordinary soldiers forgotten and forsaken. Down in Soho, bold on the map by then—the midseventies—the only visible remnant of the Art Workers Coalition was Carl in his unchanging blue workingman's garb, donned somewhere along the way. Barbara Rose, now the ex–Mrs. Stella, thought he got the overalls from the painter Courbet and the style of his beard from Monet, but she decided he would never copy someone else's way. In those days, he always topped his getup with a black fedora, black being the color many artists, male and female, wore, and you could spot him a mile away.

The primacy of minimalism was rarely disputed now. Carl, once rookie of the year, had become both an MVP and a hall-of-famer. Gone were the skeptics who said the work would never sell. Minimalists and their dealers, shipping raw but uniquely contemplated matter in every compass direction, had gotten rich, or richer beyond their best-case calculations, their prices rising ever a step ahead of OPEC's reeling pace.

Not that minimalism ever touched the people. London tabloids clamored for upper-class blood when the Tate Gallery bought 120 of Carl's bricks for $12,000, $100 a three-penny brick. Hartford, Connecticut, was outraged when a local philanthropic foundation and the National Endowment for the Arts paid $87,000 for those thirty-two boulders—$2,720 apiece—installed by Carl on a public green adjoining the seventeenth-century downtown Center Church.

Some, however, saw a haunting beauty in the candor of his work; *New York Times* art critic John Russell became his most constant proponent. Russell found "an exceptional charge of feeling" in some of the most minimal of Carl's minimalism, and on one occasion he wrote:

The thralldom of a sculpture by Mr. Andre is owed to the clarity of his intention, to the frank and unambiguous way in which the materials are assembled. It does not aim to rival the psychodramas that were acted out in Abstract Expressionism. It does not deal in an outrageous dream life [of the Surrealists]. . . . It just lies there and minds its own business.

Russell's admiration would never wane, but sometimes the praise of others came with so much quince and mince it could only be downed with a runcible spoon. When Carl's concrete poems were first exhibited in England, in 1975, one of them, the word *rain* typed 140 times in unpunctuated lines ten rains long—rainrainrain, etc.—was likened by one critic, who at least had the good sense to sign only his initials, to a Shakespearean sonnet.

Carl, showing a practical sense of humor about it all, adopted Barnett Newman's view of the critics: "Aesthetics is for the artists as ornithology is for the birds," which of course was even less true now than in Newman's stripe-painting day. Asked how he would respond to critics who viewed his work as a "put-on," Carl replied, "People who think I am putting them on believe that I have them in mind when I work. I don't." His art was intended to give pleasure and nothing else, he insisted; the trouble was that "most Americans have a deep distrust of pleasure of any kind."

In the *Stone Field Sculpture* controversy, he was anything but aloof. He had installed the Hartford work in the summer of 1977 and had been startled by people "really screaming" at him, he said. "Another slap in the face for the poor," cried one local politician on the make; "just a bunch of rocks," said the mayor running for reelection. "Ask him why," said one woman with no other apparent ax to grind, "if it's minimal art it isn't minimal pay." In November of the same year, when the town began to hold meetings to discuss having the boulders removed, Carl drove up with Angela Westwater, with whom he was living now, and volunteered his presence. They were accompanied by Calvin Tomkins, art critic of *The New Yorker*, who had decided to do a "Talk of the Town" piece about the rather whimsical crisis. In his brief article, he wrote how happy he was to report that the artist and Hartford "worked things out"; years later, he would remember Carl charming even the most hostile citizens, "being very cordial, very reasonable, not 'talking down,' " and fielding every question with aplomb. The next day, after the three of them had spent a pleasant evening together, they visited the site, where "concord reigned virtually supreme" on a warm, misty fall day. Two white-haired elderly women in the front seat of a station wagon smiled approvingly as they drove by, and a girl in a pink skirt came up to Carl to tell him she loved his work.

"WOMEN LIKE CARL," says Lucy as she looks back to memories of him being with everybody in town. "There's something about him that's extremely sympathetic."

He had left Rosemarie in 1970 or 1971, flying off to his Mexican divorce, but they never stopped meeting in the Cupping Room on West Broadway for an afternoon game of chess, and though Ana would find that insufferable, Angela didn't seem to mind, putting up, too, with his being the "man of a hundred lovers" many in Soho knew. Representing Carl's art now, Angela and her gallery partners Gian Enzo Sperone and Konrad Fischer ran the business and Carl ran around. "It seemed to be a perfectly intact and equable relationship as long as it lasted, and it went on for a long time," recalls Jeremy Gilbert-Rolfe, who socialized with the couple. "There would be Carl trotting around and there would be Angela being demure and the way she was, sort of ultra-Waspy, ultra-Westchester. Very competent and unruffled."

"He wrote incredible love letters and poetry," says another ex-lover. "I still have them. Champagne, roses, expensive restaurants.[5] He'd send me a ticket from Europe, waiting for me to join him. I'd say, 'Carl, I can't. I have obligations in New York.' So he'd fly over and show up

[5]Carl may have owed some of his courtliness to his mentor Frank Stella—or vice versa. Stella was involved in several love affairs at the same time as Carl in those years. One woman, confiding in *New Yorker* writer Tomkins for his profile of Stella, said she was surprised by his romantic gentleness and sweetness, which seemed wholly at odds with the "brusque personality" that others knew. "I don't remember ever meeting a man who had such a tender touch with regard to feminine things," she told Tomkins. "He was bluntly poetic, if one can put it that way."

at my doorstep to take me back. But when he got me, he wouldn't be all that nice to me, full of mad passion one day and withdrawn the next."

Carl, leaving Angela to mind the store, had begun to travel a great deal in the seventies, invited here for a university lecture, there for art-center panel, following his work from museum to museum, shaking the hands of a blur of people who would forever remember shaking his, and then, as it often befalls the maned lion, a girl in a pink skirt, or sometimes in hemispheric jeans, sometimes in the hottest bright color of the season, would come up to him and tell him how she loved his work. The stories are legion. In San Francisco, he is riding in the backseat of a car with the local girl in the pink skirt, on his way to a party in Berkeley given just for him by the local shaker of his hand whose calls he has never returned but who he has seen in the hotel lobby, and shaking his hand, he says, "Oh, you're the person who's making me a party." But the party has been canceled because he never returned the calls, and Carl says, "That's OK. Call everybody back. I've decided to go." So they are riding in the car and his host is worried about what his wife, busy with her teaching, will serve on such short notice, and Carl is telling the local girl that he is number thirty on a list topped by Rauschenberg of the most successful artists in all the world, and he is younger than them all, still climbing. Then they are at the late-night supper party, Carl ridiculing a guest who is stammering, ridiculing his hostess who only had time to scramble some eggs— "You promised me a banquet and you give me breakfast!"—and nobody knows in which direction to look, the local girl saying, "Carl, maybe we ought to leave." Then, some time afterward, the local shaker traveling on the East Coast tells the now amusing story to a colleague, who says, "Oh, he did it to you, too."

"I was at a party once," says Gilbert-Rolfe, recalling Carl's "playful" side in those days, "and Carl and Angela came, and there were a lot of funny people there, gay people, and he suddenly noticed there were a lot of them there, and I suppose it was some gay person's loft because there was a picture of the queen on the wall, Her Majesty Elizabeth the Second, and Carl looked at it and then said, 'You know, it's good to have a queen. And one is all you need.' He was trying to be fucking annoying. He was saying something that other people would overhear and it's just the kind of thing that Carl used to do."

Often, the playfulness was harmless, Carl doing his W. C. Fields, unable to get a joke straight, pontificating at his table at One Fifth Avenue, quoting as his favorite authors names no one else had ever read or heard of, from Joseph Ignace Guillotin back to K'ung Fu-tzu, who if you went home and looked it up found out it was Chinese for Confucius. And often, he was on the receiving end. Says Gilbert-Rolfe, "How many times was he at some rich person's house and they've all been sucking up the fucking martinis and one jerk who's married to a lady who collects art that he hates but he earns 3M or something and tells Carl what an asshole he is, and then people kicking apart his bricks all the fucking time."

HE GAVE UP bricks in the seventies. In a burst of creative experiments, piling rocks, tedding hay, pouring sand, scattering plastic, scavenging for street junk, stringing out pipes and rods, and carpeting museums with a host of different metals, he began to favor the simplest arrangements of cedar or Douglas fir, usually twelve inches by twelve inches by thirty-six inches, and steel or copper plates, usually one foot square, showing his stacked blocks and tile patterns throughout the United States and Europe year after year. Critics had earlier accused him of aesthetic truculence, going out of his way to discombobulate his spectators, and others had seen funereal, tomblike lifelessness in his work, but by the second half of the decade, rarely a bad word came to print. Tom Wolfe's *Painted Word,* which first appeared in *Harper's* in 1975, grouped Carl at the end of a kind of black hole in which avant-garde art had finally minimalized into nothingness, coming out the other side as pure theory, and the public loved it. But art-world writers, needing art of any dimension or bust, were not emboldened. As for writing about Carl, few would dare venture beyond wondering with a touch of reverence if the artist wasn't tiling himself into a corner, reduced by steady reduction to being unable to change, much less grow, without "undermining the power of his original statement," as one Carl-watcher wrote in 1976.

By then, having heard and discovered the limits of every conceivable question, Carl had not only found the answers but had, as with his art, reduced them to arresting, if not always satisfying, clarity. In a somewhat facetious interview in 1974, the following exchange took place:

Q: Your favorite [art] piece? Why? Critics' favorite piece? Why?

A: As someone else once said my favorite piece is my next one. The critics favor the ones two years ago and the collectors favor the ones eight years ago—culture lag.

Q: Do machines influence you? Movies, theater? People? Politics? Emotions?

A: I fear almost all machines except the lever, the screw, the inclined plane, and the pulley. I never go to the theater. Movies are the strongest art of our time. I am very emotional about politics—ideas without passion are trivial.

Q: What is taste for you?

A: Taste is something that happens between the nose and the mouth—otherwise it is the confidence that comes from being a slave of fashion.

Q: Do you believe posterity is a form of the spectator?

A: I do not believe any serious artist is interested in posterity—I have never known a serious artist able to delay gratification that long.

Barbara Rose, elevating him to Renaissance manness, had given him the deed to terrain from which he could, indeed was obliged to, retreat now and then, yet doing so made that ground so easy to hold. He whittled at his pithy style ceaselessly getting it to stand-up comic sharpness—a *bonne riposte* for every heckle, and to the heckler who dared say that one Carlism contradicted another, he had a third at the ready. "We have always had the historical choice of either lying through or living through our contradictions," Carl opined dryly. "Now through the genius of the bourgeoisie we have a chance to market them."

By the end of the seventies, Carl at forty-four, grown fatter and redder than ever, was a familiar and popular figure, toting his bag on his shoulder, walking down to Soho in an unmistakable lumber. He had made enemies, to be sure. New York novelist Stephen Koch, who would meet Carl at dinner parties in those years, was not alone in disliking him intensely, though he was readier to go at it than others. "I found him to be a narcissistic boor and an intellectual fraud," says Koch, "an angry and aggressive drinker who exuded a hauteur menace. He had found his winning performance, his shtick, and continually cultivated his image, quite successfully, since it was really worth about two rounds and that's all."

Says Gilbert-Rolfe: "He was his own worst enemy in some respects, using sort of fancy language to explain his work. He's done a bit too much of that and I think that's made him look like an asshole. . . . Carl used to like to do the sort of thing that people who drink like to do—which was to have a drink and then be rude to people. . . . A drunk is a drunk whether he's drinking or not. I mean, your behavior in the morning when you're an alcoholic is also probably pretty acerbic by the standards of the nondrinking world. But Carl was one of those people like myself in those days who got worse as he got more drunk."

Others, perhaps those who knew him best in the daytime, acerbic or not, had come to esteem him as a man of quiet generosities, always ready to lend a hand, giving his name, his money, and his time to the causes of the day, buying a struggling artist's work whether he liked the work or not, endorsing the work he did like to dealers and curators, nominating artists for shows, helping some by nightly company and calls through a crisis of spirit as well as need, and as ready as ever to hound the establishment bastards.

"So there are two sides," Gilbert-Rolfe says, thinking of this part of Carl. "I rather suspect that it's the bad side that gets recalled. Think of the long list of people hanging around New York, you know, who don't get exhibited very much, who don't get much attention, who nonetheless are serious artists of one kind or another, working for hundreds of fucking years and maybe they're not very good and maybe they are, and Carl knows them. He doubtless could tell you within some sort of reasonable chronology what they were doing at any moment. One could think of a lot of people who were as famous as Carl who would have lost track of those kind of friends a long time ago." Artists get places through other artists, not by the impersonal gallery system alone, and unlike dealers, collectors, and critics, artists on the receiving end never forget.

THIS WAS THE Carl who in the fall of 1979 picked up the phone in his newly moved-into apartment on Mercer Street when Nancy Spero called to ask a favor. She knew he had a busy schedule, but would he be available to be on a public discussion panel to take place in the Wooster Street gallery where she showed? Her husband, Leon Golub, with whom Carl used to play poker, would be on the panel, too, though it wasn't Leon's but Carl's name, he and Nancy both knew, that was meant to be the drawing card. Nancy had had the idea not to promote herself, but to help launch a young sculptor Carl had never heard of. It was the artist's first one-person show in New York. Nancy recommended the work highly, but, as Carl surely knew, it was so hard to get people to come downtown to see an unknown, so could he make it on the evening of November 12? Carl, as almost always, said yes, and knowing Nancy and Leon weren't selling much these days, he invited them to dinner after the meeting at the Japanese restaurant next door to the gallery.

The gallery sent Carl a copy of the press release announcing the show. It began:

ANA MENDIETA will be having her first exhibition at A.I.R. GALLERY, November 6–24, 1979. The show entitled "Silueta Series 1979" is an ongoing dialogue between the artist and nature.

—— 29 ——

Tall Jim Melchert, administrator, teacher, artist, and artist's best friend, was sitting in his corner office at the south arcade of the American Academy in Rome more on edge than his usual fussing, fidgety self. It was a spring day in April, Easter break come and gone, the sweetness of azalea and mimosa in the air, the fellows back in their studios working toward the annual May exhibition and, thank goodness, the end of this awful Academy year. At the moment, however, small pleasures were inert in the back of his thoughts; he was awaiting what at best could only be a heartbreaking visit with Ana's mother and sister, and if his fears came true, it could mean nasty business for the Academy.

He had tried from the outset, as was his nature, to do what was right and proper. First there had been the dreadful phone call from Sophie Consagra, the Academy president in New York—unspeakably horrible, because ever since Ana had married Carl the "joke" going around the Academy was, "I wonder which one is going to kill the other one first?"—and then, only a day or so before she was due back to clear out her studio for an incoming artist, with all the newly appointed fellows descending, she was dead. Her death had thrown his staff into the stupefying sorrow felt over the loss of someone with whom one fell in love after hating. But the work of the Academy had to go on, and that included the tactful, respectful, and competent removal of Ana's incumbency. He had been in frequent touch with Sophie, the Academy trustees, and the family's lawyer and had taken great care in arranging a professional inventory of her studio, worrying first about an Italian police search for evidence that had never materialized. He had had to fret nonetheless over every detail from the Academy's legal responsibilities to the whereabouts and, worse, the volatility of Ana's stock of gunpowder. Now there was Ana's sister and her mother having things moved into, not out of, the Academy, and here they were in Rome with this business of an enormous sum of money in the Academy safe, Jim alone knowing what was really there.

SHE WAS ANYTHING but just another fellow to Jim and his wife, Mary Ann. He had known her as far back as her Iowa City days, meeting her at a party given by Hans in 1977, when Jim was head of the visual arts program of the National Endowment for the Arts. She had been both sultry and aloof in his presence that evening, Jim sizing her up as a bit of an actress because she had applied for an NEA grant. When her slides came in the mail, he loved her work anyway, and some months later when she turned up in Washington unannounced, he was flabbergasted, discovering her to be the most vivacious, exciting young personality that had ever walked into the foundation's offices, though that, too, he felt, had had something to do with her act. She was a good artist, sure, but good artists compete against good artists, and, well, she got the grant. Then, though he would hear about her from time to time, he hadn't seen her again until he came to Rome with Mary Ann as the Academy's new director. Ana had already completed her year as a fellow, wanting to stay on, and he had rented her a barnlike studio out back and one of the Casa Rusticas, with its squeeze-in kitchen and sitting room downstairs and a couple of little bedrooms one flight up, a patch of garden under the leaves of old trees, everything tiny but pleasant and space enough for her and, whenever he showed up, even Carl. Jim and Mary Ann had arrived from California early in that summer of 1984 to live in Rome for the first time, the fellows gone, the staff yet to warm to them, alone, tongue-tied without the language, overwhelmed by the stunning Janiculan views, and only Ana to make them feel at home, which she at once set out to do. They had to get off the hill, she said, packing them into her speedy VW, wanting to show them every gallery in town, forgetting that most were already closed for the season, and showing them Rome instead. Everywhere she took them there was someone who smiled, sometimes opening a bottle of amber wine from the Alban Hills, but always happy to see her again. Then the Academy year began and Ana, absorbed all day with her new gunpowder sculpture, was still always fun at night. You wanted to invite Ana if you were having people up for drinks because she'd just be there sparkling and making everybody feel good. And when, exactly one month after her death, Jim and Mary Ann arranged, as the Romans do in Rome, a memorial mass—this one at the church called the Church of the Artists—Ana's friends from one circle or another could scarcely believe their eyes at the number of people who came.

These were the fond recollections he wanted to share with Ana's sister and mother, hoping that the matter of the safe wouldn't get out of hand.

ANA'S MOTHER HAD visited her in Rome in 1984, was given the grand tour in the VW, and went off on her own to see Florence, but this was the first time for Raquel. Four months ago, she had given birth to her second boy, Vitthal, giving him one of the names of Lord Krishna. The baby was still breast-feeding and with her in Rome. When she and her mother met with their Italian lawyer, he was able to report that he had successfully disposed of Golan's landlordly pretensions. He had been present during the move, had seen no water or any other damage, and the landlord had had to content himself with regaining the place emptied. There had been no signs of a break-in, so whatever was in the apartment had been crated and trucked across the Tiber to the Janiculum hill.

THE BRAND-NEW VW Polo station wagon Carl had bought Ana was still parked where she had left it in Via Angelo Masina when Raquel, her mother, and the baby arrived at the Academy. It stood at the curb outside the gatehouse, its white color flattened by time and the grime of the city. Jim Melchert received them as warmly as his nerves would allow. He would now have to tell them that, far from $33,000 in cash and jewelry, there was nothing of Ana's in the Academy safe, though there had been. She herself had withdrawn it, but even then there had been little of value other than a pair of gold earrings, a gift from Carl, Jim believed. A member of his staff had been present when Ana had taken it back, and the signed withdrawal ticket was in Jim's possession, but such was Carl's power, real or imagined, that Jim and the trustees worried that he or his lawyers would demand a full-scale investigation, which might somehow involve the Academy in a scandal.

Stammering and bumbling and looking inexplicably nervous to both Mendietas, Jim broke the news about the safe. Raquel of course couldn't speak for Carl, but while she and her mother were disappointed, she simply wanted to go on to the next order of business, recovering Ana's belongings. Perhaps some of the jewelry might still be among them, but what was uppermost in Raquel's mind was that she was closing in, finally and once and for all, on learning the fate of Ana's evidence against Carl. Indeed, she was intent on finding it. With the case currently in a nether world and Carl again unindicted, locating the evidence would be "the big thing," she hoped, to make it all go forward.

Jim escorted them out to Ana's studio, and leaving them to come and go as they pleased, they came and went over the next two weeks and sifted through the haunted substance of all her Roman things.

ANA'S STUDIO ON one of the Seven Hills of Rome, with its arched entrance, thrusting high ceilings, sprawling, mottled concrete floor, sinewy, sweaty pipework climbing the walls geometrically, was the kind of space that fills the reveries of artists dreaming of light and happiness. Obeying an unwritten code among former fellows, Ana had been preparing to cede the studio to visiting artist Varujan Boghosian, older and higher in seniority, and move her work to a more modest space on the same grounds. Boghosian, learning of Ana's death, immediately relinquished his privileges, so the studio had remained exactly as she left it seven months earlier—minus her cookie box of gunpowder and some bottles of gas and gasoline—hundreds of items partially packed and almost ready to go on her return. To this had been added the contents of her and Carl's apartment, consisting of some furniture and many cartons occupying a large quadrant of the studio.

Seated on a couple of straight-backed bentwood chairs, the two Raquels were surrounded by a part of Ana's life of which they knew little. Here was her most mature art, rising among the power tools with which it had been made. Older, pancake-flat baked-earth reliefs, somehow recalling her husband's ground-level sculpture, lay scattered on the floor, but that phase had been abandoned in 1984; it had given way to the vertical, freestanding tree trunks, more than six feet high, prototypes for taller works in the planning, simple ovals and teardrops unequivocally female fired into the raw wood, and there were other trunk surfaces engraved with life-size anthropomorphic outlines of less female, almost masculine imagery yet to be.

The baby slept in a folding travel bed while his mother and grandmother began their search through the cartons moved from the apartment. There were lots of clothing, coats and dresses and shoes, and Carl's attire, too. Ana loved going to the Porta Portese flea market on Sunday mornings in Rome, scavenging for bargains. Not long ago, she had picked up an old cashmere camel's hair coat for less than ten dollars, bundling herself in it and calling it "fantastically chic" to a friend who thought it looked ridiculous. Raquel found herself going through Carl's things, picking out what she thought he might still want to wear, discarding the rest, and piling the remainder for transatlantic shipment back to Mercer Street. It was mostly overalls.

Both women kept an eye out for the jewelry. Ana's mother had had three bracelets, simple gold bands. She had given one to Raquel, and on a trip with Ana and Carl to Spain that summer before Ana's death, she had given her one, too. Ana, slipping it on, had said she would never remove it, but it was not on her wrist when she died, and her mother, puzzled, searched for it now. Ana had also had family diamonds and platinum jewelry, her grandmother's gold ring, a gold chain, and many pairs of earrings. But nothing turned up now, and they began to wonder if it had been stolen by either the movers or a false friend to whom she had entrusted it for safekeeping while she traveled. Her mother finally gave it all up as lost. Well, she thought, Ana is lost, too.

Also gone were two artworks given to Ana by the artists, one by Carl and the other by Hans, though a watercolor, a gift to Ana on the day of her wedding, was stuck with a pushpin to a wall in the studio. It was a naive amateur work by her friend Ida Panicelli, a figurative image otherwise cryptic to the viewer, but Ida later recalled what she had had in mind, though not why: Carl sitting like a silent Buddha in the sky, Ana tossing stones at him that fell on a little house below them.

They found a diary. It was in block writing, which both Raquels, as recipients of his recent letters, recognized as Carl's without the slightest difficulty. It was among a sheaf of notes, also in his handwriting, some of them love poems to Ana. The diary had been written in an Italian *agenda,* as it is called, in this case a bound calendar for the year 1985, with each day and date at the top of a blank page about half the size of a standard sheet of typing paper. The first entry appeared on the page headed *giovedì 7 febbraio,* Thursday, February 7, and it did not take much reading to discover that this was Carl's record of their honeymoon trip to Egypt and the cruise on the Nile.

Whatever qualms Raquel had about taking possession of the diary were soothed by recollecting Carl's earlier affirmation to Gary Simon that he wanted nothing that was in the Rome apartment. She therefore considered it, along with everything else now in the studio, as part of Ana's estate, of which she had been named executor. It was not a comfortable act, but of course she read the diary to the last word of the final entry, which had apparently been made on the flight back from Cairo to Rome, twenty-one tightly penned pages and three weeks after the first.

By the time they went on their honeymoon, they had been together for more than five years, sometimes closer than others, to be sure. Nevertheless, they had been married less than a month and traveling separately much of that time. He had written her those three love poems on her thirty-sixth birthday two months before the wedding and another poem at Christmas, joining Ana with love and Rome as his destiny. A couple of weeks later, in wishing her Happy New Year, he had written how Ana, darling, sexy, Tropicanita, was his one and only beautiful love forever and forever. All this had been read by Raquel along with the diary, but it appeared from the latter that the thrill was suddenly gone. Ana was mentioned by name only twice and referred to once, when the journey was all over, as "the one I shared a cabin with." There were no love letters dated later than the diary, which led Raquel to speculate that something had gone wrong on the journey. In any case, Carl in Egypt had, with some exceptions, had a rather miserable time.

Although he traveled a great deal, he was never good at it, and Ana knew it, confiding her apprehensions about the honeymoon when speaking with Natalia in January and wondering how he would take to Third World hospitality. In a postcard to her mother written four days before their departure, she sounded happy enough about it, but not completely: "I think it'll be fun," she wrote, "if we survive the trip."

She had been right about his displeasure, but that was only part of it. Unlike his published or exhibited writings, the diary revealed as nowhere else an irascible, supercilious, and rather provincial side to its ever-articulate author. From the first entry forward, there was nothing but shallow griping about the failings of everyone in his purview, except, thanks to a romantic notion, the entire population of Rome. Carl's Rome was the only civilized place he knew, where money was unimportant, the friendly natives—who were especially disposed to dispensing hospitality pro bono publico—welcomed foreigners with open arms, and the poor man fared as well as the rich man, at least when it came to Italian food. The pages turned to the strains of mandolins.

Leaving the Rome of his fancy, however, he began at once to wonder whether Egypt would be anything more than a Gomorrah of poverty and disease. In the traveling, much of it fulfilled the expectation, Carl finding fault with every accommodation from the programs on his hotel television set to a perceived anti-Christian bias in a Moslem tour guide's spiel. Worst of all, once on the Nile, were his Western traveling companions. One day in February, after wishing his diary a happy Valentine's day, he sat on the deck, railing with his pen at the intrusiveness of the French, Italians and Spaniards and the boorishness of his fellow Americans.

Not that he was unmoved by what presumably lured him in the first place. Quite the contrary, much of the famous fixtures of Egypt and the Nile, from the Great Pyramid to the verdant floodplain and back to the "splendors of Tutankhamun,"[1] filled his trained eyes and his field glasses with pleasure, leaving him as much in awe of his place in

---

[1]Given a choice, Carl apparently always chose the more exotic spelling, in this instance Tutankhamun over Tutankhamen, elsewhere Ramesses and Rameses for Ramses, and of course old K'ung Fu-tzu.

the universe as the least-jaded traveler. Even the living aborigines, as he called them, had at least one impressive quality. That was the prowess of Egyptian seamen, their ability to negotiate the winds and currents of the Nile. It utterly surprised him.

His last impression of Egypt was his worst, driving him, he told his diary in the final entry, "almost to the point of violence." He was sitting in the Cairo airport on the morning of his flight back to Rome, forced to abide, at eight o'clock in the morning, a commercial for a men's cologne played and repeated without surcease at the highest volume on giant sized television sets. The commercial was in Arabic but would have been just as hateful in English, he said. He then went into an all-things-considered review of the whole country. If Egypt had opened on Broadway, it would have folded that morning. He disliked all of his fellow passengers in manner and in looks—except for "the one I shared a cabin with," he wrote in parenthesis—had remained indifferent to the cuisine, but hated the music, which had been inescapable through-out the journey. The dust was worse. Egypt was a country of dust. The Nile, when you got far enough from the dusty shore and the awful music, was, it seemed, worth the price of admission.

What the bride had been doing through all this punishment can almost be glimpsed in her two walk-on appearances in Carl's diary. Complaining about tedious repetition in a wall carving at Edfu, Carl noted approvingly that Ana had commented that the work must have been done using stencils, and two days later, she again met with favor, in an observation about the division of labor among the ancients, which fit his critique of the temples of Ramses II. If Ana disagreed with Carl about anything at all on their honeymoon, it was not recorded.

Ana's papers were mixed with Carl's. She also had a bound book suitable for a diary. Designed to be feminine, with sunbursts and a tropical motif on lined pages, it had almost certainly been picked up on a trip to Mexico, made with Hans in 1979. She had begun writing in it that year, in Spanish, titling it *apuntes*, or notes, but the notes, mostly about her art, grew more and more sporadic, and there was only one dated entry in Rome, January 16, 1984. That was a year and a day before her wedding, that winter she was making up with Carl after the break when she left for the Academy prize, Carl working now on a

fellowship of his own in Berlin and courting her steadily in correspondence, by telephone, and in frequent sorties down to Rome. "Making
love," Ana switching to English wrote to herself on that occasion, "is
a search for the confirmation of our being by another being. It is the
most profound experience of what *being* is and its beauty lies in that
this profound experience is shared by another." She went on to re-
phrase the same thought in several different ways, in the vein of the
very jottings made by Carl in the same batch of papers. He spoke of
love as the fulfillment of desire; she saw love as seeking and securing
the essence of existence. He wrote of dreams as giving meaning to what
would otherwise be meaningless; she declared happiness to be "an
after-image of the original shelter within the mother." She called him
"dear sweet Chino," a Spanish term of endearment.

They had risked sounding a little like Nelson Eddy and Jeanette
MacDonald, but of course they couldn't know that the pages of their
sentiments would end up stored this way, and Carl could turn the coin
of love around. He spoke of tragedy, of women being mysteries, men
and women bound only like the affinities of celestial bodies passing in
distant orbits in the night.

Both of them, culling their thoughts regularly, it seemed, would
make notes on the handiest scrap of paper, wrapping paper being good
enough for Carl. "My art," Ana pitched, aiming a little high, "attempts
to fuse in our super industrialized society, the most primary facts of
nature with the most artistic impulses of man." Carl, leagues ahead as
the better epitomist, scribbled: "My work is meaningless. This is a
property shared with the universe."

When Raquel got to some of Carl's concrete poems, with their
words split on two lines and crossword-puzzle patterns, she thought it
"cutesy," and her interest flagged. At a certain moment, however, she
suddenly came on something that might be considered as evidence.

Dated July 14, 1984, it was a card addressed to Ana from the
executive offices of the Vatican Museum, inviting her "to climb the
scaffolding in the Sistine Chapel." Raquel, growing excited, knew
precisely what that meant. When Ana was in New York in September
of that same year, she had expressed concern that her lifelong fear of
heights was developing into a serious disability. She had told her sister

of two recent incidents in which she had been physically overcome by anxiety as never before, and one of them had to do with the Sistine Chapel. The Michelangelo frescoes on the ceiling of the chapel were then undergoing restoration, and that part of the Vatican was closed to the public. Occasionally, a few persons, mostly art historians, were permitted to mount the scaffold and view the work in progress and, of course, the magnificence of the art itself up close. It was a privilege that had not been extended for more than a century, and a century might come and go again before such an opportunity would arise anew. Ana had sought and had somehow received such an invitation. Ana, Raquel was reminded now, had described how she had gone that day in July to the Vatican, hoping to hold her phobia in check, if only this one time. She had actually begun to ascend the structure, an easy climb for most people, when, a few steps off the floor, she suddenly panicked and said, "Forget this, I can't do it." Here in her sister's hands was sad proof of what she had recounted. Perhaps they were at last closing in on other evidence, too.

Instead, they found something that Ana had written that chilled their hearts even more. It had been set down in an unsteady hand, with wavy lines, words crossed out and letters misshaped and corrected, unlike anything else among her papers. It read:

> I recently yesterday had a very strange dream. You were with 3 children teaching them a map in a small room & you killed them. I came to see you knowing you wanted to kill me too, you had blood all over you.—Instead we made love. It was a strange dream.[2]

RAQUEL PLANNED TO turn over everything written to the D.A., but the prize she had come for continued to elude her. By now she had

[2]The word "yesterday" had been inserted over "recently had," and the sequence of words "them a map in a small room" had been added after "children" and a word that had been crossed out ("them").

been through all of Ana's personal effects more than once and had found no trace of the divorce evidence. Their time in Rome had all but passed, and when their lawyer agreed to arrange to ship everything back to the States, there was little more to do than pack their own things and go. On one of the walks to and from the studio, they had seen a cypress tree planted in memory of a late fellow, and speaking about it to Jim Melchert, he agreed to do the same for Ana. They asked that the tree be a palm.

There was something, an ineffable feeling—Raquel would always believe it to be Ana—that kept her from leaving the studio. Whatever it was drew her back to her sister's things, not the private papers, which had yielded little more than further mystery and sadness, but the photographs of her art. They were kept in more than one portfolio, the portable show windows artists pound the streets with. Raquel had already come across them, thinking, oh, those are the portfolios, so they needed to be stacked with the art. Now she picked them up again.

The divorce evidence Ana had been collecting so stealthily, burgling her husband's papers and pockets in New York and Rome, was in a manilla envelope tucked and hidden in a pocket on the inside cover of one of the portfolios, the only one with a zipper. It consisted of photocopies of exactly what Ana had told Natalia she had gathered, including the nude photographs of the bitch in Berlin—squatting on a polished wood floor and turning optical tricks with a large round mirror. To Raquel and her mother, all that mattered now was that they had everything to which Ana in the end had led them. As feelings of elation were supplanted by thoughts of their loved one hiding, fuming, and brooding over what she knew about Carl, they gathered it all and flew back to New York.

—— 30 ——

When Martha Bashford had the papers Raquel had brought from Rome on her desk at 80 Centre Street, she wondered what she could do with them. Loud TV commercials in Cairo might drive Carl, by his own admission, almost to the point of violence, and Ana might have held a dread so deep it could only escape in the crazy house of a dream, and hadn't Carl said that dreams give meaning where there is none, but go tell that to a judge.

Raquel herself had never believed that any part of it, with the exception of the divorce evidence, had legal value, but her purpose in turning it over to the D.A. was to help her see "how Carl's mind worked." By that time, however, Bashford needed no help. What had gotten to her much earlier was learning that Carl continued to live in 34E. She knew housing was tight in New York, but that he had the means and did not move told her as much as she cared to know about his irregular thinking style. The mind that concerned her most at the moment was Judge Berkman's, in which there seemed to be only the narrowest place for Ana's state of mind regarding Carl.

It was, however, painfully clear from these photocopies what had been so grating to Ana.

There were papers linking Carl to three women dating from May 1984, when Carl was on his sculpture grant in Berlin, to June 1985, when traveling via Berlin he joined Ana in Rome before leaving for their trip to Spain with her mother. The first 1984 document, a copy of a round-trip airline ticket from JFK to Berlin prepaid in Germany by Carl, recorded what appeared to be a one-time encounter with a woman artist fairly well known in Soho. She disappeared from the paper trail after that, but it was about the same time, probably a few days later, when Ana herself flew to Berlin at Carl's invitation—an excursion recalled with love and pleasure in a postcard shortly afterward from Carl to his Beautiful Tropicanita back in Rome. The thought of Carl placing his relationships with other women in such close proximity to his contact, even sexual contact, with her vexed her perhaps most of all. Her complaints to Natalia about hearing Carl on the phone with another woman found double confirmation in her pilfered record of both his AT&T Mercer Street and his credit card calls. In a trip they made in May 1985 to Buffalo, where Ana installed a work in a gallery group show, Carl called his woman friend in Berlin, and though his wife may or may not have been within earshot at the time, the same phone record—going back to three weeks before their marriage—revealed twelve back-to-back calls to Ana in Rome and the woman in Berlin, or vice versa, Carl often hanging up from one and immediately ringing the other.

In the same irksome vein, Carl's dutifully entered checkbook stubs showed that Ana was the recipient in April 1985 of a thousand dollars from her husband, with the very next check—for the same amount and the only one noted without an explanatory memo—going to another Soho woman artist. There was little more on her, but she was the woman Ana had connected with Carl by tracing them to their favorite restaurant when she was back in New York that May.

The woman who infuriated Ana most, however, was the Berlin liaison, Rita Sartorius, and the majority of papers related to her. They showed that Ana had managed to identify her would-be rival by matching the phone number in the AT&T calls to Berlin to the same number in Carl's address book, which revealed the woman's name and where in the city she lived. By the time Sartorius came on the scene, in terms of Ana's record (appearing first in September 1984), she had developed into a full-scale block-letter writer, an inveterate postcard sender, and a concrete poetaster either on her own or from some inspiration emanating from Carl, her Rainbow. The accidents incurred by husbands in the course of conventional extramarital flight are undoubtedly built into the tortuous adventure, but only men with recessed kinks in their inner wiring fly so recklessly. The schoolgirlish postcards and centerfold postures of the dark-haired Berliner who was so eager to end up in Carl's life could hardly be more expressive of a woman in the heat of a magnificent infatuation—presumably the state desired by the infatuator but in this case a man who evidently did not live by heat alone. Ana may have gone out of her way in search of heartache, but Carl's souvenirs were apparently never more than one scratch below every surface.

Ana's evidence surely would have added heat of another kind in a divorce court, and depending on the judge could still be useful were the case to come to trial, but Berkman, for her part, had made it one of her caveats that the spouse's motives for seeking a divorce were inadmissible. Bashford, preparing once again to face a grand jury, simply put it all aside, its true significance left to yellow along with the paper. The recovery of the photocopies in Rome was the strongest possible corroboration of Ana's claim to Natalia that there was, when she was still alive, a second set in 34E, amplified by her "photocopying like crazy" right before her death.[1] It also pounded on the door that had yet to be opened: that someone other than Gerry Rosen had gone to the apartment before him to remove it.

RAQUEL, IN A bright green short-sleeved summer dress, the same dress she had worn a few days earlier to her daughter Raquelita's high school graduation, sat on a pewlike bench in a witness room waiting to be called. It was a Friday, June 27, and sitting near her was someone who by now was a sort of old friend, Detective Ron Finelli. Looking thinner, he had recovered from lung surgery and was back on the job with a good two and a half years to go before retirement. There was not a cigarette in sight. They were alone, the first two witnesses in the second grand jury proceedings in the People versus Carl.

Bashford was inside introducing the case to the jurors, adhering as closely as she could to the script Berkman had imposed. The judge's firmest no-nos had been spelled out to the letter: strict adherence to the hearsay rules and legal instruction given not piecemeal but all at the end. The assistant D.A., fearing the possibility of failing to please Berkman a second time, had taken the precaution of going over her new presentation very carefully with her bureau chief, who became as convinced as she that it followed the caveats and would therefore stand.

Privately, Bashford believed that Berkman, living up to her reputation, had that something no one could explain against her simply because of her age and gender, but she also felt that there was more to it.

"The judge is being bitchy," she had confided when prepping Raquel the second time. "I can understand her point, but I think she has it in for me; she thinks I'm trying to make a big name for myself and

---

[1]Still further corroboration of Ana's divorce plans was found in the original of a letter recovered in Rome from her attorney in New York. It was an inconclusive response to a question she had apparently asked about what might happen to her own assets in any divorce proceeding.

she's trying to put me down. So let's play her game so that she doesn't throw it out again."

The knack of the game appeared to Bashford to lie in avoiding any mention of Ana's *past* activities regarding Carl. Information about her future was explicitly allowed by Berkman, so the key word became Ana's *plans*. Raquel, and later Natalia, could only speak of what Ana was *going* to do, and both prosecutor and witness, ever mindful of the consequences, tried as hard as they could not to falter, but in practice it did not always work very well. Thus, when Raquel was on the stand, this exchange took place about Ana's plans:

Bashford: What, if anything, did she say to you about her state of mind concerning the marriage?
Harrington: She told me . . . that she was planning on taking him to court, hiring a detective in Berlin to follow him and this other woman that she knew he had there, and that she was going to get as much money as possible from him through the courts and that she was going to ruin his reputation in the art world because she felt that people didn't know the real Carl Andre. That she was going to expose him to the world . . . and that she was going to continue to collect evidence for the divorce proceedings.

These were, of course, all plans, but at the same time they again revealed, as they had to, what lay behind them, so when Bashford got to Natalia, she grew even more watchful, both women sticking so closely to the "plans" that they continually tripped over them, producing almost comical results:

Bashford: Did Ms. Mendieta tell you anything concerning any plans she had made regarding her marriage to Mr. Andre?
Delgado: She said that she wanted to get a divorce and she wanted me to help her find an attorney to represent her. . . .
Bashford: Did she tell you anything else she was planning to do at that point?
Delgado: She said that she was planning to get information on—

evidence together that showed that her husband had been having an affair with two women.

Bashford: She had told you she was trying to—planning to—accumulate some evidence?

Delgado: Yes, she did. . . .

Bashford: When she talked to you when she said she was planning to gather evidence to help in this planned divorce proceeding, did she tell you how she planned to gather the evidence?

Delgado: Well, she had—she was planning on getting—photocopies of telephone bills that she had, phone calls—

Bashford: Don't tell us what. She was planning on getting photocopies of material?

Of course the answer was yes. Ana, it seemed, had been planning to do what she had already done. The grand jury room had been turned into an arena where fiction was stranger than truth.

SUMMER HAD BROUGHT an end to the art season and the annual exodus from Soho, but the ordeal sailed on. In some respects, the case began to transcend itself, creating a window of its own on the way people of the sixties lived in the eighties, a window on the textured landscape of human frailties. The word *conspiracy* filled the void downtown. It had a double meaning, depending on which side you stood: some saw a district attorney, driven by a cabal of feminists and Third World Latins, hungry for the red meat of a "celeb" trial; others saw an art world Mafia buttoning up and closing ranks to protect one of its capos.

The grand jury sessions—there would be eight dealing with the case—crept at a summer pace through July and August and into September, neither Carl nor the family receiving any indication of how the matter would fare. Carl, with the help of his European dealer and old friend Konrad Fischer, put together a one-man show exhibited in Brussels and Düsseldorf, which of course he could not attend. It was made up of variously arranged blocks of Belgian blue limestone, giving the show its name, "Belgian Blue Limestone." A picture postcard was printed of one of the pieces of sculpture, *Belgica Blue I,* and though in black and white, blue was the mood of the image as well. That was the card he would use for correspondence for a long time to come.

CARL WAS IN hell that summer, May Stevens told Zarina early in September. They were in Minneapolis, had run into each other at conference on women in the visual arts, and were having a drink. May was one of the main speakers on the program. Zarina had known her for a long time and thought of her as sort of patronizing but very nice. She knew that May was a very good friend of Carl's, and they had begun to talk about Ana, Zarina saying, "I haven't been in New York, has anything come up there about the trial?" By that time, Zarina, who had had her dream in which Ana had told her what had happened, had made up her mind, but still, you just don't blurt it out.

"It was a tragic accident," said May. "If anybody is in hell, it's Carl."

"I don't doubt it," Zarina said, but before very long, she revealed her true feelings.

"Oh, no, you can't think that," May said. "No one knows and no one will ever know what happened. Even he doesn't."

"May, come on," Zarina said in her Indian syntax, "he was there, and he will know."

"But he doesn't. He doesn't go out and he doesn't see anybody, but I've seen him and it's so sad. You should see him. He doesn't know what happened. No one will ever know. It's a tragedy."

"It was a tragedy for all of us," said Zarina. "We lost her."

"It was a big loss for him," said May.

ANOTHER WOMAN ATTENDING the conference was Ruby Rich, keeping a cold distance from May Stevens. She was there in her Arts Council capacity to give a talk about film, but she had another mission in mind.

She had been at work all summer preparing an article due to be published in *The Village Voice* on the first anniversary of Ana's death. She was hardly a disinterested observer, but her editors, as with past assignments, had given her free rein to be as controversial as the editorial spectrum of fair play allowed, which at the *Voice* was about a full circle. Ever the girl detective, she had combined her research for the article with her extracurricular probing for Bashford. Her latest memos to the assistant D.A. included notes about a social scientist in Denver named Lenore Walker. Walker had done studies of women murdered by their spouses and had served as an expert witness in some cases. She had found a pattern in her statistics indicating that "the point at which most husbands kill their wives is when they have got their act together and have decided to leave," Ruby had written. This had seemed relevant to Ana's determined divorce plan, though Ruby was unaware that she had actually made arrangements with Marsha Pels on the Friday before her death to move her possessions out of Carl's apartment.

When the *Voice* had insisted that Ruby try to obtain a comment from Hoffinger about the rumors of Carl's violence, she got no further than getting the attorney on the phone to deflect her questions ("That's not something we're aware of"), but the conversation produced further tidbits she passed on to Bashford. One concerned Hoffinger corroborating, in an apparently inattentive remark, that Carl had had the key to the Rome apartment all along, and thus access. Another item recorded Hoffinger's use of the word "accident" in connection with the defense, which was the first time Ruby had heard of that theory, she told Bashford. "I pounced on this right away," that memo reported, "and said I thought it was interesting that he used that term because I had heard other people close to Carl use it recently but understood it has never been a contention in the case. He was immediately defensive, tried to back off, and said, 'Well, there are three possibilities, aren't there?' "

All of this was extremely premature considering that, at the moment, Carl was not only unindicted but had won a major victory in court by getting the original charges dismissed. This state of affairs, however, had driven Ruby even farther afield from her journalism and amateur police work to pressure-group politics, and her being on every doorstep was what Carl's friends pointed to when they cried conspiracy. That was pure passion, and as for the questionable ethics in using her press credentials for nonjournalistic pursuits, she was not shooting for a Pulitzer but for quite another prize. Her own answer to her critics would come in her article. In the meantime, she had begun to organize "a whole lot of people" to write to District Attorney Morgenthau. At the Minnesota conference, she went further.

A couple of hundred high-energy women in the visual arts from all over the country were in the audience when Ruby read her paper on the role of women in films, a field for which she was known nationwide. Zarina, for example, had never met Ruby, but she was eager to hear her lecture and sorry that she arrived late, having been tied up elsewhere. She hadn't been listening very long when the talk ended to applause, Ruby thanking everyone, then quieting them and saying, "Now I want to talk to you about something else, and I hope you can give me ten minutes." The room grew silent, and Ruby spoke again. "I want to talk to you about Ana Mendieta."

She went on to eulogize Ana, the artist and the person, and publicly accuse her husband, whose name was well known to everyone present, of ending her life. There were potent forces, she said, bent on shielding Carl from the law, and women everywhere had to lend their support to assure that justice be done. By the time she had finished, many people in the room were weeping. Zarina, who had tears in her eyes, too, and Ruby both remember the powerful effect of her appeal. Ruby was suddenly surrounded by volunteers and well-wishers. Back home, however, the feelings faded, and even Zarina, who had taken Ruby's number, began to feel she didn't want to be "rounded up," and she never called.

The Village Voice carrying Ruby's article appeared on Manhattan newsstands on September 16, eight days after the anniversary of Ana's death. By the prickly cruelties of chance, it was also Carl's fifty-first birthday. The article was titled "The Screaming Silence," and the art crowd was back in town to read it.

"This is not an exercise in objective journalism," Ruby said in her first paragraph. "It's a personal meditation on one year, the legal process, loyalty, power, and the art world."

Reporting the news that Bashford expected a grand jury decision by the end of that week, Ruby also registered her fear that the case would somehow be quashed by insider power. There was a circle of Carl's dealers, friends, and collectors, the minimalist generation that "got rich while asserting that objects had no value," and this was the "new Old Money of the art world, not to be trifled with." While Carl's friends were happy that the first indictment had been dropped, she wrote, "Ana's friends feel discouraged and betrayed. They are angrily waiting for something to change, some miracle to occur." But she was pessimistic, suggesting that high stakes were at play, resulting in a cover-up of a blood crime:

> The art world is a business like any other. People are afraid to alienate their employers or jeopardize their careers by rocking the boat. Paranoia is rampant, peer pressure no less severe than at your average corporation, law office, or newspaper. Loyalty in the art world runs deep. . . . There's an understandable reluctance to get involved, a post-'60s distrust of the D.A.'s office, a suspicion of the press. "Everyone would be cautious about hurting Carl," explained one artist. But where does loyalty leave off and obstruction of justice begin?

She gave three "examples" of obstruction, which included an anonymous allusion to May Stevens backing away from revealing damaging information about Carl, and then she addressed the countercharges against herself and those with her by asking, "Is there a conspiracy to accuse Carl Andre of violence? Or a conspiracy to cover up his violence? It's hard to sort out. We don't know enough about why Ana Mendieta died. In these circumstances, silence is a terrible weapon."

She was also dismayed by the unprecedented way the art world had divided on this issue and a failure of the feminist movement:

> Ana Mendieta's death has become, for many of us, a parable of the relative power of women and men in the art world. . . . The silence of so many women who could be coming forward is another lesson, one having to do with internalized oppression, powerlessness, fear of retaliation. Is this the first postfeminist murder case? There are prominent women on both sides of the argument. Loyalties have divided less by gender than by generation. For

many of the women who came of age with the minimalists, brotherhood is outweighing sisterhood.[2]

The article, to no one's surprise, only deepened the abyss of bad feeling downtown, Lucy, for one, calling it a "lynching." Marsha, never having met Ruby, called to thank her. But Ruby was right about one thing: three days later, again on a Friday, the grand jury voted its decision. It reindicted Carl on murder two.

USING THE POWERS of electronic word processing, Hoffinger was back in court with his rewritten motions to discover, inspect, suppress, and dismiss with fifteen days lopped from the forty-nine it had taken to create the same kind of documents the first time around. He had also been spared another month of argument by Judge Berkman, who ordered the release of the grand jury minutes before he had even filed his request. Bashford, who could have, raised no objection. By taking the initiative, Berkman was signaling that she was on some sort of rampage aimed at Bashford. No one could ever know who, if any, of the grand jurors had read and was moved by the *Voice* piece, which had been published only days before the voting, but it appeared likely that the article had not escaped the notice and the displeasure of Judge Berkman.

Hoffinger, undoubtedly sensing Berkman's mood, came into court bent on delivering the *coup de grâce*. Bashford, he said, commiserating with Berkman, had ignored, flouted, and made a mockery of the judge's caveats after she had so "carefully explained what had to be avoided." The prosecutor's use of "rampant hearsay" after all Berkman had instructed "boggles the mind." The whole exercise seemed a replay of

[2]She gave as an example a conversation she had had with Joyce Wadler, who had told her about the wall of silence she had faced in researching the *New York* article. Perhaps some activist women would yet stand up, Ruby had remarked to her at the time. "Wadler laughed," she wrote now. "She remembered receiving the invitation to the giant show of women artists they organized at the Palladium last year. 'The announcement was amusing,' she told me. 'A lot of the names were familiar. They were the women who wouldn't return my phone calls.'"

the first go-around but at twice the speed and with twice the rancor. Hoffinger's briefs, which were directed at inflaming the judge's apparent indignation, went further in assailing Bashford's inexcusable blunders—such as neglecting, unlike the first time, to tell the grand jury that Natalia had spoken to Ana in a language Carl did not understand.

On November 12, Bashford replied, remaining strictly on the defensive. She had not violated Berkman's ruling about past infidelities, because "all of the questions put to the witnesses called for information with respect to Ms. Mendieta's plans for the future," which was true about the questions, but not about the answers. She charged that Hoffinger's arguments were sometimes "unfair" and sometimes "ludicrous," though she had no response to some of his strongest points. One of them was that she had told the grand jury that if it voted not to indict that would be the end of the case, failing to make clear that the prosecution still had further recourse.

On December 29, with Bashford and Hoffinger standing at the bench, Berkman gave the assistant district attorney an old-fashioned, if unseasonable, tongue-lashing. She was throwing the case out again, and her written opinion would give the legal reasons why. Berkman was furious. She scolded Bashford's performance as a lawyer and berated her as a person. Having seen Bashford's name in print once too often, she called her "publicity hungry." That was the blow that hurt most, because Hoffinger had leveled the same charge and was now at the assistant D.A.'s side to hear his accusations come home to roost.

Bashford walked out of court, out of 1986, red-faced, hurt, and annoyed, feeling personally and unjustly aggrieved by the judge. It was no way to start a new year, and her boss agreed. After seventeen months of hard and heartfelt work, she was discharged from the case.

——— 31 ———

Ana was twenty-nine years old when she arrived in the dead of winter 1978 hefting her baggage along with her branding iron, her portfolio, the phone numbers of an uncertain support structure, and barely enough start-up money to test her mettle in the hardball wonderland of the New York art world.

Almost everyone she planned to look up she had met through Hans when they had visited him in Iowa or when she had accompanied him on periodic trips back East. How they would receive her alone was one of her many preoccupations, but it was not a bad year to be trying.

While social headway for women in the art world had trailed as usual behind the rest of the culture, they had begun to make some gains earlier in the seventies thanks to the sixties feminists. Women in the movement who had been active in the Art Workers Coalition had suddenly discovered that after the strikes and sit-ins they had still been the ones who had made the coffee and gathered crumbs when the men had gone. Many of them broke away to form their own groups, WAR (Women Artists and Revolution) being the first. They had picketed, boycotted, pitched eggs, and ripped Tampax for their gender's sake, raising a consciousness here, teaming with like-minded minorities there. In the meantime, Soho had flourished; in 1978, it was moving toward a third boom year, feeling, or at least looking, slightly magnanimous. The gallery-system fraternity was still as much in place as ever, fortified and enduring, it seemed, but there were a few more slots than there ever had been for women with the right stuff. So why not me? asked each contender, and Ana joined them now.

A PACKET OF surviving letters and postcards from Ana to Hans attests to the longing and travail, the dreams and striving of the newest unknown woman artist in town. Unlike the way she composed her meditations on her art, she was a careless, unreflecting letter writer, dashing off the small news of the day and the large, uncensored feelings coming and going with it, but not at the same tempo. The news of course went the way of all news, but the feelings, being universal, gave a lasting voice to the letters. She had already found the Sullivan Street apartment when she wrote the first letter back home on February 6 and 7, 1978.

My dearest Hans,
I love you and miss you very much. You are constantly in my thoughts and with me. I hope that you are getting along and not feeling too lonely. Today we are having the *worst* blizzard. . . . So as you can imagine the snow is making me nostalgic and sad, as well as constantly cold. I wish my favorite bed warmer was here with me. . . . MOMA [Museum of Modern Art] is having a retrospective of Sol LeWitt so I will probably go uptown to see it, otherwise I don't think there is anything else going on. De Kooning is also having a big show of work from 1960–1977. I am scared and lonely about my situation but confident that I will survive. . . . I hope you don't forget me too quickly. You are probably finally having some peace of mind (without me interrupting you). But remember that no matter how obnoxious or bitchy I might be, I do love you.

A few days later, writing on the twelfth, she had moved into the tiny, one-room, ground-level apartment. New things were beginning to happen:

My dearest Hans,
Alone again, naturally, and wishing very much that you were here. Since Friday I have been staying at my place and it's hard. I don't have any furniture, so I've been sleeping on the floor. Today I spent all day hauling wood that I would find in the streets. I am quite exhausted! I drug it home all by myself. . . . I am hoping that somebody will help me build a table and shelves from the wood I've drug home. . . . I talked to Mary Beth Edelson who says

Heresies will publish 2 or 3 of my photos in the next issue as well as an article that I am in. Also I found out Lucy wrote an article in *Studio International*. . . . It has a reproduction of mine. . . . I haven't contacted anybody about my work since my place looks like a concentration camp and I don't have a phone yet. As I said I am quite lonely. Everybody has their own thing going and since my place is so desolate it is quite oppressing, but I'm strong and I guess I can make it—Although once in a while my eyes water. . . . Baby I really miss you and need you. I hope you are surviving and not falling apart. You will see that time will fly by and we'll soon be together again. . . . It looks like I will be needing a part-time job, things are so expensive here. . . . I really wish you were here. It's going to feel so good to touch you next time I see you.

By February 21, the pace had quickened. She had found a friend and neighbor in Argentinean artist Liliana Porter, an old acquaintance of Hans's. "I was one of the numbers she had for people to call, to get introduced," says Liliana. "But she didn't need me. In a very short time, she knew more people than I did. But I saw her very often. I was like family because we spoke Spanish, I was somebody she could speak to about the 'Americans.' "

Ana had managed to schedule a performance at the Franklin Furnace, and she began moving around the galleries showing the slides of her earth and body works, hunting for much-needed steadier work as well:

My dearest baby,
Boy, I am really pooped. I have been out running around all day today and just got back (7:45 P.M.). I had to go to Franklin Furnace and look at the space. . . . I got a lead from the Spanish Arts organization that there are 3 openings at the Bronx Museum. . . . Also I talked to Marina Urbach today. She has a new gallery in Chambers Street and gets a lot of publicity. . . . She is looking at my work next Tuesday. Tomorrow I have to go to an employment office . . . to get Food Stamps. . . . Also I think Thursday

I am going to take stuff to Sonnabend [Gallery]—you have to leave it while they look at it. So why not try? Enough of work talk. I am absolutely drained! I've been thinking also of new work, etc. I haven't seen Yoyo or Ted. It's like they are afraid I will become dependent on them or something. . . . I really miss you and think of you all the time. Last night I even had a wet dream. I wonder how you are doing. But I really feel un-sexed. . . . It's really amazing how much you take a fulfillingness and love for granted. We really have been together for so long. You are really part of me. . . . My evenings go by very slowly—and I am suffering from insomnia badly. I've been picking up books off the street and read late into the night. . . . Take good care of yourself since I can't. *I love you with all my being.*

Ted was Ted Victoria, whom she had met when he came as a visiting artist to Iowa. He would shortly become one of her best chums, the somebody she had been hoping for to help her make something out of the wood she had "drug" home in Iowese. "I helped her furnish that whole thing," Ted would recall many years later. "She came over here one day and she was bragging how she set up that apartment just by stuff she found in the street. How she was able to walk along the street and find a mattress—a mattress!—and so many other things, and all of a sudden I realized I had some stuff up in my storage space. I went up and I got like an architectural drafting lamp that I wasn't going to use anymore and a couple of captain's chairs and some other stuff. And she took it all home, you know, just took it right home all at once to paint it and use it right away. And as she was walking down the street—I'll never forget—she says to me, 'Oh, I love America! God bless America! Only in America could this happen!' "

As soon as she could afford one, she would buy a shopping cart, and the image of Ana, wearing artist black, moving this way and that around Soho dragging things twice her size to her nest in the Village would remain downtown longer than she would. One of the sustaining daydreams Ana and Hans had to console their separation was that an apartment in Manhattan would be their shared pied-à-terre in the art world, to and from which they would fly when beckoned by public acclaim. The pink stucco building on Sullivan Street stood behind a gate with all the charm of a Spanish courtyard going in but with somewhat less appeal looking out the barred windows of the mere closet on the inside. Yet Ana would claim, as long as she could bear it, that it suited her size and temperament, and she did her best to make it happy for herself as well as Hans when he came to town. The found mattress went on a loft bed near the ceiling, her minuscule "studio" wedged underneath it among her clothing and a homemade little altar to her luckiest saints of Santería. The kitchen was indiscernible, and when she got hungry for her own cooking, she would trot over to Ted's big loft, do up some chilis rellenos, Oaxacan style, and give him a haircut after dessert, listening to Bonnie Tyler sing "It's a Heartache" again and again until he cried uncle.

She found a job at the steam table at Food, a Soho cafeteria on Prince Street. But it was short-lived since she flew back to Iowa for the Easter break, spending "ten beautiful days in person" with the man she so cherished, and—she wrote in her next letter from Sullivan Street—"absolutely *certain* of my love and devotion for you." Apparently they had had some quarrelsome moments, Ana taking the blame for being bitchy, yet claiming that to be an immutable part of her nature:

You have to accept me the way I am. I just wouldn't want to make a mistake about us. I am being realistic and positive. I do love you and accept you like the way you are. Except for maybe I get paranoid about how you feel about me as an artist. I feel insecure and feel you don't like my work. But baby we really are good together. Don't you think? . . . I called Prix de Rome and they said I almost made it but not quite. . . . I called [dealer] Hal Bromm and he is supposed to call back for an appt. . . . I just got interrupted by a call from Hal Bromm saying they are not accepting any work and to call back in the fall. . . . Back to talking about the L.I. job, I am not going to worry or kiss anybody's ass for it. I am just going to do my work and try to get it moving. . . . I was so proud of how you have pulled your life together. I guess one

tequila drunk on the day I left is not so bad. Please baby take care.
. . . And remember that the essence of you is always with me—a
part of me. All my love and kisses. *Muchos besos.*

The L.I. job was a teaching post at the State University of New York
at Old Westbury, Long Island. She had been invited to join Ted and
Hispanic artist Luis Camnitzer, Liliana's recently estranged husband,
in a three-person show at the university that spring. "Ana was doing
this installation," says Ted, recollecting it as an episode in her fear of
heights, "and we got the groundkeepers to pull down an old dead tree.
She converted one part of the museum, the gallery space, into a kind
of environment of old leaves, and in back of one area she did one of
her bodies, which she made out of moss. And I remember specifically
Ana was deciding who was going to climb up the ladder and tie some
of the branches up to the top of the ten- or twelve-foot ceiling in the
gallery, me or her, and I ended up doing it, which I wasn't too pleased
with because I'm not too keen on heights myself, but she wasn't going
up there." Coming to her rescue, however, wasn't quite enough:

I worked very hard all last week on my piece at L.I. [she wrote to
Hans on April 27]. I wish you could see it. It was hard work and
the students were enthusiastic and helpful. It was hard emotionally for me to be there because they (Luis and Ted) were interviewing for the jobs next year (I was not interviewed). Finally after the
opening (when I was high on wine) I told Ted off, how hurt I was
and that I was taking it personally that I was not considered for
the job. . . . At least I have my job at Food back.

That was written at six o'clock in the morning. She was in a somewhat better mood later in the day:

Hi baby. I worked all afternoon and I was really beat. . . . How
is Kasper [Hans's dog] doing? Are you two going out to the lake
a lot? Are the mushrooms out already? I really wish we were
together. I miss you a lot. It has been hard to adjust after my visit

to Iowa. I really enjoyed the visit. You were wonderful and I loved being with you. Do you really love me too?

Her uncertainty about his affections and the infrequency of the affection itself did not detract from—perhaps even fueled—the first purpose of the separation, the pursuit of burning ambition. At the top of her list of influential New York people whom she had met in Iowa was Lucy, soundly established by now as a leading art-world social critic and cohesive force in uniting women artists. Warm, wide open, kindly Lucy, blaming herself and neurosis for being "one of the busiest people in this fucking city," did not have much, or enough, time for Ana, and Ted, Luis, and Liliana, while almost always available, were looking for the same sort boost as she. Two women not on Ana's phone list who she was eager to meet were Carolee Schneemann and Nancy Spero. Fortunately, they were known to two women whom Ana had met. Carolee would immediately discover a kindred soul in Ana, a sister "voyager on the despised terrain . . . of the inherited hierarchies of the male culture." Nancy Spero, as much a feminist as Carolee and more the political activist, would have a greater practical impact on Ana's life and career.

Nancy, more than twenty years Ana's senior, was one of the founders of the women's cooperative gallery A.I.R. The initials stood for Artists in Residence, the old academic qualifier adopted in early Soho to bestow legitimacy on bona fide artists occupying commercial space and adopted later by the twenty founding women for want of something better.

The nonprofit enterprise rented space at 97 Wooster Street from fellow artists who owned the building, including May Stevens and Rudolf Baranik. At the start of the fall season of 1972, they opened the A.I.R. Gallery, with the smell of fresh paint permeating the first exhibition. The group had a maximum of twenty dues-paying, selected (later elected) women members, each receiving in the bargain a one-person Soho show every two years, with the proceeds of the sales—free and clear of a dealer's standard fifty-fifty split—going directly to the artist. Using mainstream PR footwork and other power-seeking ploys learned from the art-world business, A.I.R.—the first gallery of its kind—was

the members' answer to the token changes wrought by the best efforts
of the women artists' movement. Most women still had no place to
show their art, and what was shown continued to suffer under the
pressure to conform to accepted styles, which in turn made women
appear less innovative than men.

The gallery system's answer to that answer, however, was an old-
fashioned raspberry. Before long, feeling ostracized, many A.I.R.
women were cast into the same position as one frank founder who
admitted to constantly wrestling with idealism "and my avariciousness
for my own success." Some, like Nancy, had either gotten their egos
on a leash or were still grappling, but more important for Ana, others
buckled and began using the cooperative as a stepping stone into the
mainstream—vacating space behind them. Ana, as good a wrestler as
any, was quick to grasp the dilemma as well as the opportunity.

She had two friends already on the inside, one of them, Dotty Attie,
an A.I.R. founder. But a woman needed an assenting majority of the
membership to get in, and politicking had combined with the resident
avarice to rust the girders of good intentions. Ana had met Dotty a year
or so earlier when Hans had given her a show in Iowa City. The other
woman, Mary Beth Edelson, was one of the few New York artists Ana
had befriended entirely on her own, though it was workaholic Lucy who
had had the idea and with one phone call brought them together.

Somewhat older than Ana, Mary Beth, an avowed feminist and a
handsome, bespectacled midwesterner, had been doing body art, ex-
ploring female blood taboos, sexual fantasies, and goddess mythology
throughout the seventies. So when they met in New York in 1977, they
had something to talk about. Ana had gotten Hans to invite Mary Beth
to Iowa for a performance, a "public ritual," the artist called it. She
set fire to six hundred feet of hand-braided cornstalks on a sloping hill
at sunset for her opening number. The daughter of an Indiana dentist,
Mary Beth had moved to Soho in 1975 and had begun to receive
critical notice. Ana had not yet made up her own mind about making
the same move, but her new friend urged her forward. Everything
about Ana, Mary Beth believed, suggested that New York would embrace her. She was a good artist, an attractive woman, and her Third

World origin was a big plus, Mary Beth felt. These were times when guilt-stricken people and whole institutions were out prowling for savory, media-stopping have-nots to "redress" what they had not done for, or had done to, hosts of have-nots before them. Ana had not heard any part of this for the first time, but coming straight from Spring Street made it mighty.

Calls to Dotty and Mary Beth were among the first Ana made in New York, and it was not long after that she met Nancy Spero. Nancy, also from the Midwest, born in Cleveland, was a mother of three young men, had been married for twenty-seven years, and was an artist whose work was as far from Ana's as a 210-foot-long collage of typewritten words—which was what Nancy was working on at the time—could be, though there was a strong feminist fiber woven through every inch of it. Along with her husband, Leon Golub, Nancy had had an intensely political career, both of them one-time Art Workers Coalition activists. Nancy was also a WAR veteran. In any event, she was part of a group of A.I.R. women who made a studio visit to meet and evaluate Ana as a candidate, and she was won over on the first look, saying later, "I remember being struck, dumbstruck really, by Ana's work. I felt it was extraordinary, and I felt her presence was extraordinary." With Nancy, Mary Beth, and Dotty behind her, Ana was voted in, her one-woman show scheduled for the fall of the following year.

LILIANA AND LUIS were Latin but too "American," or at least too well off, for what would develop into Ana's lust for the ghetto. "Oh, Liliana," Ana would say to one of her Third World friends, "every time she's depressed she goes and buys a mink coat." Instead, Ana pursued the New York Cubans, reaching out through them for the source. One of the first was Juan Gonzalez, who had left Cuba after Ana. Though decidedly anti-Castro, he shared her interest in revisiting their homeland.

"We were both in a group of artists who wanted to go to Cuba. She was passionate about Cuba," Juan says. "She was obsessed with Cuba, but she wasn't really political. She used the whole political thing because some of the people she'd gotten involved with in New York were radical and very leftist. And she was very conscious of her condition as a woman. But her interest was her work and making it as an artist, and that's it! The rest was just a way to get there.

"And that was what made it very difficult to be her friend. It was hard to have any kind of real human connection, because whenever you talked to her, her mind was always occupied with this one thing, making it. But yet I liked her. She could be very tender, and she really needed affection. And she would call me and she would shower me with affection and I'd be very affectionate with her, too. We'd talk about art, we'd talk about sex—we would just be Cuban with each other. And she was wild. I guess 'wild' is the wrong word. I mean, she was just on fire all the time, loud and always up—in her way of expressing herself, in her way of laughing—and when we had a party she was, well, you could not miss Ana. We became, in a way, like relatives, because we were in New York and we were here alone, so we would talk and sometimes I could sense her aloneness and her need for a family."

Hans came through New York in June on his way to visit his family in Germany and stayed at the Sullivan Street place for a few days. They made a date to meet back in Iowa City in July before leaving for Oaxaca. Two letters written in this period show Ana as unhappy when he was gone as she was regretful of the things that went wrong when he was around; however, writing from New York in the fall, she thought they had been "perfect together" on the trip to Mexico and Hans was "pretty lucky that I love you so much."

A subtle shift in the language of her letters that fall and winter told more of the story. Returning to Soho, Ana plunged into the "viable-alternative" art world, working at A.I.R. to help organize and promote the shows of her fellow members and plugging into the greater women-artists' network. She began working with *Heresies* on its upcoming Third World women issue and found herself being invited to a number of group shows, exhibiting in well-funded or well-publicized events showcasing Latin American artists. Although she would spend the rest of her life fighting the Latino label, her Third World "plus" started adding up quickly, and before very long she was planted on a certain turf with a view of the high road. These rapid gains, though she was working now as a domestic and a waitress to pay the rent, were reflected in her letters to Hans. Besides being the reporter to her loved one, Ana, who had begun as the devoted pupil, was suddenly serving as the teacher's adviser and advance woman on the New York scene, which lay beyond the confines of Hans's realm. In space in her letters taken up last spring by pining and yearning for his caresses, she was now instructing him where to send his slides and résumé and how else to jockey for a place in the downtown sun ("If you want me, I'll talk to them about you. Just give me the word"). Her love, though she claimed it was undiminished, simply took up less paper, and her interest in what was new in Iowa City, even in what Kasper was up to, had begun to wane.

"I have felt a wall go up between us since Feb. when you stopped being affectionate and personal over the phone," she wrote just before a spring trip home. When she came back to Sullivan Street, she said:

> I hope the telephone conversation helped you as it has helped me. Some things that needed to be said were said. I feel a new confidence that things can be worked out if the communication lines are opened and honest and our plans for the future clear. . . . As I stated in our talk, I am not superficial or frivolous about life. (So don't accuse me of it.) I just want certain needs that I have fulfilled. (Friends, interaction, discussion of the works.) I also want you in my life. I hope we can find a solution. Our relationship was lacking in some of the above mentioned needs. Maybe it can fulfill them now. I don't know. . . . All the best of me I give to you.

They would be together in Iowa that summer, and there would be postcards, phone calls, and visits in New York and Iowa for years afterward, but the next letter, written and sent sometime in May 1979, was the last:

> I am sitting at AIR now and can't really write you a decent letter because I am being constantly interrupted but I thought you mighty enjoy just a little note from me. Telling you (the note) that I love you and miss you. Don't forget that. Why is it that when we are together we cannot stop time and have it just be us? And

not let dumb things interfere? Human nature I guess. . . . I love you.

LARGER PASSIONS MOVED her relationship with Hans into limbo that year, the first being her upcoming show at A.I.R., set to open on November 6. An inchoate mixture of others had to do with Cuba. She yearned to return to the soil from which she had been torn and cast out. This desire had always been with her, but lately it had grown into a Januslike obsession, one face being the compulsion to touch the source of her being, the other a fear that she had somehow lost it, that going home would disenchant her, leaving her with no home anywhere. All this had been heightened by the possibility of a trip in the near future, but especially by her father's release from prison and his recent flight from Cuba.

After serving a third of his twenty-year sentence on a diet of garbanzos and water, Ignacio Mendieta had suffered a heart attack and had been placed in the care of his physician father-in-law, living under house arrest in Varadero Beach. Years of trying and a moment of governmental good feeling brought forth an exit visa, and in April 1979, the sixty-year-old nephew of the president of the republic arrived in Cedar Rapids. He had been stripped long before of his Cuban patrimony and now was penniless, toothless, without a word or token of thanks from the CIA, but at last a free and happy man—reunited with his wife and children after so many years. Among the first things he did was buy a miniature American flag to wear in his lapel, give an interview to a local newspaper, and within two or three weeks he had landed a job at Mercy Hospital of Cedar Rapids, the janitor's post.

Over the years, Ana had built up a great resentment toward her father, sometimes arguing with her mother that he had forsaken his responsibilities to his family in the name of an abstraction. This did nothing to lessen the excitement and joy she felt now, seeing him safely Americanizing in the little white house on Danbern Lane. But she had yet to fill the empty spaces in her heart, and her impulse to return to the motherland was more powerful than ever.

———

ON THE NIGHT of Ana's A.I.R. opening, Nancy and Leon threw her a party big enough to pack their huge loft one flight up on La Guardia Place, just north of Soho. Counting people at your opening and particularly your opening party was no way to count success, but Ana, who had been one of fifty or so fresh talents mentioned in a *Village Voice* article called "There's a New Kid (or Two) in Town," was surely the title kid tonight. Nancy recalls it this way: "It was very crowded. It was nice. We had a lot of wine consumed." That was six days before Ana met Carl.

Most of the time during her trips back to Iowa to see Hans had been spent at Old Man's Creek and the Dead Tree Area. She had been creating earthworks for her *Silueta Series,* begun in 1975 when she had abandoned the use of her own body. Her A.I.R. show consisted of limited editions of color photographs of her newest work. Some months earlier, she had placed a couple of them in a group show at the Henry Street Settlement, and the *Soho Weekly News,* describing her silhouettes as "vaginas on the hillside," called them "bracing" and an advance over the abstract expressionists who had tried to identify their bodies with the earth "but as men couldn't come this close." Whether that was praise or an attempt at humor, or both, it did not shade the reviews of the latest show, which were enthusiastic.[1]

Art reviews for all but the anointed, however, normally took weeks or even months to appear, generally after the show had closed. To draw real-time attention, A.I.R. had instituted a series of Monday-night panel discussions, and Nancy was head of the committee. She had succeeded in scheduling one such meeting on the Monday after Ana's opening, November 12, asking the panel to tackle the question of what male artists honestly think of their female counterparts. Among the panelists were Leon Golub and Carl Andre.

A large turnout, given Carl's name, was predictable, but even Nancy was surprised at how jammed the gallery was when they got going. Not all the A.I.R. members cared to have a basically extraneous event at the

---

[1]*Arts Magazine* found "wonderment" in "the feeling of mystery that surrounds Mendieta's silhouettes." *Art in America* called the work an "explosively sensual drama." Even more impressive was the sizable amount of review space given a first one-person New York show.

gallery during the course of their exhibitions, but Ana had been all for it, and the large audience could only help in the long run. Custom and good manners, however, demanded she take a back seat on this night. There were people in the audience who, like Ana, were too new to Soho to have seen Carl in action in his Vietnam days, but he was still the familiar blue figure at downtown public forums. Over the past couple of years, he had been active in a group called Artists Meeting for Cultural Change, art and politics their issues. Fresh faces would gather at the Artists Space a few doors down on Wooster, listen to the old hands go at the evils of the system—Carl, austere and Marxist, Leon, wry and dry, Rudolf and Lucy in there, too. When the evening's discussion was over, everyone would head for a drink at the Pool Room around the corner.

Lately, women had drifted away from this group as they had from the Art Workers Coalition; again, there was something of a man's world about the new group. That was how some of these women, Lucy included, got *Heresies* started. Carl, quietly, with no questions asked, no strings attached, had put up the five hundred dollars needed to get issue number one to the printers.

Ana may have heard of Carl Andre before 1969, but in the summer of that year, while still a graduate student studying painting, she had enrolled in a seminar given by visiting critic John Perreault—his first time out as a teacher. Contemporary art was the subject, and Carl and the other minimalists were the artists studied. The class was assigned to create a minimal or conceptual artwork, one student "turning in" a final embodying the negative concept of not showing up for class by not showing. Ana, however, had either been unmoved by the minimalists or didn't care. She produced a conventional paper on the mystical and sensual art of the Mexican painter Tamayo, his work as unminimal as sunsets and flowers. The chagrin of her young professor was overcome by the power of her conviction, her need "to get back to her Hispanic roots," says the professor—taken by Ana in the process as a lifelong friend.

By now, however, her interest in minimalism had grown, especially in Sol LeWitt's work, whose show at MOMA she had mentioned twice in her letters to Hans. Carl had not shown much that year, and not at all in New York, except for one piece in a group show. He had recently broken with Angela Westwater. First, they had parted as lovers and shortly afterward, when she married a nonartist, a businessman, he had pulled out of her gallery. Her choice of his successor had made him "very upset," according to her partner Gian Enzo Sperone, and leaving the gallery had been some sort of protest to let her know. He had moved over to old friend Paula Cooper and was preparing his first one-man show in her gallery, set for early 1980.

Facing him from the audience, Ana knew nothing of this nor almost anything else about him. Since it would take some time for her to succumb to his charms, there could have been no love at first sight on her part. Nor did Carl pick her face out of the crowd. Something else happened, and it happened so unexpectedly, so improbably, that it would reach across time to the few who were there or were told to brand their memories. In hindsight, they would see omens in the way Ana met Carl.

Suddenly, inexplicably, Ana's pictures, the mud bones and fetish pickings of her silhouettes, began to fall. The panel was speaking, and one cracking sound followed another, irrupting, demanding silence with the voice of gods, the picture frames splitting apart, the photographs peeling off the walls, tumbling, racketing, and crashing on the floor.

"It just started popping off the wall, falling down," says Mary Beth, who watched it like everyone else, incredulous. "The photographs were held by those little plastic things that you put on the side, and after a while they get tired of being there and they'll pop off. But the show had only been up a couple of days. Apparently, with all the lights on in the evening and the heat in the building, something happened all at once and they all just started popping off and falling off the wall."

Ana, mortified, leapt to the rescue, and Nancy and Mary Beth ran with her. Says Nancy: "Her pictures started popping off the wall. It was terrible. There were these photographs, maybe with plexy in the front and then a board behind, and there must have been some warping or expansion, maybe the heat of all the people that were in there. It was very bizarre. Everybody had to crowd in the center."

Ana, Nancy, and Mary Beth were quietly putting the pieces together in a corner of the gallery when the discussion ended and the audience filed out. The other panelists, invited by Carl to dinner, began to go off to the sushi place next door where he had made reservations, and when Leon came to collect Nancy, she said that if Carl didn't mind she preferred to stay behind and help Ana. The gallery would be open the following morning, and they wanted to get her work back on the wall. Carl would hear nothing of it, promptly asking the embarrassed artist to join them, though, it seemed to Nancy, he didn't know who among the remaining women she was. When the pictures were safely rehung, they joined the others in the restaurant. Ana had still not gotten over her mortification, but Carl, perhaps only now laying eyes on her for the first time, stood and welcomed her graciously to his table. They all talked about her strange bit of bad luck until Ana just laughed it away.

ANA WENT BACK to Cuba in January 1980. It was meant to be a journey of redemption, but much had been lost forever. The five-bedroom house at 837 Nineteenth Street in Havana where Ana had been born and raised was now shared by ten people. The stranger who answered her knock invited Ana inside and left her alone to wander when she told him she used to live there. "Oh, the furniture was exactly the same," she wept to her sister back in the United States ten days or so later, "everything was like we had been living there all along." Then she climbed the stairs and went into her room, and she sat on her bed, which was when she began a long, hard cry.

To the younger cousins with whom she used to build castles on the beach at Varadero, Ana had simply disappeared. They could only remember that one day they had been playing rebels with Ana, everyone dressing up like Fidel, and then she had gone home with her mother and father, and they never saw her again. They were on the castaway side of the Mendieta family, who had lived and worked with the revolution, suffering at times, rejoicing at others. When Ana came back, they longed to know how she had fared and she in the same way longed as much as they.

"Kaki" Mendieta, another Raquel christened in immediate need of a nickname, was two years younger than the big cousin who always had had the last word down at the beach. The revolution had been kind to Kaki, and she had grown up in its service to be a teacher of Cuban history and culture at the art institute in Havana. She knew the local art world and how to move through the political labyrinths that weaker countries excel in constructing. Ana, the street-smart orphanage kid, latched on to her, sensing how to get by. "I want to do my sculpture here because I was born here," she declared in Cuba with emphatic conviction, though she would never get even close to being sure. Kaki may have gotten on to her cousin, but they soon became good friends all over again.

Ana went back to Cárdenas to spend a week with her grandparents, who had recently celebrated their sixtieth wedding anniversary. Says Kaki: "She told me she had long conversations with her grandmother, whom she loved, trying to recover her background . . . at the same time, she was angry at her grandmother, who represented the rupture she had been forced to make from [her] history and the family." Ana would roam through the house, she told her cousin, resurrecting memories gone from their normal place until then, rummaging among the precious objects in the glass cabinets, walking up and down the central staircase, the steps feeling not nearly as steep as they had felt to a little girl.

Her great-granduncle had founded one of the first museums in Cuba, in Cárdenas, and as a child Ana relished going there to see living fleas dressed up in a flea circus, but when she visited it now, the fleas were gone and the museum no longer bore the family name. The old house in Varadero Beach, with its big dinner bell on the porch and the yard that went onto the sand going down to the warm sea, had been demolished by the time Ana got back. The wood had been used to build schools, and the land on which it stood was now a public park. Only the trees and the walkway to the front door were still there. Ana stood under the pine trees and walked up the path to nowhere, retreating from what had been, remembering, or trying to, what had happened long ago. She gathered up some Varadero sand and dug a fistful of Cuban soil. "Those were the two things she took back from her first trip," Kaki says. "Later on she used to tell how she kept them in her apartment in New York as one of the most important things she had in her life."

GIFTS, FLOWERS, DINNERS, and trips to Germany, was the formula that women "onto" Carl saw as his irresistible romantic strategy. Women who were swept away doubtless discovered a lot more. Ana may in the end have fallen like others for the style before the man, but in her case, Carl had another edge. To many who knew both Hans and Carl, there were remarkable resemblances between the two men, Hans somewhat shorter and darker and more fun-loving and adventurous, Carl stockier and more poised, but both were thirteen years Ana's senior, bearded and otherwise hirsute, strong-minded, hard-drinking, seasoned in all of their ways; the list, for what it was worth, went on. The Freudians among these observers sometimes saw a resemblance in both men to Ana's faraway father. The greatest difference at the moment, however, was indisputable: Carl was in New York and Hans was a thousand miles away.

With Raquel living at an ashram in Miami Beach and Natalia not yet in Ana's life, Ana had found a confidante in New York, a brand-new, neutral friend with whom she shared some of her feeling about the progress and setbacks of her romance with Carl. That was Zarina, whom she had met before her trip to Cuba, walking up to her at a meeting of *Heresies*. Ana, emotionally taxed by the visit to her home-land, had thrown herself into her work when she got back. Besides making and promoting her art and working at odd jobs to pay the bills, she had teamed up with Zarina to put together a Soho exhibition of Third World women artists living in America.

Zarina had known Carl since 1971. She had met him at a party in New Delhi when he and his work had represented the United States at an international exhibition (and where he had had his first and worst Third World traveling experience). She hadn't seen him very often since, but Carl in India had taken a liking to a friend of Zarina's, another Indian artist, and both Zarina and Carl were still in touch with her.

Ana in the beginning spoke to Zarina only of her problems with

Hans, whom Zarina had yet to meet, without letting on that the cause of her distress was Carl. "I didn't realize that she was going with Carl," Zarina says. "There was a little overlap, and I think it bothered her that she hadn't broken completely with Hans and she was seeing Carl. And as I know of her, I think she was a one-man woman. She was very loyal."

The champagne and flowers were fine. Going to dinner at places like Da Silvano, drinking a forty-dollar bottle of wine and ordering another before it was gone was good, too. Carl's charm, his sense and poetry, his way of making her feel feminine, beautiful, cherished, unique as a woman, were better. That he could be all these things and bring her to dinner with Paula Cooper and uptown collectors, that he could put her by mere nomination in a group show with himself and Sol LeWitt that very first spring of their courtship, that Sol and his wife Carol would love her instantly, that there was no museum or gallery on any continent, no Kunsthalle, Centre Pompidou, Biennale di Venezia, no place in the art-world galaxy that would not receive Carl Andre, even wearing his Marxism on his sleeve, as visiting nobility, while lesser artists obeying maddening convention stood holding their slides somewhere at the end of a line; these were good things, too.

But love came slowly. She resisted being carried off to Carl's world, keeping up her friendships with Ted and Liliana and the others who had first been friends of Hans's and were in different ways dear to her now. But she never brought Carl around. Hans came to stay at Sullivan Street for the last time that spring. Ana had made up her mind to tell him about Carl. Hans himself had said that she might find somebody else when she went to New York, and now it had happened and it was wrong to love two men. The words didn't come just that bluntly, but at end of the summer, in Iowa, they decided it was over. Somehow for Ana, however, it was not the end.

"She was not very sure of her relationship with Carl," Zarina felt even after she had begun that fall to see them together. "She had a lot of affection and love for him, but she always said, 'Oh, he's a Wasp,' and he's cold, and he doesn't respond to emotions."

But her heart said otherwise. "Because all difficulties crumble," Ana wrote to herself, "against the indescribable reality of your gaze; there all possibilities surge."

And one day she composed a poem, placing it among her papers concerning Carl:

> It was necessary to reinvent it all.
> With you all has been like the first time
> the first kiss, the insecurity
> of not knowing what to do
> the already forgotten excitement of adolescence
> It was necessary to rediscover the space of love
> to recompile the geography of the bodies
> rewrite the ritual, choreograph it
> and to find myself
> as the first time
> with the ecstasy as much as with
> the mystery

There was a note of bitter-sweetness on a separate page—and a dark reflection of what their love might be:

> And so the last acceptance
> is of the flesh
>
> And probably also
> the final rejection

For his part, Carl was ambiguous about his relationship with Ana. There were at least two other women in his life at the time, and none of the three knew about the other two. Ana was hurt, for the first time, by Carl's refusal to allow her to move some of her belongings into 34E, particularly something to change into in the morning. She complained about this to both Liliana and Zarina. "Ana said that it disrupted her," Zarina recalls. "She had to get up in the morning and then to get her messages or mail she had to go to her place. And Carl didn't want her to bring her clothes, they should live together but have sort of separate lives. And there were ups and downs because he was quite adamant." Zarina felt that Carl didn't want anyone else to know that someone was living with him, but even when she saw Carl with other women, she thought it best not to say so to Ana.

For better or worse they became a couple, Ana insisting now that Carl meet her friends, showing him off like a trophy to the troglodytes of the lower regions of the art world. To Ted, Carl was "the high priest of minimal art" because the *New York Times* had said so, and whenever Ana brought him along, Carl carrying four or five bottles of expensive wine, he was somewhat in awe. "Carl liked my cooking a lot," says Ted. "He'd love coming over. He was always very elegant, very eloquent, very much a gentleman, and very charming, and loved good food. That's one thing about Carl. He loved good food and loved good wine. So did Ana. I remember one time I made a marinated shrimp dish and he called it something like, 'Oh, this is the best tuttimari'—or something, an Italian name—'I've ever had.' " After dinner there was drawing-room conversation. "He was such an intellectual. He would say things I didn't know what he was talking about or where it was coming from."

There was reciprocation. Ana liked to entertain and cook her Mexican chilis and Cuban black beans and pesto learned from Hans, but there were no pots and pans in 34E, no solid provisions either. Ted was amazed the first time he visited Carl's apartment. "Very stark. Very clean, and very much like Carl's work. Refrigerator very empty, because he never cooked."

You went to their apartment, had a drink, and then went out, Zarina says of the routine. In the restaurant, Ana would go on about politics and Cuba and the white man, while Carl just listened and smiled. "I thought he really did care for Ana," Zarina says. "You know, he was almost fifty years old, he had lived a part of his life, he had wives, and now he was with a younger woman, almost like a child, and the way he touched her, I mean, it was with so much affection, like sort of touching her hair, putting his arm round her."

"When we are one," Ana wrote of her love for Carl one winter day at that time, "I am listening to you, we are speaking. I feel the vastness of the universe, the nothingness where all things come from. All at once it becomes. It is. Time: Past, Present, Future is Now."

———

THIS WAS A season of fulfillment and good fortune for Ana. She won the Guggenheim in 1980, a second NEA grant the same year. Still another was on the way. "Aren't you leaving anything for your old age?" Lucy asked her, Ana unable to wipe a smile from her face when telling the news. The exhibition of eight Third World women artists, though Ana refrained from showing her own work, drew her major notice in the *Voice* (titled "The Passion of Ana") as a bold polemical figure on the art scene.[2] An article only a two or three issues before that, "Ana Mendieta Plants Her Garden," glowed all over the page about the person and her work. She returned to Cuba in January, taking Lucy and a band of other artists and writers along, and in the summer she was back again, invited by the Castro government, to fulfill her ambition to work there. Carving the rock walls of caves in the Jaruco Mountains outside of Havana, she at last brought her haunting, stateless silhouettes home forever. The photographs of these *Rupestrian Sculptures*, as she called them, became the substance of her second one-woman show at A.I.R. It would be her last with the cooperative. She had come into conflict with many of her fellow members, accusing the group, particularly after they rejected Zarina as a member, as being a kind of white middle-class women's club. Their complaints about her not being a team player, failing to pay her dues, and exploiting her Third World "plus" were probably as true as hers, but Ana had begun to aim for the center of the art world, the hated-loved system, and she was leaving all the "viable alternatives" behind her, bad feelings included. When you aimed at the center, you needed steel in your arrows.

---

[2]In presenting the show, she assailed contemporary American feminism as a self-serving movement, predominantly white, middle-class, and therefore racist. She was not the first to say so, but she gave it a focus where until then it had none.

—— 32 ——

Elizabeth Lederer was slight in stature, combative by nature, an avid runner, and only two years younger than Ana at her death when she took over the case of *The People v. Carl Andre.* It would be hard, however, to find a woman less like Ana. She had a very fair complexion and a kind of Oriental look about her shining, sometimes tired-looking hazel eyes. Her auburn hair was usually done up carefully in curls. She dressed squared-off corporate fashion, with the groomed look that can only be acquired by mastering the tricky optics of mirrors reflecting mirrors, and she possessed the book-on-the-head carriage of a New England finishing-school woman. She had actually been to Boston schools—Clark University and Suffolk Law School, hardly the Yale where Bashford and Hoffinger had gone. When she smiled, she radiated warmth, but her daily overworked routine spent trying to put people in prison left her a little frugal when it came to her smile, and so she was sometimes misunderstood.

Lederer had in fact gotten out of the prosecuting business one year earlier. After more than six years downtown, most recently working in Assistant D.A. Linda Fairstein's sex crimes unit, she had quit Morgenthau's staff of 450 working stiff A.D.A.s to go over to the upscale life of a private law firm. The trouble was she hated the job, and when someone high up in the D.A.'s office found out and asked if she would care to come back to her old desk in the Motor Vehicles Building to work on the Andre case, she had said yes, but with some conditions.

ACROSS THE STREET at Hogan Place, Robert M. Morgenthau, "Bob" if you got to know him, a shirtsleeves D.A., feet-on-the-oaken-conference table, puffer of lonsdale-length cigars, surrounded by signed black-and-whites of him and JFK, had wanted a "fresh look" at the case. As usual, he had a hundred pending homicides in his hopper, and it was rare that one was treated much differently from another, if only for the regularity of the unimaginative style in which New Yorkers killed their neighbors. Unable to get past Berkman, however, the Andre case had become most irregular.

If it ever had been, it was no longer the local media's candidate for a circulation- or ratings-boosting glitz-and-grit murder case. The previous summer had produced a seemingly made-for-TV "accident" in Central Park. A nineteen-year-old photogenic rich kid named Robert Chambers had been charged with murdering his girlfriend, eighteen-year-old Jennifer Levin. The young man had captured the media's fancy with a blame-the-victim story about her being "pushy" and "sexually aggressive." Indicted on murder two, he had pleaded innocent and was awaiting trial, his plight called the "Preppie Murder Case" in *People*-ese. Later, writers would find parallels in the two cases, but Chambers's case, in the hands of Lederer's ex-boss Linda Fairstein, was lower on Morgenthau's worry list than Carl's.

The question he had faced before bringing in Lederer was three-fold: how to go up against Berkman a third time, whether the case would ever get by at all, and, depending on its chances, should it simply be dropped? Morgenthau had agreed with Bashford that the judge's remark about her being publicity hungry had been uncalled for, to say the least; her relationship with Berkman had somehow gotten "personal" and thus counterproductive. But pulling Bashford off the case was concession enough for Morgenthau. If it was true that Berkman found working with women assistants somehow not to her liking, he was not going to give into *every* judicial whim. She would have to deal with Lederer, a little older, a little more experienced, but the sex was not negotiable. The prerogatives of the front office had to be defended, win or lose a murder case or two. In the end, everything was personal.

Thus the case would have to get by on its own merits, and Berkman had told the D.A.'s office that this was its last chance. Lightening the charges to manslaughter could make it more movable and subsequent conviction more likely. Even the hardest heart might twinge seeing a Carl Andre sentenced to fifteen or twenty-five years to life, while punishment for the various degrees of manslaughter ranged downward to a mere scolding and a term of community service. But that was out of the question. Lesser charges could arise later in a plea bargain initiated by the defense, or by the grace of a merciful jury, but as far as the D.A.'s office was concerned, the crime by its very nature was murder two. If Carl had lived on the ground floor or if the event had occurred in, say, Ana's first-floor apartment, and she had been killed in a fall not usually fatal, the charge of recklessly creating the risk of death could be inappropriate. But the only way to throw someone out of 34E without "evincing a depraved indifference to human life" was by the front door.

Abandoning the case entirely was another matter. It was, in any event, a decision that could not be postponed. Berkman had set a date, January 26, on which Morgenthau had to inform the court whether he was going to seek a third indictment. There was more than just a deadline, too. No D.A. would admit to being in any way swayed by outside pressure, but heat was reaching his office and beyond. Apart from Ruby Rich's organized letter-writing campaign, which was perfectly democratic and normal, there were people who called him Bob and could get him on the phone on the first try who were urging him to bear down. He needn't have any qualms about sending Carl to jail, quipped one such friend-adviser who had known Ana in New York and Rome, because the artist could serve his time moving bricks around. Morgenthau was finding himself collared by the other side, too. During one private social evening, a senior figure in the publishing world who was very closely connected to Carl cornered Morgenthau, wanting to know how he could allow his office to hound the artist so pitilessly when the case kept being thrown out of court. No one, however, would ever be able to accuse the D.A. of succumbing to one partisan group or the other. In exchange for Lederer's fresh look, he gave her a free hand to decide whether to make a last stand for murder two or quash the People's grievance once and for all.

LEDERER DID NOT like the case. From what she had heard from Bashford, she did not like the art world, she did not like the likes of Hoffinger, and indeed, she had an inner, Little-Red-Riding-Hood fear of going up against him. True, taking charge now had the potential to be a heroic return to her career as a prosecutor, and bringing it to trial, not to speak of obtaining a conviction, meant winning win or lose; even if she could not succeed where her colleague had failed, any internal criticism would accrue to the alleged quirks of Judge Berkman, not her. What troubled Lederer most of all was her lack of conviction that Carl was guilty. Bashford, she had seen at once, was completely convinced that Ana had been murdered in the strictest sense of the law, including some measure of premeditation. Lederer's talks with Detective Finelli yielded the same degree of certainty from him ("Liz, I'm tellin' ya, he did it"), his opinion coming at the first feel of the case. All the other cops from Crime Scene back to the radio-car officers who answered the 911 call concurred. "A bear," was how one Sixth Precinct detective described Carl physically when Lederer wondered out loud whether he had the muscle to carry out the deed. She had no shortage of respect for the police's experience-based conclusions and Bashford's legal expertise, yet Lederer was left to live and cope with the rub of reasonable doubt.

She understood what inheriting someone else's "baby" and not having been in at the beginning meant. Much of the knowledge and perception gained over fifteen months by her predecessor had in effect been lost and needed whatever quick recovery was possible. But to her, the case looked like a field of wreckage, botched police work, errors in the legal work, two strikes against it in court, and, it seemed, a judge winding up perhaps with a touch of glee to pitch the third.

She continued to go about it anyway, putting one piece of paper alongside another, calling here and calling there, seeing this witness and that, trying to build on the strong parts of the case and reassemble it in a more forceful way than it was given to her. Above all, she sought somehow to "solve" the mystery so that she might purge herself of energy-sapping reservations. In the meantime, she decided to remain skeptical, a devil's advocate, until persuaded one way or another.

On the twenty-sixth, she told Judge Berkman that the People would take their chances before a grand jury once more.[1] She was unaware

[1] Her decision made a *New York Post* pun headline ("DA Again Paints Famed Artist As a Wife-Killer") but without her name or news of Bashford's replacement. Dredging up the jet-lag story again, and attributing it to Carl saying his wife "might have stumbled out an open window," the two covering reporters got a slightly unprintable

of course that her decision to proceed, no matter how carefully weighed, had made Hoffinger's private guess about the Morgenthau bureaucratic machine and how "nobody was going to take the responsibility of stopping it" come true.

LEDERER'S LACK OF enthusiasm was becoming obvious to others. Ruby had called her about a new lead—a person she interviewed who had been in the Delion grocery shortly after Ana's death and had heard a clerk speak in the plural of "witnesses to the crime." An answer that the story had failed to check out had been less than satisfying. Raquel had not had a word from Bashford after the case had been dismissed the second time until she called and learned she had been replaced. When Raquel finally met Lederer, she was disappointed. Bashford, whatever her shortcomings, had at least felt as strongly about the case as Raquel, but Lederer, though more businesslike and appearing more efficient, seemed without commitment and distant besides.

Nevertheless, the new assistant D.A. drove on in her own surgical fashion, moving quickly and incisively. If there would be passion, it would come later. She gathered and reshuffled her witnesses, replacing the person who had testified to Ana's fear of heights with someone who had more powerful and more recent testimony to reveal.[2] Ready, she went into the grand jury room on a Monday morning in March and walked out of the same room a week later with the third indictment in hand. She had studied Berkman's objections with microscopic intensity. There was to have been absolutely no mention of anything that had to do with reasons for the divorce—the use of the somehow melodramatic word "detective" specifically banned. Consequently, in

---

mini-interview with Hoffinger. He was said to have told the *Post:* "There's practically no evidence. It's conjecture and circumstantial bull----."

[2]The witness was Marsha Pels, substituting for Modesto Torre. Torre's memory of Ana some years earlier being unable to look out of his window had been challenged by Hoffinger as too far in the past to be relevant. Marsha would testify that three weeks before Ana died, they had gone on a holiday outside of Rome, and Ana had had a severe attack of acrophobia. The only access to the clifftop villa of their destination was a long, steep ascent of stone steps and she had been unable to make the climb without Marsha's assistance.

Lederer's presentation there was no talk of infidelity or any suggestion of Ana hiring detectives. If Berkman saw fit to throw this one out, too, she would have to find new arguments, and dismiss it or not, no one could say that Carl Andre had not gotten every benefit of the grand jury process.

Hoffinger told the *New York Times* on the day of the third indictment that he was not sure whether he would try for a third dismissal, but a few weeks later he was back in Berkman's court trying. Moving again to overthrow the indictment, he rehearsed all the old arguments and recited the ancient history of Bashford's failures and Berkman's own reproachful position. The only thing new was his request for a ruling on the sufficiency of the evidence. In both of Berkman's dismissals, her justification for allowing resubmission was that this was a "close circumstantial case," and she had not examined the sufficiency question explicitly. Far from accepting it as a close call, Hoffinger claimed it did not even "meet the minimal requirements" for an indictment. If it was close, he seemed to be saying, show me.

Lederer, in her first time out against her unnerving adversary, fielded the challenge smartly. Her effort, she argued, "differs markedly" from Bashford's. She had followed Berkman's earlier rulings and directions to the letter, omitting evidence deemed inadmissible and presenting evidence deemed necessary but omitted earlier. Hers was a "balanced, thorough, and fair presentation strictly adhering to this Court's guidelines." Like her predecessor, she opposed Hoffinger on every point, but with a shrewdness learned perhaps from Bashford's bad luck. Thus, in anticipating his request for the grand jury minutes, she gave them to Berkman before she could ask, saying with just a tiny genuflection that the judge did not need Hoffinger's assistance to decide on the motion. Fighting Hoffinger's persistent demand to suppress Carl's statements to the police as having somehow been coerced, she agreed to a pretrial hearing on the admissibility of such evidence.

Her terse, preemptive style breathed a new vitality into the case, and by toughing out Hoffinger's attacks, she seemed to be doing the exercises of a formidable courtroom opponent—though all of this was still only a paper war.

On June 17, Berkman agreed with Lederer in every respect. No grand jury minutes for Hoffinger, no relief granted. This was a close circumstantial case because Berkman said so; the evidence, what admissible part of it was left, was therefore more than sufficient. The twenty-month, heavy-casualty battle for dismissal was over. The third murder-two indictment was upheld. Berkman as required stepped aside. A month earlier, she had given Lederer and Hoffinger the names of three judges, saying that if they could agree on one of them, she would not send the case to a random selection from a pool of available judges. One of the three was a woman, and Hoffinger had listed her as his first choice. Lederer, wondering if her opponent knew something she didn't, chose a man, but when Hoffinger agreed with her choice without argument, she concluded that he had outwitted her and had wanted a man all along. By then it was too late to retreat. The new judge was Justice Alvin Schlesinger. In his brown courtroom, room 1333, beginning next November, Carl Andre would stand trial for the murder of Ana Mendieta. Nobody was going to call Lederer hungry for publicity. There was none.

33

Carl had begun to come out of the shell of 34E. Until lately, he would rarely be seen downtown other than on days when he had to make appearances in court. His exemplary attendance record, his presence as a quiet soul with a book bag, had been rewarded and had led to a more relaxed relationship with the authorities. At the time of the first dismissal, in April 1986, Hoffinger had asked Berkman to reduce bail, and she had, substantially, lowering it from the original $250,000 to $100,000. The difference, minus the 2 percent the city charged for the trouble of holding it, had relieved his debt to Frank Stella almost entirely, and his financial situation, which had become precarious, had been eased, too, making his life a little more livable. Along the way, Hoffinger had also succeeded in getting Carl's passport restored, and he had plans to travel back to Europe that summer, having been away for two years.

Almost all of his European friends, along with some who had been more friendly with Ana than him, had remained unswervingly sympathetic to Carl and aloof from the militant side-taking in Soho. From the beginning he had received many warm, condoling letters from abroad, and travelers to New York had sought him out to grieve with him in person. Some of them had received no response and had encountered what appeared to be strange behavior on the part of people close to Carl.[1] But that was in the early days when suspicions were at their highest and the eagerness to shelter him was less practiced. Little by little, however, he had started to respond. By now he had been seeing friends regularly in New York and had received at least two visitors he and Ana had befriended in Rome. One was French artist Veronique Bigo, the other an Italian museum curator named Ester Coen.

Veronique, living in Rome when Ana was there, had gotten very close to her, rather less so with Carl. In New York, she had found him completely changed, both physically and otherwise, and she was dismayed, the one time she saw him, by his deliberate dodging of any word she spoke of Ana. Closer friends knew better than to talk about "the accident." Ester Coen, taciturn by nature, was unsure of what to talk about, as usual, never quite knowing whether what she was saying would "get on his nerves or not." She had seen him during his anxious weeks in April while he was awaiting another fateful decision after the third indictment. They drank champagne by candlelight and talked about art, Japanese food, and the spectacular view of Manhattan from the windows of 34E.

SINCE ANA'S DEATH, Carl had had no one-man shows in the United States and very little income, but in 1987, the European side of his world began to build up to near average, with three museum exhibitions scheduled for that year in the Netherlands and Italy, as well as group shows in Germany and Switzerland. The German show, in Münster, was where Carl was reunited that summer with several old friends. Rita Sartorius flew in from Berlin. An art researcher, she had done the

---

[1]Ida Panicelli, for example, had written twice without receiving a reply, wanting to express her sorrow and ask if there were anything she could do for him in Rome. Roman artist Nunzio on a trip to New York found it impossible to see Carl. He contacted both Angela Westwater and Paula Cooper and was told by both that they had no idea where Carl was.

catalogue for the Dutch exhibition "with great dedication and meticulous scholarship," Carl had written in the introduction. She was a
relative newcomer to his German clan, the old-timers being his longtime dealer Konrad Fischer and his wife, Darte.

Their get-together was made even more like old times by the presence of Sol LeWitt, both in the same show and, with his wife, Carol,
in person. Sol, as Carl's friendly rival in art, went back, as did Fischer,
to the sixties, the beginning, and Carol had first met Carl more than
a dozen years ago. To the LeWitts, Carl seemed happy to be with "old
family" in the three or four days they all spent there, lunching or
dining, or running into one another in Münster and Düsseldorf.

Carol, however, found it hard going, growing very upset at being
with Carl and the Fischers, everyone including herself avoiding men-
tion of Ana. The LeWitts had been living in Italy when Ana was there,
and Carol had come to regard Ana as one of her dearest friends. The
Fischers had also known Ana, and Darte had gotten close to her, too.
It was bad enough to pretend that she had never existed, but, thought
Carol, it was presumptuous, even a presumption of guilt, to act as if
Carl wasn't suffering.

They had gone to a farewell dinner in Düsseldorf, the LeWitts, the
Fischers, and Carl. Both Sol and Carol had strong feelings about how
passions might have gone haywire that night, but the feelings, and their
love for Ana, came with compassion for Carl and a refusal to sit in
judgment. Carol had always been uncomfortable with Carl, afraid of
him, finding him intimidating, but when toward the end of the meal
she could bear all the make-believe no longer, she worked up the
courage to bring it out in the open.

"You know, Carl," she said while the table fell silent, "it's so hard
for me to be with you, just because I miss Ana so much, and I really
am looking forward for this to be over so we can mourn her."

To Carol it seemed that Carl almost cried as he said, "I really need
to do that." She believed him, as she believed that he truly had loved
Ana.

SPIROS PAPPAS, a strong-looking Greek immigrant with a shock of
thick hair, lived in precisely the same kind of apartment as Carl did,

in 21E. He was the building superintendent at 300 Mercer, and having received a telephone call from the district attorney's office, he was expecting a visit from Elizabeth Lederer. Pappas had been asleep in the bedroom identical to the one thirteen floors above him, when Ana, falling, had passed his closed window. He had heard nothing, either before she plunged or when she crashed directly beneath him. A few minutes later, however, he had been awakened by an intercom call from the doorman on duty at the time, and when he looked out of the window, he saw her body sprawled on the setback below.

Since the June ruling, Lederer had had the double task of catching up to where Bashford had left off and generating the much more complex presentation required for a trial. Bashford hadn't had to prepare the latter material, so to that extent, the case had now become Lederer's own.

She was aware that Bashford, using the Crime Scene photographs and measurements, had reconstructed every scenario she could think of and had found nothing to persuade her that Ana might have gone out the window alone, particularly without leaving footprints. At the time, a visit to the apartment itself had seemed as unnecessary as it was infeasible. It had already been searched by the police, Carl was securely in Hoffinger's hands, and there was no chance of obtaining a second warrant for a mere visual inspection. Lederer now faced the same problem, but she had a strong inclination to take a look for herself. Like Bashford, she had been unable to understand how Carl could remain in that apartment, starting every day by the light of *that* window, and when she discovered that Pappas happened to live in 21E, she decided to call on him at home.

There were other good reasons to interview him. It was a sure bet that Hoffinger would draw hired guns, her phrase for expert testimony, when she put the Waverly Place doorman on the witness stand. His testimony about having heard a woman scream for her life was pivotal, and it took little imagination for Lederer to envisage the defense bringing in high-priced acousticians ready to say that at the distance of more than three hundred feet between the thirty-fourth floor and street level, the chances of hearing anything was whatever percentage you wanted the guns to say. The hot summer night drone of hundreds of air conditioners and the exhaust fans of the all-night deli were a couple of other points Hoffinger could be expected to use as an awl on her witness.

Meeting with Pappas, she gained reassurance from his having lived over the Delion for almost as many years as Carl, and he had had no trouble hearing street noises from his window when open. Carl of course remained a third of the full distance still higher, but in a courtroom, that only meant that two-thirds of any defense objection would appear groundless.

If Lederer was feeling encouraged, when she saw the bedroom and approached the window she was stunned. Her entire outlook on the case turned around. She had sought for some piece of evidence that might move her, as a jury had to be moved, beyond the mighty line of reasonable doubt, and now, not by any Holmsean detection or deduction, but by the natural agency of the one thing she had most in common with Ana—her body size—she had been transported, her conscience suddenly in the safe port of certitude.

She moved slowly toward the window. She slipped off her shoes. At nearly five-feet-two, she had almost four inches on Ana's true height, and the windowsill came fully to Lederer's waist. She had no unusual fear of heights, but in that one moment she felt she understood the deepest meaning of that fear. She was looking out the window almost at Ana's eye view. Had she been taller, say, a head taller like Bashford, her perception might have been less compelling, but as it stood, she was overwhelmed. Later, she would make her calculations and conclude that Ana, 73 percent of her below the sill, would have had to bounce, rise, or, as she would put it, fall *up* three feet from the bedroom floor, and then, by the force of the same misstep, drunken or otherwise, propelled across the twenty-inch platform formed by the radiator cover, the sill, and the ledge outside—with more than half her body driven into the void—before gravity could take over.

But no amount of arithmetic could substitute for the three-dimensional geometry of standing there in her stockinged feet, her own eyes revealing truth. Walking out of Pappas's apartment, Lederer had come away with her most powerful witness as herself; anyone but a giant, conscious of Ana's height and seeing the bedroom itself, Lederer believed, could only conclude the same as she had. Were the court to allow her, bringing a jury to 34E could make the whole of the People's case.

THE FALL ART season came around for the third time since Ana's death. The condemned *Tilted Arc* had not yet been removed from Federal Plaza, and Richard Serra had still not gone into exile, but the story was forgotten. The Crispo case, too, had receded into a dark place and was even further from trial than Carl's. The Guggenheim was celebrating its fiftieth anniversary, decking out its permanent collection, including an Andre timber piece on the ramp, but the hottest, most talked-up show in town was neoexpressionist Julian Schnabel's retrospective at the Whitney, hard evidence that the eighties' new art had pushed minimalism aside.

The gallery system itself was feeling trampled on by the hyped merchandising and the outstanding success of the auction houses, which were already making front pages with the upcoming spring sale of the late Andy Warhol's estate. An art-world era seemed to be passing, yet the pro-Carl and pro-Ana encampments in Soho, though dormant all summer, had become a fixture, bursting on the scene once more that autumn.

Carl's trial was due to begin on November 23. Three days earlier, a retrospective exhibition of Ana's work opened at the New Museum of Contemporary Art on lower Broadway in Soho. The show was to run for two months, which meant that it would be on public view throughout the trial. Carl's defenders, seeing nasty intent aimed at doing him in, immediately cried foul. Moreover, during the week of the opening, Soho was mysteriously plastered with unsigned posters soliciting witnesses for the prosecution. The usual billboard announcements on the walls of Mercer, Wooster, and Prince streets in particular were all but papered over with an eye-catching ANA MENDIETA in bold black type, the text reading: "Suicide? Accident? Murder? Anyone With Information Please Call." This was followed by the D.A.'s number. Lederer's office denied having anything to do with it, as did the other suspect, the Guerilla Girls, the feminist self-proclaimed "conscience of the art world."[2] The perpetrators were never discovered. Neither was the paint-and-run bandit who splattered the word SUICIDE in black on the sidewalk in front of the New Museum the day of the opening. In the end, the trial was put off until January 19 for purely technical reasons, and it was purely accidental that the retrospective, two years in the planning, fell on the date it did. But Soho had grown accustomed to chronic conspiratorial aches and pains, which would become crippling at trial time.

UNLIKE THE TENSE Park Avenue memorial two years earlier, when the two sides had yet to congeal, the New Museum opening, a reception on November 19, was a one-sided affair. It was the largest opening the museum had ever had, the crowd reaching onto Broadway in unusually cold weather. Rumors circulated that Hoffinger had advised Carl to be seen but he had refused. In any event he wasn't there, and those close to him, wondering who on their side or still straddling might have gone, sent spies. Hoffinger sent someone from his staff who could blend in to search Ana's art for "clues."

Welcome or not, people bore witness to something entirely new: the perception of a power in Ana's work that began to surmount, if not heal, temporal wounds. No one had ever seen the body of work as a whole, drawings and sculpture filling large spaces, video screens alive with her filmed performances, photographs of her earthworks, the last ten years of her creative life. For the first time, friends and critics, some who had paid scarce attention to her work before, perhaps because of her presence, saw something in her absence that was universal and constant. With few exceptions, reviewers saw the glimmers of greatness, lamenting the loss of what might have been, but in the end, only

[2]The Guerilla Girls, a secret organization "to combat sexism and racism in the artworld," conceals the identity of its members, ostensibly to shield them from retribution from the power in the museum-gallery establishment. They thus astonished many art-world feminists by failing to take any position in the case, "even though we have a variety of individual positions," says an anonymous spokeswoman. The belief was widespread that the Girls were, in fact, in the sway of those older feminists who had sought to protect Carl.

what existed could ever have meaning.[3] It was her old professor John Perreault, co-curator of the show, who became her best interpreter. He had been among the first to write about Carl's art, and now he saw beauty again. Her work, he wrote, sought a oneness in nature and the human spirit; it was about the supernatural, and at its finest, he said, it *was* supernatural. She had gone beyond letting her soul become visible; she had been "courting the gods."

—— 34 ——

On March 10, 1987, the day after he testified to a grand jury for the third time in the case, Ed Mojzis, the doorman who heard the screams and who was one of the prosecution's most important witnesses, stepped up to a pay phone and dialed Lederer's direct number at the D.A.'s office.

When he had her on the line, he spoke with some trepidation and embarrassment, saying, "Look, I'm a vet and I have problems."

As he went on, Lederer, sagging, thinking, oh, no, made the following notes on a scrap of paper which looked something like this:

Long Is Jewish—2 mo
      2 X—1976—Oct.
        1978—Apr.
'81 NY Hosp—4 mo
    Oct.—Feb. or March
Haldol

Ten months later, at the end of the day on Friday, January 15, 1988, a package was delivered to Hoffinger's thirty-third floor office on East Fifty-ninth Street containing what lawyers call *Rosario* material, the emphasis added by custom to denote a particular case in law. That was four days before the trial was scheduled to begin, and the long battle

---

[3]Reviewing the show in the *Voice*, Elizabeth Hess made an unqualified prediction that over the years Ana's work would be judged as ahead of its time. Michael Brenson of the *New York Times* spoke warmly of the complexity, the convincing voice and presence, and the importance of her work.

for discovery—learning by entitlement everything the D.A.'s office had in its casebook on the defendant—was at last over. *Rosario* material is most easily defined as evidence gathered by the prosecution that may be considered favorable to the accused. As a result of the case for which it was named, such material must be released to the defense before the start of the trial, which in practice was usually as close to the last moment as possible. Amid the pile of documents Hoffinger had received was a copy of the half sheet of paper on which Lederer had made the above undated notes.

The D.A. was under no obligation to explain what the scribbling was all about, and it probably would have gone undeciphered by Hoffinger, though the intriguing and not completely mysterious word "Haldol" might have set him in the right direction. One day earlier, however, the trial judge, Alvin Schlesinger, had sent Hoffinger information provided by Lederer that made any detective work a lot easier. As a result, someone on Hoffinger's staff looked up Haldol in the *Physicians' Desk Reference,* which listed it as a pharmaceutical "for use in the management of manifestations of psychotic disorders."

What Judge Schlesinger had been obliged by case law and fairness to pass on to the defense was that Ed Mojzis, not very long after he had returned from Vietnam, had been hospitalized for a psychiatric disorder, and that was only the first time. Further, his medical record revealed that one of his symptoms was auditory hallucinations—language any defense lawyer could be counted on to popularize for the benefit of a jury and the media as "hearing things."

His medical history was part of what Mojzis had admitted to Lederer on the phone and in greater detail two weeks later in person. Hoffinger had no knowledge of these conversations, but another piece of *Rosario* informed him that Lederer had solicited records of an unidentified patient from the Long Island Jewish Hillside Medical Center in a subpoena issued the previous May 19. From all this, Lederer's hasty jottings suddenly became transparent. They strongly suggested that Mojzis had been hospitalized at least three times between 1976 and 1981, over a period of six months, and since the note had to have been written before the subpoena, it was equally as clear from the rest of the record that Lederer had failed to inform Judge Berkman at a time when she was still considering Hoffinger's latest motion for dismissal. Further, Lederer may have been aware of Mojzis's infirmity even while the grand jury was still in session. If so, she had withheld that information.

Hoffinger immediately set his staff to work. Lederer would have a lot to explain. In the meantime, he would move on the opening day of the trial for a full hearing of the entire affair, aimed once again at throwing out the People's case.

The discovery process had delivered two other apparent windfalls, adding firepower to Hoffinger's arsenal. Early in the investigation, Bashford and Finelli had committed a whopping blunder. She had written the search warrant for 34E and had neglected to state the first order of business of any investigation of a crime scene. Finelli, who had worked with her and had carried out the search, had failed to spot the glaring error. What was missing was any reference to "processing," looking for the simplest clues like bloodstains and other usual telltale signs. Worse, there was not a word of the most basic processing, taking photographs and fingerprints. This was so elementary as to be implicit, but usually written in anyway for safety's sake, since what was not in the warrant technically could not be carried out—or at least Hoffinger would so argue before the judge. Moreover, where the warrant had been unequivocally clear—about the search for Ana's Xerox copies—Hoffinger noted that according to the inventory of the items seized, virtually none of it had been *photocopied* material.

He would therefore go into court asking for the suppression of everything taken from the apartment, as well as almost everything else in the case, but in this instance, in spite of all his vigilance, he would do so at the risk of committing a potential blunder himself. In planning to draw attention to the absence of photocopies, he could not have been aware of their true significance: they were part of the chain of circumstantial evidence that his client had arranged for their surreptitious removal after Ana's death.

"No EATING OR drinking in the courtroom, Miss," was what Alvin Schlesinger said as he walked into room 1333, a five-thousand-square-foot satrapy all his own. He had entered from his chambers at 9:20 on the morning of the first day of Carl's trial, his hands folded in front of him to keep his black robe from swaying, his sparkling eyes spying a woman in a second-row seat sipping from a plastic container. She left.

There were few others in the 128 fraying seats behind the railing that separated the players from the spectators. Back in November, when the trial had been postponed until today, the judge had reprimanded Hoffinger for showing up fifteen minutes late, at 9:45 instead of 9:30, admonishing him to be prompt next time. Today, 9:30 came and went, but Schlesinger had sent word to the lawyers that his previous trial had taken longer than foreseen and Carl's would not be called until the afternoon, if then, so even Carl didn't show up until three. He was alone as usual, taking the farthest possible seat from the judge in a corner of the last row. A few days earlier, he had been into Paula Cooper's gallery looking rosy, thanking Paula for her Christmas presents, smiling warmly, fluffed out in brand-new or freshly laundered overalls and a long down coat. Now, however, he appeared dampened, somber, sunk into himself. Ana's mother, already seated, was in a middle row, both Carl and she avoiding any eye contact, as they would throughout the trial.

A reporter and a photographer from the *Daily News* drifted in and out. Jan Hoffman of *The Village Voice* followed the trial in progress to pass the time. A man by the name of Rodney Swift had been accused of pickpocketing a transit police decoy in the subway. He was on the stand, his Legal Aid attorney trying to show he had been framed. There had been reports in the press of cops doing just that, entrapping blacks and Hispanics to fatten their arrest records and win promotions. Rodney Swift, black, thirty-eight, looking bewildered after four months at Rikers and another jail at the old Brooklyn Navy Yard, told his story.

The undercover female police officer sitting across from him on the train, wearing plain, tight clothes, kept opening and closing her legs to entice him, said Swift, and when he finally approached her and asked her for a blow job, she attempted to involve him in a pickpocketing scheme. Schlesinger listened intently, leaning forward, leaning back, fanning himself with a legal pad. Carl watched, too, perhaps more observant than anyone else of the man who would judge him as well. Swift was an honest citizen, his lawyer contended, addressing the jury, drawing out his client to speak about his life. He was a poet, the defendant said, writing his poems in Greenwich Village. He worked with a caricaturist in Washington Square Park, selling his poetry for five dollars a poem. He had got on the subway on his way to visit his aunt, and then this had happened. He was innocent, he said, the allegedly pickpocketed wallet planted when he was arrested.

Hoffinger showed up at 3:45 and bent over the back of Carl's seat, whispering. They got up and left. Word went around the courtroom that the present case would go on until the following afternoon. Little by little, everyone departed, leaving Rodney Swift to his fate.

THE PEOPLE AGAINST Carl Andre, which was how it was announced in court—the word "versus" reduced to a "v." in the records and dead in actual speech—was called twenty-four hours later, at about three P.M. on Wednesday, January 20. Schlesinger had just instructed the jury in the Swift case and had sent them off to what he called a "nice place" to deliberate. But the Andre trial proper did not get going that day either, and indeed would not really begin until the morning of January 29. The interim, six intense court days, would be occupied by a preliminary procedure called a *Huntley* hearing to determine the admissibility of each piece of evidence against Carl. Some of the judge's most crucial decisions would be made here, but first came an old-fashioned battle for turf.

Some days back, Judge Schlesinger had given a party. As was his style in recent years, he had taken over a restaurant, inviting about sixty friends and associates, including Lederer, and, to keep it fair, Hoffinger. Schlesinger was aware that the assistant D.A. was very nervous about going up against a hard and seasoned litigator such as Hoffinger. The thought of his overpowering flamboyance had given her more than one sleepless night, and she hadn't been ashamed to admit it, not only to the judge. Hoffinger, having begged off, was not present at the party, so when it fell to the host to say a few words to his guests, he felt free to include a little roasting of Lederer's apprehensions, sending his best wishes along with it. Now, at the court clerk's call, Hoffinger, leading an entourage rolling overstuffed leather briefcases on a trolley, was first down the center aisle in a display of uptown power that captured the room, though Lederer, perhaps by design, had not yet arrived. Only

Carl, red-faced and tagging behind his three-man defense team in his stuffed overcoat and open galoshes, his book bag dangling from a drooping shoulder, punctured the class-act image, though he certainly looked the part of a man under fire two and a half years who was now going to live or die.

A few moments later, Lederer made an impressive entry herself before the same small group of onlookers, but in quite another way. Followed by a spindly assistant even younger than she, Lederer came down the same aisle handsomely, pushing a kind of a supermarket shopping cart full of manilla folders, the straight-backed young prosecutor, every nerve taut but in its place, as meticulously groomed, but not as expensively, as the big-retainer counselor she was about to face.

The three-way struggle for supremacy began. Hoffinger, who had filed his motion to dismiss the case because of Lederer's conduct regarding the doorman's illness, tried to speak first, but Schlesinger took the offensive the moment he opened his mouth. "Keep your voice up," the judge warned him, mating the defense lawyer's opening move and launching into a reprimand about the brief having been "dumped" on him at so late a date.

Lederer, not to be left behind, put her toes in, claiming Hoffinger's motion had made serious allegations. The Ed Mojzis problem, along with two other prosecution "improprieties" raised by the defense, had nothing to do with the present hearing, and Lederer asked for time to prepare a written response.

Hoffinger made a tactical retreat into silence. Schlesinger gave Lederer a week to reply, disposed of some technical matters, and adjourned. Hoffinger took his case into the corridor, filling in a journalist on the Lederer-doorman "monkey business." Carl watched from down the hall. That was day one.

THE *Huntley* HEARING got going in earnest the next morning at 10:27 when Lederer called her first witness. She had prepared herself to face three defense challenges to the evidence: that Carl's oral statements and whatever else had transpired while he was with the police that Sunday were the result of some form of intimidation; that the police reports of what he said were not credible; and that whatever had been seized in the search of Carl's apartment had violated his constitutional rights.

Accordingly, over the next few days, she presented six witnesses who had been assigned to the case, five of the cops and Martha Bashford, to show that everything had been done as properly as humans are able to do things. Hoffinger, striving to demonstrate the opposite, called five witnesses, including other cops on the case and his own predecessor, Gerry Rosen.

Rosen, as wiser as he was older and still smarting over having been stiffed by Carl, had nevertheless reentered the case as his witness. Hoffinger hoped to show that Carl's rights had been trampled on when Rosen called the Sixth Precinct that Sunday afternoon and couldn't get Finelli on the phone. The defense also claimed a second rights violation stemming from a phone conversation Lederer had had with Rosen some days back. She had asked him, among other things, if there was any basis to his statements to the press that Ana had been suffering from jet lag and he had said no, he "made it up." Hoffinger stated that Lederer's call and Rosen's "unfortunate" decision to answer her had breached client-attorney privilege law, hurting Carl "in a way that cannot be sanitized." Rosen, in spite of knowing he would appear once again in the role of the naive and bumbling lawyer, had agreed to come forward. Over the last two years, he had grown a great deal more secure about his professional abilities, even to the point of regretting having lost the case; now he wanted to "rise above it all" and simply be a witness to what he knew to be true.

As provided by law, each side cross-examined the other side's witnesses, and in the end, Schlesinger ruled on which evidence would and would not be allowed admission to the trial as well as on the question of Carl's rights. With a couple of suspenseful exceptions, notably how the judge would decide on the search warrant and Lederer's handling of Mojzis, the outcome was more or less predictable. Thus what turned out to be more engaging about the pretrial hearing was the three-way foreplay heating up for the climactic act. It would produce the biggest surprise of them all.

———

SCHLESINGER WANTED HOFFINGER to know who was boss. To his "keep your voice up" beginning, an admonition he often repeated, the judge promptly added "Stand back" whenever Hoffinger approached a witness. He also made deflating running gags about Hoffinger's celebrated cross-examination prowess.

"I used to live with the hope that there was an end to everything, both good and bad," said the judge, trying to move Hoffinger along. "I'm losing faith."

Hoffinger showed himself to be controllable but incorrigible, standing back when told, working his witness into inevitable contradictions, then swooping down, arms flailing, for the kill. "First you have to nail him," he said when holding one of his chatty little law lessons in the corridor, "then take him apart." He was all over the place when in action, advancing and retreating, glancing at his notes, pushing up his half-glasses to his forehead, charging, waving awesome reminders of the witness's oath ("You recognize that you're under oath, don't you?"). Since the hearing witnesses were mostly cops and lawyers, however, it seemed only a warm-up for what was yet to come, and even Schlesinger, sometimes visibly caught up himself in admiration, let him go. "I should sustain it," he replied to one of Lederer's objections, "but I do want to hear the answer."

But he held on to the leash. What was the relevance of his question? the judge would repeatedly ask, cutting into Hoffinger's dance with his witness. When he would decide that there was no relevance at all, he'd whip around to the witness and snap, "Don't answer that! Next question, Mr., uh, Hoffinger." He simply could not remember the famous defense attorney's name, though he had known him for years and had gotten it right when he had invited him to his party. For his part, Hoffinger ascribed to a heuristic formula: let the judge be king. When scolded, he would smile, trying his best to look sheepish in a thousand-dollar wool suit.

The Sturm und Drang of it all, the sex, in Hoffinger's phrase, seemed to relax Lederer. Every day saw her grow surer in her own courtroom manner—planted unswaying on her feet, arms folded across her chest, peering out over Elizabethan collars, winnowing her witnesses hygienically, her cries of "Objection!" coming more frequently, though she didn't win any more than before. Nor was she mollycoddled. "Miss Lederer!" Schlesinger fired at her, "I've heard your objection and overruled it! Don't look so anguished!" By the time the preliminaries were almost over, Schlesinger had begun to appear as though he had had a shrewd master plan to assure fair play, trying all the while to offset undue advantage and reset the scales of justice to zero.

THE HEARING DREW to a close and there had not been a single mention in the media, though Schlesinger's court was in the news for another reason. To the utter surprise of everyone, Rodney Swift had been acquitted of all charges, and *Daily News* columnist Earl Caldwell had written a long article praising the verdict, the jury, and the judge. The cause for astonishment, as Caldwell suggested, was that the case had hinged on the word of one indicted black man against the police, there having been no other witnesses. Caldwell pointed out that the makeup of the jury—blacks and whites, young and old—was a result of the voter registration drives of 1984, the year Jesse Jackson ran for the presidency. Jurors were selected from voter registration rolls, the composition of which had changed, resulting in a more representative social mix. This factor, as well as the shortfall in police credibility and the underscoring of Schlesinger's fairness, would soon have an almost metaphysical connection to Carl's case.

SCHLESINGER CAME INTO the courtroom on Thursday morning, January 28, and ruled on all the pretrial issues. By now, everyone had become old friends of a sort, or at least a familiar face. A crowd of regulars had been building up slowly during the hearing. Beginning with Ana's mother as the family's representative,[1] the spectators consisted mainly of Ana's friends coming and going, but the more complex nature of the audience would not take its full shape until the second or third day of the trial proper. Carl had his own routine: rarely ex-

---

[1]Raquel and Tom were scheduled to be witnesses and were thus by law prohibited from attending the proceedings.

changing a word with even his lawyers, barely looking anywhere but straight ahead, following the proceedings attentively, then sinking into his reading during every break.

The first matter of business was Hoffinger's "doorman motion" to dismiss the case. Lederer had submitted her written reply two days earlier and had made oral arguments yesterday, after Hoffinger had assailed her filed response as being "artful" and "ducking it." She hung tough. The subpoena for Mojzis's hospital records, she said, had not been answered until long after Berkman's final decision. She had not known about any medical problem before Mojzis's call, which was after his final grand jury testimony. Moreover, his disorder had been treated, was under control, and he had not had any symptoms since 1981. In any event, the law was on her side. The prosecution had no obligation to present evidence on the credibility of its witnesses; disclosing Mojzis's medical history when she did had been sufficient.

"I am constrained to conclude," Schlesinger began as soon as the court had reconvened, "that withholding evidence . . . did not materially affect the third grand jury proceedings." The tension in the room ran high. Carl, head high, one hand covering his mouth, seemed focused on every word. "The motion," Schlesinger went on after giving his reasons, "is in all respects denied."

There was no outward reaction. The judge then turned to the search warrant, dealing with the prosecution's failure to specify the taking of photographs. Once the police had legally entered 34E, he said, nothing could stop them from testifying as to what they had seen with their own eyes, which was the only thing the photographs could record. What they saw and what was on film were substantially the same things. The photographs were therefore admissible at trial.

As for the taking of fingerprints, like all prints, they had been invisible to the naked eye. Dusting, oversight or not, was not in the search warrant, and by virtue of the defendant's Fourth Amendment right against illegal search and seizure, the Crime Lab's latent fingerprint report, Schlesinger ruled, was inadmissible evidence. The *absence* of footprints on the windowsill and radiator, which, as the prosecution had maintained, was *not* something seized in the search, was again not

discernible to the naked eye. Thus, this Taoist-like example of Nothingness, so compelling to the prosecution's case, was ruled inadmissible,
too.

Hoffinger, in his oral arguments the day before, had unwittingly
made a mountain of the "Xerox copies" phrase in the warrant, which
had been reduced by time to a molehill. "They didn't seize anything
Ana was said to be collecting," he had complained, grumbling on and
on. "The material seized has nothing to do with the case. They took
whatever they could find. It was a general search. The court was misled
in issuing the warrant." Lederer, who was less familiar than Bashford
with the details of the missing photocopies, had not even bothered to
reply, and now Schlesinger, who, understandably, could see no great
difference between a copy and an original, overruled Hoffinger's objections and allowed the infidelity records to stand. They would never be
spoken of again.[2]

SCHLESINGER HAD ANNOUNCED that jury selection would begin that
morning. At 11:10 A.M., he declared the *Huntley* hearing ended, ordering a fifteen-minute recess before the start of the trial. In the corridor
just outside his courtroom, while the break stretched to half an hour,
the potential jurors, wearing little badges, drifted up and down. They
were waiting to be gathered and led in a back way and were looking
slightly lost. To some, they seemed the most concrete sign that after
all these days, weeks, and years, Carl's trial was really going to begin.

Schlesinger, looking just-rubbed with his favorite lotion, reentered
the courtroom first, turning to an aide and saying, "Clerk, you wanna
gather the Andre club?" Obeying him to the letter, the clerk stepped
outside the squeaky, swinging courtroom doors, and cried, "Andre
club!" At 11:45, everyone was in place, and Schlesinger said, "The case
is now on trial."

---

[2]Among his more or less expected decisions, Schlesinger found that all of Carl's
statements to the police had been made voluntarily and could therefore be introduced
at trial. One of the few things taken from 34E dear to Hoffinger's heart and thus
supported as admissible was the photograph of Ana and another woman with Fidel
Castro. It was among the items ruled out, however. The Rosen issues were dismissed
as inconsequential.

Papers shuffled, the words sinking in, but suddenly Hoffinger rose.

"Your Honor," he said matter-of-factly, "my client wishes to waive a jury."

Most of the spectators, if they heard him at all, seemed not quite sure what that meant, and waited for more clues, but Lederer and Schlesinger were completely taken aback. The Sixth Amendment guarantees the right of trial by jury, but according to New York State law, as in other states but far from all, that implies the right not to have a jury, and this was what Hoffinger wanted. The reason for the astonishment was that neither Schlesinger nor Lederer, much less anyone else, could remember the last time a murder case was tried without a jury. Schlesinger, doing something he had never done before, turned directly to Carl and addressed him.

"Did you hear that?"

Carl got to his feet. "Yes," he said, his voice flat and high. "I did, sir. That's my choice."

Schlesinger stared at him. He had been watching him carefully and inconspicuously from a corner of his eye all through the hearing, but he seemed to be seeing him now for the first time.

"Tell me about yourself," he said. The judge had a way of talking to defendants rather imperiously.

Carl remained inscrutable. "I'm fifty-two years old," he replied, everyone in the courtroom leaning forward. "I'm a sculptor by profession. I have a high school education. . . . I have lived since 1957 in Manhattan. . . . I've never been in court in my life."

"Listen to what I have to say very carefully," said Schlesinger. "If you don't understand, ask me and I'll try to explain as best as I can."

Carl, playing it the judge's way, nodded.

"If you had a jury trial," Schlesinger began, "you would have an important part to play in picking that jury." He pointed to the jury box. "Do you understand?"

"Yes, sir."

"In a nonjury trial, I make all the decisions. Sometimes there is an advantage in a jury trial. You get a mixed bag of people with different experiences. Twelve different people considering the issues. There is a great exchange between juries. If I try the case alone, I have only one experience. I do not have the benefit of others to call attention to certain aspects of the case. . . . It is based on one head."

Carl listened dutifully.

"I will tell you," Schlesinger went on, becoming less didactic, "that in my experience sympathy plays a part with juries, but I'm a judge and have certain obligations. If I determine that you are guilty, whether or not I feel sympathy for you, sympathy will play no part in my judgment."

"I would expect no less," said Carl, probably meaning not "less" but "more."

Schlesinger grew frighteningly grave, making a remarkable effort to attain absolute clarity. In the few minutes that had gone by, he had begun to understand Hoffinger's probable motivation for this dramatic turn in events.

"Let me tell you," he said to Carl, "sometimes lawyers are wrong in their judgments of judges. Are you willing to accept the risk? Would you want some moments to reflect?"

"I have reflected," Carl said without hesitation.

The judge instructed the clerk to prepare a waiver for Carl to sign in his own hand. The clerk drew it up and passed it to the defendant. Carl signed. The clerk handed it up to the bench.

"I'll ask you for the last time," said Schlesinger, glancing at the sheet of paper, "are you sure of what you are doing?"

"Yes, Your Honor."

It was exactly noon. Schlesinger, admitting to being taken by surprise, adjourned until ten A.M. the following morning.

"Have a very good day," he said to all.

―――― 35 ――――

Ana danced until the sequins fell from her champagne-pink dress the night of her farewell party in Soho, but her heart was full of loss when she flew to Italy for her Prix de Rome. She was one of thirty fellows taking a new turn in their lives at the American Academy in September 1983—the last one in the door. Chris Haub, who hadn't met her yet, remembers when she got there:

All of us arrived somewhere around the middle of the month. Ana was delayed, about a week or so late. We were all kind of waiting for this last person to arrive, and I remember seeing her for the first time, seeing her walking down the hall with her hair up in a towel, coming out of the shower. She disappeared into a little room, kind of mysterious. Then she made a real effort to break right in. The next day she was there, shooting pool with the guys and drinking beer and having a good time, outspoken and not shy, very much a part of things.

As I got to know her a little bit better, she talked about the delayed arrival on account of her father had died just prior to that. It was pretty common knowledge that she and Carl had broken up just before she came to Rome, and she was furious at Carl for breaking up with her the same month her father died and yet had a sense of optimism about the future of their relationship. I don't think she figured it was a final thing.

A large part of her life had crumbled that summer of her thirty-fifth year. Both of her grandparents had died in the old house in Cárdenas a few months earlier, and her father had died unexpectedly in August at the age of sixty-five. He had recently taken his oath of allegiance as a U.S. citizen, and since coming to Iowa, he had flown the flag from the front of the house every day and from his meager savings had built a garage out back to leave something of his own in America. Ana got drunk at the funeral. Carl hadn't even phoned her or sent a word of condolence. She called Hans and saw him the day after her father was buried in Cedar Rapids. She was in tears. He was sympathetic.

"Well, things are not working with Carl," she said.

He listened. New York had been a maturing experience, she said; it had allowed her to come to terms with herself as an artist. But it hadn't worked out the way she thought it would. She looked at him for a while. Probably, she said, she could only love one man.

"Our relationship was very unique," he said.

She loved Iowa, she said.

"You can't turn the clock back," he said.

He was seeing a woman named Barbara Welch now. It was good between him and her, said Hans. She was a yoga teacher, a bit of a health freak. He had given up drinking. No yoga yet, but not a drop of alcohol. They would probably marry. Barbara did not like the idea of him being alone with Ana.

They never saw each other again.

CARL AND ANA had split only days before her father's death. But for more than a year now, they had grown mean and low toward each other. He had lately seen bigger changes in his life than she had in hers. He had been the purest standard of minimalism and still was, but minimalism, many declared, was dead, and the obtrusive, bulldozing new art of the eighties seemed proof enough. The reviews, interviews, and other column inches, which he had once in jest admitted to measuring with a ruler, were scaled back and more often than not had to be paid for, hiring the usual writers for ads and catalogues. Sales declined, his U.S. income slumping to three thousand dollars in a recent year; only the slower recession of minimalism in Europe kept his life-style afloat. Minimalism itself lost no ground as a respected art movement, nor did Carl or the rest of the young Turks grown middle-aged diminish in critical esteem. But minimalism and even the newer, so-called postminimalism were simply no longer avant-garde, and few of the originators, who had cleaned out the Augean stables of the art world, could bear it. They feared erosion as much as death and worried about their place in art history as much as the flab in their mirror. Some like Donald Judd had taken to publishing hysterical attacks on neoexpressionism, and Carl did the same kind of self-serving whining at his table.

Even the table was not the same. Mickey Ruskin, up one notch from bankruptcy, had opened a new "store" on University Place in the Village. Chinese Chance was what it came to be called, and the artists of old, those who were still alive, had followed him as usual, Carl making it his "hang." It was set up like a smaller version of Max's Kansas City, the paintings on the wall bartered for food and drink good and cheap, the waitresses hired for looks and brains. But the scene was stale, no one made to wait outside, the room half-full with a dull nostalgia for the days when ideas and ambitions were young. The Neos, in a suit, a shave and a haircut, acted out success-in-the-eighties in their own places in the East Village and Tribeca, while at Mickey's there was acrid-smelling burn-out in the air and a mood of the party being over. The party *was* over, Mickey himself, grown paranoiac, the once teetotalling "rabbi" sitting coked out in his office, a loaded shotgun leaning on a wall, staring at his death by an overdose in 1983.

Carl never brought Ana to Chinese Chance. It was another space in that part of his life in which she had nowhere to hang her clothes, where nobody knew her name or what she meant to Carl. He would go there alone, eat dinner alone, and meet friends Ana did not know. One of them was an artist named Frances Bagley, whom he had met after Ana, had put in a show, and had given champagne and flowers, fine dinners, and a trip to Germany. She was a Texan, doing sprawling outdoor sculpture with flags in the wind, a strong, attractive woman who could drink as hard as either Ana or Carl but she, too, had a fear of getting near the open windows in 34E.

Ana in 1984 was shocked when she heard specific information about Carl having an affair with another woman, but she had never had trouble sensing it. He was not adult enough, she complained to Lucy, and Carl gets lonely, she told Raquel, and after all they were not exactly husband and wife. But when the rationales wore off and the wine spritzers no longer eased the pain, she would reach for the sheathed knives of sarcasm and cut Carl down in company. His work, his career, his everything, were in decline, she would tell him, so why not be content with being a famous has-been. And they would drink on, Carl, smiling first, then arguing back to show her where she was "wrong" until she gave no sign of letting up, beginning too many sentences with "Oh, Carl, you know that's not true," and suddenly he would want out and turn redder and cry, "Shut up!" but she would not shut up until her eyelids and his would begin to droop and after Carl picked up the tab for the whole party they would help each other up or down the stairs, leaning together for support all the way home. On the Soho street scene, it began to look as if crusty old Carl had taken up with some loony Cuban.

SHE HAD WRITTEN him a good-bye forever letter when she went off to Rome. Her sister would find a rough copy one day, as though Ana had drafted it many times to get it right. "You don't have to make any excuses for leaving now," it read in part. "I have enough vanity and I can live without you. I must confess that you are not so important to me anymore." What she finally wrote, only the recipient knew when he made his first approach to win her love once more.

He was in France and she was in Italy, only a few days settled into her room at the Academy. Carl, watching a swan on the park lake rear in Lyon wrote her his reply. She had used a phrase about "getting over" him, and now he hoped she was managing to do so, if that was what she really wanted. For his part he declared that he could never get over her. He was, he said, relieved by their separation, but only because their love had become momentarily difficult. But a love such as theirs was everlasting and could not simply vanish in one stormy moment. Rome, he was sure, would give her a new perspective, especially with regard to her mixed emotions about America and Cuba. Her destiny lay with Cuba, he was sure, imagining her as the José Martí of Cuban art. But Martí had died young, and Ana needed time, and he wanted her to live to enjoy her destiny. Rome, he predicted, would be the place where she would build that future. He wondered what her impressions were of the city, and sounding eager to hear from her, he ended the letter writing LOVE @.

At the moment she was sharing her impressions on a Roman hill with someone else and making a few impressions of her own on others at the Academy. According to Chris Haub:

Ana was a tremendous gossip, and we used to get together and talk a lot about our impressions, speculations, opinions, criticism, things like that. She really didn't care what people thought. She would say just outrageous things about people.

You say less is more and in her case less was more. She was more angry, more antagonistic, felt more strongly. And also more in the middle of things than the rest of us had been. She was one of those small big people who came in and took up a lot of space for her size, needed attention, attracted attention, but as a result alienated the rest of the group. For some reason she didn't take anyone else in the place seriously when she first got there. That changed. She got to be friendly with people whom she hadn't thought much of at first.

So she would show up in my studio, sit down and talk for three hours. We talked, but basically she talked. She'd come in and get stuff off her chest. And I was interested and I liked her. It was curious: generally she was right in her criticism. She would criticize our friends. She would say things that you yourself wouldn't say, wouldn't feel a need to say, but when she said them, you knew there was a lot of truth to what she said. She called a spade a spade. She didn't hold back. I liked her spark. She had this thing about being confident and projecting confidence. It was more important to be confident than to be right sometimes. And yet it wasn't a flimsy confidence. She wasn't afraid to speak in public. She wasn't afraid to take control of the situation. She wasn't afraid to be very vocal. She wasn't confident and arrogant in private and shy in public. She was consistent.

Like so many travelers before her, she fell in love with Rome and Italy and Italians. She bought her VW, came off the hill, signed up for lessons in the language, and learned the gestures and the curse words on the crooked streets, winding through the town and the countryside in circles that brought her to Pisa and Pompeii in the first month, making her thirst, salivate, for duomos, frescoes, and *pasta alla matriciana.* *"Roma es bellissima,"* she wrote to her mother in Spanish mixed with Italian, inviting her to come. "It fascinates me."

Carl showed up the first time at Christmas, bearing gifts. It was a trial reconciliation. What had touched off their separation had been his insistence that she turn down the Prix de Rome and remain with him in New York. She had refused and he had walked out. Carl's career was slipping, and, the way Ana saw it, the threat that she might pass him by on her way up was eating the flesh of his self-regard. "Are you going to still talk to me when you're famous?" he had asked her, trying to be funny. In tender moments before the break, she had sought to convince him to apply for a grant in Europe so they could at least be on the same side of the Atlantic that year. She had resolved to treat him more thoughtfully, and it had been she who had discovered the funding program in Germany, gotten the application, and encouraged him to fill it out. Winning the award would make him feel better, she had thought, would soothe his big white ego, but by the time he had in fact won, she was gone, so he left, too, taking up residence in a street called Storkwinkel in Berlin.

They were good to each other for a while. They went up to see the LeWitts that Christmas. Sol and Carol had bought a little house in Spoleto, less than a two-hour drive north of Rome. Carol had opened a little wine shop in town, and Sol's art was well represented in Rome. They had built a home in Italy with a young child more Italian than American and plans for more. Carl seemed shaken by it all, as though, Carol thought, the idea of Sol having something that he didn't have had made him uncomfortable. It was not long afterward that Carl began to speak to Ana about buying a place in Rome. Ana was thrilled. She started looking right away. He flew in whenever he could now, and she flew back to visit him, too. He became a welcome asset at the Academy, someone to build an evening around, and the friends Ana was piling up in Rome were as pleased as everyone else to have him there. The other fellows, however, seemed to have felt a little cheated.

I think people might have been jealous of her relationship to Carl and whatever else that meant, too [says Chris]. Everybody would say she used her association with Carl to give herself credibility. But why shouldn't she? He was her boyfriend. I was surprised: they seemed to be such different people. Not that I knew him, but from what I knew it seemed like a strange match. But she was definitely not in his shadow. I think she felt herself to be his equal. She probably felt that she was a better artist than him.

It was that spring that Natalia came to Rome to visit and told Ana of the rumor that Carl, the new Carl of their reconciliation, was having an affair. Months went by, Ana holding back her displeasure. By the summer, she suspected who the second woman was—the woman whose paintings he had bought and hung on the living-room wall of 34E. Ana held that in, too, rage in a chamber of her heart, love remaining in another. Carl had been so wonderfully perceptive about the business of her destiny. Rome had indeed become the setting where she was altering her life and work. Italy, for Ana, became a glorious compromise in Latinity, a midplace in the geography of her soul between Cuba and America, neither motherland nor fatherland, a kind of sisterland in which she felt strong and free. She developed a newness to her art, making portable, studio sculpture, the despised yet adored art object that artists had to make to remain and feel alive, working her way up from the floor pieces to the fire-engraved tree trunks standing tall. She gave up smoking, ran every day under the umbrella pines of the Villa Pamphili gardens, got a little more vegetarian than before, and watched Carl's diet, too, both of them on a hundred-dollar-a-month habit of vitamins with rutin and hesperidin, popping them until their breath went bad. She took up yoga, adopting her teacher's family as her own, a home to come home to on Sunday afternoons and play board games with the children on the living-room floor of a Renaissance palazzo. But the champagne and Frascati, the Chianti and the spritzers stayed, and sooner or later she would start going at him in company— "Oh, Carl, you know that's not true"—and he would smile for a while, but only a while.

Back in New York, after she had tracked him to the chess-playing receptionist at Paula Cooper's, she confronted him, eliciting only his adamantine refusal to confirm or deny. That was early in the fall of

1984, Ana walking out this time, getting into her cab to catch her flight back to Rome and advising him to fill his lonely days with the woman he would kiss and never tell. Then came the phone calls professing his love for Ana only, and then the second reconciliation, Carl once again on his side of the bed on the Academy hill, writing poems of Ana dreaming of Egypt on the morning of her thirty-sixth birthday. And the dream came true.

Then the word "Berlin" was somehow too often in the air, raining on Ana's fantasy of what their marriage, the Commitment, had been about. There were the tip-off phone bills, the prepaid tickets, the matching number in his book, the postcards, Rainbow, the nude photographs; Ana, snooping, uncovering all the rankling bits and pieces, stealing off to the copy shop, bit and piece piling up inside that envelope slipped into a secret pocket of her portfolio.

She feared retribution. Women do not go through their husband's pockets with a sense of impunity. He would "really blow his top" she had told Natalia that May of 1985 when she had proposed her half-jesting, daredevil scheme to disguise themselves and catch Carl with a woman. He had a terrible temper. She had said it repeatedly to Natalia, and Ana believed that she was engaged in an ongoing act that might trigger it. The "yesterday" of her written dream that making love to Carl somehow diverted his intention to kill her can only be traced, and without much return for the effort, to sometime when she was in Rome. But it was on that same trip to America in May and June that she expressed her premonition that she was going to die "very soon." That was what she told Carlos Alfonzo when she was visiting him in Miami and confiding how she had been spying on and gathering divorce evidence against Carl. She told someone else, too.

Either a few days before or after her trip to Miami, Ana in New York spoke of similar forebodings at greater length to an old friend of Carl's, Alice Weiner, Larry Weiner's companion of twenty years. They had gone to a party for a mutual friend. Ana had grown fond of Alice's daughter, Kirsten. Alice herself was no great friend, but Ana hadn't seen any of the Weiners for a while, so when the party was over the two women went to the Ray Charles Café in the Village and talked. They brought each other up-to-date. Ana spoke of her breakthrough tree-trunk sculptures, the big commission of her career to be done in Los Angeles's MacArthur Park, the good side of life with Carl in Rome, and their honeymoon travels. Suddenly, she said she wanted to get a lot of work done because she didn't think she had a lot of time left in life. Alice wanted to know why.

"I have a funny feeling," Ana said. "I don't know, I think it has something to do with heights."

"How could you live in that apartment?" Alice asked.

"I don't know, it gives me the creeps."

CARL DIDN'T STOP calling that number in Berlin. Ana went for the jugular. By that last summer, going out with the Andres in Rome was certain to be an unforgettable night on the town gone wrong, the two of them boozing along raucously, bickering, kicking up to rough stuff, and skewering each other with insult, all to the mortifying displeasure of the rest of the party. It had never been this bad before. Marsha Pels remembers one of those summer nights. They had gone to eat from the silver platters of the Trattoria del Pantheon, a place to be seen at where Ana loved to go:

> They drank a tremendous amount. On one level it was enjoyable: we had great discussions, like arguing whether Antonio Gaudi was as good as Frank Lloyd Wright, but as they proceeded to get drunk, there was that kind of strange neurotic interaction between them that you would witness. When we were getting up to leave, Ana dropped her earring, and when Carl went to pick it up she was hostile, saying, "Oh, leave it, you can't do anything; you can't even put it in." She kept at it, "You don't know how to put it in," she kept saying. "You don't know how to put it in." It was incredible. Carl turned beet red and clenched his fists like a little boy and just said, "Oh, shut up! Shut up!"

> She wouldn't shut up.

THE MOON REACHED its last quarter and the sun set at 7:17 on the last night of Ana's life. The doorman at 300 Mercer Street saw her go and come back sweating from jogging that evening, and if she had followed routine she had run the half-mile perimeter on the pavement around Washington Square Park five or six times. Carl watched the men's semifinals of the U.S. Open coming from Flushing Meadows thanks to Channel 2. The delivery person at the Chinese take-out place on Broadway brought the phoned-in order up to 34E, knocking on the door at about 10 P.M. By that time the Yankee game was on, New York versus the Oakland A's, Carl, an enthusiastic baseball fan, having switched to Channel 11. Ana ate a green vegetable.

Carl rarely failed to read the *New York Times,* read it hard, doing the crossword puzzle, almost never skipping a page. He had already digested the TV listings no later than the early afternoon, which was when he had answered the telephone and spoken briefly with Raquel, telling her that Ana and he planned to stay home and watch *Dracula* on Channel 13. It was the *Times*'s TV highlight of the late evening: "A Transylvanian success story, almost. At 'em you old bat." It went on at eleven o'clock. The Yankees had won, besting the A's three to two. A second bottle of wine had been opened. Ana was mixing hers with mineral water.

THE BAT HAD already been at 'em, the old favorite nearly over, when Natalia, who had just gotten into bed with her husband, dialed the 212 number from the north side of Chicago.

They had seen a movie themselves, had been to a theater for their Saturday night out. They had seen *The Kiss of the Spider Woman,* and Natalia had been struck by the resemblance between the actress Sonia Braga and Ana; the vibrancy of her character in the film juxtaposed with the cold elegance of her German lover had reminded her of Ana and Carl. Natalia's husband, Rodrigo del Canto, agreed, though he didn't regard Ana the way Natalia did. He and Ana did not get along very well. They had only met a few times and found each other "headstrong," poles apart in their taste in art, and Ana also didn't care for the way he treated Natalia. Natalia sensed a certain jealousy on her husband's part whenever she seemed to him to be overly devoted to Ana. Now, on *their* Saturday night, here she was again, in their very own bedroom, on the phone to New York, getting toward midnight Chicago time, and it was the eve of their first wedding anniversary.

Natalia had planned the late call on purpose, knowing Ana and Carl were always up until the small hours. She had tried to call several times during the week either without being able to reach her or catching Ana on the way out and unable to talk. They had yet to really speak about Ana's troubles with Carl, and Natalia, who had been Ana's confessor from the start, wanted to know what was going on and how she might help her dearest friend.

"Hello."

She recognized the voice. "Hello, Carl. This is Natalia. May I speak with Ana?"

"How are you?" asked Carl.

She was fine, so was he, and Ana got on the phone.

The two women chatted idly for a while, Natalia telling her that she looked like Sonia Braga, and Ana, laughing, saying she had heard that from other friends, too. Ana, who had solved some work problems that afternoon, was full of excitement about how that part of her life was going. She wanted to know how Natalia was getting along with her husband. Ana seemed in a good mood, a little garrulous, the way she got with wine, so Natalia said, "Let's talk," and Ana knew what she meant.

So they started, Ana saying she had "all this information," the photocopies in Rome and in New York, right there with her things in 34E, and that on this trip she had been "photocopying like crazy" because she had discovered new stuff that made her "very happy" in terms of clobbering Carl in court. As she spoke, her anger heated up, Natalia growing concerned that she might get carried away into saying something she would regret.

"Isn't Carl there?" she asked, thinking he might be overhearing what she was still keeping secret. When Ana said he was, Natalia cautioned her, saying, "Let's switch into Spanish."

Ana, standing or sitting at the only phone, which was on a table near the front door, had been speaking about the woman in Germany, and Carl, watching television, was only about twelve or fifteen feet away from her. Going into Spanish, she picked up where she had left off and now referred to her sarcastically as *"esta mujer del país de los Nazis"*—that woman from the land of the Nazis.

"Ana!" Natalia warned again, "he can understand that."

She rattled on anyway, about seeing Abramowitz, suing, getting the apartment in Rome, about hiring someone to photograph them in the act, the words *detective* and *Berlin,* which are precisely the same in Spanish, creeping in along with *divorcio,* which could hardly be closer to its English counterpart.

Natalia thought her friend was making a mistake in the way she was going about it. She told her that she knew of a woman with an unfaithful husband who decided to stick it out so she'd be well off, but ended up being miserable. It would be better if she would talk it out with Carl, bring everything out in the open.

Ana had had similar advice that afternoon from Raquel, but she remained leery. "Oh, I don't know," she said. "I don't know if I would want to do it now. He'll get so angry, I'd feel safer doing it in another place."

That last remark made Natalia think that Ana was merely putting off what ought to be taken up without delay. "Well," said Natalia, "I don't know, I think you have to do it at some point. I don't see why you keep putting it off."

"You don't understand," Ana said, "I'm scared. He gets very vengeful and vindictive. He's just going to blow his top when he finds out that I have all this information."

"Well, Ana, he's going to find out in court anyway. At some point you guys are going to have to talk about this. It seems to me that you're better off trying to resolve it now rather than going to court. Maybe this will work out. Maybe not. But just talk about it. The whole thing of running around surreptitiously collecting all this evidence on him, I mean, it just seems so ridiculous. I think you should confront him."

"Well, this whole thing is hard to figure out." She just didn't know how to deal with it, she said. "Do you really think I should talk to him?" Ana went on.

"Yes. I think you should confront him and try and work it out."

By now they had been speaking for more than half an hour, and

Natalia's husband had been growing steadily more annoyed, signalling her to get off the phone. Leaving the matter where it was, Natalia told Ana she had to hang up and would phone her again tomorrow.

"Well," Ana said, "don't call me early in the morning because I want to sleep late."

WHEN ANA HUNG up, the Tracy-Hepburn film *Without Love* was about to go on. It started at 1:10. The 1945 comedy, based on a play about the life and manners of the socially privileged, apparently failed to amuse either Carl or Ana, but it had a striking effect on both of them. His memory of Ana getting up from her chair at three o'clock and declaring, before going to bed, that the acting was good and the plot and dialogue "absurd" put her in accord with the critics forty years before her.

The story they watched together, at least for a while, takes place in wartime Washington, where a housing shortage causes a beautiful widow (Hepburn) to allow a brilliant inventor (Tracy) to move in with her, quite platonically and only after she learns that he is from as fine a family as she. Tracy carries a torch for one Lila Vine, the woman who jilted him in Paris, and Hepburn cannot love another either, her husband, who succumbed in a fall from a horse, having departed in her arms with these dying words, "What a dirty trick on us, Jamie, but don't think we end here." After a few TV commercials, it becomes a capital idea for them to marry, but not until they renounce love forever. Tracy says he'd rather have a good book than love, and Hepburn, who had wanted to "live life with a great big *L*," agrees, saying, "By gum." They have some fun together: "You slay me," says Tracy; "Jiminy Cricket," Hepburn says. Not very long after he begins saying, "By gum," just like her, she falls madly in love with him. But he is chagrined and indignant about her failure to keep the bargain.

If Carl had the timing right up to this point, it had to be about here that Ana got up and left in some kind of huff, Carl hanging on for the finale.

Heartbroken, Hepburn on the rebound now takes up with a suave European, while Tracy, at the last moment coming to his senses, realizes that he loves her after all and snatches her away from temptation before any damage to virtue is done—or so he prefers to believe. "You're like the tower of Pisa," he tells her at the end, cocksure that nothing took place in her moment of weakness, "you have certain leanings but you remain upright." A final shot of Tracy finding Hepburn's shoe in a slightly suspicious place, however, rings down the curtain on a small intimation of doubt, leaving Carl alone with the glow of the screen, the empty bottles, the night as hot as ever. His reflection of a few hours later that this minor romantic comedy of a woman who loves more enduringly and more profoundly than a man paralleled their lives, "only the other way around," would always remain a rare illumination of how he saw his own love for Ana.

Without Love went off the air at precisely 3:24. Later, at the trial, strong but not conclusive evidence would arise that Ana got up from bed and came out of the bedroom at about 4:15. Not until two hours and five minutes after the end of the film, however, did the next wholly unequivocal piece of information emerge from that final darkness. That was when Carl called 911 to report what he termed a suicide, saying that they had quarreled and Ana went to the bedroom and he went after her and that she went out of the window.

———— 36 ————

The one head, the one life experi-
ence in the universe that would decide Carl's fate belonged to a rather
lonely man whose wife had died a while ago and who in many ways was
still grieving.

Alvin Schlesinger was sixty-four years old, lived by himself uptown,
and had lately been renting a house in Vermont where he would go
these winter weekends to ski and get his fine color. When Dorothy was
alive, they had a big, rolling farm in Bucks County, Pennsylvania: a lot
of land, small house, and they used to travel until he became a judge.
He was a lawyer in private practice then, and when he got a job working
for a steel multinational, they went abroad and lived in Italy for a year,
five months in Rome. He could still speak some Italian. He lost her in
1982, and then, whenever he could get away from the bench, he would
go traveling again: to India, the Himalayas, anywhere exotic and far
from all the gentrified places where he felt too much alone without her.

He had sold the farm not long ago and moved some of the art and
the folk art to his justice's chambers in the New York County Court
House across the street from 1333. In the infinity of ways odd things
happen, he had roundabout connections to the art world. There was
a distant family tie to the well-known color field painter Jules Olitski,
a contemporary, though no friend of Carl's. When Dorothy was alive,
they had begun to collect art and art objects in a desultory way, and
many years back they had bought a painting in New York by Jim
Leong. The artist was a longtime resident of Rome who had gotten to
know Ana when she was there. But Schlesinger had never met Leong,
had forgotten all about the painting, had not seen Olitski in ages and
none of these coincidences were known to him nor would be until long
after the trial.

Perhaps because he had a few more empty hours than other state supreme court justices, and because it only took a few, he was an exceptionally dedicated man who brought the office home with him after court adjourned. He had started out as an interim judge in the Bronx, got elected in 1980 to a fourteen-year term, and by now, halfway through, he knew he would never run again. He had sent too many woeful souls through the door to prison that lay off to his right behind his bench, where the latest writing on the cinder-block wall just over the threshold said: "25 to Life Goodbye Scumbag." It made no sense to get it scrubbed. Among his professional affiliations, he was a director of the Fortune Society and Green Hope, criminal rehabilitation programs, and whenever the law gave him leeway, he chose to sentence an offender to do time there rather than in prison or the streets where, he knew and advised his felons, you either got worse or got killed.

Sympathy would play no part in his judging Carl was what he had told him, but that was like saying a man like Schlesinger had no heart. On the other hand, he had not welcomed the sudden, unexpected shift of the entire burden of judgment onto him. He much preferred being the mediator in a jury trial and letting the twelve jurors battle over the decision. This turn of events meant he would have to play two roles, both judge and jury, which also meant more work, making for a harder trial and more homework, as if there wasn't already enough. Worse for the accused, Carl had not yet made a good impression on him. He found him peculiar.

WAITING FOR THE judge on the morning of the first full day of the trial, people in his courtroom were still talking about the surprise decision to go the rarely traveled nonjury route. Going down in the elevator yesterday afternoon, Ruby Rich had told Tim Clifford, a reporter covering for *Newsday*, that she thought Carl's move was "elitist" and typically arrogant, and today there were already others joking about a "minimal" trial, as if Carl were going to have some sort of sweetheart, gallery treatment. True, he had elected not to be judged by your everyday Walkman-walkers wearing Reeboks with buzzing coming out of their ears, freshly peeled off the Jesse Jackson voter registration drives; no blacks, Latinos, or any people of color were going to size up weirdo Carl against Tropicana. But the price paid for the "privilege" was very high. In a then-recent study of thousands of jury trials, a survey of the trial judges revealed that in criminal cases they would have convicted at a rate 20 percent higher than the jurors. More important, the overwhelming majority of all appeals after conviction are based on either alleged mistakes made by juries or by judges instructing juries. Unless Schlesinger were to commit a gross error in competence, the chances of his verdict being overturned in appeal would be next to nil. Whether Carl knew it or not, agreeing to Hoffinger's choice meant agreeing to one quick game of Russian roulette with more than one chamber loaded.

Carl liked the judge, as much as a man could like his executioner. He had watched him painstakingly in the proceedings prior to his. He had decided that Schlesinger was a roughhewn, uncultured sort of fellow but far from a hanging judge. He was in perfect accord when Hoffinger, making his own final assessment, counseled waiving a jury. His confidence in Hoffinger, no literatus either, had grown in recent days as he observed him in court spinning his spidery antiwitness snares and then "closing the web," as Carl called it, telling him so with what Hoffinger took for admiration. "Listen," Carl had said approving the nonjury strategy, "you call the shots."

Hoffinger's colleagues at the office, however, had opposed him. They were skeptical. It was a red-or-black bet, odd-or-even, and they were wary of betting wrong. He had gotten the itch to go for a bench trial eight months earlier, after Berkman had dismissed the first indictment, calling it a close circumstantial case. Carl was a "very private man," Hoffinger felt and said every time he could, but perhaps a little too "private" to suit the sensibilities of a Jesse Jackson jury. His final decision depended only on who the trial judge would be and how he operated. At the pretrial hearing, he had liked what he saw, but played his cards close to his chest. Many times, lawyers hinted at opting for a nonjury trial to test the waters of the judge's predilections. But most judges, like most other people, got grumpy about working harder than they had to, and hardly anybody ever actually put them to the task. Thus Hoffinger, unsubtlety his specialty, had preferred surprise attack.

Elizabeth Lederer, in a pin-stripe suit under a fur-collared cloth coat, came down the aisle with her "second-seater," Mark Sullivan, a lot of paper between them, and a small surprise all her own to spring later in the morning. In the meantime, when the court was called to order and Schlesinger asked for opening statements, she led off.

In the name of the people of the State of New York, she accused Carl, reading the text of the indictment in her strongest, most sobering voice, of the crime of murder in the second degree. His victim, she said, had been a vibrant, resourceful, and independent woman. She was mortally afraid of heights. "She loved life but met evil."

Carl remained impassive, pinching the bridge of his nose now and then, stroking a folded hand. The courtroom was more crowded than it had ever been, in a telling, lopsided way. An artist friend of Ana's named Juan Sanchez had held a meeting at Cooper Union, trying to organize a sizable and constant presence of her friends in court. This had brought in a group of regulars, including Ruby and her group, who congregated around Ana's mother on the side of the courtroom behind the prosecution's table and the vacant jury box. They were mostly women, feminists, blacks, Hispanics, many, including Ana's mother, scribbling a lot more notes than the few reporters and generally looking quite engaged. The other bank of public seating, the right side walking in, where supporters of Carl, getting the picture, might have been expected to sit, stayed empty, looking by contrast like tundra. Before the trial, Carl with an assist from his closest friends had made an effort to discourage attendance, just as he had done for two-and-a-half years keeping the same people from speaking about the case, particularly to the press. No reasons were given; none was asked for. It was something slightly mystical, having to do with respecting Carl's privacy and his yearning for his private nightmare to end. "One did not have any contact with any of the principals involved in the trial," Larry Weiner remembers. "It was like a gag rule, a total gag rule. It was not a proper thing to be discussed at a table. It was not a proper thing to be discussed. As hard as it was, because one would always want to know how it was going, no conversations at all."

After a summary of how the prosecution would prove its case, Lederer concluded, speaking of Ana's demise and declaring categorically,

> She didn't fall. She didn't jump. She was pushed. She died because Carl Andre forced her out of that window. For her it was the most horrifying and terrifying way to die, moment by moment, living her worst fear as she fell to her death.

The assistant D.A. had traveled far since she first took on the case. Schlesinger turned to Hoffinger. The defense had no opening statement, he said. Lederer called her first witness: Natalia Delgado.

Natalia, wearing a string of pearls on a blue dress and looking too gray for her thirty-five years, had given birth six weeks earlier to her first child, a girl, naming her after Ana. "She was my very dear friend," she said in reply to Lederer's first question about her relationship with the deceased. That morning, Schlesinger had ruled, like Berkman, that any mention of Ana's plan to divorce Carl was inadmissible. It fell short of establishing a motive, he had explained, because the prosecution had no evidence that Carl knew about Ana's intention and no one could assume how he would have reacted if he had known.[1] Natalia's testimony was therefore limited to showing Ana's nonsuicidal "forward-looking conduct" and, after Hoffinger's objection was overruled, her fear of heights, to which she added something new.

"She never opened windows," Natalia stated.

That final, long telephone call, full of Ana's fear and tension, was reduced to a couple of sentences. Natalia believed in her broken heart that she had finally come to understand what Ana had been trying to make her understand that night when she said she was afraid to confront him, that she didn't want "to do it now," that she would "feel safer doing it in another place." Not in 34E. But Natalia could not say any of that.

---

[1] Although Schlesinger did not say it in court, his reasoning was that some men might be delighted to learn that their wife wanted a divorce; if there had been a witness to Carl threatening to harm his wife if she divorced him, he would have allowed the divorce testimony.

"We spoke about her work," Natalia said of the phone conversation, tears in her eyes. "She was in good spirits. She spoke of *my* relationship with my husband." She was anxious to get back to Rome. Her voice was "upbeat" and "lighthearted" when she heard it last.

Had she had occasion to call her again? asked Lederer, looking for her answer about Carl's strange reply the following morning, when Ana was already dead.

Yes, said Natalia. Carl responded saying that, "She's not here right now," and, yes, he would tell Ana to call her when she got home.

Lederer, introducing the Crime Scene photos as the State's first exhibits, also used the occasion to elicit testimony from Natalia about Carl's neatness. She had been in 34E on several occasions between 1983 and 1985, said the witness, and had stayed there with Ana once for several days. It had never looked anything like the mess in the photographs, she said. She had seen Carl's "attic room" too, and everything in the apartment had been in perfect order.

Heeding a first principle of first-year law—raising a potentially damaging aspect of the case oneself to take the sting out of it being revealed by the opposition—Lederer asked about Ana's drinking habits. Ana got caustic yet "happy, slaphappy" when she drank, said Natalia. Once she sang in a restaurant. Natalia had never seen her stumble or fall.

Lederer turned her witness over to the defense.

The master cross-examiner rose but did not otherwise move from behind the defense table, Carl seated at his right hand, two assistants, Mike Sherman and Steve Weiner, on his left. He spoke softly, maintaining the low-key demeanor with which he had begun this important day.

"I'm going to stay right here," he said in deference to earlier admonitions about his courtroom peregrinations.

"That's where I prefer you to be," Schlesinger replied with a half smile.

HOFFINGER HAD ELABORATED a very precise strategy by which he would conduct the defense. Its uncomplicated foundation was inherent in every purely circumstantial case where there was little more that could be done than seek to undermine the import of the circumstances. Breaking a single link in the chain was often enough to create the necessary reasonable doubt. In this case, if evidence was introduced by the prosecution that increased the difficulty of believing that Ana had committed suicide or met with an accident, Hoffinger's counterattack had to be centered on impeaching that evidence. Judging the charges against the defendant depended directly on the strength of those two precepts. If Lederer's case were to convince Schlesinger that Ana had not jumped or fallen on her own, there could be no reasonable doubt that Carl was guilty.[2] Further, whatever physical evidence was put forward as consistent with homicide, like the "fresh, bleeding scratch" of which Lederer had spoken in her opening summary, tended to reduce the other two possibilities. Thus, this category of proof had to be discredited, too. Finally, since the discrepancies between the 911 call and Carl's handwritten account some hours later could only be reconciled by some theory of confusion in Carl's mind, the entire sequence of events on that Sunday had to be made to appear fuzzy, particularly the police recollections of Carl's oral statements and the credibility of the police themselves. The more than two years and four months that had elapsed since the events in question weakened the persuasive powers of memories and appeared as a godsend now.

The best evidence against suicide and accident was the victim herself. Her persona in life was paramount among the mainstays of the People's case, and from the defense's point of view, unfortunately, it had to be spattered and stained. Hoffinger's detective had been out sleuthing for damaging information, and Ana's museum show, which had closed less than a week ago, had proved to be a usable source. It was dirty but necessary work. One life had been lost in a tragedy; another life was at stake. The fight to save it, however, had placed the person in jeopardy in a most unenviable position, forcing him not only to sanction the operation but to turn principal informant himself

---

[2]Stated another way, no matter how guilty Carl might have appeared, if the other two possibilities were not ruled out beyond a reasonable doubt, Carl would have to be acquitted. There were no other alternatives that were not simply a complication of these conditions.

against the woman he once loved. Who knew better than he what foibles beset his wife, and where but in privileged conference with his client could Hoffinger learn best what they were?

Hoffinger had his own pet theory that Ana may have been a lesbian. She hung around with homosexuals, he had heard, male and female, particularly when Carl was away. She would also bring some of them around for a free dinner in a fine restaurant, usually Sabor, when she and Carl were together. At first he hadn't been sure of what he could make of that, finally deciding that it would not go very far because she was an artist, but it remained on file with other items of eccentricity, such as her being cast out from her Cuban heritage, her interest in Santería, which he invariably called "voodoo," as well as her past works in blood.

All of these theories were put to practice now as he launched the defense's strategy in cross-examining the state's first witness.

WITH A COUPLE of quick questions, Hoffinger brought out that Carl had been in Europe and not yet married to Ana when Natalia stayed with Ana in the one-bedroom, one-bed apartment and that they had gone to a restaurant with a couple of her Hispanic gay friends (though only their names were mentioned), one of whom would be a prosecution witness. Then he took off for less nebulous skies, asking the witness if she was familiar with Ana's art, to which she answered yes.

"Do you know the art where she used her own body to make impressions on the ground?"

She did.

"And the work with blood running down her face?"

Anyone who had seen the New Museum show might have known that one; there had been a continual screening of the performance videos, including the rather startling illusion piece in which she "sweat" blood.

Was the witness familiar with Ana using her own body "impacting on earth?" asked Hoffinger.

It was the death-foretold approach, but there were no objections from the prosecution. Schlesinger listened with apparent full attention. Carl, who used to argue so vehemently against interpretation, sat like a stone upon a stone, in no way visibly stirred. The artists who half-filled the courtroom were accustomed to naive, even fatuous "critiques" of art, and the feminists knew all about blaming female victims for their own misfortunes, but not many could have experienced a concoction of the two clichés like this. Hoffinger bore down.

What about the work where she was "melding into earth . . . work in which she depicted the body of a woman lying face down with blood coming out?"

Natalia answered as best as she could, but it was not her answers but his questions that were meant to be mighty.

When he was satisfied with this as a beginning, he turned the witness back to Lederer, for the post-cross-examination curative called "redirect" questioning. She attempted to place all of the work mentioned by Hoffinger, whether done by Ana or not, into the context of one period in the seventies, which was true, but even she spoke of "bodies impacting on surfaces," unwittingly adding to the whole obnoxious exercise, which was about as relevant as Carl pouring sand from high places in his gravity pieces of the late sixties.

Hoffinger picked up the same shovel in "recross."

To make certain, it seemed, that the judge had not missed his point, he asked once more, "Was Ana interested in the wedding of the human body with the earth?"

"She was interested in the cycle of life," said Natalia in her sharpest answer yet.

"What about the body in the earth?"

Finally, Lederer fired off an objection. Schlesinger sustained it. Natalia, who had been a witness to Ana's deepest feelings in life only to be a witness in death to what she thought of her art, was dismissed.

LEDERER CALLED ED Mojzis. That was her surprise. It sent Hoffinger scurrying to his notes. Both sides had informed each other of their witnesses and their scheduled appearances, but it was part of the game of trying to get an edge to "forget" this or that detail—the disadvantage being that your opponent could be equally as "forgetful," or worse.

It was half-past noon now, and Mojzis, waiting to be called, had been extremely nervous, though he didn't look it as he took the stand and swore to tell nothing but the truth. He was often jittery. It was one of the side effects of Haldol, about which the doctors had told him, but this was something else. Counting the three grand juries, this made the fourth time he would have to testify, not to speak of how many other times he'd had to tell his story less formally. He didn't mind all the phone calls, the prepping, going back and forth to Elmhurst on the F train when he ought to have been sleeping. Ever since Harry, the night man at the Delion, had gotten him into this, he'd just been doing his duty as a citizen, and from what little he knew from the D.A. about the art world running the other way, he felt good about himself. This had really shaken them up, he'd heard. Someone in the building at 11 Waverly had told him that people were wearing T-shirts saying, "No, no, no, no." Never once had he doubted hearing those words that morning. But he had never been cross-examined, and from what he had learned of Hoffinger, the guy sounded scary. Hoffinger had sent around a private detective to question his boss in the building when Mojzis wasn't around, wanting to know about his background, his habits, his drinking. The lawyers had all the records of his mental history, the whole problem, and who knew what Hoffinger would ask him in public? So Mojzis was little shaken when Lederer called him to ask for his testimony the very first day. But it was OK with him. He was happy to get it over with.

He sat erectly in the witness chair, a chubby, round-eyed figure, his pudgy hands folded in his lap. He was wearing a gray V-neck sweater and a tie, and he stared straight ahead, looking a little like he was getting ready for a haircut, as Lederer approached him.

She led him through his memory of going out to Harry's for coffee at 5:30 that morning of his thirty-eighth birthday. Hoffinger rose in objection when Mojzis repeated what he had said to the night manager about how maybe somebody threw somebody out of a window because he just heard a woman screaming. No one had asked for Mojzis's "maybe" and Schlesinger struck the doorman's opinion from the record. The rest of the direct testimony went smoothly. Lederer had brought in a plywood model of 300 Mercer Street as seen from Waverly Place, and Mojzis was asked to identify his positions when he had heard the screams and when he had heard the crashing sound. She sought to establish that the distance the doorman covered between the two points agreed with the four seconds of silence between the two sounds. That would place the origin of the screams as close to the windows of 34E as physically possible. As for the closet of Mojzis's medical history, Lederer would let Hoffinger be doorman on that one.

AFTER LUNCH, THE litigator was ready. The medical record was, of course, the lever with which he hoped to pry loose and discard one of the cornerstones of the case, the closest thing the prosecution had to an eyewitness to murder. That a star witness, the only person to hear screams, had a history of auditory hallucinations seemed lifted right out of an old Perry Mason script. But as a second-act curtain line, it promised more than it could deliver, and Hoffinger knew it. His own investigation had revealed that Mojzis's symptoms could be activated by drinking, which was one reason why his investigator had questioned Mojzis's employer, but the doorman had not had a recorded hallucinatory episode in more than six years, exactly four years at the time of Ana's death. More important, Mojzis was not some post-factum crackpot with a cut-and-paste story. He had described the screams of a woman, their nature, the direction they came from, and the critical four-second silence between the final no and the "explosion" *before* he knew, or could have known, either that a person had been killed in a fall or that the person was a woman. Hoffinger needed a more general approach to his witness.

Where was he that morning when he first started to hear "sounds"? Hoffinger began, speaking softly, the way some well-meaning fellow might talk to a person known to have heard things.

He had just crossed Mercer on Waverly.

He had called them "screams" this morning, Hoffinger said, picking up a sheet of paper, yet at the first grand jury he had said the woman was "saying" no, not "screaming" no. Hoffinger flashed the transcripts. The same was true for the second and third grand juries. Saying, not screaming.

Mojzis shrugged. "I might have used the word 'saying.' "

That was confusing, wasn't it? asked the lawyer. Mojzis was confusing the court. "You're confusing me," Hoffinger said.

Schlesinger barked. "Your confusion is irrelevant," he said to the lawyer. Hoffinger deferred with his boyish smile.

That morning, Mojzis had testified that four seconds had elapsed between the screams and the explosion, yet to the grand jury in 1985 he had said "three or four" seconds.

Mojzis remained unruffled. Hoffinger kept at it.

"Are you a little confused?" he asked after a barrage of other "contradictions" plucked from his various testimonies.

"Yes," said Mojzis with nothing more than candor.

Hoffinger glanced at the reporters seated in the front row, flashed a wry smile, and, after failing to confuse Mojzis about when he first learned that the victim was a woman ("I read it in the papers"), he plunged into the medical records.

Mojzis had had a couple of years of college, yet until his present job, he had not risen higher than being a janitor, and he had been in hospitals, hadn't he?

Yes, said Mojzis, for "psychiatric care."

"What does that mean?" Hoffinger asked.

"You tell me," said Mojzis, the courtroom erupting in laughter.

"What was wrong with you?"

"I was never told what was wrong with me."

"You were never told you were a paranoiac schizophrenic?" Hoffinger asked, reading from the record. "With symptoms of paranoia and false ideation?"

Schlesinger broke in, objecting that Mojzis was not a physician and thus not competent to describe his illness. He could however describe the symptoms.

"I had auditory hallucinations. You hear voices and things like that."

The last time was in September 1981. He had gone against the doctors ("What do they know?"), had stopped taking his medication, and had been drinking when it happened. Hoffinger, seeing an opening, jumped four years to the night of Ana's death, asking Mojzis how many hours he had been working when he heard the screams.

He had been on duty all night, Mojzis recalled.

"And it was your birthday, wasn't it?" said Hoffinger, with the clear implication that he might have been celebrating.

"It was the *morning* of my birthday," Mojzis replied smartly.

"You do like to drink, don't you?"

"I like to eat, too," said Mojzis.

Again the room broke into rolling laughter, the corpulent doorman stealing the show. He quickly gave a clear denial that he ever drank to excess or that he drank every day.

The defense had no further questions. Lederer, in redirect, tried to reiterate strong points, but it was Schlesinger, as judge and jury, who brought out something new. He asked Mojzis how his auditory hallucinations had been manifested.

"You thought you heard people whispering. Always people I knew," said Mojzis. He described the mumbling in his ears of friends, some he could not identify. "You become very paranoid and begin to think that the voices are plotting against you, directed against you." A moment before, under Lederer's questioning, he had said that the scream on Waverly Place had "sounded like a person pleading for her life or trying to stop someone from doing something."

Schlesinger thanked the witness and released him. It was 3:20 on Friday afternoon. The sky in the high windows on his left was darkening. He had planned to get away this weekend for skiing, but it was too early to quit. He called a five-minute break.

"THE GUY IS sick," Hoffinger said, talking with reporters during the brief recess. "Did you see his eyes? Two years of college and he's a lobby attendant?" He had gone too easy on him, he said. "If there was a jury, it would be a different ball game." Carl read his *Times Literary Supplement.*

LEDERER SUMMONED BOBBY Baumert, the young cop who had found Ana's body, had touched her neck and her wrist for a pulse, and had covered her with a sheet. Ana's mother held back tears as he went through the details, but his main function as a witness was to show that Carl, back at the Sixth Precinct, had been read his Miranda rights at 6:45 in the morning. Hoffinger used the cross to point out that the police had made no measurements of the position of the body, particularly of how far it lay from the building line. The theory in this instance was that a jumper would land in a different place from someone who had been forced out of a window, and though no one could tell which would be nearer or farther, it added to the confusion.

When Baumert was told to step down, Schlesinger adjourned saying, "Have a nice weekend," and headed for a little house in Vermont. But there was something disturbing the judge, something he had seen repeatedly at the edge of his eye he kept trained on Carl.

37

Hoffinger gabbing with the press was something entirely new in the case, but it was not incompatible with his grand design. You could curtail public attention in the pretrial period simply by sitting out the tango, as he called it, which meant embargoing whatever information in your control. But it was all happening in open court now, the court documents suddenly public, so it was better to give your own spin to whatever media coverage there would be. Even Carl was taking direction. As he was coming out of court earlier in the week, a *Post* photographer had sought his picture, and Carl, surrounded by his lawyers, tried to get lost in the usual dash for the elevator. The lensman, who had been trying for a shot on the run, collared Hoffinger, stating his case. "You don't want him to look like a gangster, do you? Lemme do my job; I wanna get outta here, too." Hoffinger turned to Carl, and without a word exchanged, Carl stood zombielike against the elevator doors and let the man do his job.

On the other hand, the earlier no-press policy, and a little luck, had paid enormous dividends in terms of keeping the case all in the art-world family. Twenty-eight months of managed scarce coverage had yielded scarce interest. Schlesinger, acceding to a request from the media, had taken the unusual step of opening his court to television, but there had been no follow-up. Early interest by CBS had been withdrawn, and Canadian television, in search of the larger story, had sent reporters who had given up when they ran into the wall of silence.[1] The judge had also authorized news photography during the proceedings, and this had actually produced a camera now and then, Carl being photographed in a few days more than in his whole lifetime. But only reporters from the *Post,* the *Daily News, Newsday,* and *El Diario* had become media regulars, their editors (except for *Diario*) giving them little space for their efforts. Of the art-world press, a far-flung institution of hundreds of art writers, only Judd Tully, New York editor of the *New Art Examiner,* was putting in appearances, notebook in hand. The most regular of all was Jan Hoffman of *The Village Voice,* who would, or if she failed to find her "angle," would not write a post-trial article. The *New York Times* couldn't make up its mind whether the news was fit to print or even whether it was fit to send a reporter.

The lucky part, as far as Carl's desire for as little exposure as possible was concerned, was that in media terms his bench trial had become only a sideshow of the "real" trial taking place in the very next courtroom, some fifty feet down the corridor. There sat young Robert Chambers, defending by the wits and craft of his lawyer, Jack Litman, his story of how Jennifer Levin died by a mishap from being overly demanding of his genitals, and there was where your first-bite news was. The trial-watching public alighting on the thirteenth floor had a choice: either go to the left and get a guaranteed front-row seat at the Carl Andre did-he-kill-his-wife trial or turn right and stand in line for hours waiting for a single seat to empty before passing through a portable metal detector to get a live look at the preppie woman slayer and a lesson in "the fast-paced world of sex and under-age drinking in which the defendant and victim moved," in the words of the *New York Times.* Almost everyone, including WCBS and the *Times,* turned right, and

<hr>

[1]The CBS turnabout had somehow disappointed Schlesinger, who on noting the letter of withdrawal remarked with a touch of sarcasm, "I guess they have more important things to cover." Ana's friends and family were less generous. Since there were board members of CBS who were also board members of MOMA and the Met, the Mendieta circle saw the withdrawal as an extension of the wall of silence protecting Carl. Considering the tenacity of the art-establishment will, this was not impossible, but neither the television network itself nor its CBS News division had made the original request; it had come from the local outlet, WCBS.

a paper-bag lunch was a good thing to carry along. Sometimes the overflow drifted into Carl's trial, wondering, no doubt, where it was.

SOME NEWERCOMERS TO Soho, those who had arrived with the neoexpressionist eighties, were perplexed by the way the case in its most dramatic moment seemed to be dimming like twilight. Writer Gerry Marzorati, who had worked for the *Soho Weekly News* until it folded in 1982, was one of them. What surprised him was that the feminists were not making it a cause; he thought they would "turn it into a metaphor of men and their women." The truth was that throughout the trial, the feminists, or at least many of the sixties-generation originals, those old artworkers dressed in black, the giant killers chopping at the beanstalk of the phallocentric system, were suddenly out of town or lying very low. Lucy was in Colorado, getting reports and a tongue-lashing from Ruby by telephone ("I was terrified I was going to be asked to come and talk"). May Stevens, who had said she hadn't seen the scratches but now couldn't bring herself to repeat it, was nursing a knee injury, receiving news-bearing visitors. Dotty Attie decided not to attend the trial because she feared having to sit in a seat that would mark her as being with one side or the other. Ana had been a woman of a thousand friends; most of them preferred to follow the trial in the newspapers, except there was next to nothing in the newspapers.

Lederer had come up against the same art-world Invertebrata as her predecessor. She had searched the whole kingdom for a single authority who would testify to Ana's place as an artist in the aesthetic hierarchy. Not even Lowery Sims, who had bought Ana's drawings for the Met, her "conspiratorial" sister of color in promoting minority artists, had felt free to oblige her. Lowery had in fact been pressured by the museum not to do so, and when she suggested the names of others to Lederer, she was shocked to learn that they had already refused or evaded the D.A. before her. "I really understood the nature of evil," said Lowery, "very subtle but very frightening." Women stopped Lederer in the courthouse corridors requesting anonymity ("I don't want my husband to find out"), eager to pass on stories of Carl pushing this person or that but refusing to testify. The powers of subpoena were of little value in such cases. A witness cannot escape being summoned to the stand, but lawyers recognize reticence as the first symptom of incipient courtroom amnesia. Lederer had hoped, and continued to hope, to sway one or two women, even the ex-lover of Carl's who had gone as far as coming to her office to be interviewed. She had arrived wearing dark glasses in the shadow of a big-brimmed hat, and in the end decided that she would not cooperate. She said, "Ana is dead. I want to live."

It was not gross fear, however, but thirty years of love, affection, admiration, gratitude, and an overpowering wish to believe in the fundamental goodness of his spirit and the everlasting purity and rectitude of his art that bound the nobility, the clergy, and the merchants of the art world to Carl. That art world *was* Carl. Unlike Lederer, Hoffinger found witnesses galore.

A PIMP WITH a ten-thousand-dollar-a-night business was the first case to come before Judge Schlesinger back from the slopes shining Monday morning, February 1. Whenever he found himself waiting for the "Andre club" to gather, he rarely lost a chance to roll up his sleeves and funnel justice along. In the first forty minutes of this judicial day, he managed to dispose of five cases, receiving a minor surprise when an addict, given a choice, picked prison rather than rehab at the Fortune Society, claiming that he couldn't control his habit if the judge freed him. He was ready for the club at 10:37.

Lederer called twenty witnesses over the next four days, then rested the People's case. She revealed a pattern, mixing each day, as she had the first, with tales of Ana's outlook for the future and the police investigation, saving Tom and Raquel for a strong ending. Faithful to his own style, Hoffinger continued his broadcast strategy of sowing doubt on every landscape.

The first two witnesses this morning, friends and associates of Ana's, were called to attest to her career being on the rise and that committing suicide was not in her busy schedule.

Al Nodal, the Los Angeles curator who had commissioned Ana's projected MacArthur Park sculpture, testified that he himself had once contemplated suicide over marital problems and, as a friend and fellow Cuban émigré, had confided in Ana. "If things don't work out, I'll kill myself," he had told her, to which she had replied, *"Eso no se hace—* That we do not do."

By now this was a famous exchange, having appeared in both Ruby's and Joyce Wadler's articles, and Hoffinger, in cross, was ready for it.

Much had been made about Ana planning for her immediate and distant future. Both Bashford and Lederer had wanted to bring in a suicidologist as a prosecution witness, but in the end, Lederer's skepticism about the value of hired guns had changed her mind. She had done her own homework and had learned that far from making plans, one of the most common symptoms of imminent suicides was canceling engagements. Hoffinger, who had his own research, knew this, too, and the first question he put to Nodal sounded learned and canny.

"Were you," he asked the witness, "also making plans for the future when you spoke of suicide?"

"Yes."

The lawyer moved off from that one like a modest cager who had scored a three-pointer. But the witness of course had not killed himself, so both question and answer were irrelevant.

Picking up a few affirmatives to the questions about "the work in which she depicted herself lying on the roof dead and bleeding," Hoffinger took a new direction.

"Was she interested in voodoo?"

"We discussed voodoo figures."

"What about casting spells?"

They had discussed that, too, said Nodal. Ana had once sent him a postcard with a picture of a tongue on it. That, she said, would stop the criticism Nodal felt he was receiving at the time.

Hoffinger dropped a name, a "voodoo" god he called "Jemaya," as a subject in which Ana may have been interested. It went no further now. It was a plant meant to bear fruit when the defense would present its own witnesses.

LEDERER, IN A way having to reach across the Atlantic, had finally found an art-world authority competent to put Ana's and Carl's careers in context. She now called Ida Panicelli to the stand. Ida had arrived from Rome the past November to take up the New York–based job of editor of *Artforum,* one of the world's leading art journals. As a critic and museum curator, she had written about Carl and, having done the inventory of Ana's studio in Rome, was thoroughly familiar with her work.

Under questioning from Lederer, she described the rise and decline of Carl's art, the downward spiral of interest having begun in the eighties. Ana's career was growing, getting attention, and she was "doing very well." As a person, she was "passionate, giving, lovely, and sometimes very funny." She had a "positive response to life."

How about when she was intoxicated? Hoffinger asked when it was his turn.

Ida, who spoke English well but not perfectly, seemed momentarily unsure of the word "intoxicated," and Schlesinger jumped at the chance to use his Italian: *"Ubriaco,"* he said in translation.

"She spoke loudly, even more passionately," said Ida. When she went to dinner with Carl and Ana, they both "drank a good deal."

As he had done with Natalia and Nodal, he asked Ida if she had ever seen Ana stumble or fall after a night of drinking. Like the others, she replied no, but this too was Hoffinger planting.

LEDERER CALLED BUILDING superintendent Spiros Pappas next to show that street noises reached at least as high as 21E. Hoffinger wanted to know if the ducts on the deli roof "throw out sound on the streets," only to be reminded by Pappas that it was the motor, not the duct, that made noise. Of which there was more than one, Hoffinger shot back. Harry Leandrou of the Delion followed. He confirmed Mojzis's story about hearing a woman's voice from "high up": "He said he heard some screaming, a scream." Hoffinger had no questions.

TO MAKE HER case against accidental death, Lederer relied on Modesto Torre and Marsha Pels, the eyewitnesses to Ana's fear of heights who had testified before the grand jury. Hoffinger, as Lederer expected, kept going back to Ana's drinking, so the prosecutor offered testimony from the biochemist at the medical examiner's office who had measured the alcohol content in Ana's brain tissue, "the organ of choice," he called it. He estimated that she had probably had six or seven glasses of wine during the course of that night, and as an experienced drinker had "much more tolerance" to the effects than an occasional drinker.

Joacquin Gutierrez, the pathologist who did the autopsy, testified, too, describing the condition of the body minutely. Ana's mother cried softly. Carl pressed his eyes. He remained impassive when the 911 tape was played twice, then a third time, when Schlesinger wanted to hear it again.

THE POLICE TESTIMONY began in earnest with Officer Mike Connolly taking the stand on the second and third days. Lederer moved it all along intermittently but chronologically until ending seventy-two hours to the minute later with Martha Bashford on Thursday. Pieced together, it told the prosecution's side of the story from the moment Connolly came to Carl's door at dawn to Martha Bashford's "Fuck him, he's under arrest" that evening.[2] Most of the people in the courtroom were hearing all this for the first time, but to those to whom little was new, Hoffinger's cross-examination was more telling. It was the surest indicator of the points where the defense felt weakest.

He played his faulty-memory cards hardest here. By now he had all three sets of grand jury minutes, the transcript of the pretrial hearings, and all the police reports in which to find inconsistent statements by the same witnesses or something said now and not before. What he found appeared to be trivial more often than not, but he searched for them endlessly, hinting at conscious deception, even a plot; in any event, piling them on would have a cumulative effect.

When Connolly, in an obvious lapse, stated that Carl had showed him his catalogue when they returned to the apartment and not in the first encounter, Hoffinger "caught" him. Connolly had just called the open cut on Carl's face a scratch, but elsewhere he had called it a scrape. Carl having asked to wash his hands as his first request when Connolly and Capolupo entered the apartment seemed in need of particularly heavy defense correction. Carl was upset, Connolly had

---

[2]The line, first introduced at the preliminary hearing, became the tacit punch line of one of Schlesinger's running gags. When Finelli testified at one point that in turning his Polaroids of Carl over to Bashford he felt they were in safe hands, the judge remarked, "Even though she used such language?"

testified, but became very calm "right after he washed his hands." Yet, said Hoffinger, he hadn't mentioned anything about the washing of hands in his report or in his first grand jury testimony. The hand-washing scene had come later, he noted, implying that it had somehow been added to color the tale blacker. Carl never wept, asked to see the body, or looked out the window, Connolly had said in direct testimony, but Hoffinger pointed out that in his original report he had quoted Carl as saying, "She was everything to me."

"How would you like to have your life on the line based on some-body's memory?" Hoffinger asked in his corridor talk that day.

Officer Capolupo, who hadn't testified before the grand juries, was less vulnerable. He corroborated Connolly's testimony, hand washing and all, and drew little fire in cross. But on Wednesday, Hoffinger went after what he regarded as the weakest link, Detective Finelli.

In the pretrial hearings, Finelli had showed himself to truly have a memory problem. On more than one occasion, he had gotten the times mixed up with regard to the sequence of events, and Hoffinger had never missed snaring him and closing the web. Hoffinger had also gotten him to admit after a flat denial that he had backdated one of his reports. Lederer had rushed to his rescue, attributing his memory shortcomings to having gone off the case for cancer surgery, which had been followed by months of convalescence.

Finelli was in a blue pin-striped suit, his gold badge at his lapel, as he took the stand. "He was just sittin'," he said, beginning his testi-mony with the moment he first laid eyes on Carl in the squad room. He raised 911, listened to Carl's story about how they stayed home, ordered in, and watched TV while Ana got tipsy, and then he brought out the contradictions in Carl's story ("Did you think she took a pill and disappeared?"). The detective, only a year away from retirement now, went through the rest of that long blue Sunday in 1985, Carl making his laconic phone calls, showing Finelli his bales-of-hay cata-logue, going to sleep on the boss's cot, writing his statement, balking at the video cameras, Bashford finally ordering his arrest. Having been warned in jest by Schlesinger not to repeat Bashford's order word for word, Finelli simply concluded there.

Hoffinger approached him, a three-point-fold white handkerchief in his breast pocket. Everything he had just recounted was from memory, right?

Finelli agreed, saying, however, that he had made notes.

Hoffinger, aware of the answer, wanted to know when.

"Two, two and a half weeks ago . . . in the wee hours of the morning."

Had he talked with his partner Detective Nieves? Had he seen his notes?

Yes, he had Nieves's notes of what Carl said.

Even the notes hadn't helped, though. In direct testimony, Finelli only moments earlier had said that he had called the Crime Scene Unit at 11:25 that morning before leaving for Carl's apartment; the precinct record showed he had signed out at 10:50. It seemed like quibbling, but Hoffinger, hurling dire reminders at the detective that he was under oath, was seeking to show both embellishment and collusion.

That business about her being "tipsy," Hoffinger pressed on. "Did that come from Nieves?"

The old cop could not be fazed. He toughened, sounding dead sure on this one. "That came from Carl Andre's mouth."

Hoffinger pulled out Finelli's grand jury testimony from 1986 and 1987. There was "drinking," but no "tipsy."[3] Finelli didn't look bothered.

How much Hoffinger believed that the police had sat around only recently trying to script a better story, and trying, miserably, to get it straight, was hard to assess, but he certainly grew vocal about it in his unprintable corridor press conferences. "They're framing an innocent man," he complained during one recess that day. "I'm not surprised, but the D.A. is letting them do it! I'm jaded. I don't care. But Steve Weiner, Mike Sherman, they come out of the D.A.'s office, and they say they can't fucking believe it!"

---

[3]"Tipsy," that fine old Miltonian word, had, however, been long present in Carl's vocabulary. Remembering Robert Smithson in the "stews of Max's," Carl remarked in 1978, "Bob's capacity for Budweiser beer was beyond description or belief—he would be tipsy for hours but only rarely if ever soused."

RAQUEL, DRIVING DOWN with Tom to Manhattan the next day to be the state's last major witness, worried that her testimony might provoke a mistrial. She had seen Lederer a few days earlier and had told her she could not simply say that Ana had been in fine spirits, free of care, was happy with life and every prospect for her future. Her mother taking trains and buses to and from Spring Valley to be present at the trial had provided daily reports, and Raquel had been disheartened to hear that Natalia had not been allowed to utter a word of Ana's true feelings about Carl. Lederer wanted to bring up the final phone call between the two sisters that Saturday afternoon to show Ana's state of mind, but, as she told Raquel, any mention of infidelity or divorce was taboo. But that had been the whole substance of the conversation, Raquel had insisted, and if someone were to ask her, she would have to say that Ana's mood had been rotten, pissed off, really angry, and that she had been saying she wanted revenge. Lederer had warned her of the consequences, and Raquel had promised to do her best, but this morning she couldn't say what she would do when called.

By the time she got to Tom and Raquel, her twenty-first and twenty-second witnesses, Lederer had covered most of her ground, though she was saving a couple of unannounced witnesses in reserve—and was still trying to break the recalcitrance of others—depending on how Hoffinger fielded the defense.

Tom, first of the two on the stand, recalled how Carl hadn't notified the family, saying days later that he didn't have the phone number. But he had waived any claim on the estate, hadn't he? Hoffinger said.

Raquel followed. Word had gotten around and the media presence thickened, the well-known columnist Murray Kempton taking a front-row seat; the *Times* was still contemplating the merits of the story uptown.

Lederer had had more than enough time to study her opponent's attack pattern, so she removed the dressing on the unhealable trauma of the sisters' upbringing before he could. She brought out how the girls had been dispatched from Havana to St. Mary's Home in Dubuque, and had grown up piecemeal in Iowa. "You don't have to write often," Raquel recalled Ana telling her when she went off to New York to her calling, "because what we feel for each other will always be in our hearts." She began to cry, the judge calling a brief respite so she could pull herself together.

Lederer took Raquel through the years to when she had met Carl, visiting 34E, which was always "very neat, very organized, and simple, very simple"—not anything like the mess in the prosecution photos. Carl had once given her his catalogue and signed it. When she got to the final phone call, Raquel was still unsure of what she would say, and Hoffinger was already on his feet objecting.

Taking no chances, Lederer asked for a conference with the judge. It had to do with the substance of the witness's conversation with her sister, she said. Hoffinger continued to oppose, but Schlesinger consented and both sides followed him to his chambers. Inside, Lederer argued that Hoffinger had been the one to open the door on Ana's relationship with her husband, beginning with his cross-examination of her very first witness. Schlesinger said she had a good point. Hoffinger insisted he was blameless. Schlesinger made his ruling.

Coming back into the courtroom a few minutes later, Lederer went by Raquel and whispered in her ear. "He's going to admit your saying that Ana was angry at Carl," she told her.

Hesitant and still wary of erring, Raquel managed to say that her sister said she was "very angry" at Carl. "Although she seemed angry and spiteful toward her husband, she seemed happy about the rest of her life." It came out awkwardly, but the underlying passion of Ana's last day of life had at last bent iron in the rules of hearsay.

Hoffinger advanced softly in his cross, dwelling nevertheless on Ana's childhood wounds and her left-wing politics. She was pro-Castro, wasn't she?

"She was pro-Cuba," said Raquel.

Lederer called a young man named Eli Lederman. He was a graduate student in physics at New York University with a BA from Brown. He had calculated how long it had taken Ana to fall the 269 feet from the window in 34E: 4.21 seconds, he reported now. When he stood down, the prosecutor made an application, as it was called, petitioning the court "to visit the scene of the crime."

"A visual inspection," she maintained, "will show conclusively the impossibility of an accident." For her, it had been a life-altering experience, and she hoped it would be so for the judge.

Hoffinger opposed.

Schlesinger thought it over for a minute or so. "The application is denied," he said.

Lederer rose, standing stark. "The People rest."

Hoffinger got to his feet, too. He made a motion for dismissal, as though there were nothing to defend. "There is suspicion, surmises, perhaps," he said, "but there is no proof."

Schlesinger withdrew, obstensibly to reflect. Truth to tell, he was as curious as anyone else to see the trial of Carl Andre played out to the end, and in his unsought role as all twelve parts of the jury, many parts were still a long way from deciding the outcome. Remaining out for a proper count, twelve minutes, he returned and invited Hoffinger to begin the presentation of his best case for the defense.

38

The trial was getting Carl down, or so he told a close friend halfway through that week. He didn't think the prosecution had much of a case, "but you never know." At every break in the proceedings, he would reach for his *Times*, *TLS*, or *New Republic*, by reflex, it seemed, but he was doing more than only reading. His eyes moved imperceptibly over the top of the pages to observe others, a periscope on who and who was not in the courtroom. No one who had been told had failed to respect his wish that they not attend, but he had been very upset on Tuesday by the presence in the courtroom of Yvonne Rainer. The renowned dancer and choreographer was one of the old school, a rare equal among women as an avant-garde artist, a radiance of the minimalists' seventies adored and pursued by the founders, Carl included. It had probably been Ruby, he guessed, who had gotten her to come, knowing it would hurt him. He was right. Ruby's own accusatory presence bothered him, too, he admitted, and she was there with her Third World assembly every day. You never knew when you might get on the same elevator with her or Ana's other friends.

It had already happened with Zarina, whom he had known since that

trip to India in the sixties, the two of them alone the other day riding
up to the thirteenth floor. They had made small talk, and he had then
gone to take his place beyond the railing and she to hers on "Ana's"
side of the courtroom. He had written her a kind note when she had
come to New York, had given her a signed catalogue, and she had
admired his work, respected him all these years—but no longer. Even
the word "minimal" grated on her now and always would, she felt,
watching Carl sitting without expression, Zarina thinking, "there is the
one person who knows."

If Yvonne Rainer had broken the ranks, the line was still being held
with reinforcements added, real and symbolic. Paula Cooper, keeping
the faith and her fingers crossed, kept a $16,000 Carl Andre tile
sculpture permanently installed in a corner of the gallery floor throughout Carl's courtroom ordeal. Donald Judd, who had storefront studio
on Spring and Mercer, had placed a stack of eight pink bricks like a
raised right fist in the street-level corner window. On February 10, an
exhibition of five of Carl's sculptures would open in Madrid's Crystal
Palace. Paula had told Carl she would fly over to be there, and she was
no ordinary presence. Gian Enzo and Angela planned to show Carl's
work at their gallery in Soho that same month, and MOMA had a piece
currently on display, alongside Sol LeWitt, Judd, and some of the other
masters. Dealers were saying that minimalism was coming back, and
dealers were usually the first to know. This was good news. According
to the books at Paula Cooper's, Carl had been $240,000 in the black
before this all began; now he had nothing but goodwill.

The feeling among Carl's friends was that the nonjury decision had
been a "good move," in Paula's phrase. The first proof being cited was
the cherished dearth of public and media attention. That much could
not be disputed. Carl's art-world image, from what little was being
written, simply wouldn't travel north of Soho. The courtroom photographs, uncommon in any trial, were news in their own right; they were
getting a play in the tabloids, taking more space than the stories, and
Carl, unfriendly as he was by nature toward cameras, was just not
coming through as simpatico. *El Diario* had made the case a major
story for its readers, shifting journalistic objectivity to other pages. Carl,
on the first day, had slighted the Spanish-language daily's veteran

courthouse reporter, Antonio Santurio. Introducing himself, Santurio had assured him that he would treat him fairly and Carl had refused to shake his hand, leaving him standing in the corridor with his arm extended.[1] Whatever that did to change the color of his reports, it was probably independent of the daily *el caso Mendieta* logo the editors ran alongside them: it showed a woman going out of a window, a hulking figure lurking just behind her. Nor could he be blamed for headlines like this: "Carl Andre: Ana Killed Herself Because I Was Not in Bed with Her."

Murray Kempton's scathing *Newsday* column, published the day after his courtroom visit, had more circulation in the general community, however. He had dropped in on both thirteenth-floor trials and in a somewhat figurative way had linked Carl with young Chambers as murder suspects "inescapably guilty" of an unpardonable trespass: vainglory. The day before Kempton showed up at the trial, Officer Capolupo had testified that Carl had said Ana was despondent because he was a better artist than she. The columnist had evidently found that remark as insufferable as Chambers's tender-genitals defense, and therein lay his story. He wrote:

Carl Andre says his wife defenestrated herself after he reminded her that he was a better artist than she. Evidence of deplorably bad manners aside, it takes a towering self-esteem to ask us to believe that the shock of recognizing her own incurable inferiority on no one's say-so but yours was enough to cast a strong and sane woman into suicidal despair. . . . Anyway, there Andre and Chambers sit with no song to sing to us except the one that asks, "Why Didn't She Leave Me Alone?" To think of oneself as the planet in whose orbit everyone else is but a satellite is finally to be not worth thinking about.

---

[1]"These things you do not do," Santurio lamented that day, but at least Carl was democratic about it, giving the same treatment to *Newsday*'s Tim Clifford. He complained that he "almost caught a cold" from Carl's icy refusal to respond to him.

THE SCALES OF justice, so to speak, were kept in an apartment on the Upper East Side and taken out every night after court to weigh the case against Carl Andre. Schlesinger made copious notes all day, and once not long ago his memory had retrieved data faster than Lexis—computer software used in law research—so weighing the case at home, relaxing with a cigarette and a nip of whiskey, was fair enough. Mulling, he called it.

He would have liked to have known Ana. She must have been a vital, passionate woman who could excite the full range of a man's emotions intensely. Fiery. Lederer was doing a good job, working very hard, getting over her nervousness. Hoffinger was overloading. Trying to turn Ana's art against her was absurd. It had no bearing on the case. But he was cautious and thorough. The old war horse. He could be quite tough on a witness, yet know when to go easy, like with the doorman. Carl certainly looked suspicious. He showed no emotion. No wonder Hoffinger had waived a jury. Then there was that thing Carl was doing in the courtroom. Scratching. Schlesinger would catch sight of him and see it again and again, Carl scratching himself all over, but mostly on the top of his left wrist. It didn't look natural.

HOFFINGER TRIED TO turn the prosecution case around by breathing life into the suicide and accident theories, though the final scenario he offered in his summation—the defense's solution to the puzzle of how Ana died—would be not quite one and not quite the other.

He composed a strong overture to begin with. Of his first five witnesses, three told rather outlandish tales attesting both to Carl being framed and Ana being insanely suicidal. The other two were conventional accident-support witnesses.

First came Carl's ex–cleaning woman, Alison Bierman. She was a plain but pleasant-looking young woman who had worked for him for five years. His apartment, she testified, often looked as it did in the Crime Scene photographs, she said, the overturned chair included. Messiness was "Mr. Andre's environment." Carl told her never to straighten up, never to touch anything, and never to go into his "chaos room," which was what he called the storage room, never by any other name. Her only job was to dust. Two hours of dusting every Monday or Tuesday. The windows were always open in the summer, the air-conditioning never on. Perhaps that was why it was so dusty. If something were out of place, which was usual, she would dust around it, never under it, which would have required moving it. Once, when nobody was home, curiosity had gotten the best of her and she opened the door to the chaos room. It was messy. Just like in the photo.

Lederer, in her first cross-examination, was ready. She had herself interviewed Bierman. She attempted to show now what kind of person would make such an extreme claim to Carl's slovenliness so unsupported by any other testimony, the rest of the defense's own witnesses included. She elicited a little love story of Carl being Bierman's "hero" and she being "like his psychiatrist." Bierman had come to New York as an aspiring artist hoping, after corresponding with Carl about the "politics of art," to become his assistant; he didn't use assistants, he said when she showed up, but needed a cleaning woman. She had started at twenty dollars a week and had worked in 34E for five years, dusting, vacuuming, and throwing out empty bottles. Now and then she would show him her artwork, and he was always kind, she said, telling her how nice it was to have somebody coming in to clean on a regular basis. Once, he took her to a "fancy restaurant," just him and her.

Lederer used the occasion to force Bierman to admit that she couldn't bring herself to go back to the apartment after Ana's death, though on objection from Hoffinger this was stricken from the record. On her way out of the courtroom, the cleaning woman's eyes met Carl's, and, in his only courtroom reaction, he smiled.

Hoffinger's second witness was Carl's next-door neighbor from 34F, Bobby Tong. His testimony, by subsequent developments in the trial, would create a mystery within the mystery. Tong said he had been up all of that Saturday night, having gotten home around midnight. He shared the apartment with his secretary, Angela Wu, he said, and she slept in the living room. They had been up all night sending telexes to Hong Kong. Sometime before 5:30 A.M. while he was by his bedroom window, kept open because he smoked, he heard two noises. No screams, no voices, only "a very distinct sound . . . like a suction." As a tenant, the noise was unmistakable to him: someone in a neighboring apartment was opening or closing a window. The second sound, a few seconds later, was like "a car backfiring" or the "lid on a garbage can crashing." Later in the morning, he had been questioned by the police, and he had had a "slight argument" with them. They had tried to make him say that he had heard a woman screaming, said Tong. "It was all whacko."

Tong's testimony, whatever else it was worth, scored one for Hoffinger in the game of launching surprise witnesses. Lederer had had no notice from the defense that Carl's neighbor would testify. Having read the police reports, she was almost certain that Tong's courtroom account was not the same story he had told the detectives who had called on him, but until she could verify this she was hamstrung. She limited her cross to drawing out information Hoffinger hadn't covered, notably that Tong had only been a tenant for two months when he heard the "unmistakable" window sound. He further admitted to being able to hear normal street noises, which augmented the superintendent's testimony. Tong had also been one of the two neighbors who had heard the Thursday-night fight at the Andres and had seen Ana in the hallway. He had followed behind her, he said now, and she was hysterical, weeping, and saying, "I'll do it. I'll really do it."

The next two were the pro-accident witnesses. Ronnie Ginnever, the owner of Sabor, testified that Ana would get drunk and "walk into tables, walk into walls." Lederer showed that Ginnever was an old friend of Carl's dating back to the early sixties, but this witness was followed by someone who had never met Carl. Bridget Knapp was a young woman who had once lived twenty floors below Carl in 14E. She was just under five feet tall—too short, she said, to reach the central latch that opened her bedroom window. Sometimes, when the window got stuck, she said, she would crawl onto the radiator to get to the latch "jerk it with one hand, then pull it with two hands to open it." She never stood on the sill because "that would be foolish." Lederer, showing herself sharpest at cross, disposed of Knapp in three quick questions that worked for her side. They brought out that the windowsill was breast-level on the witness, that she had never seen, much less tried, the windows in 34E, and that she had no fear of heights.

The fifth and most bizarre of this series of witnesses was a Cuban émigré named Cesar Trasobares. He was an art-funding administrator in Miami and had been rather close to Ana since the early eighties. He was branded a traitor now by her family and her friends even before he opened his mouth. In Hoffinger's book, he was one of Ana's gay friends whom she would get Carl to take to dinner at Sabor. Trasobares, looking a little uneasy with both labels, told of Ana drinking a half-gallon of wine, her speech becoming "a little blurred," getting a little clumsy on her feet, and falling "a couple of times." He last saw her in the spring of 1985 on her trip to Miami—"alone without her husband," Hoffinger interjected—and she wasn't all that sanguine about her career. But the uniqueness of Trasobares's testimony was his purported knowledge of Ana's interest in a "female force" and her relationship with the voodoo god Jemaya, as Hoffinger called it.

"She would speak of Jemaya," Trasobares said.

There was something particular about Jemaya, wasn't there?

Yes, there was.

Hoffinger asked what it was.

"Jemaya is a deity that takes flight," said the witness. "She was interested in researching it."

Hoffinger moved in on the witness. "When," he asked, "does Jemaya take flight?"

"September 7. The deity takes flight."

There was a brief moment of silence. Then Hoffinger moved on, but the date lingered like spilled wine. Ana had "taken flight" on September 8, not the seventh, but a little too close for comfort. Had she been the victim of some self-cast voodoo spell? Casting spells, after all, had been one of her interests, according to Hoffinger's information.

Here was what all the careful planting had at last sprouted. Lederer tried to uproot the whole dwarfish growth, getting the witness to state that Jemaya was only one in the whole church of Afro-Caribbean deities in which Ana had been interested and, to make it sound kosher, that they were associated with Catholic saints, but the entire spectacle remained most unholy.[2]

[2]No one had done the research, and the flight was a flight of someone's imagination. Jemaya, usually spelled Yemayá in Santería (Agwe in voodoo), is a wingless water-bound goddess, the goddess of protection, matron of the seas and motherhood. There is, *santeros* believe, no sickness of the heart that she cannot wash clean, no desert of

In the corridor, after Trasobares was dismissed, Hoffinger replayed it more "softly" for reporters. All he had wanted from Trasobares, he said, was to show that even Ana's friend would say she stumbled. He didn't care about the rest of the stuff, just the stumbling and that her career was going nowhere. Ana was on the margin; Carl was "a giant among sculptors," world famous ("You're talking Tate"). Who was Ana Mendieta? Carl didn't want all this to come out; he didn't want to "besmirch her reputation." It was a tragedy for everyone, but he gets a murder charge pinned to him to boot.

THE PREVIOUS SUNDAY, January 31, 1988, at 5:30 A.M., a woman had stood at the open window of Carl's bedroom, screaming. Sticking her head into the winter air outside, she screamed one word one time as loud as she could: "Ho!" She had been told to scream "ho" rather than "no" because a certain Dr. Robert Knaff told her to do so. He was on Waverly Place below her, standing in the dark where Ed Mojzis had stood on the night he heard a woman scream "no" several times. Ho travels better than no, according to Knaff, a consultant on "human factors engineering," which is "the study of humans and systems." Dr. Knaff barely heard the screaming woman's "ho," so imagine if she had screamed "no."

These were the results of an experiment that Hoffinger attempted to enter into the record on Friday afternoon when Dr. Knaff took the stand as an expert witness. Lederer objected to his very presence.

"Did you know how loud Ana Mendieta could scream?" she asked him, questioning the parameters of his test.

He did not.

"Did you know anything about Mr. Mojzis's hearing?"

He did not.

Schlesinger, who at first believed he was going to be asked to rule

---

despair that she cannot flood with hope. Her favorite animals are creatures of the shore, one of her favorite places in the house is the bathroom, and she probably would delight in a hot tub. Her birthday is September 8, her lucky number seven, her lucky day Saturday. In Santería, incidentally, the Ninth Commandment of the Creator of the Universe states: "You will neither fear death nor take your own life."

on the admissibility of a new technology only to learn that it was nothing but somebody shouting "Ho" out of a window, thought the witness ludicrous. Giving a brief lecture on how some people may have unknown quantities of wax in their ears, he sustained the prosecution and threw Dr. Knaff and his testimony out of court. Hoffinger was red-faced but quick to back off, and inculpable of not trying everything.

Knaff, though he could no longer be tallied, marked the beginning of the final group of defense witnesses, the hired guns. First, however, came a challenge to the origins of Carl's scratches, particularly the one on his nose. Larry Weiner, in his baggy gray Brooks Brothers suit, took the stand to declare that he had run into Carl on Eighth Street in the late afternoon of either the Friday or Saturday before Ana's death. Carl looked terrible. He was sweaty and seemed to be suffering from jet lag. His face was pimply, as if from prickly heat, and the pimples looked like they had been scratched, but he was not one to stare at such things because, he said, his own complexion was not so wonderful either. Lederer, less concerned with Larry's face, asked him where Carl's pimples were. He pointed to his earlobe. "Somewhere around the sideburn, where it stops."

The next defense witness on the scratches contradicted Weiner, which might seem an act of ineptitude but not in the process of raising doubt. Her name was Elaine Miner, and she testified to being certain she saw Carl in the late afternoon of that same Friday. Miner had worked at Paula Cooper's as a bookkeeper, and she had the Soho gallery-worker look, young, attractive, oversized bright turtleneck, wide studded black belt. Carl had come into the gallery bearing his note of apology to Paula for having given her a "hard time" in a recent phone call. He had an "abrasion on his nose," said Miner, "like he could have gotten hit by something." Hoffinger handed her the official police mug shot made at seven-thirty in the morning on Monday, September 9, 1985. It showed a scab on the lower part of his nose. This was the way he looked on Friday, said Miner.

Lederer asked whether Carl had any other marks, pimples, or prickly heat. Weiner notwithstanding, Miner hadn't seen anything red but Carl's nose. Was there anyone else in the gallery at the time? asked Lederer. Yes, another employee, named Marika Bergman.

Lederer already knew this and had spoken to her. Bergman had seen no scratch, not to speak of prickly heat, but had been reluctant to testify. The prosecutor knew now that she would have to somehow win her over.

BETWEEN MINER AND Larry Weiner, Hoffinger summoned Alice Weiner to tell the story about Ana's premonition of not having much time left in her life. He also used her to bolster Carl's version of how he got the nose scratch. No amount of testimony could reconcile his claim of running into a door on his terrace while his passport showed him still in transit from Europe, but it could be left unmentioned. Alice Weiner, in a gray suit herself, said that Carl always kept the windows open. While this was another chip in the Bobby Tong suction story, Alice added that open windows caused "lots of wind" in the apartment and made the doors slam. Carl was also "accident-prone"; he would "fall off a sidewalk," would cut his fingers, and though she didn't quite say it, running into a door, or a door running into him, was part of his style. Ana "bumped into things," too, but that was when she drank. When Carl drank he became "a little pussycat."

MONDAY, THE DEFENSE'S last day, was the day of the doctors, doctors of art included.

"Take your mind back to September 1985," Hoffinger instructed his witness, critic David Bourdon, who had been praising Carl in print since 1966. "In terms of exposure to the public and success, compare Carl Andre's and Ana Mendieta's respective statures in the art world."

Schlesinger, rather bothered, wondered out loud how this expert related to the case. The issue, he said, was what Carl and Ana thought of the matter of fame and not the truth of what they thought.

Nevertheless, what Bourdon thought was allowed, and he said that the difference between the two was that Carl was a "modern master" and as for Ana, "I knew the name but never saw the work."[3] Lederer had no questions for Bourdon.

[3] He may have forgotten his 1977 *Village Voice* review of an A.I.R. group show, in which he singled out and described Ana's *Tree of Life* series, but probably not the phone call he had made to Mary Beth Edelson a few weeks earlier in which he discussed his impressions after a visit to Ana's New Museum retrospective.

A similar evaluation of Carl and Ana as artists was given by Filip Bool, who added an anecdote meant to cause further damage. Bool, wearing a double-breasted blazer and carrying a leather shoulder bag, had just flown in from the Netherlands. He was one of the Dutch museum curators who had been showing Carl's work with dedication since the beginning, though he had only known him personally for seven years. Citing his expert credentials, he omitted one of his most recent contributions to promoting Carl's oeuvre: his sponsorship of Rita Sartorius's 1987 catalogue of all of Carl's work. Carl, he said, was "one of the most important sculptors since the Second World War," and Ana was "on the way up."

At this point, Lederer leapt to her feet in protest. By now she had completely lost her fear of Hoffinger as the invincible grand master, and it showed. "I don't understand this ranking of artists! They're not like baseball players!"

She, of course, had cast the first stone in calling Ida Panicelli, and Bool had spoken an indisputable truth, but the main purpose of his testimony came next. Bool had been present at a March 1984 dinner party in Amsterdam after a Sol LeWitt opening, seated at a table with Carl and Ana. Everyone was eating rijstafel and drinking beer, but Carl and Ana were drinking wine. "At a certain point," Bool recalled, "in front of seventy-five people, Ana Mendieta stood up on her chair, very excited, very unexpected, and she did fall down with this chair."[4]

How was Carl, asked Lederer, "was he clumsy or accident-prone?"

"No," said the witness, unaware of Alice Weiner's claim.

How had the couple behaved toward each other that night of the dinner?

"Carl wasn't too glad about the food. I don't know what she was doing. She was kind of excited. She was a Latin American, South American type."

"Thank you so much, Dr. Bool."

THE FIRST OF the medical doctors was Dominic de Maio, a former chief medical examiner of New York City, retired since 1978. He had

[4]Bool had some problems with his English and it may have affected his description of the incident. Sol and Carol LeWitt, seated at another table, did not witness any of this, though Carol saw a commotion and concluded that Ana had fallen.

two main roles as a witness. One was to attest that the scratch on Carl's nose in the mug shot could have been made by running into the wall on his terrace. This, however, backfired when Schlesinger, sustaining Lederer's objection, pointed out that Carl had said he had been hit by the door, not the wall. The second objective was to underscore the significance of a line in the autopsy report stating that the bladder was "devoid of contents." Since the bladder normally refills at the rate of one cubic centimeter per minute, de Maio informed the court, it meant that the moment before Ana died she had urinated. This was very suggestive. Reasonable people do not take time out in a life and death struggle to go to the bathroom.

When Lederer got the witness, she asked him if he had examined the deceased's panties to determine whether urine had been released on impact. He had not. She then produced a piece of evidence equally as intriguing as the empty bladder. This was in a document called an autopsy worksheet. Unlike the autopsy report, which had been typed by a secretary from Gutierrez's dictation, it was in the pathologist's own handwriting. Further, the typed report was dated December 24, 1985, and the worksheet September 9, 1985—the day after the autopsy. It revealed that he had sent seventy cubic centimeters of Ana's urine to the toxicology laboratory along with other contents of the body. Using the refill rate cited by de Maio, this figure meant that Ana had urinated seventy minutes before her death, at about 4:15 A.M., but everything depended on which of the two contradictory documents was the best evidence. That was left undecided.

DR. DAVID PREVEN took the oath and described himself as an educator and a psychiatrist. Suicide was one of his major interests, he said, its study being "more of an art than a science." There were intentional suicides and subintentional suicides, an example of the latter being someone killed when driving a car while intoxicated. Schlesinger stopped him here and said that such an event could also be caused where the driver was not at fault, but Preven's point was made. Subintentional suicide types, he said, could easily say that they had plans for living, were not overtly depressed, and not even a psychiatrist could predict their behavior, especially under the influence of alcohol.

Lederer, citing other authorities, tried to show that suicide was indeed predictable. and normally accompanied by such activities as canceling appointments, giving gifts, assigning responsibilities to others, and, above all, experiencing depression. Preven admitted being familiar with this work, but he was from another school. Depression and alcoholism were the biggest factors, he said, particularly in falls.

"Let me tell you about falls," he said, as long as he was on the subject. "Forty percent of falls are felt to be alcohol related. . . . It is a very unusual event to be pushed from a window."

This last remark was so blatantly inadmissible that it was immediately ordered stricken from the record, but Lederer seized the moment to underscore whose side the witness was on and why. She asked him how much he was being paid by the defense for his testimony.

Preven stiffened, the hackles of his integrity as a scientist rising along with him. "Two hundred and fifty dollars an hour."

Schlesinger smiled. "I'll take a three-hour recess and make you a rich man," he said.

The doctor, however, was actually being shortchanged. Lederer, having rejected the hired-gun approach, had also felt free to ask the same question of Dr. de Maio. His services cost three hundred dollars an hour—"at least," he said.

The final defense witness, Dr. Kurt Dubowski, a jovial professor from Nebraska and an expert on alcohol abuse, had settled for the bargain price of $160 an hour, but he had had to be flown in, had spent the night in a $235 room at the Waldorf-Astoria, and had contracted for a surcharge "appearance fee" of $1,850.

Dubowski told everything you already knew about the effects of alcohol but were afraid to ask. A 0.18 brain alcohol level generally, he testified, would put the subject, depending on drinking experience, in an excited, confused state—the midrange of effects. It would affect emotions and awareness and impair memory, comprehension, and judgment. The lesser-known pieces of information that Hoffinger wanted to bring out, undoubtedly for his final scenario, were that the subject would feel warmer, would suffer a loss of visual acuity ("like dropping a curtain in front of the eyes"), and that if Carl had drunk as much as Ana that night, she was drunker than he.

Lederer asked if drunken behavior tended to vary from episode to episode.

It did not, said Dubowski. "A happy drunk is a happy drunk."

Was there an attenuating effect in coordination in coping with a physical struggle?

There would be difficulty in recognizing danger, said the witness. "You might try to claw his eyes out, and you might miss and slip and fall down. . . . The ability to defend would be impaired."

Dubowski, sensing Lederer was finished, joked about having to catch a plane and was dispatched. Steve Weiner, making his debut for the defense, asked that judicial notice be taken of the weather on September 8, 1985. He submitted a weather map and an hour by hour report on conditions.

Schlesinger accepted it with glee. "I like to read the symbols," he said, "because I was once a meteorologist."

Hoffinger stood. "The defense rests, sir."

Carl rubbed his eyes and pinched the bridge of his nose.

Lederer asked for a rebuttal. She had new witnesses. She also wanted to recall Bobby Tong. He had lied on the stand, she charged, and she would prove it in further cross-examination.

The judge granted her request, stating firmly, however, "This trial will not go on beyond tomorrow morning if I have anything to do with it."

39

Lederer's first-day ploy of springing Ed Mojzis unannounced boomer-anged. Hoffinger had complained to the judge, and after he had used the same dodge and she had complained about him, Schlesinger had finally ruled—with Lederer opposing—that she had to supply him with the complete list of her rebuttal witnesses that evening. It contained five names: Bobby Tong, Detective Nieves, Nancy Spero, Marika Berg-man, and Rudolf Baranik.

The last three had been subpoenaed to refute the testimony about Carl having a scratch on his face in the late afternoon of that last Friday. Larry Weiner's pimple testimony was worthless, if only because he had placed the scratch near the earlobe, but Elaine Miner, the gallery bookkeeper, had at least gotten the position correct, though she admitted under cross-examination that she had previously discussed the matter with Hoffinger "ten to fifteen times." Discussion with Hoffinger was the very reason the assistant D.A. had hoped to turn the surprise-witness trick one last time. She feared that he might somehow influence her witnesses before she could get them safely on the stand the following morning.

Nancy, along with Leon, had seen Carl and Ana on Thursday night; Bergman had seen him in the gallery the same Friday afternoon as Miner; and Rudolf, of course, had been with him at dinner, with Ana and May Stevens, on Friday night. Not one of the three witnesses, plus the two spouses, had seen any scratch. The Baraniks had, to be sure, repeatedly refused to testify, but something had occurred recently that made Lederer summon Rudolf to court anyway.

Village Voice critic Elizabeth Hess, Betsy to friends, had reviewed Ana's New Museum show enthusiastically in December, and thinking that she might write something further, had gone on to become a regular at the trial. She was a good friend of Rudolf and May's, and some days back had had a conversation with Ruby about her being unfair to the couple. Betsy had visited May in the hospital, and May had made a remark that had impressed her. Although Carl was one of the Baraniks' oldest and dearest friends, Hoffinger would never call her or Rudolf as witnesses, May had said to Betsy. That was because they had not seen any scratch on Carl, and indeed, May was sure, there was none. This was what Betsy had told Ruby, the moral of the story being that in spite of their love for Carl, they could not accommodate the defense. Ruby had been more taken by May's clear admission to another party than by Betsy's argument, and had passed the information on to Lederer. Lederer, who had inherited the Baraniks' problems with their loyalties and had not seen a clear way to relieve them, suddenly pounced on the moment. She felt that forcing Rudolf to appear in an eleventh-hour situation might break the logjam of his conscience.

It still seemed like a long shot, but she was far more confident about Marika Bergman. After speaking to her again since Elaine Miner's testimony, Lederer felt that she now had her locked in, a damn-sure witness to Carl not having a scratch. Bergman hadn't seen any scratch on his face, and, she told Lederer, had it been there, that was the kind of thing she would notice. As for Nancy Spero, the prosecutor had no doubts at all. Before the trial, however, Hoffinger had listed Nancy and her husband as defense witnesses; he had not called them, but he had apparently thought they might be useful, and Lederer could not be sure why.

BOBBY TONG WAS gone. Witnesses had to be available throughout the trial, but he had not been heard from since his testimony five days earlier. Lederer had discovered his disappearance shortly afterward, and when Hoffinger said he knew nothing about his witness's whereabouts, she had put the police on it. Tong currently lived on East Broadway, but there was no sign of him there, and the police had begun to search the city. They had managed to trace his secretary, Angela Wu, the woman with whom he had shared the apartment at 300 Mercer Street. She told them that Tong no longer worked for the firm. He had been fired for stealing checks. Moreover, Wu further repudiated Tong's testimony. Despite Tong's claim, she had not been in the apartment the night of Ana's death, she said. She was in Hong Kong at the time.

LEDERER CAME INTO court that Tuesday morning with no further news about Tong, but she was greeted with another twist in events. Visiting the witness room to check on the rest of her rebuttal witnesses, she found everyone else in place but not in order.

Baranik would not be moved. He was a Lithuanian, he told Lederer, and Lithuanians always look at people in the face, not in the nose.

"But his nose is in the center of his face," Lederer said.

If she were Lithuanian, perhaps she would understand, but she yielded instead, deciding to concentrate her energies, in the few moments left before the case would be called, on trying to plug a bigger hole in the dike. Marika Bergman had had an overnight change of heart. She was no longer damn sure that Carl had not had a scratch.

Lederer stood over her as Bergman, seated on a hard chair, hung her head, her eyes cast at the floor. The prosecutor had been stunned and deeply frustrated by her sudden about-face.

"But you told me you didn't see it!" she said in a low, angry voice. "Why are you changing your story now?"

"Well, I don't think that's what I said," the young woman murmured.

"I absolutely know what you said," Lederer insisted.

There was no audible answer. Lederer tried to convince her by telling her that she was a critical witness and that she had a duty to testify to the truth of what she had seen. Bergman muttered something about not being sure of anything anymore.

So, Hoffinger had got there first, Lederer imagined.[1]

WHEN THE ANDRE club had been gathered and Hoffinger's opening objection to the whole idea of a rebuttal had been overruled, Lederer called Nancy Spero. The slender, frail-looking artist was dressed in gray slacks and a black shirt, her hair cropped very short. She showed every bit of the fright she was feeling. She had been in the witness room with Rudolf, whom she had known as a fellow in politics and art since the sixties, both pretending the other wasn't there. She had overheard Bergman's recantation, and now, rattled by Carl's presence, she knew she was the only witness left.

They had gone to dinner at Janice's Fish Place that Thursday evening, Nancy said under questioning, a foursome together for about two hours. They had talked about what they always talked about, art and politics, everyone in good spirits.

"Was there anything unusual about Carl's appearance?" asked the prosecutor.

"No."

Lederer handed her the Polaroid exhibit of Carl's face and told her to examine it. "Did he look any different?"

Nancy stared at the photo, her hands shaking slightly. "Yes," she said. "He didn't have a scratch on his nose."

Hoffinger went for her memory bank. Did she remember where she

[1]He had in fact spoken to Bergman the previous evening. As a result of the conversation, he said later, he knew why she wasn't called by Lederer: Bergman, her memory somehow refreshed, realized she hadn't even seen Carl that day; while he was in the gallery, she happened to be in the back room.

was Wednesday, the night before that dinner? She did not. Where was she Friday? She would have to look at her date book. Ana was a very great friend of hers, wasn't she? Yes, said Nancy.

THE BOBBY TONG minisaga came up next, Detective Nieves taking the stand. Nieves had knocked on Tong's door that Sunday morning. There was no one else in the apartment, Nieves said, and Tong had not claimed to have been up all night. He had told Nieves that he had gone to bed early and had gotten up at five-thirty in the morning. He had heard "something," a noise. No suction, no garbage can lid. Tong told him he had seen Ana crying the Thursday before. There had been no argument between Tong and Nieves. The talk had lasted five minutes.

The people rested, or rather rerested. So did the defense.

Lederer reported to the judge that the police were still looking for Tong. She asked that his testimony be stricken from the record. Hoffinger called the whole thing a "last-minute ploy." Schlesinger called for summations first thing the next morning.

The war of the evidence was over. The warring ground was red. There remained only advocates to pick from the bones and a one-headed jury to eat the flesh.

"THE PRECISE QUESTION in this case," Hoffinger began, speaking before a sparsely filled courtroom at 9:53 the following morning, "is not what occurred, but whether there is proof beyond a reasonable doubt."[2] He then began his examination of what was known of "what happened that tragic night."

First, he said, there was the bedroom—that of "two artists living together on their way shortly to Rome"—in disarray. Alison Bierman, who came to clean, said this chaos was normal. Did she have a motive to lie? he asked. This bedroom was not the scene of a struggle. There

[2]This was of course a statement of fact, and the best definition of "reasonable doubt," above all in this case, was Judge Schlesinger's. In the Swift decision, he had instructed the jury on the meaning of the term: reasonable doubt, he said, means you cannot simply have a doubt. You must have a *reason* for a doubt and it must agree with common human experience of what is considered reasonable.

would have been clearer signs. Ana was a "vital, forceful, feisty, animated woman, especially when she was drinking." Yet there were no other signs of struggle.

Then the scratches. The police saw something on Carl Andre's nose. Elaine Miner saw the scratch on Friday at the gallery. Nancy Spero didn't see it on Thursday night. The fact that people don't see something doesn't mean it wasn't there.

Finelli—"the man who has no memory"—said he saw a scratch on Carl's right arm. Martha Bashford said left arm. If Ana Mendieta was involved in a life and death struggle, with her long nails, you would expect some clear evidence of it on his body. There was some blood under the left fingernails, but the report didn't say whose blood.

The scream. What did Mr. Mojzis tell us? He heard "No, no, no, no." This is supposed to be a woman screaming? Mojzis's memory can't be trusted. That scream was heard at a distance of three hundred feet, "longer than a football field away." Mojzis continued to walk toward Broadway. He didn't look up. "Obviously he was used to such voices. I'm sure he heard them before."

Was the crash four seconds from the first no or the last? People were not standing with a stopwatch. Tong did not hear the scream. He heard two noises, a window opening and a crash. Where were the noises accompanying the struggle? Tong's window was only twenty feet away. Tong had no reason to lie. Tong heard a quarrel a few nights earlier, so why would he lie? Is Detective Nieves's report sufficiently reliable?

Can we rely on any of these police reports? But large portions of police testimony are not actually in the reports. They are taken from memory. What are we being asked to accept? No notes. All memory. "None of what the police are telling us, Your Honor, is reliable."

What was left were Carl's statements to the police. They were said to be incriminating because they were inconsistent and they showed consciousness of guilt. But consciousness of guilt is the weakest form of evidence and must be supported. Even innocent people hide things.

"I'll say this in due respect to the court. It is frightening, Your Honor, to have to rely on the police. . . . We don't dare rely on such memories that could affect Carl Andre's entire life."

From the 911 tape, Hoffinger went on, it would appear that Carl was actually in the room, but the photos, which show an indentation in one pillow, prove that Ana did in fact go to bed. They also show a white T-shirt hanging on the doorknob. She took off her T-shirt. This wasn't like the 911 tape. Did she say to Carl in the middle of a fight, "Wait, I'm going to take off my T-shirt and hang it on the doorknob"? The urine not being in the bladder is very important, Hoffinger maintained. Did they take time out from their struggle so that Ana could go to the john? "I submit that the only evidence that can be relied upon in this trial is the autopsy report."

What other inconsistency was there? There was a supposed one-and-a-half-hour gap between the time Carl said he went into the bedroom and the time he called 911. But Carl didn't have a watch. He had lost his sense of time. It was a hot night. They had been drinking. Carl mentioned twenty minutes in the statement, but that was as it seemed to him. He called moments after hearing the crash. They were probably the longest moments of his life as he tried to grasp the enormity of what had occurred. These statements were not inconsistent. If they were, they were not incriminating. "They do not show consciousness of guilt of *murder*."

The attorney paused for a moment and said, "In an ordinary case, we would stop here. We are not Perry Mason. We do not have to demonstrate what happened." Nevertheless, he felt obliged to describe what the evidence pointed to and he proceeded to do so, laying out a vivid scene:

Ana went to sleep. It was after a hot night of eating and drinking. She awoke in the dark. She went to the bathroom. It was 75 degrees, 88 percent humidity, a 3 knot wind. She took off her shirt. It was dark inside and outside. She had come out of the light. Her eyes had not yet adjusted to the glare. She went to the window to open it. She was too small to get leverage on the sill, so she stepped on the chair. The window was stuck. She used both hands. She slammed the window open, her body swiveling, and she lost her balance. She hurtled out of the window accidentally.

Hoffinger picked up the photos and showed them to Schlesinger. True, the overturned chair was nowhere near the window, but, Hoffinger said, the later set of photographs proved that the police had moved things. They had failed to preserve the scene.

"It is very rare in a criminal trial for the defense to put together what occurred," Hoffinger concluded. But the story was not complete:

> There is a final chapter to be written in this tragic book. Your Honor will be writing it. . . . Ana Mendieta was not the victim of a homicide. She was the unfortunate victim of either an accident or subintentional suicide.

Schlesinger took a drink of water. He turned to Lederer. When Hoffinger was seated, she rose and addressed the bench.

"MAY IT PLEASE the court," she began. "On September 8, 1985, Carl Andre murdered Ana Mendieta."

The evidence spoke for itself. Four-fifths of Ana's body was below the sill level. She was afraid of heights. There was no furniture near the window. All the windows were already open. Every single witness testified about her high spirits and lack of depression. These were very different types of people. Ana was proud of her accomplishments. Her future was clear. "Based on everything we know about suicide, Ana did not choose to end her life. . . . The defendant in this case is guilty beyond a reasonable doubt."

The prosecutor then offered her own theory of the case: "The defendant is a man who chooses his words carefully," she said. In his first statement, to the 911 police operator, there was a quarrel, she committed suicide, and "he was in that bedroom with her when she went out the window." Within ten minutes of the 911 call, he made a different statement. He began to back away. He said now, "I *think* she committed suicide." To Connolly and Capolupo, he didn't say he had a quarrel. He distanced himself yet further with Finelli. He *denied* the quarrel now. His written statement showed a careful account of what they ate and when, and what and whom they saw on television, and what they thought of the plot and the actors. Yet his description of his wife's death went from precise to cloudy. He came full circle. He went from suicide to accident.

Now it was her turn to offer a scenario:

> We know Ana was angry at Carl . . . that when intoxicated she became aggressive and caustic. . . . Perhaps it was Ana who was first to become physical. It escalated to a fight and the fight moved into the bedroom. Something cut him to the quick. He was able to overpower her. . . . She screamed for her life. She was unable to save herself. In the hours that followed, Carl Andre thought about how to save *himself*. He realized no one would believe his suicide story.

His account of a quarrel about being more exposed to the public demonstrates "unbelievable conceit and arrogance." Lederer asked: "Are we honestly to accept that it would cause her to get up from the table, walk into the other room, climb up on the sill, and dive out that window?" Yet the 911 statement came closest to what happened. He saw Ana go out the window because "he caused her to go out the window."

Consider the conduct of the defendant, she said. He did not display any behavior of a man who had lost his wife. He did not look out of the window. He did not call the family. He lied to Natalia Delgado that morning and instead called friends to cancel a dinner engagement. Consider his audacity toward Tom Harrington, she went on, telling him days later that he did not have his phone number.

The prosecutor concluded:

> The defendant has shown no remorse, no guilt, no contrition. He must not be allowed to walk away from this. We ask the court to find him guilty.

She was flushed when she finished. So was Carl.

———

SCHLESINGER ASKED THE lawyers to gather the exhibits and documents so that he could have them all together. When it was all handed up, he had a few words of his own to add.

"I am indebted to both of you," he said to Lederer and Hoffinger, "for your many courtesies and for being so professional. . . . I try a lot of cases. From a professional point of view, I enjoyed working with you. We will adjourn until ten o'clock tomorrow morning. I expect I will have a verdict."

He gathered up his papers, pressed them against his black robe to keep it in place, and went out. It was a little like the last day of school. He was going to mark the papers now.

LEDERER CAME OUT of the courtroom carrying the plywood model of 300 Mercer Street. She seemed very alone. She was surprised that Schlesinger had adjourned for a whole day. It was not yet noon. He had needed time. She sensed it was very close. Corridor pundits thought Hoffinger had won, but Hoffinger knew better. He had worked all this time, twenty-nine months tomorrow since he had first come on the case, giving it all he had, the product of what life and thirty-three years at the bar had taught him, winning and losing, working to save a man from years of prison, staying up late, giving up family time, taking leave from his classes at Columbia Law, seeking, raising, nurturing every tiny doubt only to find just one, which was all you needed, but you could never know, could you, until the foreman stood up and told you. Hoffinger was in the emptying corridor when his eyes caught sight of a writer covering the case. The old war horse's shoulders hunched up revealing a doubt of his own. He asked, "Whaddaya think?"

——— 40 ———

Schlesinger knew what the scratching had been all about, or at least what it might have been, Carl scratching all over, scratching the top of his left wrist. It seemed staged, he thought, meant to convince him that the scratches in the Polaroids had been self-inflicted. Lederer had done a very good job, working right down to the wire to bolster her case. Looked a little haggard at the end. Hoffinger's scenario of subintentional suicide was ridiculous. He was very meticulous, though. The doorman separated those voices; the ones that were directed at him were different from the screams. He was very effective, credible in spite of his handicap. Bobby Tong. That story about hearing the window. Not credible. The goddess taking flight. There was Hoffinger overloading again. Odd sort of person, Carl. He probably did it. Fifteen years was the least he would have to serve, if found guilty. Interesting case. Very close call.

The telephone brought bad news. A friend had died, a fellow judge. He would have to go to the funeral tomorrow morning. He made a few phone calls himself. He postponed handing down the verdict to 12:30 the next afternoon, Friday, February 11.

VERDICT DUE TODAY IN DEATH OF ARTIST

With that headline, the *New York Times* finally broke its silence with a story that Friday morning. They had sent their art-page man downtown a couple of days earlier, Douglas McGill, who usually wrote the "Art People" column in Friday's entertainment section. His article was a balanced report of what Hoffinger and Lederer had said the day before, but today the *Times* was represented by a more experienced courthouse reporter. He sat in the front row with the regulars, reading notes to catch up.

Word had spread that the decision would be delayed, but by noon there were about sixty people in the public part of the courtroom, more than ever before; the right side, "Carl's" section, remained almost empty. There was a day off in the Chambers trial, President's Day coming up, and a long weekend for many. Three weeks of looking at the same faces made it all feel like a family affair in 1333. All of the witnesses had been relieved of their obligations, and some of them were in the courtroom, Raquel and Tom seated alongside her mother. Hoffinger's wife, Bunny, sat on the right side with their daughter, Fran, a Legal Aid attorney who was waiting for one of her own cases to be called. Gerry Rosen looked on from an aisle seat.

Schlesinger was in place, sentencing a second-offender drug dealer who could speak no English. A Spanish-language court translator told him he got four and a half to nine. Carl showed up three minutes before the appointed hour of judgment. He found a seat in the last row, unfolded a back issue of the *Times Book Review*, and appeared to be reading. His Crystal Palace show had opened in Madrid the day before. He looked well scrubbed, his hair and his beard freshly trimmed. If he was going to prison today, he was going clean.

The People against Carl Andre was called at 12:37. No matter what, it was the last time. A media-pool photographer named Monica Almeida trained her camera on the defense table. She started shooting when Carl sat between his lawyers. He had taken off his padded overcoat, revealing a crisp pair of blue overalls. He stood when the judge began to speak. Hoffinger stood alongside him. Lederer, looking composed to the quick in her dark suit, watched from the prosecution's side. Carl's hands were deep in pockets deeper than the reach of his arms.

Schlesinger apologized for the delay and explained that a friend had died. "I have reached a verdict in this case," he said next. Every soul living and dead was still. He had chosen the words he was about to say with care; they were intended to reflect the closeness of his decision. "I have concluded that the evidence has not satisfied me beyond a reasonable doubt that the defendant is guilty."

Nothing that was Carl but his skin showed on the outside. Hoffinger turned loose a small smile and cuffed his client on the neck. Tears rolled from Raquel's eyes. The silence persisted. Hoffinger asked that Carl be "exonerated" from bail. Schlesinger of course granted that. Hoffinger then wanted the record of the case sealed. As required in a favorable judgment by New York State law, Schlesinger granted that, too. There was nothing more he could grant.

"Have a good day," said the judge, turning to the next case on his endless docket.

Carl gathered up his coat, scarf, and cap, slung his book bag over his left shoulder, and rushed up the center aisle toward the double swinging doors. Hoffinger, Weiner, and Sherman flanked him, the press trailing and gaining. Artist Barbara Kruger pushed her way through to Carl as he started through the doorway.

"Congratulations, Carl," she said sarcastically, "it's the best press you've had in ten years."

He was a free man now. He shot a remark right back at her, sharply, proudly. "Justice has been served!"

By now he was surrounded by journalists soliciting comment. Carl and his lawyers broke through.

"Justice has been served," he said again.

He went off in the wave to the bank of elevators down the hall and around a bend. They caught one going up. They were headed for the green door of the lawyers' lounge on the sixteenth floor to celebrate the justice that had been served.

The reporters in the corridor regrouped around Raquel and her mother now.

Ana's mother said, "I know he killed my daughter."

Raquel said, "He's getting away with murder now. But no one gets away with anything in this world. He'll get his just rewards sometime. Just wait and see."

CARL DIDN'T CELEBRATE for very long. Hoffinger continued taking calls from the press, praising the system for having worked, because you never knew whether it would or not. But Carl left by a back exit and walked home alone to 34E. Paula called from Spain. He said he was relieved. She said the show in Madrid was beautiful. He was glad to hear that. He made a call to Chester, Connecticut, to Sol LeWitt. Sol wasn't home, and he left a message with Carol's mother. Sol called back a little later.

"Justice has been served," Carl said.

"I congratulate you," said Sol.

There was nothing but silence after that. Carl said good-bye and hung up.

EPILOGUE

—— 41 ——

I have only a few vague recollections of Ana alive. She is always at a distance, never closer than at the opposite end of a long table, ten or twelve of us eating out one night in Rome; she is always a dark-haired, high-key presence engaged with the people around her. I had heard about her sometimes boisterous ways. Distance was fine with me. When she died, and the news and gossip were everywhere you went that season in Rome, I was rather astonished by the number of people whom I knew well who had gotten to know Ana and Carl. Only much later did I discover what a collection of friendships she gathered wherever she went, but at the time, when my wonder subsided, I simply never thought of her again.

Months later, in the winter of 1986, a woman who had been close to Ana approached me with a suggestion that I write a book about the case. She was quite partisan about it, and though a writer herself, she admitted to being too emotionally attached to her dead friend to do the job as she thought it ought to be done. Fairly early in our conversation, I asked the regulation first question of my inquisitive profession: did she know anything about the events that was not already known? When she said no, we spoke of other things and lost touch after saying good-bye.

More than a year passed before I heard even a mention of either Ana or Carl. I was in New York in March 1987 when an acquaintance with whom I was discussing other matters quite unexpectedly made a similar recommendation. The bits of lodestone attracting these propositions, I gathered, were my knowing those people in Rome and, to a lesser extent, in New York who had been friends of the couple. Once again, I asked the same old question, but unlike the bearer of the earlier proposal, his answer was yes.

"Tell me," I said.

"Well, the poor guy is being victimized by a feminist cabal," he said.

Intrigued, I was suddenly brought up-to-date in one sitting by an extremely knowledgeable observer on much of what had transpired in the interim. What had probably started it all in the first place was that on that very day, the *Times* had run a story I'd missed about Carl being indicted for the third time. My informant, I learned, not only knew Carl personally but had recently married a woman who had been a very close friend and associate of Carl's for many years. I met her shortly afterward, and because of what followed, I must have passed, as pass we must, a first screening.

There was of course no doubt where their sentiments lay. They were solidly in the camp that viewed Carl as suffering a grave injustice. He had become the innocent prey of a high-flying district attorney propelled by the twin engines of a media-class defendant on one wing and women's rights activists on the other. This being a far better story than day-to-day murder, I was very attentive to what they had to say, and I imagined that they saw in me a disinterested writer who might air Carl's ordeal and set the record "straight." What was implied in the bargain, though never actually stated, was access to Carl himself and thus a journalistic exclusive. Having gotten this far, I was, at my request, provided with copies of all the press clippings on the case until then, the most comprehensive being Joyce Wadler's article in *New York,* an anathema no less on Carl's side than on Ana's. I was also given some important introductions and privileged documents as well, though meeting Carl still lay in the future.

A difficulty arose when my reading of the material to which they had steered me did not agree with theirs—not that anyone ever asked my opinion. Nevertheless, I simply didn't see Carl as being persecuted by adversarial scheming. To be sure, there were people who in their passions had suspended the notion of fairness, but I was more inclined to agree with those who, like Gerry Marzorati, saw the feminists as being strangely silent. Not being far enough inclined, however, I made no effort to try to learn why. I took a beaten path instead, saying nothing while retreating.

Word reached me in Italy that summer that Carl's trial was scheduled to begin in November. Again, many months had passed in which

Breaking the Seal, 1988–1990

my interest in the case, such as it was, had been diverted, but I decided to attend the trial to witness, for one thing, the best presentations of the advocates on both sides of the story. I arrived some days in advance of the appointed hour only to learn of the two-month postponement. Hoping to turn my personal inconvenience to some benefit, I proceeded to use the waiting period for independent research.

I used the information in Joyce Wadler's article as a guide to some of the players, and before long I began to run into some of the same problems she had had two years before me, namely hostile silence. I had some small but critical advantages, however. First were those personal relationships with friends, or friends of friends, of the protagonists.[1] Second, I was under no pressure of anything like a deadline or any other kind of commitment. I could bide my time. Third, the case was at the end of a particularly long cycle; a court decision, one way or the other, could be expected to weaken resolves of silence. When people know something that other people do not, it seems safe to state as a general rule, eternal reticence is a rare response. I therefore continued my research with a certain amount of confidence gained from having been in similar positions before.

Before long, however, I discovered that I had been living in, or at best in the neighborhood of, a fool's paradise. I had underestimated the old-boy insularity of the art world, where a suspicion of strangers had been ingrained long before my time; these old boys and old girls were more attached to the code of *omertà*, as it is called in the Cosa Nostra, than the Cosa Nostra. To complicate matters, I was caught unprepared by my own ignorance of one of the provisions of the New York State Criminal Procedure Law; it permits the sealing, indeed resealing, of court documents *after* they have been made public. When, following Carl's acquittal, Judge Schlesinger adhered to the defense request to seal the records, he in effect turned back the clock on the case to the

[1]This led to an introduction to Carl shortly before the trial. He was less than receptive. A series of letters over time, requesting an interview and offering all ethical guarantees regarding its presentation, brought only one postcard in reply. I had sent him a copy of my biography of filmmaker Rainer Werner Fassbinder, to which he responded: "2 APR 88 . . . THANK YOU FOR YOUR BOOK ON FASSBINDER. HE WAS TRULY A MASTER OF HIS AGE. PAX. @ carl andre."

moment *before* Carl picked up the phone and called 911. There is, according to state law, no record of the call, no record of the trial, and no record of anything in between.

By the self-contradictory nature of this regional law, at the moment of the sealing I was suddenly catapulted into a rather unique position. If you eliminated the judge, the prosecution, and the defense, I was the only witness to virtually all of the records now entombed like the pharaohs for all time. The only other person I could think of who had attended every moment of the trial and the preliminary hearings was Ana's mother. But apart from my being an outside observer, I, unlike her or anyone else to my knowledge, had had access to the pretrial records, a mass of material that included a significant part of the grand jury minutes.

Carl had excluded his own friends from the courtroom. Small groups of Ana's friends had sat in at various times during the proceedings. Scanty and sporadic press coverage had relayed little more than the box score. The defendant had in fact had the closest thing to a secret trial on this side of the world. In his case, that may have pleased him, but now no independent investigator starting fresh could ever learn anything from the primary sources about the twenty-nine months of inquiry into Ana's death. Her death had by default been declared by the state as having been caused by forces not only unknown but unknowable. There was something medieval and musty about it all.

It was under the impact of this singular state of affairs that, shortly after Carl's acquittal, I decided to write this book.

I SET OUT to break the seal, to recover as much as I could about this woeful story so that it would not die with the victim. I had no other intention. My ignorance of the law did not extend to the United States Constitution, and I knew that the Fifth Amendment protected Carl Andre from ever being placed at legal risk again. People who have in fact experienced double jeopardy in countries where the provisions of the Fifth Amendment are nonexistent cherish that law as much as anyone can, and I, it so happened, am one of them. Moreover, I believed that in Carl's case, in spite of being characterized by what might be termed an *absence* of justice, the system as a whole had worked. The search and seizure provisions of the Fourth Amendment, the Fifth Amendment right of the accused not to bear witness against himself, and his Sixth Amendment right to counsel had joined together to tip the scales in a way that failed to satisfy the judge of the defendant's guilt beyond a reasonable doubt. Tipping the scales, sometimes more than other times, is their precise function. Whatever one thought about guilt or non-guilt in this case, the precious principle that it is better to set ten guilty people free than to convict one innocent person had been safeguarded. What a thrill it was to sit in court day after day during the hearings observing judge, prosecution, and defense put forward the finest points of the Bill of Rights, all for the benefit of one accused party. People had gone to the electric chair and the gas chamber when those very amendments had been abused. Carl was partially right. Justice was served. Justice for future defendants was reinforced. Justice for Ana Mendieta, however, was buried alive.

Time in the end proved to be a friend in my travels. A month or so after the trial, Jan Hoffman published her long and thorough article in the *Voice*. Most of her interviews had been conducted after the acquittal, and though she had met up with the usual inhospitality from those closest to Carl, she found people to talk to who had been silent while the case was still in the courts, including three or four of Carl's ex-lovers and "one influential art world figure" who claimed to have witnessed Carl striking a woman in public. They all requested anonymity ("If my name is used, I'll never get shown at Paula Cooper"), but she had found the atmosphere in Soho somewhat less stifling than it had been. A few weeks later, Judd Tully published in the *New Art Examiner* what became the last article on the case. Even Ana's friends were more outspoken than ever, and both Hoffman and Tully had gotten sharp quotes from a couple of Carl's friends who had allowed themselves to be identified. After almost three years of mum as the word, it sounded almost like an open debate.

By then, I had been at it myself for months, and my experience agreed with theirs. As more time went by, I was, with the help of old friends and new, able to develop fresh sources of information. I also succeeded in amplifying my personal library of the official record. It was substantially complete.[2]

In Iowa, interviewing Ana's friends and family in June 1988, I discovered an important piece of new evidence. It had been lying among papers that Ana's brother, Ignacio, had long forgotten. It consisted of eighteen pages of handwritten notes spanning the first several days after Ana's death—the notes Ignacio had begun to take down the night Raquel called from Spring Valley to tell him the terrible news. Part of their significance related directly to the trial. These notes formed a contemporaneous record of what the police, mostly Detective Finelli, were telling Raquel about the case, particularly about the events of the day that led to Carl's arrest. The defense challenge to police credibility on the basis of faded memories, a major undertaking throughout the case but especially at the trial, loses its force entirely with one reading of Ignacio's notes. Almost every major and minor detail in the entire police testimony is corroborated. Had this document come to light six months earlier, it would have been admissible at the trial.

Ignacio's notes are of even greater consequence in terms of completing the story. They coincide with Natalia's account of her last phone call with Ana as she told it to Finelli and Bashford in Raquel's presence on the Monday after Ana died. Although it would have been inadmissible as evidence at the trial, the following section of these notes made on the same Monday (to which I have added punctuation only) is certainly pertinent:

Natalia called. Talked at 1:00 A.M. Ana was going to divorce, get detective. Photo copies, all in Rome. Photo copies of recent trip in Mercer St. Very mad, was talking. Was not drunk. Organized. "Should I say something to him?" Was scared. Karl [sic] vengeful, vindictive. End of conversation.

It was Jack Hoffinger, when he sought to suppress the infidelity records, who first drew my attention to the photocopies by insisting there were none. The police, he had argued, had violated the terms of

[2]See the section Sources and Notes for a description.

the search warrant by seizing material other than what had been stipulated. No one paid him much mind, but he was right. In my posttrial research, new evidence emerged demonstrating that the missing photocopies had been removed or destroyed sometime between the late afternoon of the Sunday of Carl's arrest and midmorning of the next day.

Here, once again, is the sequence of events: At the pretrial hearing, both Finelli and Nieves testified to witnessing Carl give the keys to his apartment to an unidentified friend sometime between 3:30 and 4:00 P.M.[3] Natalia Delgado, on Monday morning, called Ana, hearing from Gerry Rosen that she was dead, that Carl had been arrested, and that he was his lawyer "looking for some things." Aware of the photocopies both in 34E and in the apartment in Rome, Natalia alerted the police in New York that afternoon. Bashford and Finelli obtained the warrant and that evening 34E was searched, but the photocopies were gone. Bashford suspected that Rosen may indeed have removed them, but since he was Carl's lawyer, client-attorney secrecy laws would, she felt, prevent her from getting any further, and she dropped the matter. Rosen, however, did not remove them. He retrieved the keys to 34E, along with Carl's bag of personal papers, at eleven o'clock Monday morning from Carl's friend Nancy Haynes. Once inside the apartment, he removed only what Carl instructed him to—his financial portfolio. Since Rosen held onto the keys until he was fired, by the time he got to 34E, the photocopies were already gone.

What does all this mean? As a result of the ruling that the divorce issue was inadmissible, the infidelity records were never introduced at the trial, and neither was the set of photocopies found in Rome. As the proof they were meant to be, they were innocuous, but the absence of the photocopies in 34E, like the absence of footprints, was strong negative evidence. It showed that sometime after Ana had hung up after speaking to Natalia for the last time, Carl learned of their existence. Ana had taken Natalia's advice not to put it off, and she did indeed "say something to him." No one on that Sunday could have

---

[3]This testimony was unrelated to the photocopies. It was meant to affirm that Carl was not yet in custody and was free to do whatever he pleased.

known the import of the photocopies. They had to be concealed. That Carl was concealing something is indisputable. When after washing his hands that morning he saw Officer Connolly looking into his storage room he said, "I don't want you in there" and closed the door; his written authorization some hours later permitting Finelli and the Crime Scene Unit into 34E singled out the same "attic room" as off limits. It was not until the warrant was executed that the room was searched—ten hours after even Gerry Rosen had gone. At the trial, Hoffinger had argued that "even innocent people hide things" and that consciousness of guilt is the weakest form of proof. Fair enough, but this one brings us a step closer to what happened in 34E.

I HAVE COME no closer than what has been set down in this book. Much remains sealed, perhaps forever. The law on sealing public records, however, which runs so contrary to the modern concept of the First Amendment freedoms of information and the public's right to know, is of course amendable. It is not a tried and tested statute, and while other states have similar provisions, it is far from being the law of the land.

This statute arose as an outgrowth of the 1964 Civil Rights Act. It was originally meant to protect people accused and later exonerated of wrongdoing from wrongdoing on the part of the police and other law-enforcement agencies. It provided for the destruction of the acquitted person's fingerprint files and police photos, which, by virtue of the exoneration, the authorities had no legitimate business possessing. This was a commendable, long overdue advance of individual freedom. It could only enhance and in no way impinge on the freedom of others. In the New York State version, this right is guaranteed in the first two operative paragraphs of the law.

It was adopted in 1976 along with a third paragraph, later revised, closing *all* the records in criminal cases that end in acquittals. The well-meaning intention was to protect the privacy of the individuals concerned. Only the person acquitted has the power to grant access to the records.[4] To a large extent, this too may be considered as progress

---

[4]There are a few narrow exceptions that apply to law-enforcement authorities only. In my final letter to Carl, I appealed to him, in the interest of completeness, to exercise

regarding the freedoms upheld in a democratic society, though the possibility of a conflict of interests between individual privacy and the right to information is well recognized as inherent. Where, however, a part of that law allows the individual to *remove* documents that once belonged to the public from its domain, it comes up against the force of logic and does impinge on the freedoms of the community at large. Until the seal is evoked, the transcript of any trial in progress and the pretrial records of the case are public documents. They can be freely consulted and copies can be purchased from the court. This is a guarantee of the First Amendment. The seal law ought not be allowed to become a license to make certain trials secret. The public has the right to know how justice is being dispensed in *every* criminal case, particularly murder, not just the ones the state wins. No one protected by the Fifth Amendment, no matter how private a person by nature or desire, needs that much privacy. It is an insult to the First Amendment. In this case, it was also the final insult to Ana Mendieta.

SOMETIME AFTER THE trial, a meeting was held at Paula Cooper's Gallery. It was attended by Paula, Carl, and others whom I have failed to positively identify. It was decided that no one among the participants would ever speak again of the case. There was nothing new about this except its being a posttrial renewal of the strategy of silence to support Carl's understandable wish to get on with his life as a free man. His ordeal was over, and Carl hoped, in Paula's words, "it would all go away." It was to be the start of a new era of one kind or another. Minimalism was making a strong comeback, and Carl needed, not the least financially, to come back, too.

In the spring of that year, he had his first one-man exhibition in the United States since Ana's death. It was a very private, unusual affair, somewhat reminiscent of the installation of the travertine cross in Rome after she died. It took place in an annex to the Soho gallery run by Julian Pretto and was not open to the public. One received an

---

his right to open the files. It was unacknowledged. But his was not the last word. In January 1989, through a third party, I was offered a copy of the official trial transcript at the standard court cost, about $3,500; since it would have been tantamount to bribing a public official, I refused.

R.S.V.P. invitation, and there was no formal opening. It consisted of three pieces, all of them very unlike Carl's normal work, and they lent themselves to manifold interpretation. One was a mason's trowel without a handle, another an abstract crucifixion, but it was the third, or rather the most prominent piece, that received the most attention. It was a real window. A wood-frame window, four feet, nine inches high and two feet, seven inches wide, hung on a blank white wall. There was no pane, but it was closed and made opaque by metal screening. In the lower part of window, the screen was torn.

One of Carl's admirers found it "gutsy"; others who were less impressionable considered it yet one more oddity. Of the many critics who viewed it, all but one preferred not to comment in print. The reviewer who did, Alfred Mac Adam, writing in the art magazine *Contemporanea,* not surprisingly saw death as its central theme. He wondered if Carl was speaking of "our own death . . . or is it the death of others that grants us a postponement, a displacement to someone else of the inevitable?"

By the following spring, Carl was back to his old self again, at least artwise, with a perfectly conventional, highly advertised one-man show of new sculpture and old poems at Paula Cooper's. In the meantime, he had been in many group exhibitions in the United States and Europe. His sales had picked up sharply. His prices at auction followed the general explosive trend and continue to do so. With the passage of time, the pact of silence was breached here and there, but most of the stalwarts remained true, trying at times to plug the holes. The relevance of their efforts, however, beyond pleasing Carl, grew increasingly obscure.

The sculptor-poet recovered a lot of old ground, getting out to his old haunts in Soho, visiting the galleries to see the work of others, and contributing his name and his work to the latest good causes. His old champion John Russell of the *Times,* admiring the show at Paula's, returned to his side after a long absence in which he was reviewed critically by other *Times* writers or ignored by the newspaper. Last summer, after so long a hiatus, Carl was back on the interview circuit, sounding a little rusty but tossing off self-effacing epigrams once more. "I feel much more comfortable in Europe than I do in most of Amer-

Breaking the Seal, 1988–1990

ica," he told a young artist-interviewer. "But then my work went out of fashion 3,000 years ago." His grandfather, some of his readers learned for the first time, was a bricklayer and his father had worked in the shipyards. There was never a time in his childhood when poetry was not part of his family life. To have been born and raised before the advent of television was an incalculable blessing. "When people ask me what my art communicates I cannot help but think of what the gravestone says to the corpse beneath."

He had been through the system as few men before him, and he was back.

THREE DAYS AFTER the trial, at a garish East Village night place called the Chameleon Club, a benefit was held to aid Nicaraguan artists. In all the raucous sound and darkness, it was hard to figure out what it consisted of, but at one point in the evening, a woman dressed in black named Nancy Berliner got up on the platform and began shouting at her loudest, "History get back!" Truth to tell, she didn't exactly rivet everyone's attention, the room proving to be a tough one, but the history she was warding off in a scheduled performance piece was, she explained, the history of women "flying out of windows." Although she had not known either Ana or Carl, she had just spent the past two weeks or so attending the trial, taking notes, and writing the work she was now enacting. It was a long poem, part pamphlet, part ballad, one artist's protest of the outcome of the trial. Since every woman, she said, was a potential candidate for "having an accident with a man," it was her outcry as a woman, too. Another woman that same month entered Angela Westwater's gallery in Soho, where an Andre sculpture was on exhibit, and attached a sheet of paper to it, a passage from *Crime and Punishment*. Artist Howardena Pindell, when asked by Judd Tully for his posttrial article if she viewed the decision at the trial as in some way symbolic of the position of women in the arts, particularly women of color like herself, replied, "Oh, sure, I see it as totally symbolic: your life isn't worth shit." She voiced the anger of many minority artists, saying, "The art world is segregated as it is. I know if Ana had been an Anglo and if Carl had been black, the art world would have lynched him."

There was a fear, and in some quarters a hope, that Ana would become a kind of Third World martyr, but before very long it subsided. More predictable things happened. Ana's art continues to be made known. Recent exhibitions have been held in galleries and museums in New York and Los Angeles and elsewhere. Many more are planned. A documentary video made about Ana's life and work, titled *Fuego de Tierra* and first shown at the New Museum retrospective, circulates nationally. The film contains vivid footage of interviews with Ana shot by Cuban television, Ana recalling her origins, remembering the stories she heard as a child of her great-grandfather General de Rojas, still a national hero of the War of Independence, remembering, too, how she and her sister were sent away to grow up in a distant land. The spirit of her ways, which bore on so many lives, reshaping some forever, is visible.

THE LIVES GO on, of course. The art world, or that portion of it that tore apart, has not yet knitted together again very well. Few mention the case anymore, but people in Soho continue to shun others who were once old friends. At openings, you can still sense ripples of tension when certain familiar faces appear. Men and women walk down some streets not to chance down others, trying to avoid being seen or seeing what they hope they will never see again. It is hard to find peace in a place of silent hearts.

SOURCES AND NOTES

The primary sources of this book are more than two hundred interviews, unpublished correspondence and other privileged documents, pretrial records, and extensive notes made during my full attendance of the preliminary hearings prior to the trial and the trial as well. I have also had access to notes made at the trial by Judd Tully and Raquel Oti Mendieta and notes made as a result of discussions with others who attended the trial both as observers and participants.[1]

The vast majority of the interviews were conducted between November 1987 and December 1989. Some of them, which took place between friends and acquaintances, may be better described as conversations. Everyone knew in advance what the information related was for. More than 95 percent of the people involved did not ask for any restrictions regarding the way their interviews would be presented. They spoke freely of what they knew, some more comfortably than others. With the exception of one person who had personal knowledge of Ana's Iowa period, no one was promised total anonymity.

Of the balance of less than 5 percent, there were three categories of requests for conditions: subjects who during the course of the interview asked that their names not be cited regarding parts of what they were about to say; subjects who would agree to speak only if all of what they said were not attributed directly to them; and a very small number

---

[1]The pretrial records acquired consist of the 911 transcript, the original felony complaint, transcripts of the bail hearing and a second pre–grand jury hearing, the indictment, the autopsy and other forensic reports, and the entire set of eighteen documents filed by the prosecution, the defense, and the court in connection with the outcome of the three grand jury proceedings and the pretrial hearings. These contain large portions of the grand jury minutes as well as material appended from other records in the case.

of persons who sometime after they had spoken unconditionally had second thoughts—in one case more than a year later—and sought to withdraw parts or all of what they had said. A journalist's only obligation is to respect the wishes of the persons in the first two categories. Unlike the laws on the sealing of public records, the ground rules of interviews do not provide for the purging of information once it has been freely divulged.

On the other hand, there may have been dire personal circumstances that led to these unusual turnabouts, though if there were, they are known only to the individuals involved. In view of this possibility, I will adopt the following method of citing my sources. Where I use the letter *I* for "interview" (or, as the case may be, "conversation") followed by a person's name, the reader may take it to mean that there is a more than 95 percent chance that the source is the actual person cited. There thus remains a less than five percent chance that the source was someone else: an unidentified person—to employ a journalistic convention—close enough to the person named to know the information related. In this way, anyone who feels that he or she may have committed an indiscretion has the option, should that be the person's desire, of claiming to be among the very small group who from the outset truly felt and expressed a need to remain once removed.

Let it be said, however, that nothing in this book, unless it is clearly stated, is further than once removed. Every spoken word or inner thought was either told to me directly by the person concerned or to someone else who told it to me. Nothing is the product of my imagination.

SOURCES

Abbreviations

Sources of Material

AEAM = Archives of the estate of Ana Mendieta
FC = Felony complaint (9/8/85)
GJM = Grand jury minutes
I = Interview

IMN	=	Ignacio Mendieta's notes in AEAM
L	=	Letter, memo, or other correspondence
LHB	=	AM's letters and postcards to Hans Breder, 1978–1979
PHN	=	Preliminary hearings notes
PTR	=	Pretrial records
T-1	=	Transcript of 9/9/85 (bail hearing)
T-2	=	Transcript of 9/13/85
TEX	=	Trial exhibit
TN	=	Trial notes

Interview Sources Cited

DAt	=	Dotty Attie	SK	=	Stephen Koch
MB	=	Martha Bashford	DK	=	Dieter Kopf
NB	=	Nancy Berliner	BKt	=	Barbara Kruger
HB	=	Hans Breder	AK	=	Annette Kuhn
RB	=	Romolo Bulla	EL	=	Elizabeth Lederer
RoB	=	Rosalba Bulla	SL	=	Sol LeWitt
LC	=	Lucy Clink	CL	=	Carol LeWitt
ECo	=	Ester Coen	LL	=	Lucy Lippard
PC	=	Paula Cooper	JM	=	Jack McRae
EC	=	Eduardo Costa	GM	=	Gerald Marzorati
AC	=	Alvin Curran	JM	=	James Melchert
ND	=	Natalia Delgado	MAM	=	Mary Ann Melchert
SD	=	Stavros Deligeorges	IM	=	Ignacio Mendieta
WE	=	Wendy Evans	RMH	=	Raquel Mendieta Har-
DF	=	Daniela Ferraria			rington
RF	=	Ronald Finelli	ROM	=	Raquel Oti Mendieta
AF	=	Andrew Forge	AM	=	Ann Minich
JG	=	Joan Geller	RMM	=	Robert Morgenthau
JGR	=	Jeremy Gilbert-Rolfe	FM	=	Francesco Moschini
LG	=	Leon Golub	EM	=	Ed Mojzis
JuG	=	Juan Gonzalez	MPN	=	Mary Perot Nichols
TH	=	Tom Harrington	GO	=	Gerry Ordover
ZH	=	Zarina Hashmi	IP	=	Ida Panicelli
CH	=	Christian Haub	MP	=	Marsha Pels
EH	=	Elizabeth Hess	JP	=	John Perreault
JSH	=	Jack S. Hoffinger	JeP	=	Jeff Perrone
JH	=	Jan Hoffman	HPt	=	Howardena Pindell

LP	=	Liliana Porter	MSu	=	Mark Sullivan
RR	=	Ruby Rich	GS	=	Gary Simon
GR	=	Gerry Rosen	LSt	=	Lowery Sims
WR	=	Warren Rosen	NS	=	Nancy Spero
AR	=	Alex Rosenberg	GES	=	Gian Enzo Sperone
RR	=	Robert Rosenblum	MTt	=	Modesto Torre
AS	=	Alvin Schlesinger	CT	=	Calvin Tomkins
ES	=	Edith Schloss	TV	=	Ted Victoria
CSt	=	Carolee Schneemann	JW	=	Joyce Wadler
JS	=	Julius Schmidt	PW	=	Pat Weaver
MAS	=	Mary Angela Schroth	LWt	=	Lawrence Weiner
MS	=	Mike Sherman	JWt	=	John Wessel
		t	=	Interview by Judd Tully	

Witness Testimony

Pretrial Hearing, January 20–28, 1988

Witnesses	Date Testified
P.O. Michael Connolly	1/21/88
P.O. Robert Baumert	"
Det. Ronald Finelli	1/21–22/88
P.O. Louis Capolupo	1/25/88
A.D.A. Martha Bashford	"
Det. Anthony J. Amplo	"
Det. Gary Ward	"
Det. Richard Nieves	1/26/88
Sgt. Joseph Ayers	1/27/88
Douglas Ohlson	"
Gerry Rosen	"

Trial, January 29–February 11, 1988

Principal Witnesses	Date Testified
Natalia Delgado	1/29/88
Edward Mojzis	"
P.O. Robert Baumert	"
Al Nodal	2/1/88
Ida Panicelli	"
Spiros Pappas	"

Harry Leandrou	"
P.O. Michael Connolly	2/1–2/88
Modesto Torre	2/2/88
Marsha Pels	"
Craig Vaughn	"
P.O. Louis Capolupo	"
Det. Gary Ward	"
Dr. Donald B. Hoffman	2/3/88
Det. Ronald Finelli	"
Dr. Joacquin Gutierrez	"
Martha Bashford	2/4/88
Det. Anthony J. Amplo	"
Tom Harrington	"
Raquel Harrington	"
Eli Lederman	"
Alison Bierman	"
Bobby Tong	"
Ronnie Ginnever	"
Bridget Knapp	2/5/88
Cesar Trasobares	"
Dr. Robert Knaff	"
Lawrence Weiner	"
Alice Weiner	"
Elaine Miner	"
Dr. Dominic de Maio	2/6/88
Filip Bool	"
David Bourdon	"
Dr. David Preven	"
Dr. Kurt Dubowski	"
Nancy Spero	2/9/88
Det. Richard Nieves	"

Negative Sources

The following persons refused to be interviewed for this book:

Carl Andre (on being told that the book was being written): "A pity."

Rudolf Baranik: "I have nothing to add."

David Bourdon: "I am reluctant to be probed with 'what ifs?,' 'isn't it possibles?' and 'why do you thinks?' "

Rosemarie Castoro: "I don't think we should meet."

Emile De Antonio: "Carl will be very upset when he hears about this."
Nancy Haynes: No response to follow-up letter.
Brenda Miller: "I don't want to talk to you about it, OK?"
Mary Miss: "I wouldn't feel comfortable."
Douglas Ohlson: "I cannot be of help."
Julian Pretto: "I don't wish to quote Carl [hangs up]."
Frank Stella: No response.
May Stevens: Claims not to have received mail or phone messages.
Marjorie Strider: "I don't want to be involved."
Angela Westwater: "I'm sorry. Good-bye [hangs up]."

NOTES

Mercer Street: Sunday, September 8, 1985

One

1:    "a jumper down": Connolly in PHN.
1:    "small shake": Leandrou in TN.
2:    "voice from high up": ibid.
2:    touched for a pulse: Baumert in PHN.
3:    "My life is over": Connolly in PHN and TN.
3:    wash his hands: Connolly and Capolupo in PHN and TN.
3:    "maybe I did kill her": Connolly in PTR, GJM, and PHN.
4:    "I just know": Capolupo in PHN.
4:    description of bedroom: photos in TEX.
5:    "a bunch of boulders": Connolly in PHN.
5:    "No, no, no, no": Ed Mojzis in PTR, GJM, TN, and I-EM.
6:    A sharp "No": I-EM.
6:    "heard a woman screaming": Mojzis in PTR, GJM, TN, and I-EM.
6:    "do the paperwork": Capolupo in PHN.
7:    "read me my rights": Baumert in PHN.

Two

7:    AM's return to New York: in PTR, GJM, and I-ND, I-RMH, I-MT, I-EC, I-MP, I-JP, et al.
7:    the last evening in Rome: I-ECo and I-JWt.

9:	"Dear Passion Flower": L in AEAM.
9:	"I'm FULL": ibid.
9:	"Carl gets lonely": I-RHM and I-ND.
9:	"again and again,": L in AEAM.
10:	"I want to marry": I-ROM.
10:	"Don't we look good": I-MP and I-RMH.

Three

10:	alone on a bench: Finelli in PHN and I-RF.
11:	raise 911: Finelli in PHN.
11–12:	911 tape: transcript in PTR; the actual tape was played three times in PHN and TN.
12:	"pedigree": Finelli in PHN.
13–14:	Carl's story: Finelli and Nieves in PHN, Finelli in TN; also IMN.
13:	piece of skin: I-RF.
13:	"happened to her": Nieves in PHN.
13:	"took a pill and disappeared": Finelli in PHN.
14:	Listen, pal: I-RF.

Four

14:	conversations she had with others: I-MT, I-TV, I-LP, I-RR, I-EC.
15:	lawyer who was working: Bernstein in PTR and GJM.
15:	both of them offered: I-MT and I-MP.
15:	One of those mornings: I-HB.
16:	"Ani, I don't think": I-RMH.
16–18:	autopsy report: PTR and AEAM.

Five

18:	moment of terror: I-RF.
19:	"cancel our dinner": Finelli and Connolly in PHN and TN.
19:	"unmendable": Finelli in PHN and TN; Ginnever in TN testified that she received a call with the word "unmendable."
19:	seven photographs: Ward in PHN.
19:	"this is Natalia": I-ND.
20:	violent argument: Nieves in PHN, Coler in PTR and GJM, and Tong in TN; also IMN.
20:	"the word get-go": I-RF.

20:       scrambled eggs: I-RF.

21:       dinner for twelve: I-AK, I-MPN, I-WE, I-LP, I-LW.

21:       "quite feisty": Ginnever in TN.

21:       "gonna-be-famous": I-WE.

21:       the Andres shouting: Coler in PTR and GJM.

21:       "just another weirdness": I-WE.

22:       "Ana is dead": Ohlson in PHN.

22:       "later this afternoon": ibid.

22:       "know a good lawyer": ibid.

23:       "passing his visitor": Finelli and Nieves in PHN.

23:       "English better than me": Finelli in PHN and TN.

23:       "the horrible belief": statement in PTR.

24:       trying to outfox them: I-MB, I-EL, and I-RMH.

24:       Ayers told his men: Ayers in PHN.

Six

25:       "dentist at three": I-RMH.

25:       "all this stuff": I-RMH and GJM.

26–28:   Rosen's background: I-GR.

27:       "Something terrible has happened": Ohlson in PHN.

28:       "Carl really needs help": I-GR and Rosen in PHN.

28:       "hot-shot artist": I-MB.

29:       "a cat scratch": Bashford in TN.

29:       how she would proceed: I-MB.

29:       "this looks serious": Finelli in PHN.

30:       "no problem": Rosen in PHN and I-GR.

30:       "Can you believe": I-MB.

30:       "very, very fresh": I-GR.

30:       "homicide is greater": I-GR; also I-MB.

31:       "He's under arrest": Finelli in PHN.

31:       "Do me a favor": I-GR.

32:       arcade photo booth: photos in AEAM.

32:       she would tease him: I-LP.

33:       third scratch: Finelli in PHN.

33:       imagined Ana's arms: I-RF.

Seven

33:	the Lion's Head: I-AK and I-MPN.
34:	calls kept coming: I-WE and I-LP.
34:	Finelli's call to Raquel: I-RMH.
36:	"very bad to tell": I-IM.
36:	he feels guilty: I-ROM.

Havana: 1948–1961

Eight

37:     sit there enthralled: I-RMH.

38:     gifts to adorn: interview in Cuba with Raquel "Kaki" Mendieta in the documentary film *Fuego de Tierra*. It also contains interviews with Ana Mendieta, Raquel Mendieta Harrington, Raquel Oti Mendieta, and Raquel Costa Mendieta. A partial transcript of the interview with Kaki Mendieta, by Nereyda Garcia-Ferraz, which is longer than the one in the film, appears in the literary quarterly *Sulfur*, Spring 1988, pp. 57–65, a special issue "featuring a tribute to Ana Mendieta."

38:     stories the children heard: I-RMH and I-ROM.

38:     permission to marry: I-ROM and I-RMH.

38:     baby book: AEAM.

39:     "was already black": Raquel Mendieta Harrington in *Fuego de Tierra*.

39:     "happiest day in my life": L in AEAM.

39:     madder than ever: I-RMH.

39:     out of the water: interview with Kaki Mendieta in *Sulfur*, Spring 1988, p. 59.

40:     "page is missing": I-RMH.

40:     "have some respect": ibid.

41:     "Look at all the bullets": ibid.

42:     "against my belief": I-ROM and I-RMH.

44:     keeping the family together: I-ROM, I-RMH, and I-IM.

45:     many evacuations: I-RMH.

46:     "tie me up": ibid.

46:     the only dollars: I-ROM and I-RMH.

47:     "I'm free": I-RMH.

Rikers Island: September 9–10, 1985

Nine

49:     "That's not true": Rosen in T-1.
49:     crossed out: FC.
49:     "until further notice": L I-GR.
49:     one of the first: I-GR.
51:     "looking for some things": phone call reconstructed from I-GR and I-ND; also Lederer in PTR and Rosen in PHN.
51–52: Natalia's background: I-ND.
52:     "these gringos": ibid.
53:     "do lunch": I-LSt.
54:     "something really happened": ibid.
54:     comforting Carl: I-GR.
55:     "Before you know it": I-MB.
55:     "asking me to overrule": Sayah in T-1.
55:     "poor Joe": I-GR.
56:     "That's your ruling": Rosen in T-1.
56:     "I want to retain": I-GR.

Ten

57:     "not a rubber stamp": Sayah in T-1.
57:     spent the morning: Bashford in T-1.
58:     no objection: Bashford in T-1.
58:     "No woman commits": I-RMH and I-TH; also IMN.
58:     "stop himself": I-TH.
59:     "I didn't talk": ibid.
59:     "That's not true": I-RMH; also IMN.
60:     "going to expose him": I-RMH and GJM.
61:     helped Bashford make sense: I-MB.
61:     photocopied an array: I-MB, I-ND, I-RMH, I-TH, Finelli in PHN and TN, and Bashford in TN; also IMN.
62:     "photocopying like crazy": I-ND; also IMN.
62:     Bashford assured her: I-MB, I-ND, I-RMH, and I-TH; also IMN.

Eleven

64:     "monolingual by choice": I-WE.
64:     "getting home scared": ibid.

65:      "The plans have changed": I-MP.
65:      "We're getting married": ibid.
65–69:   Rosen at work: I-GR.
69:      at 10:30 P.M.: Finelli and Ayers in PHN.
69:      going to Italy: I-MB.
70:      crime scene measurements: Amplo in PTR, GJM, PHN, and TN.
71:      infidelity records: PHN.
71:      "whole schmeer": Finelli in PHN.

Twelve

72:      "jet lag": *New York Post,* 9/10/85.
72:      "cash bail": New York *Daily News,* 9/10/85.
73:      "gifted and serious": *New York Times,* 9/10/85.
73:      aesthetic sister: I-CSt.
74:      "I kept listening": I-LL.
75:      Jane had not been flattered: I-GR.
75:      "got to get me out": ibid.
75:      until tomorrow: I-GO.
76:      expecting Carl: I-GES.
76:      yelled at his lawyer: I-GR.
76:      "I'll be back": ibid.
76:      the terse message: L, 9/10/85.
77:      Ordover's background: I-GO.
77:      "lawyers to Tahiti": ibid.
78:      sudden suicide: ibid.
78:      one of the friends: I-LW.
79:      his former client: in I-GO, Ordover did not identify his client, always referring to him as "this person," but Stella was identified by many others including in I-PC—the only "secret" revealed being that he put up *all* of the money; when asked in I-GO whether "this person" was Stella, Ordover neither confirmed nor denied it.
79:      he identified her: I-TH.
79:      see his wife's body: Finelli and Ayers relayed this to the Harringtons, I-RMH and I-TH; also IMN.
80:      "Don't cop out": I-GR.
80:      temporary insanity: ibid.
80:      "money on his art": I-GR.
81:      had called twice: I-GR and I-GO.

81:     "I always look": I-GR.
81:     "Good luck": ibid.

Thirteen

82:     interviewing the lawyers: I-GO.
82:     Paula Cooper's background: I-PC; see also J. Howell's cover story,
        "Quite Contrary," in *Art News*, 3/89, pp. 153–157.
83:     She had met him: I-PC.
83:     "give them away": ibid.
83:     "verbally very acerbic": ibid.
84:     "cantankerous attitude": V. Raynor (review) in the *New York
        Times*, 1/11/85, p. C18.
84:     grim company: I-GO and I-LW.
85:     "that's sculpture, too": quoted in C. Tomkins, "The Space Around
        Real Things," in *The New Yorker*, 9/10/84, p. 65. This is still the
        best profile of Stella and contains much about Carl Andre, who was
        a major contributor to it (hereinafter cited as Tomkins profile); see
        also P. Cummings, *Artists in Their Own Words*, New York, 1979,
        p. 190, where it is quoted the same way (Cummings's is the edited
        transcript of a long interview conducted with Carl Andre
        in 9/72—a valuable source hereinafter cited as Cummings
        interview).
85:     "prophetic remark": Cummings interview, p. 190.
85:     without further delay: I-GO and I-PC.
85:     computer went down: I-GO.
86:     "Thank God": ibid.
86:     "bitchy": I-LW.
87:     "I didn't mean that": ibid.
87:     "gotta get him back": I-GO.
87:     looking the happiest: ibid.
87:     "know what happened": I-LW.
87:     room for Carl: I-GO.
88:     "Carl's out": ibid.
88:     Stella also felt good: ibid. Ordover's account of his actions 9/10–
        11/85 is based on a memorandum he dictated for his own files on
        9/12/85.
88:     "Carl's lucky": I-PC.

Quincy, Massachusetts: 1935–1964

Fourteen

89:   "I have told them so": "An Interview with Carl Andre," p. 3; this is an unsigned catalogue introduction to a 1984 Andre exhibition at the State University of New York at Stony Brook (hereinafter cited as 1984 interview).

89:   "not attempt to supply": 1984 interview, p. 3.

90:   "become a secretary": A. Gould, "Dialogues with Carl Andre," in *Arts*, 5/74, p. 27 (hereinafter cited as Gould interview).

90:   against the moon: D. Bourdon, *Carl Andre*, New York, 1978, p. 18.

90:   "any Puritan land": H. Adams, *The Education of Henry Adams*, Boston, 1974, pp. 9–14; quoted in Bourdon, *Carl Andre*, pp. 17–18.

91:   "lying in the weather": Bourdon, *Carl Andre*, p. 18.

91:   "salty eroticism": in "Robert Smithson: He Always Reminded Us of the Questions We Ought to Have Asked Ourselves" (an unsigned interview with Carl Andre), in *Arts Magazine*, 5–6/78, p. 102 (hereinafter cited as 1978 interview).

91:   winter memory: poem dated 2/20/65 in *Carl Andre*, a 1969 exhibition catalogue published by the Haags Gemeentemuseum, The Hague, Netherlands, and "republished by Daled Brussels in February 1975 with the approval of Carl Andre," p. 36 (hereinafter cited as 1969 catalogue).

91:   "sumac bushes": Gould interview, p. 27.

91:   "you on fire": Tomkins profile, p. 58.

92:   form and standards: Cummings interview, pp. 173–174.

92:   independent sources: Frampton's letter is in 1969 catalogue, pp. 7–13.

92:   "greatest pleasure": Cummings interview, p. 177.

93:   "school spirit": Frampton in 1969 catalog, p. 7.

93:   first checks: Cummings interview, p. 173.

94:   "might call 'reality' ": Rose in Bourdon, *Carl Andre*, p. 9.

94:   "take care of me": quoted in J. Wadler, "A Death in Art," in *New York*, 12/16/85, p. 41.

94:   "reason and squalor": Cummings interview, p. 179.

95:   "eat what they kill": Rose in Bourdon, *Carl Andre*, pp. 9–10.

95:   "and I quit": Cummings interview, p. 178.

95:   "resigned from": Rose in 1969 catalogue, p. 40.

95:   One such opus: J. Siegel, "Carl Andre: artworker," in *Studio International*, 11/70, p. 175 (hereinafter cited as Siegel interview).

96:   "A-1 Steak Sauce": Frampton in 1969 catalogue, p. 7.

96:   "very Orwellian": Cummings interview, p. 178.

96:   "time together": Frampton in 1969 catalogue, p. 8.

97:   "or a beer": quoted in R. Sukenick, *Down and In: Life in the Underground*, New York, 1987, p. 57.

99:   on Rauschenberg and Johns and the birth of pop art: see C. Tomkins, *Off the Wall*, New York, 1980 and C. Tomkins, *The Bride and the Bachelors*, New York, 1968.

99:   struck young Stella: Tomkins profile, p. 61.

100: "just looked blank": Cummings interview, p. 184.

100: "what you see": quoted in Tomkins profile, p. 81.

100: "tremendous impression": Cummings interview, p. 190.

101: wrote to Castelli: Frampton in 1969 catalogue, p. 11.

101: surges of envy: J. Gilbert-Rolfe, *Immanence and Contradiction*, New York, 1985, p. 170n. (This is a 1976 interview with Carl Andre—hereinafter cited as Gilbert-Rolfe interview).

101: "written by Dean Swift": Frampton in 1969 catalogue, p. 9.

101: *Billy Builder:* this was published in three installments in *Tracks*, Spring and Fall 1976 and Spring 1977.

102: "too long": Frampton in 1969 catalogue, p. 9.

103: "blond Smith girl": Rose quoted in Tomkins profile, p. 73.

103: "cramped quarters": Frampton in 1969 catalogue, p. 9.

103: "light black woman": I-LL.

103: "dismissed as pointless": Frampton in 1969 catalogue, p. 11.

103: "Things that are unthreatening": Cummings interview, p. 191.

104: "polymorphous perverse carpentry": Frampton in 1969 catalogue, p. 11.

104: "bad breath": C. Andre and H. Frampton, *12 Dialogues: 1962–1963*, New York, 1981, p. 88.

104: "shine on her nose": Andre and Frampton, *12 Dialogues*, p. 60.

105: "powerful as a glacier": 1984 interview, p. 6.

105: "put to use": Lao-tzu, *Tao Te Ching*, quoted in Bourdon, *Carl Andre*, p. 19.

105: "hole in a thing": quoted in 1969 catalogue, p. 41.

Spring Valley, New York: September 11–14, 1985

Fifteen

106:	"USA on a BSA": I-RMH.
107:	view the deceased: I-RMH and I-TH.
107:	"that'll be enough": I-TH.
108:	about AIDS: I-RMH.
108:	thoughtless "quips": I-JGR and I-JWt.
109:	"the truth as I know it": I-RMH.
109:	doubly sure: ibid.
109:	"I'm innocent": I-JSH.
109–111:	Hoffinger's background: ibid.
111:	"call the shots": ibid.
111:	"making out a will": I-ROM and I-RMH.
112:	"He killed her": I-LP.
112:	"about what happened": I-TH; also IMN.
113:	"Ana's to give you": I-TH.

Sixteen

113:	wanted to throttle: I-MB.
115:	alcohol content: PTR.
116:	She had wished: I-MB.
117:	Interpol was working: I-MB.; also IMN.
117:	"didn't notice": Finelli's report in PTR.
117:	greater certainty: I-RF.
117:	"How could you notice": I-RMH.
118:	didn't press them: I-MB.
118:	Tom Harrington's background: I-TH.
119:	"let us know": I-TH.
120:	"can't bring myself": I-TH.
120:	"until you get home": I-TH.
121:	afraid of dying: I-JSH.
121:	"this kind of thing": I-TH; also IMN.
122:	"not at this time": I-TH.
122:	"much shorter": I-RMH.
123:	"search for origin": AEAM.
123:	"to my love": AEAM.

124:     "to our future": AEAM.
124:     "roots to my dreams": AEAM.
124:     "ANA FELL": L, 9/12/85, AEAM, also IMN.

Seventeen

125:     "him coming back": Sayah in T-2.
125:     "the appropriate time": Bashford in T-2.
126:     "What else do you need": Sayah in T-2.
126:     "give it to him": ibid.
126:     Hoffinger agreed: Hoffinger in T-2.
126:     aesthetic sisters: I-CSt.
127:     "we can do it": ibid.
127:     die twice: I-RR and I-CSt.
128:     "inherited hierarchies": I-CSt.
128:     women were saying: I-CSt, I-RR, and I-MBE.
128:     Ana and she: I-CSt.
129:     changed his mind: I-RMH.
129:     lost her faith: ibid.
129:     "going to kill me": ibid.
129:     orphange life: ibid.
130:     empty hearse: ibid.

Iowa: 1961–1978

Eighteen

132–135: Ana Mendieta growing up in Iowa: I-RMH.
135–136: Ignacio Mendieta in Cuba: I-ROM and I-IM.
136–137: Ana Mendieta in high school: I-RMH.
137:     Ana Mendieta's mother and brother in Iowa: I-ROM, I-IM, and
         I-RMH.
138:     kleptomania: I-IF.
138:     "aesthetic fascism": quoted in J. Paoletti, No Title, Middletown,
         CT, 1981, p. 100.
139:     trend-watching piece: H. Junker, "The New Sculpture: Getting
         Down to the Nitty Gritty," in the Saturday Evening Post, 11/68,
         pp. 42–47.
139:     "imprints of reality": Sukenick, Down and In, p. 54.

140:     "body beautiful": L. Lippard, "The Pain of Pleasures of Rebirth:
         Women's Body Art," in *Art in America*, 5–6/76, p. 75.
140:     hidden penis: ibid.
140:     "society can admit": quoted ibid.
140:     Halloween party: I-HB, I-RMH, and I-IF.
141:     Breder's background: I-HB.
141:     "AH-na not Anna": I-IF.
142:     "Masturbation can be an art": I-HB.
143:     "just worshiped him": I-RMH.
143:     some who were there: I-JS, I-WR, I-TV, and I-IF.
143:     "exploded off the canvas": H. Breder, "Ana Mendieta: Imprints/
         Student Years 1972–1977," in *Sulfur*, Spring 1988, p. 75.
143:     "to mother earth": in AEAM; see also "A Selection of [Ana
         Mendieta's] Statements and Notes," in *Sulfur*, Spring 1988,
         pp. 70–74.
143:     "innumerable ways": Breder, "Ana Mendieta," p. 75.
144:     "had dark skin": quoted in J. Wilson, "Ana Mendieta Plants Her
         Garden," in *The Village Voice*, 8/13/80, p. 90.
144:     "all sexual violence": quoted in N. L. Harris, *The Female Imagery
         of Mary Beth Edelson and Ana Mendieta*, a 1978 unpublished
         Master's thesis at Louisiana State University. This informative
         sixty-nine-page essay, with comments by Ana Mendieta from an
         interview with the author, is not listed in the otherwise thorough
         bibliography prepared by Cristina Delgado Olsen in the catalogue
         for the 1987–88 New Museum retrospective.
144:     "somehow suggesting rape": I-HB.
144:     too ashamed: I-RMH.
145:     "love in this house": I-HB.
145:     "consumed by fire": Breder, "Ana Mendieta," pp. 75–76.
146:     "seen that close": I-SD.
147:     to write about her: see her articles in *Ms.*, 10/75, and *Art in
         America*, 5–6/76.
147:     "back together": I-HB.
147:     "to begin life": Breder, "Ana Mendieta," p. 76.

West Broadway: September 16–23, 1985

Nineteen

148:	front of silence: I-JW.
148:	Andre Defense Fund: Wadler, "Death in Art," p. 40.
148:	"vengeance and violence": Wadler, "Death in Art," p. 43.
148:	"love and rage": ibid.
149:	"solemn compromise": quoted ibid.
149:	"by renewing": quoted ibid.
149:	"envy at the rain": in 1969 catalogue, p. 25.
149:	"a death foretold": Wadler, "Death in Art," p. 41.
149:	"Absolute garbage": quoted in Wadler, "Death in Art," p. 43.
150–151:	Rich's background: I-RR.
151:	Raquel and three others: I-RR, I-ND, I-GS, and I-RMH.
151:	Bashford's cases: I-MB.
152:	"with so and so": I-ND.
152:	tracked her down: I-RMH.
153:	"in CA life": AEAM.
153:	"blow his top": I-ND.
154:	"through so much": ibid.
154:	jealous of Nancy: I-RMH.
154:	"hugs and kisses": PHN.

Twenty

154:	three love poems: AEAM.
155:	Ana had had a dream: I-RMH.
156:	Sperone's background: I-GES.
157:	"Pay me in copper": ibid.
157:	"a real artist": ibid.
158:	destino contro: ibid.
158:	Schloss's background: I-ES.
159:	"artist with a beard": ibid.
160:	"I'm gonna smash": I-AC; also I-ES.
161:	"He would boycott": I-AC.
161:	people who attended: I-DF, I-FM, I-RB, I-RoB.
161:	seemed nervous: I-DF.
161:	gutsy: ibid.
162:	"book with you": I-RB and I-RoB.
163:	"everything is OK": I-RB and I-JWt.

Twenty-one

164:    "maybe he'll show up": I-RMH and I-LL.
164:    one more impiety: I-ROM.
164:    "Carl is coming": I-RMH and I-LL.
164:    "freaking and thinking": I-LL.
165:    Each of the three: I-CSt and I-LL.
165:    Lucy grew angry: I-LL and I-RHM.
165:    "Carl's here": I-LSt.
166:    "turbulent world": I-MP.
166:    her efforts: I-RR.
167:    "murderer has dared": I-CSt.
167:    "a little bit": ibid.
167:    "I said, Wow": I-LSt.
167:    "swat him or something": I-MPN.
168:    "got run over": I-AMi.
168:    "of their daughter": I-JP.
168:    "did nod hello": I-LG and I-NS.
169:    "nobody's knows": I-RHM.
169:    "moved to say": I-CSt.
169:    "some poetry of Ana's": I-RMH.
170:    "on is victory": poem dated 6/1/81 in AEAM; there is an earlier version written in Spanish dated 3/20/81.
171:    "just walked out": I-TV.
171:    "as a person": I-LSt.
172:    "pull behind her": I-AMi.
172:    profoundly moved: I-ROM, I-RMH, I-TH; also I-GS.
173:    "say hello to Carl": I-EC and I-RMH; see also Wadler, "Death and Art," p. 46.

Twenty-two

174:    "masterpiece or junk": H. Rosenberg, *The De-definition of Art*, New York, 1973, p.12.
174:    certifiable denizens: for the best sociological study and history of Soho until 1980 see C. Simpson, *Soho: the Artist in the City*, Chicago, 1981.
178:    "rejected with impunity": R. Hughes, "The Artist as Entrepreneur," in *The New Republic*, 11/14/87, p. 24.
178:    "Should I buy": I-RR.

179: outsiders like Tom Wolfe: see especially T. Wolfe, *The Painted Word*, New York, 1975.

179: "well-shrunk *Dental* Surgeons": R. Hughes, "The Sohoiad," in *The New York Review of Books*, 3/84.

179: promoting stereotypes: see the reaction to Hughes of *Artforum* ex-editor Ingrid Sischy in J. Malcolm, "A Girl of the Zeitgeist," in *The New Yorker*, 10/27/86, p. 64 (part two of a two-part article that began 10/20/86).

Centre Street: October 1985–April 1986

Twenty-three

181: "trial of any defendant": Bashford in GJM.

181: "sets me back": I-JSH.

183: buttoned up: I-MB.

184: would go co-op: GJM and PTR.

184: opened an account: ibid.

184n minor skin growth: medical bill dated 9/4/85 in AEAM.

184: had been mailed: L, 9/8/85, in PTR.

184: "long ride down": PTR and GJM.

184: fifth-floor window: Torre in PTR and GJM.

186: butler do it: see, e.g., J. Romano, *Strategic Use of Circumstantial Evidence*, New York, 1986.

186: Bashford had become convinced: I-MB.

187: three-dimensional picture: PTR, GJM, and I-MB.

Twenty-four

187: registered letter: L, 9/23/85, in AEAM.

187: "repays them financially": I-RMH.

188: "I have to give": I-RMH and I-TH.

189: "WE OWE TO ANA": L, 9/23/85, in AEAM.

190: "decent human being": I-MP.

190: "I'm responsible": I-CH.

191: "I was drunk": I-GES.

191: Lippard's background: I-LL.

192: "be nice to Carl": ibid.

192: clashing with Ruby: I-LL and I-RR.

193: "statement of fact": I-RR.

193:     even hauled off: I-LL.

193:     just didn't know: ibid.

194:     "sadomasochistic slaying": M. Chambers, "City Art Dealer Charged in Case of Sex Torture," *New York Times*, 5/18/85, p. 28.

195:     The Serra affair: the literature here is abundant; see, for example, R. Hughes, "The Trials of *Tilted Arc*," in *Time*, 6/3/85, p. 78, and Malcolm, "Zeitgeist," part one, pp. 61–67.

196:     "a total split": I-AK.

197:     "not that healthy": I-LW.

197:     "weren't in the room": I-CSt.

197:     grand jury completed: PTR

Twenty-five

198:     "planned murder": quoted in F. Faso and P. Meskil, "Sculptor Charged In His Wife's Death," the New York *Daily News*, 10/22/85, p. 12.

198:     "Carl is very upset": I-RMH.

198:     extralegal activities: L, 10/19/85.

198:     "less than helpful": ibid.

198:     "part of the difference": L, 11/8/85, I-GR.

199:     "just and proper": PTR.

199n: "was pretty good": G. Gorgoni, *Beyond the Canvas*, New York, 1985, p. 12.

201:     "loony Cuban": quoted in Wadler, "Death in Art," p. 40.

202:     "shocked by that": I-LSt.

202:     wouldn't need lawyers: I-JSH.

202:     "public figure": PTR.

203:     "respectfully prayed": ibid.

Twenty-six

204:     called their lawyer: I-GS.

204:     in the vault: I-GS, I-RMH, and I-TH; also IMN.

205:     "her worry list": I-RMH.

205:     make no claim: I-RMH, I-TH, and I-GS.

205:     nobody had the key: I-GS

205:     "we deserve it": I-JWt; also I-GES.

206:     Bashford had been told: I-MB and I-RMH.
         which was true: I-WR.
206:     heard from the maids: I-IF.
206:     "heart would pound": ibid.
206:     "incredibly sexy dream": I-MP.
207:     "ghost was with me": ibid.
207:     "Oh, my God": Edelson's diary entry 11/86 and I-MBE.
207:     "you cannot breathe": I-IP.
207:     "not unhappy": I-ZH.
208:     "wanted to assume": I-CSt.
208:     "an antidote": J. Tully (review) in *The New Art Examiner*, 5/86,
         pp. 59–60.
209:     "fear every day": quoted in Tully, *New Art Examiner*, p. 60.
209:     "patently deficient": Hoffinger in PTR.
210:     "traumatic experience": ibid.
211:     "held for trial": Bashford in PTR
211:     jumped onto the radiator: Hoffinger in PTR.

                         Twenty-seven

212:     "piece of the pie": Rich's memo to Bashford and I-RR.
213:     "lived for her work": ibid.
213:     confirming Ana's premonition: C. Alfonzo, "El Dia Que Ana
         Mendieta Le Trajo Un Regalo a Eleggua," unpublished statement
         in AEAM.
213:     held a meeting: I-RR, I-RMH, and I-MB.
213:     art con man: see J. Perrone, "Carl Andre: Art Versus Talk," in
         Artforum, 5/76, pp. 32–33.
213:     no qualms: I-JeP.
213:     seen Carl strike Angela: the incident was related anonymously in
         J. Hoffman, "Rear Window: The Mystery of the Carl Andre
         Murder Case," in *The Village Voice*, 3/29/88, p. 28.
214:     "Carl wasn't one of them": I-PC.
214:     beyond verbal abuse: I-SC.
214:     "Carl has suffered": I-RMH and I-ROM.
215:     "feeling among people": I-LP.
215:     called Hoffinger: I-GS.
215:     "a pipe broke": I-RMH and I-RR.
216:     four-page opinion: PTR.

Park Avenue South: 1965–1979

Twenty-eight

218:     the rabbi: Sukenick, *Down and In,* p. 210.

218:     "and had moved": Sukenick, *Down and In,* pp. 203–204.

219n: contractual: Sukenick, *Down and In,* p. 203.

219:     "almost carnivorous": T. Southern in J. Stein and G. Plimpton, *Edie,* New York, 1982, p. 278.

220:     hipoisie: Sukenick, *Down and In,* p. 214.

220:     adding more than subtracting: Frampton in 1969 catalogue, p. 10.

221:     caught the eye: J. Myers, *Tracking the Marvelous,* New York, 1983, p. 234.

221:     She lifted Carl: L. Lippard, "Rejective Art," in *Art International,* 10/66, pp. 33–36.

222:     "solution was *Lever*": Bourdon, *Carl Andre,* p. 26.

222:     "run along the earth": quoted in D. Bourdon, "The Razed Sites of Carl Andre," in *Artforum,* 10/66, pp. 14–17.

222n: "great resentment": quoted in Cummings interview, p. 195.

223:     stubbing his toe: I-AR.

223:     "edge clay beam": poem dated 2/8/66 in 1969 catalogue, p. 37.

224:     like a dandy: I-LG.

224:     "and so nice": I-PC.

224:     "Euclidean isles": Bourdon, *Carl Andre,* p. 14.

225:     "my ideal piece": quoted in Bourdon, *Carl Andre,* p. 17.

225:     probably more effective: Lippard, "Rejective Art," pp. 33–36.

225:     word "Renaissance": B. Rose, "Shall We Have a Renaissance," in *Art in America,* 3–4/67, p. 31.

225:     capping it all: L. Lippard, "Rebelliously Romantic," in the *New York Times,* 6/4/67, p. 25.

225:     "in the nose": quoted in Wadler, "Death in Art," p. 42.

226:     "strawberry shortcake": quoted in Sukenick, *Down and In,* p. 221.

226:     "art and life": I-PC.

226:     "could be amusing": I-JP.

226:     "our art battles": quoted in Sukenick, *Down and In,* p. 220.

226:     drunken argument: Carl Andre's diary in AEAM.

227:     "didn't belong there": I-JP.

227:     "wheeled up the aisle": quoted in Sukenick, p. 233.

227:     "can't sit here": quoted in Sukenick, *Down and In,* p. 219.

227:    "major setback": quoted in Sukenick, *Down and In*, p. 219.

228:    "amount of bullshit": I-JGR.

228:    "involved in any": I-PC.

228:    but its politics: for the politics being rejected see especially S. Guibaut, *How New York Stole the Idea of Modern Art: Abstract Expressionism, Freedom, and the Cold War*, Chicago, 1983.

229:    "those we despise": quoted in Andre and Frampton, *12 Dialogues*, p. 92.

229:    "dictatorship of bourgeoisie": quoted in Siegel interview, p. 175.

229:    "not petty ambition": quoted in L. Lippard, "The Art Workers' Coalition: Not a History," in *Studio International*, 7–12/70, p. 174.

230:    "fascist lie": quoted in Siegel interview, p. 176.

230:    "thoroughly segregated": quoted in Siegel interview, p. 177.

230:    "isn't worth having": quoted in Siegel interview, p. 177.

230:    "taken from him too": Lippard, "Art Workers'," p. 174.

231:    "charge of feeling": J. Russell (review) in the *New York Times*, 4/4/80.

232:    "minds its own business": quoted in Wadler, "Death in Art," p. 42.

232:    Shakespearean sonnet: "A.M.G" in LeWitt, *No Title*, p. 17.

232:    "for the birds": Gould interview, p. 28. Carl (or Gould) had the quote garbled, but the reference is clear.

232:    "pleasure of any kind": P. Sutinen, "Carl Andre: the Turner of the Matter," in *Willamette Week's Fresh Weekly*, 8/12/80, p. 9.

232:    whimsical crisis: *The New Yorker*, 11/21/77, pp. 51–52, and I-CT.

233:    "not talking down": I-CT.

233:    "Women like Carl": I-LL.

233:    "competent and unruffled": I-JGR.

233n: "bluntly poetic": quoted in Tomkins profile, p. 87.

234:    "withdrawn the next": quoted in Hoffman, "Rear Window," p. 28.

235:    "Carl used to do": I-JGR.

235:    "all the fucking time": ibid.

235:    "black hole": see Wolfe, *Painted Word*, p. 101.

235:    one Carl-watcher: see R. Smith (review) in *Artforum*, 1/76, p. 62.

236:    "gratification that long": Gould interview, p. 28.

236:    "chance to market them": Gilbert-Rolfe interview, p. 172.

268:      "my own success": quoted in "Lucy Lippard on A.I.R." (A.I.R.
          document), p. 1.
268:      Everything about Ana: I-MBE.
269:      "presence was extraordinary": Spero in *Fuego de Tierra;* also I-NS.
269:      "buys a mink coat": I-ZH.
270:      "need for a family": I-JuG.
270:      leaving for Oaxaca: I-HB.
270:      "pretty lucky": LHB.
271:      "I give to you": ibid.
272:      "Human nature I guess": ibid.
272:      free and happy man: I-ROM and I-RMH.
273:      threw her a party: I-NS and I-LG.
273:      "a New Kid": D. Bourdon, "There's a New Kid (or Two) in
          Town," in *The Village Voice,* 6/13/77, p. 67.
273:      "wine consumed": I-NS.
273:      "come this close": W. Zimmer (review) in the *Soho Weekly News,*
          5/31/79.
273n: reviews: J. Heit, "Ana Mendieta," in *Arts Magazine,* 1/80, p. 11,
          and G. Coker, "Ana Mendieta at A.I.R.," in *Art in America,* 4/80,
          pp. 133–134.
274:      Fresh faces: I-EH.
274:      "her Hispanic roots": I-JP.
275:      some sort of protest: I-GES.
275:      "falling off the wall": I-MBE.
275:      "in the center": I-NS.
276:      joined the others: I-NS and I-MBE.
276:      "living there all along": I-RMH.
277:      "I was born here": Ana Mendieta in *Fuego de Tierra.*
277:      "history and the family": interview with Kaki Mendieta in *Fuego
          de Tierra.*
278:      "had in her life": ibid.
279:      "She was very loyal": I-ZH.
279:      "respond to emotions": ibid.
279:      "all possibities surge": AEAM.
280:      "the mystery": poem by Ana Mendieta in AEAM.
280:      "the final rejection": AEAM.
280:      "quite adamant": I-ZH and I-LP.

281:     "coming from": I-TV.
281:     "he never cooked": I-TV, I-ZH, and I-LP.
281:     "future is now": AEAM.
281:     "his arm round her": I-ZH.
282:     "your old age": quoted in E. Costa in *Sulfur*, Spring 1988, p. 80.
282:     "passion of Ana": C. Rickey, "The Passion of Ana," in *The Village Voice*, 9/10/80, p. 76.
282n: Ana Mendieta's statement: AEAM and in *Ana Mendieta: A Retrospective* (catalogue), New York, 1987, p. 17.
282:     "Plants Her Garden": J. Wilson, "Ana Mendieta," p. 90.

Broadway and Houston Streets: 1987

Thirty-two

283:       Lederer's background: I-EL.
283–285:   Morgenthau's dilemma: I-RMM.
286:       "Liz, I'm tellin' ya": I-EL
286–287:   Lederer's dilemma: I-EL.
286n: "DA Again Paints": *New York Post*, 1/27/87, p. 14.
287:       "to the crime": I-RR.
287n: gone on a holiday: PTR and I-MP.
287:       Hoffinger told: "Sculptor Indicted for 3d Time in Wife's Death," in the *New York Times*, 3/19/87, p. B6.
288:       "meet the minimal": PTR.
288:       "this Court's guidelines": Lederer in PTR.

Thirty-three

290:       "get on his nerves": I-ECo.
290n: Panicelli and Nunzio: I-IP and I-RB.
291:       "meticulous scholarship": Carl Andre in the introduction to catalogue: *Carl Andre: Haags Gemeentemuseum*, The Hague, 1987.
291:       seemed happy: I-SL.
291:       "we can mourn her": I-CL.
291:       "need to do that": I-CL and I-SL.
292:       expecting a visit: I-EL; also Pappas in TN.
293:       her outlook on the case: I-EL.
294:       "Crispo Case": the case went to trial after Carl's, and on 10/17/88 Crispo was acquitted.

294:        office denied: I-EL.

295n: "individual positions": L, 2/21/89, to author (signed: "Love, Gue-
            rilla Girls").

296:        "courting the gods": J. Perreault, "Earth and Fire," in *Ana Men-
            dieta: A Retrospective* (catalogue), New York, 1987, p. 17.

296n: reviews: E. Hess, "Out of Body," in *The Village Voice*, 12/8/87,
            p. 119, and M. Brenson, "Works by Ana Mendieta in a Retrospec-
            tive," in the *New York Times*, 11/27/87, p. C30.

                            Thirty-four

296:        "I'm a vet": Lederer in PHN and I-EM.

296:        *"Haldol"*: Lederer's document in PTR.

297:        "psychotic disorders": Hoffinger in PTR; also I-MS.

298:        Xerox copies: warrant in PTR; also PHN.

298:        "No eating or drinking": PHN.

299:        told his story: ibid.

300:        had given a party: I-AS.

301:        "dumped" on him: Schlesinger in PHN.

301:        "monkey business": Hoffinger in PHN.

302:        "made it up": Rosen in PHN, Lederer in PTR, I-GR.

302:        "unfortunate" decision: Hoffinger in PTR.

302:        "cannot be sanitized": ibid.

302:        "rise above it": I-GR.

303:        "I'm losing faith": Schlesinger in PHN.

303:        "take him apart": Hoffinger in PHN.

303:        "want to hear the answer": Schlesinger in PHN.

303:        "Don't answer that": ibid.

304:        "look so anguished": ibid.

304:        praising the verdict: E. Caldwell, "The Jury's Message is in its
            Verdict," in the New York *Daily News*, 1/25/88.

305:        "ducking it": Hoffinger in PHN.

305:        "in all respects denied": Schlesinger in PHN.

306:        "misled in issuing": Hoffinger in PHN.

306:        "now on trial": Schlesinger in PHN.

307:        "waive a jury": Hoffinger in PHN.

307–308:   dialogue between Schlesinger and Carl Andre: PHN.

Rome: 1983–1985

Thirty-five

309:     "a final thing": I-CH.
310:     at the funeral: I-RMH.
310:     "not working with Carl": I-HB.
310:     Barbara did not like: ibid.
310:     income slumping: I-LG and I-NS.
311:     sitting coked out: Sukenick, *Down and In*, p. 276.
311:     fear of getting: I-MP.
312:     "I must confess": document in AEAM.
312:     ended the letter: L, 10/1/83, in AEAM.
313:     "she was consistent": I-CH.
314:     "It fascinates me": L, undated but late 1983, in AEAM.
314:     "when you're famous": I-RMH.
314:     the idea of Sol: I-CL.
314:     she started looking: I-JG and I-RMH.
315:     "better artist than him": I-CH.
315:     habit of vitamins: I-RMH.
315:     adopting her teacher's family: I-JG.
317:     "gives me the creeps": Alice Weiner in TN.
317:     going out with the Andres: I-DK, I-AF, I-JG, I-LC, I-ECo.
317:     "Oh, shut up": I-MP.
319–321:   the last phone call: I-ND, PTR, GJM, I-MB; also IMN.

Centre Street: January 29–February 11, 1988

Thirty-six

323–324:   Schlesinger's background: I-AS.
324:     typically arrogant: Rich and Clifford in PHN.
325:     Carl liked the judge: I-JM.
325:     "closing the web": I-JSH.
325:     "call the shots": ibid.
325:     His final decision: ibid.
326:     "but met evil": Lederer in TN.
326:     trying to organize: I-RR and I-ZH.
326:     "no conversations": I-LW.
327:     "fell to her death": Lederer in TN.

327:       "very dear friend": Delgado in TN.
327n: delighted to learn: I-AS.
327:       "never opened windows": Delgado in TN.
328:       "upbeat" and "lighthearted": ibid.
328:       "happy, slaphappy": ibid.
328:       "stay right here": Hoffinger in TN.
328:       "prefer you to be": Schlesinger in TN.
329:       undermine the import: I-JSH.
330:       not go very far: ibid.
330–331:   Hoffinger's cross-examination of Delgado: TN.
332:       happy to get it over: I-EM.
333–335:   Hoffinger's cross-examination of Mojzis: TN.
335:       "different ball game": Hoffinger in TN.
336:       disturbing the judge: I-AS.

Thirty-seven

336:       "Lemme do my job": TN.
337n: "more important things": Schlesinger in PHN.
337:       find her "angle": I-JH.
338:       "into a metaphor": I-GM.
338:       "I was terrified": I-LL.
338:       sit in a seat: I-DAt.
338:       felt free: I-LSt and I-EL.
338:       "nature of evil": I-LSt.
338:       "husband to find": I-EL.
339:       "I want to live": ibid.
340:       "we do not do": Nodal in TN.
340:       Hoffinger's cross-examination of Nodal: TN.
341:       "drank a good deal": Panicelli in TN.
341:       not the duct: Pappas in TN.
341:       "screaming, a scream": Leandrou in TN.
342:       "much more tolerance": Donald Hoffman in TN.
343:       "based on somebody's memory": Hoffinger in TN.
343–344:   Hoffinger's cross-examination of Finelli in TN.
344n: "tipsy for hours": quoted in 1978 interview, p. 102.
344:       "can't fucking believe": Hoffinger in TN.
345:       do when called: I-RMH.
346:       "in our hearts": Raquel Harrington in TN.

346:     "He's going to admit": I-RMH and I-EL.
346:     "angry and spiteful": Raquel Harrington in TN.
346:     "visual inspection": Lederer in TN.
347:     "there is no proof": Hoffinger in TN.

Thirty-eight

347:     "you never know": I-PC.
347:     very upset: ibid.
347:     He was right: I-RR.
347:     bothered him, too: I-PC.
348:     made small talk: I-ZH.
348:     "the one person": ibid.
349:     refused to shake: Santurio in PHN.
349:     "Not in Bed": A. Santurio, "Carl Andre: Ana se mató porque no
         fui a la cama con ella," in *El Diario*, 1/26/88, p. 5.
349n: "caught a cold": Clifford in PHN.
349:     "worth thinking about": M. Kempton, "Of Murder, Pride and
         Presence," in *Newsday*, 2/5/88, p. 6.
350:     didn't look natural: I-AS.
350–351: Bierman's testimony: TN; also I-EL.
352:     "It was all whacko": Tong in TN.
352:     "had no notice": I-EL and I-MSu.
352:     "I'll do it": ibid.
352:     "walk into walls": Ginnever in TN.
352:     no fear of heights: Knapp in TN.
352–353: Trasobares's testimony: TN.
354n: "neither fear death": M. Gonzalez-Wippler, *Santería*, New York,
         1973, pp. 24–25; see also Gonzalez-Wippler, *The Santería Experi-
         ence*, Englewood Cliffs, NJ, 1982, and L. Teish, *Jambalaya*, San
         Francisco, 1985.
354:     "besmirch her reputation": Hoffinger in TN.
354–355: Knaff's testimony: TN.
355:     "where it stops": Larry Weiner in TN.
355–356: Miner's testimony: TN.
356:     Alice Weiner's testimony: TN.
356:     Bourdon's testimony: TN.
356n: call he had made: I-MBE.
357:     Bool's testimony: TN.

357n: Bool had some problems: I-SL and I-CL.
358:      "devoid of contents": autopsy report in AEAM.
358:      autopsy worksheet: AEAM.
358:      "two main roles": De Maio in TN.
358–359: Preven's testimony: TN.
359:      "a rich man": Schlesinger in TN.
359–360: Dubowski's testimony: TN.
360:      "beyond tomorrow": Schlesinger in TN.

Thirty-nine

361:      "ten to fifteen": Miner in TN.
361:      one last time: I-EL.
361:      Betsy had told Ruby: I-EH and I-RR.
361:      break the logjam: I-EL.
361:      damn-sure witness: ibid. and I-MSu.
362:      repudiated Tong's testimony: I-EL and Lederer in TN.
362:      "center of his face": I-EL.
362:      change of heart: ibid.
363:      "I absolutely know": ibid.; also I-MSu and I-NS.
363n: in the back room: I-JSH.
363–364: Spero's testimony: TN; also I-NS.
364:      no argument: Nieves in TN.
364:      "last-minute ploy": Hoffinger in TN.
364–367: Hoffinger summation: ibid.
367–368: Lederer summation: TN.
369:      "have a verdict": Schlesinger in TN.
369:      "Whaddaya think": Hoffinger in TN.

Forty

370:      Very close call: I-AS.
370:      "Verdict Due": D. McGill, "Verdict Due Today in Death of
          Artist," in the *New York Times*, 2/11/88, p. B5.
371:      "not satisfied me": Schlesinger in TN.
372:      "the best press": Kruger in TN and I-BKt.
372:      "Justice has been served": Carl Andre in TN.
372:      "killed my daughter": Raquel Oti Mendieta in TN and I-ROM;
          see also R. Sullivan, "Greenwich Village Sculptor Acquitted of

Pushing Wife to Her Death," in the *New York Times*, 2/12/88, p. B3.

372: "getting away with murder": Raquel Harrington in TN, I-RMH; see also Sullivan, "Sculptor Acquitted," p. B3.

372: "I congratulate you": I-SL and I-CL.

Epilogue: Breaking the Seal, 1988–1990

Forty-one

377: "I'll never get shown": quoted in Hoffman, "Rear Window," p. 26; also I-JH.

377: last article: J. Tully, "Andre Acquitted: Trial Kindles Sexual Politics in New York's Art World," in *New Art Examiner*, 4/88, pp. 22–24.

378: "End of conversation": IMN.

381: "all go away": I-PC.

382: "of the inevitable": A. Adam, "Carl Andre," in *Contemporanea*, 11–12/88, p. 112.

383: "corpse beneath": D. Batchelor, "3000 Years: Carl Andre Interviewed by David Batchelor," in *Artscribe International*, Summer 1989, pp. 62–63.

383: "flying out of windows": I-NB.

383: "accident with a man": ibid.

383: "lynched him": quoted in Tully, "Andre Acquitted," p. 24, and I-HPt.

ACKNOWLEDGMENTS

I would like to thank the following people for their contributions to this book: Dotty Attie, Helen Aylon, Will Barnet, Frank Barron, Martha Bashford, Stephen Black, Romolo Bulla, Rosalba Bulla, Barbara Cavalieri, Susan Cheever, Lucy Clink, Ester Coen, Maria Colau, Paula Cooper, Eduardo Costa, Alvin Curran, Cheryl Doering, Mary Beth Edelson, Clayton Eshelman, Wendy Evans, Daniela Ferraria, Ronald Finelli, Andrew Forge, Joan Geller, Jeremy Gilbert-Rolfe, Frances Cohen Gillespie, Leon Golub, Juan Gonzalez, Tom Harrington, Zarina Hashmi, Christian Haub, Joe Helman, Elizabeth Hess, Jan Hoffman, Kate Horsfield, Peter Ibarra, Ruth Felicity Kligman, Stephen Koch, Dieter Kopf, David Korzenik, Annette Kuhn, Susan Levinstein, Carol LeWitt, Sol LeWitt, Lucy Lippard, Jack MacRae, Cornelia McSheehy, David Marlowe, Gerald Marzorati, Donna Masini, Nicolette Maus, James Melchert, Mary Ann Melchert, Branda Miller, Ann Minich, Edward Mojzis, Ron Morason, Robert M. Morgenthau, Francesco Moschini, Mary Perot Nichols, Cristina Delgado Olsen, Gerry Ordover, Ida Panicelli, Spiros Pappas, John Perreault, Ren Pierson, Liliana Porter, B. Ruby Rich, Warren Rosen, Robert Rosenblum, Angelica Savinio, Alvin Schlesinger, Edith Schloss, Julius Schmidt, Carolee Schneemann, Mary Angela Schroth, Mike Sherman, Joy Silverman, Gary Simon, Lowery Sims, Sandy Skoglund, Holly Solomon, Nancy Spero, Gian Enzo Sperone, Monroe Studell, Mark Sullivan, Donna Thurman, Edith Tiger, Calvin Tomkins, Carmine Tornincasa, Modesto Torre, Robert Tyne, Ted Victoria, Joyce Wadler, Pat Weaver, Lawrence Weiner, Steve Weiner, Barbara Welch, and John Wessel.

Thanks are due to my students at the University of California at Santa Cruz who participated in the research: Sheila Albright, Melinda Ault, David Batchelder, Barbara Becker, Matthew Brenner, Robert

Bulterman, Lynn Hobel, Scott Lichtenstein, Kathy Smith, and Zoe Wiese.

In the category of family and friends who are like family, I owe a lot to Niki Berg, Peter Berg, Alice Cicconi, Didi Lorillard Cowley, Rob Cowley, Steven Kartagener, Alan Katz, Jonathan Katz, Stephen Katz, Antonia McElrath, Dennis McElrath, Michael Mewshaw, Dale Norman, Alex Rosenberg, Carole Rosenberg, and Barbara Steinman.

I am especially grateful to Nancy Berliner, Hans Breder, Natalia Delgado, Jack S. Hoffinger, Elizabeth Lederer, Ignacio Mendieta, Raquel Oti Mendieta,[1] Marsha Pels, and Gerry Rosen. Further special thanks go to my editor at Atlantic Monthly Press, Ann Godoff.

Raquel Mendieta Harrington gave so much so selflessly that any expression of appreciation falls much too short. It is rare in the course of one's research that a writer meets a person as resourceful as she, one with a memory for detail that not only reaches back as far as memory can but that withstands every test of confirmation. Over a period of two years and numerous long interviews evoking a wide range of emotions, she proved to be by far the richest source of information about her sister and the events in which she herself was involved.

Judd Tully, art critic, curator, and journalist with credentials of the highest caliber, worked with me on this book. He conducted preinterviews and some of the interviews with admirable skill and sensitivity. They are credited, where possible, in the Sources and Notes section of this book. His additional contributions, leading me with a smart flashlight through the tortuous byways and dimly lit back alleys of the New York art world, were inestimable.

Last, but always first, I thank my wife, Beverly Gerstel Katz, for making the impossible possible.

[1]Mrs. Mendieta died in Chestnut Ridge, New York, on November 29, 1989, at the age of 68.

INDEX

Abramowitz, Alton, 59, 62, 153, 320
Acconci, Vito, 140, 142
Adam, Alfred Mac, 382
Adams, Henry, 90
AIDS, 108, 127
A.I.R. gallery, 267–70, 272–76, 282
Alfonzo, Carlos, 212–13, 316
Allen, Verl, 137, 141
Almeida, Monica, 371
American Academy in Rome, 63, 239–40,
    309
Amplo, Anthony J., 70
Andre, Carl,
    art world and, 21, 58–59, 175, 226n,
        285, 289–90, 374, 381–83
    as artist, 138–39
    first success, 220–25
    minimalism and, 231–32, 310–11
    in *Saturday Evening Post*, 139
    artworks and/or shows by, 290–91
    "Belgian Blue Limestone" show,
        254–55
    Crystal Palace exhibition (Madrid),
        348, 371, 372
    Equivalents, 224–25
    Joint, 18
    Lever, 222–24
    opening in Rome, 157–61
    Stone Field Sculpture, 4–5, 231–33
    styrofoam sculptures, 83
    Art Workers Coalition and, 228–30
    Frances Bagley and, 311
    birth and childhood, 89–91
    with Bulbas in Rome, 162–63
    compared to Hans Breder, 278
    Paula Cooper and, 82–84
    in custody, 29–33, 48–49, 54–56,
        87–88
    Natalia Delgado on, 52
    drinking and, 149, 150, 356

Wendy Evans and, 63–64
Ronald Finelli on, 58–59
Hollis Frampton and, 91–93, 95–96, 99
as freight brakeman, 103
Tom Harrington and, 111–13, 118–22
at hearing, 125–26
Jack Hoffinger and, 110–11, 325
grand juries and indictments, 181–87,
    197–99, 216–17
interviewed (1974), 236
Robert Katz and, 375n
Brandon Krall and, 152–54
Lucy Lippard on, 191–93
at Max's Kansas City, 22, 226–28
Mendieta and (relationship), 7–10,
    14–15, 152–54, 154–55, 312
    affairs with other women and,
        311–12, 315–16
    breaking up, 309–10
    Natalia Delgado on, 318–19
    first meeting, 273–76
    Chris Haub on, 314–15
    honeymoon in Egypt, 244–46
    Marsha Pels on, 317
    reconciliation in Rome, 314
    wedding, 163
Mendieta's death and
    behavior following, 189–91
    emergency call to police, 11–12,
        23–24, 75, 113–15, 322
    at memorial service, 164–69, 173
    reaction, 255, 290, 291
Raquel Mendieta and, 25, 59–61,
    187–89
New York Daily News story on, 72–73
New York magazine cover story on,
    199–202
New York Post story on, 72–73
New York Times story on, 73
Doug Ohlson and, 22

Andre, Carl *(continued)*
  Gerry Ordover and, 77–78
  Marsha Pels on, 65
  personal characteristics, 233–38, 233*n*
    temper, 316
    violent behavior, 148–49, 160,
      213–15, 249
  poetry, 92, 148–49, 154–55, 223, 247
  with police after Mendieta's death,
    2–3, 6–7, 12–14, 18–20, 22–24
  Ruby Rich on, 150–51
  Barbara Rose on, 93–96
  Gerry Rosen and, 66–69, 75–76, 79–81,
    198
  Rita Sartorius and, 251
  Rome apartment and, 204–05, 215–16
  Alvin Schlesinger and, 325
  Edith Schloss on, 159–61
  Gian Enzo Sperone and, 156–59
  Frank Stella and, 84–85, 99–105
  as student at Kenyon College, 92
  as student at Phillips Academy, 91–92
  trial of, *See* Trial
  in *Village Voice* article, 257–59
  Larry Weiner on, 196–97
  as writer, 95*n*, 101–02, 104
  as young man in New York, 93–97,
    99–105
Artforum magazine, 78, 207, 224, 341
Art in America magazine, 147
Art International magazine, 225
Art Workers Coalition, 82, 228–30, 261
Attie, Dotty, 268, 338
Ayers, Joe, 24, 69–71, 107

Bagley, Frances, 311
Baranik, Rudolf, 81, 108, 117–18, 267,
  360–61, 362
Bashford, Martha, 28–32, 69, 151–52,
  213, 256, 257, 292, 298
  Andre case and, 57–58, 205–06, 212,
    249–52, 284–88
  Carol Berkman and, 216–17, 259–60
  evidence gathered for case against
    Andre by, 113–18
  at grand jury, 181–87
  at hearings, 54–56, 125–26
  Jack Hoffinger and, 199, 202–03, 211
  Raquel Mendieta and, 61–62, 109
  at trial, 302, 340, 342–43, 365, 378–79

Batista, Fulgenico, 40–41
Baumert, Robert, 1–2, 4, 6–7, 335–36
Baxter, Douglas, 78
Bay of Pigs invasion, 43–44
Bellamy, Richard, 220
Bergman, Marika, 355–56, 360–62, 363*n*
Berkman, Carol, 199, 202–04, 209, 211,
  216–17, 250, 251–53, 259–60,
  284–89, 297–98, 325
Berliner, Nancy, 383
Bernstein, Joel, 183–84
Betty Parsons gallery, 91
Bierman, Alison, 350–51, 364
Bigo, Veronique, 290
Billy Builder, or The Painfull Machine
  (novel by Andre), 101–02
Boghosian, Varujan, 242
Bool, Filip, 357
Boone, Mary, 176
Bourdon, David, 90, 221, 224–25, 356
Brancusi, Constantin, 104–05
Brassel, James, 5–7
Breder, Hans, 15–16, 79, 206, 240, 243,
  261–65, 268, 270–72, 279
  Andre compared to, 278
  Mendieta and, 140–41, 142–43, 145,
    310
Brenson, Michael, 296*n*
Brook, Terry, 102
Bulla, Romolo, 161–62
Bulla, Rosalba, 161–62
Burden, Chris, 26, 76
Butler family, 133–34

Caldwell, Earl, 304
Caldwell, Susan, 27
Canto, Rodrigo del, 318
Capolupo, Louis, 1–4, 6–7, 12, 342–43,
  349, 367
Castelli, Leo, 77, 98, 101, 176, 178
Castoro, Rosemarie, 78, 81, 104, 157,
  214, 233
Castro, Fidel, 38, 40–45, 71, 136, 306*n*
CBS, 336–37
Cedar Rapids Children's Home, 134
Cedar Tavern, 97, 226
Chamberlain, John, 77, 228
Chambers, Robert, 284, 337, 349
Chapman, Michael, 93–94, 96
Cheever, Susan, 214

Chinese Chance (restaurant), 65, 311
Clifford, Tim, 324, 349n
Coen, Ester, 290
Coler, Mark, 20, 184, 209n
Connolly, Michael, 1–5, 6, 10–12, 18–20,
    186, 342–43, 367, 380
Consagra, Sophie, 239
Contemporanea magazine, 382
Cooper, Paula, 67, 76, 78–79, 81, 161,
    176, 214, 218, 226, 279, 290n,
    Andre and, 82–84, 86–88, 224, 299,
    348
    gallery, 175, 275, 355, 377, 381–82
Cortez, Jayne, 24
Costa, Eduardo, 71
Crispo, Andrew, 80, 194–95, 200, 294
Curran, Alvin, 159

Damon, Betsey, 209
Delgado, Natalia, 52–53, 69, 71, 117,
    186–87, 204–05, 210, 253–54, 315
    Martha Bashford and, 151–54
    at grand jury proceedings, 316, 318–19
    Mendieta and, 14–15, 61–62, 378–79
    at trial, 327–28, 330–31
Deligeorges, Stavros, 146
Delion Delicatessen, 1–2, 115
El Diario, 337, 348–49
Dubowski, Kurt, 359–60

Edelson, Mary Beth, 207, 262–63,
    268–69, 275–76, 356n
Edwards, Mel, 24
Evans, Wendy, 21, 33, 63–64, 215

Fairstein, Linda, 283–84
Fassbinder, Rainer Werner, 375n
Feldman, Jane, 28
Ferraria, Daniela, 161
Finelli, Ronald, 18–20, 48, 55, 61, 117,
    183, 252, 286, 298
    with Andre at precinct headquarters,
        10–14, 22–24, 28–33
    Andre's apartment searched by, 69–71,
        379–80
    Tom Harrington and, 107, 119
    Raquel Mendieta and, 34–35, 58–59,
        108–09, 378
    at trial, 343–44, 365, 367
Fischer, Darte, 291

Fischer, Konrad, 76, 78–79, 233, 254, 291
Flavin, Dan, 225
Frampton, Hollis, 91–93, 95–96, 99–100,
    103–04, 229
Franklin Furnace, 26, 263

Gilbert-Rolfe, Jeremy, 227–28, 234–35,
    237
Ginniver, Ronnie, 21, 33, 352
Goetz, Bernhard, 111
Golan, Joseph, 205, 215, 241
Golub, Leon, 168, 224, 238, 269, 273,
    361
Gonzalez, Juan, 165, 269–70
Goosen, Eugene, 220
Gorgoni, Gianfranco, 199n
Gorman, Dennis, 135
Grau, Paulita, 44
Green Gallery, 220
Greenberg, Clement, 97
Guerilla Girls, 294–95, 295n
Guevara, Che, 40–41
Guggenheim Museum, 138, 157, 230
Gutierrez, Joacquin, 16–18, 341–42, 358

Harrington, Tom, 24–25, 34–35, 58–59,
    106–07, 173, 187–88, 304n
    Andre and, 111–13, 118–22, 124–25
    Mendieta's body identified by, 79
    at trial, 345, 370
Hashmi, Zarina, 122, 207, 255, 257,
    278–82, 347–48
Haub, Christian, 190, 309, 313, 314–15
Haynes, Nancy, 7, 49–50, 54, 67–68, 75,
    154, 379
Helman, Joe, 176
Heresies magazine, 53, 192, 263, 274,
    278
Hess, Elizabeth, 296n, 361
Hoffinger, Bunny, 370
Hoffinger, Fran, 370
Hoffinger, Jack S., 109–11, 115, 120–22,
    198, 199, 215, 256, 287, 295,
    299–300, 361, 369
    at Andre's hearing, 125–26
    Andre's indictment attacked by,
        202–04, 259–60, 288–89
    defense strategy of, 181, 209–11,
        297–98, 325, 328–30
    press coverage of trial and, 336

Hoffinger, Jack S. *(continued)*
  at trial, 300–03, 305–06, 327, 330–35,
    339–44, 346–47, 350–57, 359–60,
    362–68, 378–80
Hoffman, Jan, 299, 337, 377
Hofmann, Hans, 91
Holmes, Don, 142, 144–45
Holt, Nancy, 227
Hughes, Robert, 177, 179–80

Interpol, 117, 206

Jemaya, *See* Santería
Johns, Jasper, 99, 178
Jones Matson, 98–99
Judd, Donald, 222, 311, 348

Kahlo, Frida, 52, 136
Kempton, Murray, 345, 349
Kleiman, Alfred, 48, 54
Klein, Bernie, 118
Klein, Yves, 139–40
Knaff, Robert, 354–55
Knapp, Bridget, 352
Koch, Stephen, 237
Kooning, Willem de, 98–99, 219
Kosuth, Joseph, 225–26
Krall, Brandon, 152–54
Kruger, Barbara, 371
Kuhn, Annette, 33, 196
Kunstler, William, 69, 75

Lao-tzu, 104–05
Leandrou, Harry, 1–2, 5, 6, 332, 341
Lederer, Elizabeth, 283–89, 292–94,
    296–98, 301–02, 303–06
  Markia Bergman and, 361
  at trial, 326–28, 331–33, 335, 339–43,
    345–46, 350–52, 354–60, 362–64,
    367–68, 362
  witnesses from art world sought by,
    338–39
Lederman, Eli, 346
Leong, Jim, 323
Lever (sculpture by Andre), 222–24
Levin, Jennifer, 284, 337
LeWitt, Carol, 279, 291, 314, 357n
LeWitt, Sol, 274, 279, 291, 314, 348,
    357n, 372
Lichtenstein, Roy, 178

Lippard, Lucy, 74, 82, 126–28, 147,
    164–65, 171, 191–93, 198, 215,
    221, 225, 230, 233, 259, 338
Litman, Jack, 337
Logemann, Jane, 56, 72, 75
LoGiudice, Joe, 227

Machado, Gerado, 44
Mahoney, Detective, 19
Maio, Dominic de, 357–59
Mancini, Marc, 64
Manson, Charles, 26
Marden, Brice, 228
Marzorati, Gerry, 338, 374
Max's Kansas City, 22, 83, 218–20,
    225–28
McGill, Douglas, 370
McGowan, Patricia, 6
McGurk, Harriet, 85
Melchert, Jim, 239–42, 249
Melchert, Mary Ann, 240–41
Mendieta, Ann, 24–26, 373
  A.I.R. gallery and, 267–70, 272–76,
    282
  Andre and, 7–10, 154–55
    breaking up, 309–10, 312
    Andre's affairs and, 9–10, 311–12,
      315–16
    on Andre's dress, 32–33
    Andre's girlfriends and, 250–52
    Natalia Delgado on, 318–19
    divorce plans, 251–54, 252n, 256,
      319–20, 327n
    falling in love, 279–81
    feelings for Andre, 123–24
    Chris Haub on, 314–15
    honeymoon in Egypt, 244–46
    love letters, 9
    Marsha Pels on, 317
    problems in, 59–60
    reconciliation in Rome, 314
    wedding, 160, 163
  art and, 123, 136, 145–47
    art world, 21
    body earthwork, 15–16, 143–44
    career, 282, 341
    MacArthur Park sculptures, 64
    Natalia Delgado on, 330–31
    Rape Pieces, 144, 147
    retrospective exhibition at New

Museum of Contemporary Art,
    294–96
  Situeta Series, 273
  Tree of Life series, 356n
birth and childhood in Cuba, 37–47
Hans Breder and, 15–16, 140–41, 145,
    261–67, 270–72
Romolo and Rosalba Bulla on, 162
in Cedar Rapids, 137–38
childhood in Iowa, 132–35
Cuba and, 269–70
  return visit, 276–78
death, 1–2, 16–18, 322
  autopsy, 358
  circumstances surrounding, evaluated
    by Martha Bashford, 115–18
  friends in art world and, 73–74,
    126–28
  Jack Hoffinger on, 328–330
  Elizabeth Lederer on, 327
  mass, 129
  memorial service, 163–73
  plans in New York immediately
    preceding, 14–15
  premonitions of, 316–17
  scenarios of, presented at trial,
    366–68
Natalia Delgado and, 51–52, 61–62,
    152–54, 319–21, 327–28
diary, 246–48
dreams and, 206–08
drinking and, 328, 352–53, 356
Wendy Evans and, 63–64
father and, 272
first days in New York, 262–71, 273–76
Tom Harrington on, 118–19
Zarina Hashmi and, 278–82
Chris Haub on, 309
homage to, by women artists, 208–09
love for Rome and Italy, 313–14, 315
Raquel Mendieta and, 122
New York magazine on, 200–01
Al Nodal and, 339–40
Ida Panicelli on, 341
Marsha Pels on CA and, 64–65
personal characteristics, 183–84
  fear of heights, 247–48, 317
  Chris Haub on, 313
  sensitivity about height, 16
poetry, 123–24, 169–70, 280

Rome studio, 242–43
Santería religion and, 144, 265, 330,
    340, 353
Edith Schloss on, 159
Gian Enzo Sperone on, 157–58
in Village Voice article, 258–59
Larry Weiner on, 86–87
Mendieta, Carlos (Ana's great-uncle), 38
Mendieta, Concha, 44, 136
Mendieta, Ignacio (Ana's brother), 35–36,
    136–37, 378
Mendieta, Ignacio (Ana's father), 38–39
  arrested in Cuba, 135–36
  Cuban revolution and, 40–46
  death of, 309–10
  heart attack, 272
Mendieta, Laurie, 35–36
Mendieta, Raquel (Ana's mother), 36,
    38–39, 44, 107, 111–12, 153–54,
    241–43, 249, 304, 372
  arrival in Cedar Rapids, 137
  at trial, 326, 335, 370
Mendieta, Raquel (Ana's sister), 14,
    24–26, 106–09, 118–19, 151–52,
    172–73, 204–06, 210, 213, 304n,
    372, 378
  Andre and, 107–09, 124–25, 187–89
  and Andre's apartment in Rome,
    215–16
  childhood
    in Cuba, 37–47
    in Iowa, 129–35
  Ronald Finelli and, 58–62
  Elizabeth Lederer and, 287
  before grand jury, 186, 252–53
  marriage to Don Holmes, 142, 144–45
  memorial service for Ana, 163, 169–70,
    172–73
  news of Ana's death, 34–35
  relationship with Ana, 122
  in Ana's Rome studio, 241–49
  Ignacio Mendieta (brother) and, 35–36
  as student at Briar Cliff College, 137
  at trial, 345–46, 370
Mendieta, Raquel "Kaki" (Ana's cousin),
    276–78
Miller, Brenda, 166–67, 173, 215, 227
Miner, Elaine, 355, 361, 365
Minich, Ann, 167–68, 171–72
Minimalism, 138–39, 231–32, 310–11

Miss, Mary, 21, 33–34, 126–28, 164, 166, 215

Mojzis, Edward, 5–6, 24, 49, 186, 292, 296–98, 305, 354, 360, 365, 370
   at trial, 331–35

Morgan, Maude, 91

Morgan, Patrick, 91

Morgenthau, Robert M., 73, 198, 202, 283–85, 285, 287

Morris, Robert, 222

Moschini, Francesco, 162

Ms. magazine, 147

Museum of Modern Art, 229, 262

Myers, John, 221, 224

New Art Examiner, 337, 377

Newsday, 324, 337, 349; *See also* Kempton, Murray

Newsweek, 26

New York art world, 173–80, 193–97, 294
   on Andre, 196–97
   in late 1950s, 96–99
   in late 1960s, 138–40, 225–30
   Max's Kansas City and, 218–20, 226–28
   reluctance to testify at trial, 338–39

New York Daily News, 54, 72–73, 299, 304, 337

New Yorker, 85

New York magazine, 374
   cover story on Andre, 148, 199–202

New York Post, 54, 63–64, 72–73, 75, 82, 148, 286n, 336, 337

New York Review of Books, 179

New York Times, 73, 84, 194, 281, 288, 296n, 318, 337, 345, 370, 374, 382

Nichols, Mary Perot, 33, 167

Nieves, Richard, 11, 13–14, 18–20, 23–24, 58, 183, 186, 344, 360, 364–65, 379

Nizer, Louis, 181

Nodal, Al, 184, 339–40

O'Connor, Sandra Day, 26

Ohlson, Douglas, 22, 27–28, 30–31, 54

Oldenburg, Claes, 139–40, 178, 189, 195

Olitski, Jules, 323

Operation Peter Pan, 45–46, 136

Oppenheimer, Joel, 219n

Ordover, Gerry, 77–79, 81, 84, 85–88, 195

Our Lady of the Angels Academy, 134

Panicelli, Ida, 207, 243, 290n, 340–41, 357

Pappas, Spiros, 291–93, 341

Pels, Marsha, 64–65, 165–66, 170, 190, 206–07, 256, 259, 287n, 317, 341

Penny, Dick, 137

People magazine, 195

Perle, Quimetta, 209

Perreault, John, 168, 226–27, 226n, 274, 296

Perrone, Jeff, 213

Picasso, Pablo, 206

Pietre e Foglie, 162

Pindell, Howardena, 383

Pollock, Jackson, 97

Porter, Liliana, 33–34, 214–15, 263, 269

Pound, Ezra, 92, 95, 104

Preven, David, 358–59

Protetch, Max, 213

Rainer, Yvonne, 214, 347–48

Rape Pieces, 144, 147

Rauschenberg, Robert, 99, 178, 228

Rehnquist, William, 26

Rich, Ruby, 151, 166, 192–93, 211–15, 285, 287, 324, 338, 340, 347, 361
   on Andre, 150–51
   at trial, 326
   Village Voice article by, 255–59

Rivera, Diego, 52

Rodelli, John, 1–2, 6, 186

Rojas, Carlos Maria de (Ana's great-grandfather), 38, 40–41, 384

Rose, Barbara, 77, 93–96, 102–03, 175, 191, 225, 231, 236

Rosen, Gerry, 26–28, 30–31, 51, 61, 72–73, 79–82, 117, 125, 195, 198, 379–80
   with Andre after arrest, 48–50, 54–56, 74–76
   defense strategy, 66–69, 181
   Jack Hoffinger and, 109, 302
   at trial, 370

Rosen, Jane, *See* Logemann, Jane

Rosen, Warren, 206

Rosenberg, Alex, 223

Rosenberg, Harold, 97, 174
Rosenthal and Rosenthal, 80–81
Ruskin, Mickey, 218–20, 225, 311
Russell, John, 73, 231–32, 382

Saddler family, 135
Sanchez, Juan, 326
Santería religion, 37, 40, 144, 206,
    212–13, 265, 330, 353, 353n
Santurio, Antonio, 349
Sartorius, Rita, 153, 154, 251, 290–91,
    357
Saturday Evening Post, 139
Sayah, Max, 54–56, 57–58, 67–68, 110,
    125–26, 182
Schjeldahl, Peter, 226
Schlesinger, Alvin, 289, 297, 300–02,
    323–24, 337n, 350
  Huntley hearing and, 300–08
  sealing of court documents and, 375–76
  at trial, 298–99, 326–28, 330–32,
    334–36, 339, 342n, 346–47,
    354–55, 358–60, 364, 367,
    369–70
  verdict announced by, 370–71
Schlesinger, Dorothy, 323
Schloss, Edith, 159–61
Schnabel, Julian, 294
Schneemann, Carolee, 73–74, 97, 126–28,
    140, 164, 167, 197, 207–08, 215,
    226, 227, 267
Serra, Richard, 194–95, 294
Shafrazi, Tony, 77
Shapiro, Mark, 96
Sherman, Mike, 328, 344, 371
Simon, Gary, 151, 188, 204–05, 215,
    244
Sims, Lowery, 53–54, 165, 167, 171–72,
    201–02, 338
Smithson, Robert, 139, 226, 226n, 344n
Soho Weekly News, 273
Span, Paula, 73
Spero, Nancy, 168, 170, 213, 238,
    267–69, 273, 275–76, 360–65
Sperone, Gian Enzo, 76, 156–61, 190–91,
    233, 275, 348
Sperone Westwater Gallery, 156
St. Mary's Home, 129–31, 132–33
Stella, Frank, 77–79, 84–88, 91–92, 96,
    99–105, 233n, 289

Stevens, Dorothy, 17
Stevens, May, 81, 108–09, 117–18, 215,
    255, 258, 267, 338, 361
Studio International magazine, 263
Sukenick, Ronald, 218–20, 227
Sullivan, Mark, 326
Swift, Rodney, 299–300, 304, 364n

Tanager Gallery, 96
Tate Gallery, 231
Tibor de Nagy gallery, 221, 224–25
Tomkins, Calvin, 85, 232, 233n
Tong, Bobby, 20, 351–52, 356, 360, 364,
    365, 370
  disappearance of, 362
Torre, Modesto, 184, 287n, 341
Trasobares, Cesar, 352–53
Trial, 299–308, 326–72
  Andre's behavior at, 347
  Martha Bashford and, 302, 340,
    342–43, 365, 378–79
  decision to relinquish jury, 324–25
  defense strategy, 325, 328–30
  documents from, sealed according to
    New York State Criminal
    Procedure Law, 375–77, 380–81
  press coverage of, 336–37, 348–49
  reluctance of art world to testify at,
    338–39
  scenario of Ana's death presented at,
    366–68
  verdict announced, 370–71
  Larry Weiner on, 326
  witnesses at
    Robert Baumert, 335–36
    Alison Bierman, 350–51
    Filip Bool, 357
    David Bourdon, 356
    Louis Capolupo, 342–43
    Michael Connolly, 342–43
    Natalia Delgado, 327–28, 330–31
    Kurt Dubowski, 359–60
    Robert Finelli, 343–44
    Ronnie Ginnever, 352
    Joacquin Gutierrez, 341–42
    Tom Harrington, 345
    Robert Knaff, 354–55
    Bridget Knapp, 352
    Harry Leandrou, 341
    Eli Lederman, 346

Trial *(continued)*
  Dominic de Maio, 357, 359
  Raquel Mendieta, 345–46
  Elaine Miner, 355
  Edward Mojzis, 331–35
  Richard Nieves, 364
  Al Nodal, 339–40
  Ida Panicelli, 340–41
  Spiros Pappas, 341
  David Preven, 358–59
  Nancy Spero, 363–64
  Bobby Tong, 351–52
  Cesar Trasobares, 352–53
  Alice Weiner, 356
  Larry Weiner, 355
  See also Hoffinger, Jack S.; Schlesinger,
    Alvin
Tully, Judd, 208–09, 337, 377, 383
12 Dialogues (book by Andre and Hollis
    Frampton), 104

Urbach, Marina, 263

Vaughn, Craig, 184
Victoria, Ted, 170, 264, 266, 281
The Village Voice, 255–59, 282, 296n,
    299, 337, 356n, 361, 377

Virginia Dwan gallery, 225
Voodoo, *See* Santería

Wachtler, Sol, 182
Wadler, Joyce, 259n, 340, 374–75; *See
    also New York* magazine
  Andre's violent outbursts investigated
    by, 148–50
Walker, Lenore, 256
Ward, Detective, 19
Warhol, Andy, 178
Washington Post, 73
Weiner, Alice, 139, 316–17, 356
Weiner, Kirsten, 316
Weiner, Lawrence, 78, 84, 86–87, 139,
    171, 196, 326, 355, 360–61
Weiner, Steve, 125, 328, 344, 360,
    371
Weinstein, Jeff, 168
Welch, Barbara, 310
Westwater, Angela, 81, 157, 213, 232–35,
    275, 290n, 348
Williams, Neil, 228
Wolfe, Tom, 179, 235
Wu, Angela, 351, 362

Zeus-Trabia gallery, 208